Samuel Beckett's

Crosscurrents: Comparative Studies in
European Literature and Philosophy

Edited by S. E. Gontarski

*Improvisations on Michel Butor: Transformation of
Writing,* by Michel Butor, edited, annotated, and with
an introduction by Lois Oppenheim; translated by
Elinor S. Miller (1996)

*The French New Autobiographies: Sarraute, Duras,
and Robbe-Grillet,* by Raylene L. Ramsay (1996)

The Ghosts of Modernity, by Jean-Michel Rabaté (1996)

Carlo Emilio Gadda and the Modern Macaronic,
by Albert Sbragia (1996)

*Roland Barthes on Photography: The Critical Tradition
in Perspective,* by Nancy M. Shawcross (1997)

Lévinas, Blanchot, Jabès: Figures of Estrangement,
by Gary D. Mole (1997)

*Samuel Beckett's Hidden Drives: Structural Uses of
Depth Psychology,* by J. D. O'Hara (1997)

Samuel Beckett's
HIDDEN DRIVES

Structural Uses of Depth Psychology

J. D. O'Hara

UNIVERSITY PRESS OF FLORIDA

Gainesville Tallahassee Tampa Boca Raton
Pensacola Orlando Miami Jacksonville

02 01 00 99 98 97 6 5 4 3 2 1

Library of Congress Cataloging-in-Publication Data
O'Hara, J. D. (James Donald)
Samuel Beckett's hidden drives: structural uses of depth psychology
/ J. D. O'Hara
p. cm.—(Crosscurrents)
Includes bibliographical references (p.) and index.
ISBN 0-8130-1527-8 (clothbound: alk. paper)
1. Beckett, Samuel, 1906– —Knowledge—Psychology. 2. Psychology
and literature—History—20th century. 3. English literature—
Psychological aspects. 4. Beckett, Samuel, 1906– —Technique. I. Title.
II. Series: Crosscurrents (Gainesville, Fla.)
PR6003.E282Z7824   1997
828'.91209—dc21   97-16090

Publication of this project was made possible in part by a subvention
from the University of Connecticut.

The University Press of Florida is the scholarly publishing agency for
the State University System of Florida, comprised of Florida A & M
University, Florida Atlantic University, Florida International University,
Florida State University, University of Central Florida, University of
Florida, University of North Florida, University of South Florida, and
University of West Florida.

University Press of Florida
15 Northwest 15th Street
Gainesville, FL 32611

Contents

Foreword

Although Samuel Beckett may have emerged as a singular literary figure in part by separating himself from the monumental influence of James Joyce, his admiration for the older Dubliner never wavered. While Beckett finally rejected the bulk of the Joycean encyclopedic method, preferring his own brand of desiccated minimalism, he nevertheless learned much about artistic integrity and creative methodology from the indefatigable Joyce, particularly a reliance on systems of thought and a tendency to read almost cannibalistically. As James Knowlson concludes in his recent biography, *Damned to Fame: The Life of Samuel Beckett,* Beckett adopted Joyce's habit of "reading books primarily for what they could offer him for his own writing": "Beckett's notebooks show that he too plundered the books he was reading or studying for material that he would then incorporate into his own writing. Beckett copied out striking, memorable or witty sentences or phrases into his notebooks. Such quotations or near quotations were then woven into the dense fabric of his early prose" (109). Knowlson goes on to cite the example of Beckett's reading the *Confessions of Saint Augustine* just before writing his first novel, *Dream of Fair to Middling Women,* in 1929 (published only in 1993): "A private notebook of Beckett gives chapter and verse to his many borrowings from St Augustine. It is not that he plagiarizes; he makes no attempt to hide what he is doing. Anyone familiar with Augustine's book would recognize the passages involved" (112). Knowlson confirms what a number of critics have been slowly demonstrating: like Joyce, the early Beckett relied more heavily on sources and systems of thought than critics had heretofore suspected, and the identification and close study of this source material can reveal much not only about Beckett's creative methods but about the completed works themselves.

We have known for some time, for instance, how heavily Joyce relied on *The Spiritual Exercises* of Saint Ignatius Loyola to structure chapter 3, the retreat at Belvedere, of *A Portrait of the Artist as a Young Man.* James R. Thrane has further demonstrated the scope of Joyce's use of a 1688 text by an Italian Jesuit, Giovanni Pietro Pinamonti, *Hell Opened to Christians, To Caution Them from Entering into It* (English translation, Dublin, 1868) in that same chapter of *Portrait* (see, for example, Thrane's "Joyce's Sermon on Hell: Its Sources and Its Background" in *A James Joyce Miscellany, Third Series,* ed. Marvin Magalaner [Carbondale, Ill., 1962], 33–78). J. S. Atherton has demonstrated in the notes to his 1964 edition of *A Portrait of the Artist as a Young Man* that all of Stephen Dedalus's quotations from John Henry Newman derive from a single source, *Characteristics from the Writings of John Henry Newman* (London, 1875). Atherton also discovered Joyce's principal sources for the "Oxen of the Sun" chapter of *Ulysses:* Saintsbury's *History of English Prose Rhythm* (1912) and Peacock's *English Prose: Mandeville to Ruskin* (1903) (see particularly Atherton's seminal essay "The Oxen of the Sun" in *James Joyce's "Ulysses,"* ed. Clive Hart and David Hayman [Berkeley: University of California Press, 1974], 313-39).

Beckett seems to have adopted (and adapted) this part of Joyce's method, at least for his early work, when, as he said, he was "a very young man who had nothing to say and an itch to make." In his first separately published work, the longish poem *Whoroscope* (1930), Beckett relied heavily on several external sources. The received wisdom about *Whoroscope,* which features details from the life of René Descartes, is that Beckett's primary resource was Adrien Baillet's *La vie de Monsieur Des-Cartes* (1691), which Beckett acknowledged having read just before composing the poem. But Francis Doherty discloses at least one repressed source. As he convincingly demonstrates in his essay "Mahaffy's *Whoroscope,*" "Some of the footnotes Beckett gave to the poem seem to be drawn, often verbatim," from J. P. Mahaffy's *Descartes* (1901), "and some of the poem's text could well have been generated from the same source" (*Journal of Beckett Studies,* n.s., 2.1 [Autumn 1992]: 28). Mahaffy was not only a more current and shorter source for Beckett (Baillet's is a two-volume work), he was a member of the Trinity College teaching faculty.

In Doherty's detailed comparative analysis of *Whoroscope,* he finds Beckett's direct debt to Mahaffy incontestable:

Lieder! Lieder! she bloomed and withered,
a pale abusive parakeet in a mainstreet window.
(*Whoroscope,* lines 70–71)

In Mahaffy, Doherty discovers most of the source of those lines: "Also on Petit he [Descartes] says, 'I think no more of him than I do of the abuse given to me by a parrot hanging in a window as I pass the street'." And the poem's "Fallor, ergo sum!" (line 73), attributed directly to Saint Augustine in Beckett's own note on that line, seems to have come through Mahaffy as well. Even the title *Whoroscope*, Doherty suspects, may have been generated by Mahaffy and Baillet. Beckett's introductory note to the poem is as follows: "He [Descartes] kept his own birthday to himself so that no astrologer could cast his nativity." The following sentence occurs in Mahaffy: "He objected to his birthday being noted under his picture, because it exercised idle people in superstitions about his horoscope" (9). "In Baillet's index," continues Doherty, "the relevant comments are noted under [the rubric] 'Horoscope', and we can see that Beckett saves the word 'horoscope' for his own poem, and substitutes 'nativity'" (45). "The poem," concludes Doherty, "for all its haste, is a remarkable accomplishment, but it was made all the more possible because of Mahaffy's little book" (46).

The essay that follows Doherty's in that issue of the *Journal of Beckett Studies* is J. D. O'Hara's "Freud and the Narrative of 'Moran'" (47–63), in which O'Hara suggests that Beckett's method of relying heavily on sources was not limited to his early work, but carried over into what is generally considered Samuel Beckett's most important novel, the diptych *Molloy*. The O'Hara essay is actually the second part of his study of *Molloy*. The first half, "Jung and the Narratives of 'Molloy'," appeared a decade earlier in the *Journal of Beckett Studies* 7 (Spring 1982): 19–47, and then in a revised and expanded form as "Jung and the 'Molloy' Narrative" in *The Beckett Studies Reader* (Gainesville: University Press of Florida, 1993), 129–45.

These essays, however, were a mere aperçu for the current volume, *Samuel Beckett's Hidden Drives*, the most comprehensive study in print of Samuel Beckett's use of source material, particularly the works of Freud and Jung (and their predecessor Schopenhauer), whom Beckett used extensively as what O'Hara calls "scaffolding" or "structures of thought that uphold Beckett's literary works." O'Hara's method is to trace Beckett's "use of Freudian psychology, moving from the many specific details in his texts to their actual or probable sources in Freud's writing." In his inimitable and eloquent style, O'Hara covers not only the whole of *Molloy*, but also the critical work *Proust*; the prose fictions *Murphy*, "First Love," and "From an Abandoned Work"; and the radio play *All That Fall*. Such structural emphasis in Beckett's work, moreover, confirms at least Beckett's early affinity with the modernists, but the preoccupation persists as well into his late career as a director of his own plays, when it becomes almost obsessive. What O'Hara discovers in his parallel readings is something like Beckett's own "discourse on method," intensely through *Molloy*, and then sporadically until the mid-1950s in the short story "From an Abandoned Work" (1954–55) and the play *All That Fall* (1957).

Such a comparative, parallel reading as O'Hara offers, then, constitutes an exemplary addition to the Crosscurrents series, which is designed to feature comparative studies in European art and thought, particularly the intersections of literature and philosophy, aesthetics and culture. Without abandoning traditional comparative methodology, the series is also receptive to the latest currents in critical, comparative, and performative theory, especially those generated by the renewed intellectual energy in post-Marxist Europe. It takes, as well, full cognizance of the cultural and political realignments of what for the better part of the twentieth century were two separated and isolated Europes. While Western Europe is now moving aggressively toward unification in the European Community, with the breakup of the twentieth century's last major colonial empire, the former Soviet Union, Eastern Europe is subdividing into nationalistic and religious enclaves with the collapse of the communist hegemony. The intellectual, cultural, and literary significance of such profound restructuring, how history will finally rewrite itself, is difficult to anticipate. Having had a fertile period of modernism snuffed out in an ideological coup not long after the 1917 revolution, the nations of the former Soviet Union have, for instance, been denied (or spared) the age of Freud and Jung, most modernist experiments, and postmodern fragmentation. While Western Europe continues reaching beyond modernism, Eastern Europe may be struggling to reclaim it. Whether a new art can emerge in the absence—or from the absence—of such forces as shaped modernism is one of the intriguing questions of post–Cold War aesthetics, philosophy, and critical theory. These questions gain renewed currency in studies like O'Hara's demonstration yet again of how central Freud and Jung are to the Zeitgeist of Western Europe.

O'Hara's close comparative readings and source study form precisely the sort of comparative philosophical and literary study that the Crosscurrents series fosters. The series continues to critique the developing, often conflicting, currents of European thought in literature, philosophy, and theory.

S. E. Gontarski
Series Editor

Introduction

Those who have read many of Samuel Beckett's writings know that he was capable of a breathtaking control of language, gesture, tone, and structure. Among his short late pieces are fictions that cannot be faulted, dramas as finely orchestrated as a musical composition, and monologues in which the choice and placement of a term can touch the heart. But few readers responding to one of these late texts would present that text to someone who had read no Beckett. Great writers train their audiences, beginning with their early works. Such works as "Stirrings Still" and "What is the Word" are not meant for beginners, just as Rembrandt's late self-portraits are not meant for art-school students.

We also know that Beckett was not always in complete control of his materials. He put himself at risk again and again when he began a work, and the body of his writings contains ample evidence of beginnings that did not pan out, broken lines of development, fizzles and *têtes-mortes* and *disjecta membra* and *textes pour rien*. He was sometimes motivated to write a new work by the desire to reject an old one. "The thing to avoid, I don't know why, is the spirit of system," says the Unnamable (292).

Of course, the Unnamable is already being systematic by laying down that rule. He has just wondered, "Can one be ephectic otherwise than unawares?" It is a problem that may have troubled his author. To devise new artistic structures is relatively simple. Structures of thought, however, are not so easily built or razed, and Beckett's writings require such scaffoldings even when the systems cannot be trusted.

The present study is concerned with those incredible and inescapable systems, the basic structures of thought that uphold Beckett's literary works. It concentrates on the earlier works, especially the fiction. In them we can see most clearly the external sources. What we see there not only explains those works; it also clarifies the later works in which Beckett's own developments overlie these sources. What is more, the structures of thought will turn out to be largely unnoticed, almost completely implicit, and consistent with themselves through the years.

* * *

Beckett grew up among believers, as did most of us. In his case the most influential beliefs were religious. His parents were orthodox though not intense Protestants. Early on, he studied the King James Version of the Bible, and he retained it in his capacious memory all his life. He attended a very respectable public school and Trinity College, Dublin, both transmitters of conservative beliefs. Much of his earliest literary admiration was given to Dante and especially to the *Commedia,* which also stayed with him all his life.

Perhaps Beckett's primary image of the writer was not Dante but James Joyce, another writer much given to the use of systems of thought. Joyce did not have Dante's scholarship, but his rejection of religion was so complex that it required of him almost a theologian's knowledge, much of it gained in his childhood at Jesuit schools. Joyce supplemented that material with the secular theologies of philosophy. He required of Beckett an essay on the use of Giordano Bruno's and Giambattista Vico's philosophical systems in the *Wake.* Dante and Joyce thereby emphasized for Beckett the importance of systems of thought as bases for serious artistic work.

Beckett grew up among systems of thought and belief to a degree uncommon in the twentieth century. He learned his Protestant Christianity and Joyce's and Dante's Catholic Christianity early on. His first philosophical readings took him to Descartes and Schopenhauer, quite different men but each as systematic as possible. In his youth, as later, Beckett collected vivid aphorisms and insights, but his primary concerns took him to writers by whom life was presented steadily and whole.

Beckett was not satisfied or persuaded by any of these systems. His sometimes intense objections to them suggest a desire to believe that could find no object, rather than the lukewarm indifference of people for whom no explanations of life are necessary. Biographer James Knowlson reports Beckett's loss of religious faith while in college (80). Offered many structures in which to contain life, dubious about all of them and especially about any implicit optimism, Beckett was least unhappy with Schopenhauer's philosophy. His preference was not grounded in any rigorous evaluation of that philosophy's professional merits. Schopenhauer, like Dante and Joyce, presented qualities that especially struck Beckett from the start. More than half a century after his early immersion in *The World as Will and Representation,* he used characteristic terms to praise its author: "He's not just a philosopher, he's a *great writer."*

For the young Beckett, great writers were those whose writings immediately moved him by their eloquence and by the often painful accuracy of their statements. On what subjects? Seeking for a term with which to suggest to Beckett his possible interests when, as a young man, he had sought out new authors, I hesitated. Beckett had no trouble filling the silence. "Pessimism," he said. "Pessimism."

In Schopenhauer's pessimism Beckett found not a rejection of system but a denial of the implication that, thanks to God or nature or reason, the system of life is a good one. Years later, Beckett would contrast to the mess that is life the need for an artistic form in which to contain that mess. Years earlier, Schopenhauer had offered him a dualistic structure within which he could organize that ephectic hesitation, that unwillingness to believe. The form of Schopenhauer's philosophy contained the mess, but it did not strive to make the mess acceptable.

One general subject for Beckett's doubt, then, was a central interest: system. His skeptical hesitations on that subject recur throughout his writings. One might expect that such rejections would lead to the rejection of systematizers, but this is not the case. Young and old, he respected many writers, and he gave that respect often to the makers of systems. Dante, Schopenhauer, and Joyce are obvious examples; Proust is a later addition.

Perhaps Beckett was less a pessimist than a skeptic, insofar as the two positions can be separated. Certainly he retained a skepticism about the validity of his own judgments and understandings. Perhaps a skeptic requires judgments, understandings, and systems of belief in order to exercise his doubts. They serve to sharpen the horns of every dilemma. Beckett was drawn to systematic explanations of life even though he could not make an act of faith.

Because early commentators knew of his close readings of the Bible and Dante and Descartes, they sometimes sought to show that he was religious and a Cartesian. His references to Schopenhauer, especially explicit in *Proust,* attracted little notice, perhaps because Schopenhauer's fame and ideas have faded from cultural awareness since the opening decades of the century. Meanwhile, for many critics, the intellectual movements of Beckett's own time took the place of historical sources. Dadaism, the absurd, the death of God, Marxism, existentialism, Husserl, Sartre, Wittgenstein, and many other systems and antisystems were invoked to explain Beckett's writings. Lately, even newer literary and linguistic systems and historical and psychological notions have been applied to his works like leeches. Many positive results have ensued. (Leeches still have medical uses.) A deconstructionist reading of a Shakespeare play may also prove useful, although there is no reason to identify Shakespeare as a deconstructionist *avant l'anti-lettre.*

The present study, however, takes the position that most profit is to be gained from approaches to literature that most reveal the artist's own intentions and concerns. Such approaches do not assume that the artist's intentions are praiseworthy or that they equal achievements. Many a novel intended to be great has fallen stillborn from the best-seller lists. Nevertheless, the continuing wide disagreements about Beckett's works and their intentions and even their subjects have kept alive and unanswered that basic question, what does he have in mind? Some critical responses recall the blind philosophers and the elephant. *Ex ungue leonem,* one used to say. Many a critic has found in a Beckett work this or that body part, and from it has constructed a lion or a gazelle. A common implication of such discoveries is that Beckett deliberately planted clues to guide the waterproofed detective through the spray of phenomena thrown up by each text.

This study unearths many clues pointing like arrowheads toward larger meanings, but it does not accept this detective-story model. This study's assumption, sketched above, is that Beckett needed intellectual structures for his art. These structures were needed but not easily found; a systematic skeptic is an oxymoron. They were also not to be trusted credulously. There is also the matter of respect, especially during the formative years of Beckett's career. He deferred to the thought of his early models rather than competing with them or undercutting them. He would not contrive his own system rather than use Schopenhauer's, for example. Nor would he, in his youthful twenties, set his own knowledge of the emotional complications of love and friendship above Proust's knowledge. Rather, he learned from his masters, even while darkening knowledge with his own gloom. Of course, he did not use those materials as an academic of our own time would, trailing clouds of footnotes and bibliographies. Instead of his own inferior ideas and words, he would use, often tacitly, the ideas and words of the masters. We see him doing so especially in *Proust,* where the fine formulations so applicable to his own writings often vary Schopenhauer's and Proust's phrases.

The young Beckett relied upon Schopenhauer and Proust as aids to the work of critical analysis, as he had obligatorily relied upon Dante and Vico and Bruno in analyzing Joyce's *Work in Progress.* When he turned from criticism to the writing of fiction, however, these were not so immediately applicable. (Dante, Joyce, and Proust are no models for beginners.) Nor did another source of artistic or philosophic structure offer itself. One result is that the confusions of *Dream of Fair to Middling Women* and the almost conventional structures of the stories in *More Pricks* are as unpromising as their emphases upon society and drinking and courtship are irrelevant. A conventional cliché asserts that the author had not yet found his voice. More accurately, he had not found the language his many voices would speak. He needed new structures for the new subject matter that strove to achieve expression.

It may be at once surprising and obvious that these new structures would be firmly based on depth psychology, that Beckett would resist their use, and that he would find their elements primarily in the slowly accumulating works of Sigmund Freud.

* * *

At the end of his career, Beckett's writing takes as a recurrent subject the troubles of a solitary person haunted by the past and by a sense of things done wrong or undone—a person not made suddenly and traumatically aware of these problems but troubled obsessively and cumulatively, as it were, by failure, guilt, spoiled or unachieved relations, and a wasted life. These are materials of which Beckett became a master, in the sense in which one might speak of an anonymous painter as the Master of the Seven Sorrows.

These materials are so clear to the reader of the later works that their presentations may call for no explanation. When the speaker of "The Calmative" remarks that "we are needless to say in a skull" he is right; for the experienced reader this observation is indeed needless. To reach that understanding and that cranial location, however, starting from the early works, is not easy for the unguided reader. It was much more difficult for the writer. The difficulty is not merely a question of first-person narrative. Such narratives have existed, in literature as in life, since communication was first achieved. They are directed toward the outer world, they describe that world, and they are spoken by and to inhabitants of that world.

To turn that world inside out and then to populate this new outside with materials from inside—that is no easy task. William Blake, an obvious forerunner, spent years in contriving heavy and complex machinery, appropriate for the Industrial Revolution, in order to embody his psychic characters and to locate them in a psychic universe. (It is often a skull, made by Los under Urizen's direction and evoked in Blake's drawings.)

In personifying parts of the mind, Blake anticipates Beckett. He also anticipates Mary Shelley's far less extreme characterizations in *Frankenstein.* When Frankenstein's monster describes his first sensations, he anticipates the first sensations of the Unnamable. Proust's young Marcel, awakening in a strange bedroom, also anticipates those first sensations. Like footnotes below the text of *The Waste Land,* such varied anticipations accumulate below Beckett's writings. He did not, however, achieve the means with which to express his psychological subjects by any jackdaw-like accumulation of details. He needed whole structures, not fragments. He needed Sigmund Freud.

* * *

The pages that follow contain Freud's works and ideas in abundance, leaving neither need nor space for any general review here. Nevertheless, a few topics might be raised and then lowered until their time comes.

Freud was the dominant pioneer in the creation, description, and therapeutic application of a sense of the psyche characterized in part by certain qualities. His sense of the psyche did not depend upon biology and did not locate its materials in specific parts and functions of the physical body. (Freud often suggested that such knowledge might be achieved in the future, but he disclaimed his own ability to achieve it.) His psychology separates the psyche into parts. It reports that these parts often fail to work together satisfactorily. They struggle for control and may even attempt independent existence. Freud dramatizes the relations and inadequacies of these parts, making them at once fixed entities and continuous processes. He often personifies them. He emphasizes, especially to the lay audience, the term "depth psychology," stressing that most of the mind's entities and processes exist beneath one's consciousness of them. (The term "the unconscious" suggests something asleep or comatose; Freud's term "das Unbewusste" is better translated as "the unknown" or "the unknowable." What goes on beneath one's consciousness is lively and aware, in its own ways.) Finally, Freud's sense of the psyche re-enacts a distressing part of Darwin's evolutionary ideas. As Darwin suggested that humans evolved from apes, so Freud suggests that humans still possess a bestial ancestral mind. The concerns of the psyche, he found, are simple, basic, amoral, and emotional.

High-minded people reacted against Darwin's ideas by emphasizing not the body, with its resemblance to the ape's, but the mind. They turned the chanciness and spatial limitations of Darwinian physical evolution into generalities about cultural and spiritual progress. They stressed the necessity of control. We must move upward, work out the beast, and let the ape and tiger die. A Christian society such as that into which Beckett was born in 1906 could not accept a less positive interpretation.

Freud's assertion that we contain our own apes and tigers, that man is a wolf to men, was shocking—so shocking that the general negative reaction to it focused on lesser matters—not on violence but on sexuality, for instance; not on his report of the damage done by repression but on the high-mindedness of sublimation; not on the internal struggles among parts of the psyche but on the individual's necessary shaping by and accommodation to society.

No history of depth psychology and of Freudian psychology can be attempted here, nor is one needed. Freudian and Jungian psychologies have been superseded in our time by more complicated analyses, by an emphasis on biological causes and treatments, and by the simplifying of their ideas, often into the metaphors that illustrate them. The lay notion that problems classified as psychological are shameful, revelatory of personal criminality or sinfulness, does still persist, but less and less among educated people. That notion is worth mentioning, however, because it pervaded the societies in which Beckett lived. It helped to give depth psychology something of the aura of impropriety and revolution that Darwinian evolution had and that, for the cultured few, Schopenhauer also had. (The Parisian journal *transition* claimed as a central part of its avant-garde position its emphasis on Jungian myths.) The bad name given to depth psychology necessarily encouraged people to keep any personal involvement with therapy a private matter.

Beckett knew and consulted professional psychologists and psychiatrists when young, and he studied Freud's and Jung's works very carefully. He kept these consultations and interests to himself, however, or at least he kept them from casual acquaintances and strangers. Even his notebooks, in which he transcribed passages from sources as diverse as the daily newspapers and Kant's writings, contain nothing from texts of psychology. (But see Knowlson [172] for concealed notebooks on Beckett's own therapy and reading. "Psychoanalysis was not allowed in Dublin at that time," Beckett told Knowlson [167].) Nor does the subject appear explicitly in his works, except for the briefest and most scattered of references. Because of its invisibility on the surface, perhaps, Beckett's interest in psychology received little attention before the appearance of *Damned to Fame*. Now, thanks to Knowlson, the centrality of psychology in Beckett's personal life cannot be denied. The biography has prepared fertile ground for the reception of this present study, which reports in depth the depth psychology on which Beckett based many texts after his experience of therapy.

It may be useful to recall Beckett's cautionary introductory remark in *Film*. Having cited and developed Bishop Berkeley's "esse est percipi," Beckett concludes: "No truth value attaches to above, regarded as of merely structural and dramatic convenience." The technician's clipped sentence is amusing, and the disclaimer is curious. The structural and dramatic uses of the idea are clear but not "mere," and audiences ignorant of that idea must puzzle themselves profitlessly over many details of *Film*. Beckett also found Berkeley's idea convenient in many other works, works in which its "truth value" is important enough to be given consideration. Berkeley may be wrong, but Beckett often presents the sense of an inescapable judge as psychologically valid. Perceived, as by a glaring superior eye or superego, we must confess our being to that audience.

We know that Beckett offered a similar disclaimer with regard to the Christian elements in his works. He told Colin Duckworth: "Christianity is a mythology with which I am perfectly familiar, so I naturally use it" (Duckworth, lvii). What the skeptical Beckett diminishes by such terms as "mythology" and "structural and dramatic convenience" may yet be a matter of serious concern for him. Structural convenience is, after all, a basic necessity for thought.

Such is the bleak situation with regard to Beckett's use of Freudian and other psychological materials. He will offer the investigator no footnotes and no encouragement. No truth value may attach to those materials. Nevertheless, his uses will reveal his serious involvement with them. Indeed, no major writer has made such extensive and such profitable uses of professional depth psychology as has Beckett. For most of his career he held that mirror up to nature.

*   *   *

That Beckett was deeply interested in depth psychology is scarcely surprising, despite his silence on the subject. That he took seriously Freud's exploration of that subject follows from the first assertion. That he used some Freudian ideas in shaping and clarifying his understanding of psychological topics is equally probable. Most of us have done the same, if only because of our shared zeitgeist.

Beckett also absorbed many current ideas about politics, history, economics, physics, and sporting activities, but there needs no volume of several hundred pages to reveal his references to such ideas. Readers sense themselves competent to deal with those topics as they arise, without any detailed map of the territory. When the narrator of Fizzle 2 concludes glumly: "My fortieth year had come and gone and I still throwing the javelin," we do not consult a history of the Olympics before smiling and understanding.

One may, easily enough, make general statements of a psychological nature about any Beckett work: "In *Endgame* Beckett presents an old man withdrawn from the outer world and exhausting the resources of his memory and his libidinal desires." "In *Waiting for Godot* the protagonists encounter each other within a skull, having spent the 'night' among people in the daytime social world." "Murphy is a narcissist." Such assertions, however, are of a type with arbitrary impositions of subjective concerns upon a work of art, such as making the Pyramids forecast events in American history and Kafka predict the Second World War. Such subjective interpretations cannot persuasively reveal an artist's intentions or a text's concerns. (A friend of Beckett, hearing about his use of Freud in *Murphy,* dismissed the subject. Freud wasn't necessary, she exclaimed, because Beckett was himself a narcissist. Perhaps, but Freud on narcissism was valuable to Beckett's understanding of it.)

Beckett's uses of psychology are intentional, deliberate, calculated. He did not merely look into his heart and write. Thomas Mann studied musical theory and criticism closely before writing about a composer in *Doctor Faustus*. Melville did not rely on his own experiences aboard a whaler when he wrote *Moby Dick*. Even though he was Irish, Joyce spent many years and the time of many researchers, including Beckett, in accumulating the materials of *Ulysses* and *Finnegans Wake*. Beckett studied astrology in order to incorporate it in *Murphy*. Authors behave responsibly in their use of important materials.

For Beckett psychological matters were far more important and immediate than astrology, even in *Murphy*. He could not have settled for common knowledge in any case, since depth psychology was not commonly known. He also needed much more help than any survey could have given him. Freud told stories about odd human behavior and irrationally motivated pains and fears, and he persuasively explained these inexplicable matters. He mixed his explanations with history, literature, and myth, demonstrating that neither his stories nor his explanations were new and arbitrary. And he spoke harshly of the writers of fiction who attempted to use depth psychology without understanding the subject. Freud knew, and therefore he could; Beckett did not know, and therefore he had to play the sedulous student. (*Murphy* shows him burning his fingers by attempting to be psychological on his own, before calling Freud to his aid.)

Sedulous students can often be identified by the bits and pieces of their studies that they have transferred into their own works undigested. So it is with Beckett. He does not seek to invent his own neuroses and symptoms and symbols; he turns those he has studied to his own use. Freud lists possible objects of narcissistic love, for instance, and Beckett draws on that list in contriving his own characters and situations. It is a process as straightforward as Shakespeare's use of history, Joyce's of the *Odyssey,* and Mann's of the symptoms of syphilis in *Doctor Faustus*. A map of Dublin clarifies *Ulysses* for the reader; Freud's maps of the psyche will do the reader of this study a similar service.

Beckett's imagination was vividly specific. Buildings, roads, details of clothing, gestures—such matters required exactness, and he often turned for models to the facts and scenes of his own life. This study shows such details increasingly put into the service of his psychological themes. This does not mean that either Beckett or Freud believed that psychological situations were to be revealed by a few deeply meaningful clues. We are all trained, in this post-Freudian world, to notice simple psychological details: this slip of the tongue, that insistent phrase, this recurrent dream, and that pairing of emphatic hostility and absent desire. As isolated details in real life, they may suggest curious discrete insights. If we wish to pass for psychoanalysts, however, we must notice all of them, remember all of them, and rearrange their relationships until we may contrive a tentative analysis.

Murphy rejects an affair with a homosexual. Dan Rooney insists on counting. Molloy takes sucking-stones seriously. Moran broods about bees. Such odd details proliferate in Beckett's writings. They remain odd details until Freud demonstrates for us the underlying psychic situation—different in each case—that creates them. Beckett's uses of Freud required him to perceive or conceive many such odd details, and also to understand the general structures of neuroses, repressions, and symptoms within which such details have a place. We must reproduce Beckett's dual training in order to trace his use of Freudian psychology, moving from the many specific details in his texts to their actual or probable sources in Freud's writings.

This tracing separates discoveries of Beckett's uses of psychology from those arbitrary and subjective claims about the Great Pyramid of Giza. This study does not claim symbols where none are intended, perhaps, and it does find evidence of intent. Gaber's inability to remember his message when he looks away from his notebook, an amusing bit of characterization, becomes reassuring as well because it connects with important meanings in *Molloy.*

This assertion about Gaber is a test case. John Aubrey tells about Thomas Hobbes's coming upon Euclid in middle age. Hobbes opened the *Elements* toward the end, read a proposition, and swore that "this is impossible." Readers of this introduction may be imagined as reacting similarly upon hearing of Gaber. "So he reads the Demonstration of it," Aubrey goes on, "which referred him back to such a Proposition; which proposition he read. That referred him back to another, which he also read. *Et sic deinceps* that at last he was demonstratively convinced of that trueth. This made him in love with Geometry."

Beckett's presentations of psychological matters proceed by details, although at times—as with Murphy in his rocking chair and Molloy in his mother's bed—he will begin by dramatizing a thesis. Like Hobbes in pursuit of Euclid and Freud in pursuit of a patient's neurosis, we must move cautiously through each text, avoiding hasty conclusions. (Unlike Hobbes and Freud, we can generally move forward.) The assertions made in this introduction can be of no value to the Beckett reader until they are proved on the pulse. Beckett's precise and careful making of individually meaningful texts obliges us to find each text's specific concerns. These texts do not merely intone "Freud" over and over. Each freestanding entity works out the expression of its own materials.

The study of each text therefore provides Beckett readers with a solid foundation for their own speculations. Having followed with proper skepticism each analysis of psychological structures and details, readers will find that each text has renewed itself, become both more lucid and more complexly problematic than it had seemed to be. The experience of many expositions makes persuasive the idea that someone clearly himself and unique, Beckett, could be so cautiously respectful of and indebted to other men and their ideas.

This sense of the Beckettian world should become firm enough and clear enough, even though that world continually shifts from text to text, so that works not even named in this study will also reveal senses and significances that had previously been only obscurities. In Beckett's texts, psychology turns out to be not reductive and simplifying but valuably intertwined with philosophy and aesthetics and (no surprise) life itself.

The examination begins with *Proust,* an apparently irrelevant text that is concerned not with Proust's complete oeuvre but with *A la Recherche du temps perdu.* That novel is certainly a fair field for psychological investigation, but readers of *Proust* know that Beckett does not take that approach. Instead, he offers what appear to be his own terms and then discusses themes and analyzes scenes. *Proust,* however, leans heavily upon Schopenhauer, although he is named only three times, and it borrows extensively from Proust himself. Both the monograph's subjects and Beckett's reliance on authorities turn out to be useful to us.

Chapter 2 then turns to Beckett's earliest writings that make some use of psychology. Chapter 3 examines *Murphy,* which emerges as more confused than it may have seemed but also as Beckett's first elaborate presentation of materials taken extensively from Freud. Especially we find him developing the subject of narcissism, which will continue in his writings for the rest of his career.

The following chapters examine his returns to Freud in such later texts as "First Love," *All That Fall,* and "From an Abandoned Work." The first of these works shows Beckett still a beginner, patching materials together. The second shows him in complete command of his materials. The third, something of a farewell to his dependence upon Freud, is an obsessive presentation of Freudian ideas.

The examination of texts closes with two substantial chapters devoted to *Molloy*. That dual novel is shown not only to make by far the most developed and insightful use of Freud, but to expand Beckett's interests to include the psychology of C. G. Jung, obliging readers to go much deeper into depth psychology than before. *Molloy* reveals itself as a tightly organized novel in which depth psychology at once explains the unhappy self and is itself the object of critical analysis.

With all these examinations at hand, we can say something about Beckett's artistic concerns. His emphasis upon the individual self can be understood not as repetitive but as exploratory, and his explorations can be understood not as presentations by a writer in complete control of his knowledge but as tentative actings out of possibilities. What one is and how one might perhaps alter or escape that identity are topics that motivate many texts. The necessity for love and the difficulty of loving characterize a remarkably extensive exploration of love.

Explaining Beckett's works may seem a form of disobedience or deliberate distortion. In the third of his *Three Dialogues* Beckett says that "there are many ways in which the thing I am trying in vain to say may be tried in vain to be said. I have experimented . . . under duress, through faintness of heart, through weakness of mind, with two or three hundred." This study shows that he did not try in vain by showing within his texts "the thing I am trying in vain to say," or at least a major part of that thing.

1.

Proust

As a young man, Beckett associated with very impressive people—Descartes, Schopenhauer, Dante, Joyce, and Proust chief among them. He went on to become impressive himself, but he was not always so. The young Beckett was quite aware of the disparity between himself and the company he kept, aware especially of his dependence upon the ideas of others. The nature of this intellectual dependence and the slow development of his artistic independence constitute materials for a study more complex than the present one.

Beckett spent most of the summer of 1930 in the composition of *Proust*. He had just turned 24 and had finished his last semester at the Ecole Normale Supérieure. He had just written his long, obscure poem about Descartes, *Whoroscope*. "Dante . . . Bruno . Vico . . Joyce," his essay on the future *Finnegans Wake*, had been published in May of the previous year. That essay had offered little training for a study of Proust. It appeared in a collection of essays, *Our Exagmination Round His Factification for Incamination of Work in Progress*, designed by Joyce to call attention to his still incomplete *Wake*. Joyce chose the essay topics, assigning Beckett Giordano Bruno and Giambattista Vico. Beckett may have suggested Dante himself. (In college we both majored in French and Italian, Beckett later explained, so it was natural that Joyce should have given me the assignment. The necessary texts were available at the Ecole Normale.) Beckett was instructed to show how *Work in Progress* developed and dramatized the basic ideas of the three earlier writers.

"Dante" suggests that Beckett did not pull easily in harness, and its weaknesses may have motivated his dependence upon others when writing *Proust*. He begins the earlier essay with a warning that implicitly applies to his whole project, although it is given a narrower meaning: "The danger is in the neatness of identifications." The two items specifically not to be identified are Philosophy and Philology. (Here the second term means perhaps no more than literary criticism. It is not used again.)

In the essay, organized explanations of the philosophies of Bruno and Vico appear only fragmentarily. "He found me short on Bruno," Beckett told Terence McQueeny. Indeed, Bruno appears only as lurking behind "Browne & Nolan" and as remarking on the coincidence of contraries. Beckett gives more time to Vico—perhaps necessarily, in view of Joyce's interest in taking the Vico road through Dublin and cyclical history. Vico, too, however, is fragmentary here, even though Beckett uses Benedetto Croce as an aid.

If the danger is in the neatness of identifications, "Dante" is not a dangerous work. It is interlarded with many explicit refusals of identity: "These two aspects of Vico have their reverberations, their reapplications—without, however, receiving the faintest explicit illustration—in '*Work in Progress*'" (5); "At this point Vico applies Bruno—though he takes very good care not to say so" (5–6); "This social and historical classification is clearly adapted [adopted?] by Mr. Joyce as a structural convenience—or inconvenience" (7).

Beckett's essay on common elements in Dante, Bruno, Vico, and Joyce persistently interposes separations among them. His interest in the thoroughly imperfect "identification between the philosophical abstraction and the empirical illustration" (3) demonstrates a clear preference for the illustration. The necessary result is an almost incoherent general discussion. The structure of the *Wake,* its characters and their relations, and the setting of the novel are given no description, much less explanation. Details abound; their place in Joyce's still incomplete whole is scarcely even sketched. Beckett states his approach at the beginning of the essay: "And now here am I, with my handful of abstractions, among which notably: a mountain, the coincidence of contraries, the inevitability of cyclic evolution, a system of Poetics, and the prospect of self-extension in the world of Mr. Joyce's '*Work in Progress*'" (3). We can find these abstractions in the essay. The mountain is Dante's Purgatory, and "self-extension" probably refers to Joyce's use of "type-names" to generalize individuality without metaphysics (16–17). Beckett is warning us, however, about the disorganization of his materials, not their tractability.

"Dante" could not have given Beckett himself much assurance of his critical and academic competence. He acknowledged his unclear exposition of its materials. He knew that recurrently and often silently he had taken sentences and passages from Croce, Francesco de Sanctis, J. L. McIntyre, and other critics. The essay is only prentice work. Writing the monograph on Proust, Beckett was on his own.

* * *

Proust had died in 1922, with only the opening volumes of *A la Recherche* published or revised. The final volumes, pieced together from sometimes confused and repetitious manuscripts, were published in 1927. Once again, therefore, Beckett was obliged to deal with a work in progress. Proust criticism was already a growth industry, however, and, as before, Beckett would use, often silently, ideas and passages from earlier critical works. In writing "Dante" Beckett had been obliged by Joyce to use Vico and Bruno. He said later that he would not have included them if left to himself. In *Proust* he makes no mention of them or of Joyce, nor does he speak of life as cyclical or purgatorial. He does, however, find another authority whose interpretations of life he adapts or adopts.

In recent years Beckett had been reading extensively in philosophy as well as literature. Most obviously, as *Whoroscope* shows, he had been studying Descartes, but "Dante" suggests that he was not attracted by the organization and mechanical coherence of the "scientific historians," such as Vico and Marx, or by the quantity surveyor's factuality, and certainly not by the rationalizing and justifying offered by theologians and philosophical optimists like Descartes. (He would read Kant at length in the 1930s.) Beckett had a quite different category from which he drew the information about life he was seeking: "pessimism." Pessimism consists in the stating of truths, not facts, and its expression requires rhetorical skill to be effective. Henri Bergson explains that the purpose of thought is to prepare us to act. We read his explanation much as we read explanations of the spark plug— passively. Arthur Schopenhauer, taking up the same materials earlier, locates life in a workhouse where we must, under threat of ennui, direct our thoughts to the accomplishment of actions that might momentarily satisfy the tyrannical will. We read his explanations with admiring groans. So, one suspects, did Beckett.

After sixteen volumes of Marcel's attempts to acclimate himself to the world, to wring the proper responses from his mother and grandmother and mistress, to become known and to rise in society, to bend to his will this woman and that man, and to overcome the sense that age and illness and change—Time, in short—had fragmented his life and his identity—after sixteen volumes of such troubles, read twice, it is no surprise that Beckett found Schopenhauer's descriptions of the human condition appropriate for his monograph. This time, as not with Bruno and Vico, he found that the appropriate descriptions were correct.

* * *

Regrettably Schopenhauer is read far less widely now than when Beckett was young. In fact, Beckett may have participated in the last years of Schopenhauer's wide influence. Bryan Magee has identified his effects on Wittgenstein and Wagner and on such writers as Tolstoy, Turgenev, Hardy, Conrad, Zola, Maupassant, Borges, Thomas Mann, and Proust. After World War I, however, Magee says, "acquaintance with his work declined to the point where even most professional philosophers ceased to study it" (262). Schopenhauer's influence on Proust can indeed be seen throughout *A la Recherche*. Curiously—perhaps because he is unwilling to make any neat identification of philosophy and literature—Beckett never notes that influence, despite his own persistent application of Schopenhauer to the text.

Because Schopenhauer is little read now, some hasty survey of his ideas, so far as they are central to Beckett's interest in him, should be afforded those who have not studied *The World as Will and Representation*. This section provides such a survey, warped to fit Beckett's interest in Schopenhauer's ideas. Arthur Schopenhauer (1788–1860) bitterly opposed the Hegelian orthodoxy of German philosophy in his time. As a result he was kept from teaching and had little professional success until late in life. Strongly influenced by his mother, with whom he was on bad terms, he spent most of his time in thinking and traveling. Admiring Kant, he persistently criticized and corrected Kant's ideas. As Descartes and Kant had done, he emphasized the central importance of the individual, although his typical model is a superior man. He connected that superiority with the practice of philosophy and of art (more extensively than any earlier philosopher had done) and with the renunciation of life, which he was unable to renounce himself.

Schopenhauer wrote well. "He's not just a philosopher," Beckett said. "He's a *great writer*." He enriched his texts with citations from dozens of writers. Perhaps best of all, Schopenhauer was not a conventional philosopher, by the rigorous standards of academe. Rather, like his own sometime follower Friedrich Nietzsche, he was what teachers of philosophy describe pejoratively as a "wisdom writer," someone all too willing to abandon detached rationality for rhetoric, emotion, and appeals to personal experience, and willing also to assert that he does not know and that we cannot know any ultimate truths. He even asserts that our entire conceivable existence is constituted not of substantial realities in a verifiable universe, but of mere phenomena or representations, subjectively perceived. This existence can be validly understood as the illusory maya of Vedantic and other Eastern thought, he says; and the nothingness lying beyond it is its better half, its complement, the nirvana from which our existence would itself appear as nothingness.

Like Descartes, Schopenhauer begins with the individual human. He replaces Descartes's "cogito ergo sum" with a formulation emphasizing the subservience of the thinking self, the intellect, to the eternally desiring and impersonal will. It wishes, therefore I exist. Schopenhauer finds the motive for human existence and for all existence in this persistent force of wishing, desiring, willing. This force is the single will, or will-to-live, as he some-times calls it, that impels everyone and everything. Whether in a human being or in a rock or in the force that through the green fuse drives the flower, it is the same impulse, free from any constraint or rationale that we can know. It manifests itself in all its phenomena, and it uses the human intellect in order to see itself in its representations, in the mirror of phenom-enal existence.

Like Beckett, Schopenhauer is given to duality. He sets the will against its representations, for instance, and he presents the human individual as com-pounded of will and intellect. Using its body's senses, the intellect forms its representations with reference to certain necessary ways of perceiving. These consist especially of time, space, and causality. The will is one and univer-sal; the individual intellect is not. It is limited by what Schopenhauer calls the "principium individuationis." Therefore what the intellect re-presents — that is, what each individual can know about the world — is necessarily dif-ferent from the noumena and the (Platonic) Ideas that lie beyond these rep-resentations.

The will exists out of time and space, and we can know it only in its separate acts of willing. It is causeless, but our intellect conceives of all actions as motivated. It is "an endless striving," but in us it appears as discrete goal-oriented activities, with ennui as their negative incentive and happiness as their ostensible end. Intellects display the will to itself. "The sole self-knowledge of the will as a whole is the representation as a whole, the whole world of perception. It is the objectivity, the revelation, the mir-ror of the will" (*WWR* I, book II, § 29). No intellect, however, can perceive that display, because each is limited by its "principium individuationis." As the will is beyond knowledge, so it is beyond control. The will is free, but we are not free, since the will possesses us. We are individuals defined pri-marily by our limitations, the principium again, and each individual is shaped in part by an intellect unable to know itself or the will motivating it. We perceive incompletely a world totally the representation of one will and yet perpetually at war with itself because its representations prey on or flee from each other.

Whatever it may be in itself, in its representations the will expresses itself as the will-to-live. Its central interest is the perpetuating of its living repre-sentations, and therefore sexual desire is its strongest expression. The will is free. Freely desiring sexual union, it demands that the individual intellect achieve that union. An animal's intellect responds directly. A human being's knowledge-inhibited intellect makes such a direct response impossible. There-fore, the intellect must temporize, must tell itself stories about romance, love, marriages made in heaven, lasting satisfaction—stories that in the end permit the will to have its way. The extended result, however, is always the same: the intellect suffers from its labor, and the insatiable will continues its demands after the briefest of respites. The intellect serves the will. Consciousness observes the results passively or even approvingly, caught up by the hope of better things. Schopenhauer sees no reason for such hope. He does, however, find a weakness in the will's control of the intellect. An extraordinary individual can on occasion detach his pragmatic intellect from the service of the will.

In ordinary existence the will's phenomena are perceived by each intellect, each "subject of knowing," as relevant "objects of knowing." The subject of knowing seeks in these objects some relevance to the will's concerns: should they be acquired, attacked, or escaped? When this subject of knowing is detached from the will, however, it is purified of its limiting individuality, and the subject-object relation gives way to disinterested perception. This subject can see in the will's representations their (Platonic) Idea rather than their usefulness, their desirability. Like the perceived Idea, the purified subject is freed from time, space, and causality. When so perceived, such Ideas become the material of the highest art, to be given representation by the disinterested artist. Experiencing them as represented in the work of art, spectators too can be freed briefly from the domination of the will. They can share something of the artist's purified vision. As Schopenhauer memorably puts it, art's audience finds in the aesthetic experience "the Sabbath of the penal servitude of willing" (*WWR* I, book III, § 38). Moran in his garden and the Murphy of Fizzle I in his "vaguely prison garb" (7) echo the two terms of this phrase.

The great work of art is not a link in the will's chain of causes and effects. It is an end in itself. Even the impossible translation of its Ideas into concepts for the reason would constitute a denial of its true value. While acting as an artist, the artist is also free from that chain of cause and effect. Schopenhauer is of two minds, however, about the condition of the artist (and of the philosopher, whom Schopenhauer links with the artist). The artist is fortunate in being, at times, free of the will. His freed perceptions are not of nirvana, however, but of the Ideas behind the phenomena, the representations, that make up life. These perceptions expose him to more pain and suffering than ordinary people experience, because the artist then knows not merely individual pains but the very Idea of pain.

A permanent escape from individuality and the will's demands is possible (but not through suicide, which Schopenhauer opposes). The escape is possible only for the saintly person who can merge his self, though limited by the principium individuationis, with the whole of the phenomenal world.

Such a person can say, as Schopenhauer phrases the Sanskrit terms, "tat tvam asi" (that too is me): "For the veil of Maya has become transparent for the person who performs works of love, and the deception of the *principium individuationis* has left him. Himself, his will, he recognizes in every creature" (*WWR* I, book IV, § 66).

We have gone beyond Schopenhauer himself now. He could conceive of such an existence, but he could not achieve it. He remained, at his best, a philosopher. We have also gone beyond our two artists, Beckett and Proust. Beckett will find no such escape from life for his characters. Proust's Marcel seeks none, even while understanding that his vocation as a writer demands of him "cette vie sans amis, sans causerie." Marcel even promises his imagination some sensual vacations in his youthful world: "De légères amours avec des jeunes filles en fleurs seraient un aliment choisi que je pourrais à la rigueur permettre à mon imagination semblable au cheval fameux qu'on ne nourrissait que de roses!" (*TR* II, 172–73). Needless to say, Beckett's imagination was neither enticed nor amused by these rosy girls.

* * *

Beckett sought widely for help before beginning his discussion of *A la Recherche*, the only text by Proust he would consider. Schopenhauer and the text itself constituted his major sources, but he also read current discussions of the novel and used some of their passages and terms. As in discussing *Work in Progress* he had supported Joyce's interpretation of life, so here he described and supported Proust's, but now with a recurrent darkening of its negative elements and with near indifference to the great positive discoveries of the Guermantes matinée.

Beckett begins *Proust* by giving an extensive description of human life, with examples from the novel. He discusses time, the transient self, the pain of desire, subject-object relations, habit, and memory. Most of these topics are Schopenhauerian as well as Proustian and are treated as Schopenhauer treated them. Then these brief examples give way to an extended consideration of three parts of the novel: "Les Intermittences du Coeur," Marcel's liaison with Albertine, and the dual discoveries of the Guermantes matinée. The Albertine affair leads to general remarks about love, friendship, and tragedy. The Guermantes matinée is followed by a scrambled discussion of Proust's style and aesthetics. The brief and rhetorical conclusion is an unpredictable, heavily Schopenhauerian discussion of music. The sense of patchwork cannot be evaded. The patchwork is not a serious defect, however, nor is it surprising in a critical text by a 24-year-old would-be academic. There is at least as much of critical value in *Proust* as in the earlier commentaries.

Space does not allow a thorough discussion of these matters. Fortunately most of the materials for such a discussion are to be found in Edith Fournier's fine translation of *Proust* into French. In its annotations she identifies many of the references—often silent—to other discussions of *A la Recherche*. Even more valuably, she identifies the many passages in which Beckett silently uses ideas and phrasings from *A la Recherche* itself as he analyzes and evaluates Proust's writing with Proust's own tools.

*   *   *

Beckett names Schopenhauer only three times, twice in connection with terminology. Discussing habit, the transient self, and the relations between the self and the world, he speaks of that world as "a projection of the individual's consciousness (an objectivation of the individual's will, Schopenhauer would say)" (8). Discussing Proust's impressionism (by paraphrasing Proust), he notes that "we are reminded of Schopenhauer's definition of the artistic procedure as 'the contemplation of the world independently of the principle of reason'" (66).

Habit and the transient self are Proust's topics rather than Schopenhauer's, but Beckett makes no distinctions between his two sources and among their terms. Discussing habit, he speaks of the transitional period between one habitual identity and the next as a time "when for a moment the boredom of living is replaced by the suffering of being" (8). This ennui is a central topic for Schopenhauer, and "the suffering of being" may be derived from Schopenhauer's remark that "the non-appearance of satisfaction is suffering" (*WWR* I, book III, § 52). Proust's Marcel is seldom bored—even the occasional tediousness of life in society interests him—and before his involvement with Albertine he experiences little suffering so long as his mother will kiss him good night. Beckett's use of these Schopenhauerian topics, here as elsewhere, is a central part of his intensifying and darkening of Proust's presentation of life. Marcel's response to the belated realization of his grandmother's death provides an instance. The intensity of that response fades, Beckett says, because "will, the will to live, the will not to suffer, Habit . . . has laid the foundation of its evil and necessary structure . . . " (29). Here Schopenhauer's will and Proust's Habit are linked, although actually Proust's phrase speaks not of habit but of "l'instinct de conservation" (*S & G* I, 218). The "evil" is Beckett's addition.

Sometimes Beckett seems to be summarizing Proust's presentation of a topic when he is actually explaining that presentation with Schopenhauer's aid. An example may be found in his long paragraph (53 ff.) explaining the action of involuntary memory. For the most part, Beckett is drawing on Proust's own explanation (*TR* II, 12). Proust is concerned to show that this involuntary experience evades the censorship of the intellect, but Beckett also has in mind Schopenhauer's description of the artist as able to perceive Ideas because he has escaped the demands of the will. Thus in describing the censorship to be evaded, he uses "will" three times, and he describes Proust's involuntary memory as "a pure act of cognition" in which "a subconscious and disinterested act of perception has reduced the object . . . to its immaterial and spiritually digestible equivalent" (54–55). Proust speaks a few pages later of "la malaise provoqué par l'ingestion d'une nourriture abjecte" (*TR* II, 19); Beckett transforms this indigestible nourishment into its complement, the spiritual Idea. The dual objectivity he finds in the event—that of the subject of knowing and the object of knowing—is Schopenhauer's.

His next paragraph continues to draw on Schopenhauer, and he concludes by reporting Proust's list of five images and describing the experience of each as "the baffled ecstasy . . . when the mystery, the essence, the Idea, imprisoned in matter, had solicited . . . a subject" (57). Schopenhauer would approve, of course. Proust would not. True, Proust connects these perceived images with "de lois et d'idées" (*TR* II, 24), but he associates these laws and ideas not with the objects perceived but with the subjective self, the perceiver, the timeless Marcel. The objective (Platonic) Ideas of cloud, triangle, spire, and so forth are irrelevant. Nevertheless, it will take Beckett many years to overcome the hope for disinterested and objective truths with which one might correct subjective and painful psychological error.

As these scattered illustrations suggest, Beckett draws more or less simultaneously upon Schopenhauer and Proust in his central discussions. The results sometimes report confusion and sometimes something more complex. One more example must suffice. In discussing those images of cloud, triangle, spire, Beckett says that they "had solicited the bounty of a subject passing by" (57). That metaphor is echoed later, when he speaks of homosexuals and plants: "they seem to solicit a pure subject, so that they may pass from a state of blind will to a state of representation" (69). It seems enough to trace this metaphor to Proust, who employs it for an extensive comparison of homosexuals with certain plants (*S & G* I, 42–45), but the solicitation described by Proust has no connection with Ideas. Schopenhauer, describing plants, writes that "these organic beings . . . need the foreign intelligent individual in order to come from the world of blind willing into the world of the representation. Thus they yearn for this entrance, so to speak . . . " (*WWR* I, book III, § 39). They do so out of a desire to communicate their Idea. Here, as elsewhere, one must trace Beckett's use of the metaphor and probably Proust's as well to their reading of Schopenhauer (who himself acknowledges Saint Augustine as a predecessor).

As Beckett's topics become more abstract and general, his need for Schopenhauer increases. The topic of the will, which is primary in Schopenhauer's thought, causes Beckett some difficulties when he interprets Proust. For Schopenhauer the will is an affliction. For Proust's French critics Marcel's lack of will is a weakness. Arnaud Dandieu, for instance, speaks of "une lâcheté secrète ou une faiblesse constitutionelle de la volonté" (200). Beckett, who almost invariably equates Marcel with Proust himself, wishes to defend Proust against this charge. He does so not by defending the strength of Proust's will, but by applying Schopenhauer's description of the artist as evading the will in order to raise himself above his mere self, his principium individuationis.

Describing flowers and homosexuals as seeming to "solicit a pure subject, so that they may pass from a state of blind will to a state of representation" (69), Beckett echoes both Proust and Schopenhauer. The "pure subject" is intelligible only by way of Schopenhauer's explanation that the ordinary relation between the subject of knowing and the object of knowing, imposed by the demanding will, is evaded by the artist. With this understanding, the reader can follow Beckett's continuation: "Proust is that pure subject. He is almost exempt from the impurity of will. He deplores his lack of will until he understands that will, being utilitarian, a servant of intelligence and habit, is not a condition of the artistic experience." Beckett completes that explanation in strict Schopenhauerian fashion, but then he becomes puzzling. Accusing Spenser, Keats, and Giorgione of "collapse of the will," he exempts Proust, without explaining what makes this "collapse" different from an escape from the will. He takes as his example Marcel's studying all night a branch of apple blossom: "The Proustian stasis is contemplative, a pure act of understanding, will-less, the 'amabilis insania' and the 'holder Wahnsinn'" (70).

This conclusion comes straight from Schopenhauer (WWR I, book III, § 36), including its phrases from Horace and Wieland, but it is applied to a quite irrelevant passage. Proust there shows us Marcel as merely a would-be artist, an imitator, who in fact is deliberately contriving an experience based on a secondhand view of the world. Marcel's study is methodical and repeated: "Combien de fois à Paris . . . il m'arriva d'acheter une branche de pommier chez le fleuriste et de passer ensuite la nuit devant ses fleurs," he begins, and then he evokes their beauty. He has a purpose, a thoroughly willed act of understanding; he wishes to paint a landscape in the modern style: "je cherchais à les reporter sur cette route [the "route campagnarde" outside Balbec mentioned in the previous paragraph] par l'imagination, à les multiplier, à les étendre dans le cadre préparé, sur la toile toute prête de ces clos dont je savais le dessin par coeur . . . au moment où avec la verve ravissante du génie, le printemps couvre leur canevas de ses couleurs" (*Ombre* II, 147).

The next paragraph describes a similar act of deliberate composition, this time of a "tableau de mer." Proust is presenting Marcel at a time when he was absorbed in landscape painting, under the influence of Elstir, and was translating nature into a style learned secondhand. No search for or discovery of Ideas is implied. (When, a few pages later, Marcel visits another scene for which he has prepared himself, it appears quite different from his expectations.) Beckett therefore inadvertently re-enacted Marcel's experience by imposing upon the blossom-studying an interpretation he had learned from Schopenhauer, rather than perceiving Proust's witty enactment of a quite different topic.

Where Beckett seeks to find in the character Marcel the impersonal artist reporting the Ideas of existence, Proust before the Guermantes matinée seeks to convey the immature individual, at this or that stage of his existence, interpreting the world according to the demands and limitations of his present identity. (The timeless self is the maker of the whole novel, not of these individual perceptions.) The difference between Proust's and Beckett's interests might be merely curious, except that it bears upon our future concerns. Beckett's sense of the Schopenhauerian will as something troublesome and limiting (and painful in human relations, especially), and his expectation of a meaningful external reality to be discovered objectively, during the Sabbath of willing, must be translated out of their present senses as philosophy and aesthetics and into psychological terms before he can manage his own works of art. Relevantly, Beckett's Molloy and Moran, like Proust's Marcel, will develop over time, discovering truth after truth, as it were, as they move on—often to contradictory truths. Beckett will recognize the subjectivity of truth, in short.

Love and friendship, in *A la Recherche,* connect the individual with the external human world. Beckett's extensive description of the Albertine affair certainly makes persuasive his Schopenhauerian idea that love is a disaster. (Fournier's fine notes show the extent to which Beckett appropriated Proust's own comments in describing the Albertine affair.) Friendship encourages Beckett to extend himself more on the subject of the sensitive and isolated individual. Contrasting friendship with love, he asserts that "the failure to possess may have the nobility of that which is tragic, whereas the attempt to communicate where no communication is possible is merely a simian vulgarity, or horribly comic, like the madness that holds a conversation with the furniture" (46). Proust's "cette douce folie" (*TR* II, 19–20), unlike "horribly comic," suggests no Beckettian intensity.

In denouncing friendship (47 ff.), Beckett intensifies the negative throughout, bringing together a remarkable range of passages from the novel to do so. Much of what he uses is concerned not with mankind in general but with the artist, who is now a curiously two-sided type. He is a Schopenhauerian purified subject of knowing, as when Marcel "visits Balbec and Venice, meets Gilberte and the Duchesse de Guermantes and Albertine, attracted not by what they are but impelled by their arbitrary and ideal equivalents." This claim of ideal equivalents is puzzling; the reader has just heard in detail about the constantly shifting images of Albertine that exasperate Marcel's always vain attempts to know her real self. Beckett's assertion, however, is followed immediately by what seems a complete contradiction: "The only fertile research [this technical term refers to the artist's search for "their arbitrary and ideal equivalents," it seems] is excavatory, immersive, a contraction of the spirit, a descent."

This excavatory research does not have as its aim the characters of a work or the friends and lovers of a life, whether as their multiple appearances or their Platonic Ideas. Rather, the aim is the individual artist's true self: "the ideal core of the onion would represent a more appropriate tribute to the labours of poetical excavation than the crown of bay" (16–17). Here Beckett turns to Proust for yet another vegetable image: "'Man,' writes Proust, 'is not a building that can receive additions to its superficies, but a tree whose stem and leafage are an expression of inward sap'."

Again Beckett is recalling Schopenhauer in making the artist the ideal equivalent of "man." In the passage that is his source, Marcel discusses the unprofitability of conversation not for mankind but for artists. He is not damning friendship; he is noting that the artist's materials are elsewhere: "La marche de la pensée dans le travail solitaire de la création artistique se fait dans le sens de la profondeur, la seule direction qui ne nous soit pas fermée." He adds, still speaking only of artists, that they are "ceux d'entre nous dont la loi de développement est purement interne." This being so, artists are not shaped by society and social experience but by their internal nature: "nous ne sommes pas comme des bâtiments à qui on peut ajouter des pierres du dehors, mais comme des arbres qui tirent de leur propre sève le noeud suivant de leur tige, l'étage supérieur de leur frondaison" (*Ombre* III, 188–89). In applying to "man" what Proust says of the artist, Beckett may recall, as Proust before him, Schopenhauer's observation that the will, "developed and drawn out in time, space, and all the forms of the principle of sufficient reason, is the empirical character" of a man. "The whole tree is only the constantly repeated phenomenon of one and the same impulse . . . repeated and easily recognizable in the construction of leaf, stem, branch, and trunk" (*WWR* I, book IV, § 55). Schopenhauer, however, does not consider that contemplation of his empirical character is important for the ordinary individual, and certainly it is not a concern of the selfless artist.

Beckett does not suggest that this research into the depths of the self can provide any reassuring reports. Indeed, he treats the notion of arboreal development as evidence only that "we are alone. We cannot know and we cannot be known." And with a surprising leap he arrives at the implication that Proust's subject is tragedy, "completely detached from all moral considerations." (We will see that this final phrase is linked to Dandieu.)

Beckett spoke of the failure to possess, in love, as possibly tragic. He had already claimed that "the tragedy of the Marcel-Albertine liaison" is "the type-tragedy of the human relationship whose failure is preordained" (7). Now this quite limited sub-category has expanded to include all humanity:

> Tragedy is not concerned with human justice. Tragedy is the statement of an expiation, but not the miserable expiation of a codified breach of a local arrangement, organised by the knaves for the fools. The tragic figure represents the expiation of original sin, of the original and eternal sin of him and all his "socii malorum," the sin of having been born.
> "Pues el delito mayor
> Del hombre es haber nacido." (*Proust*, 49)

Proust is not to be found in these statements. He appears to have had no interest in tragedy and certainly not in connecting it with sin. For Proust it is merely individual and a matter for the theater. As for any belief in original sin, when Marcel speaks about Bergotte's death and connects it with Bergotte's desire to imitate in his writing Vermeer's patch of yellow wall, Marcel speculates that "tout se passe dans notre vie comme si nous y entrions avec le faix d'obligations contractées dans une vie antérieure; il n'y a aucune raison . . . pour que nous nous croyions obligés à faire le bien, à être délicats, même à être polis . . . " (*Prisonnière* I, 247). Such innate social obligations have nothing in common with sin.

When Beckett first read the novel, however, he had tragedy in mind, at least for a while. The young Marcel speaks gloomily of two separate difficulties, that of communicating ideas to another person and that of achieving happiness (*Ombre* II, 19, 36–37). Against both passages Beckett wrote "Tragic." Many pages later Marcel notes that our imagination contributes much to the charm of barely glimpsed beauty (*Ombre* II, 155). Again Beckett wrote "Tragic." This time, however, he crossed the term out and substituted another one that must remind us of Schopenhauer: "Pessimist."

Such notes prepare us to understand the appearance in *Proust* of his paragraph on life as tragedy. Finding love, communication, beauty, and happiness so difficult, Beckett found the promises of life untrustworthy. Schopenhauer stood waiting to be used. The materials of Beckett's passage come from *The World as Will and Representation* (I, book III, §§ 59–61). Life is "a tragic state in every way," Schopenhauer says, a state in which "the will performs the great tragedy and comedy at its own expense." Every individual re-enacts Adam's suffering, having shared "the sin of Adam," which is "the satisfaction of sexual passion."

Schopenhauer distinguishes between "human justice" and "eternal justice" (he thinks much more highly of the first than does Beckett), and in quoting Calderòn's verses, he describes them as expressing "the Christian dogma of original sin." Beckett uses these notions. Even his apparently gratuitous phrase "socii malorum" comes from Schopenhauer, from "Additional Remarks on the Doctrine of the Suffering of the World" (*Parerga and Paralipomena* II, 304).

Almost half a century later Beckett would admit to John Pilling that "perhaps I overstated Proust's pessimism a little" (Pilling, *Samuel Beckett,* 16), itself quite an understatement. Nevertheless, Beckett was faithful to Schopenhauer's pessimism and to his ideas about the will and the intellect.

The monograph ends with one more central debt to Schopenhauer, to which we and Beckett will recur. Abruptly and unexpectedly Beckett ends *Proust* with a discussion of music. "A book could be written on the significance of music in the work of Proust," Beckett begins. Such a book had been written: Benoist-Méchin's *La Musique et l'immortalité dans l'oeuvre de Marcel Proust* (1926). Arnaud Dandieu had also discussed the topic, and Beckett borrows from both of them. But Proust's Mme de Cambremer says, "Relisez ce que Schopenhauer dit de la musique" (*TR* II, 195), and Beckett took her advice.

Much of what Schopenhauer says about music is contained in volume I, book III, § 52, and with that section Beckett makes "the influence of Schopenhauer on this aspect of the Proustian demonstration . . . unquestionable" (70)—unquestionable, that is, to those who do not read Schopenhauer. Such readers might make no complaint about Beckett's assertion that music is "apprehended not in Space but in Time only, and consequently untouched by the teleological hypothesis." They could also accept his assertion that "music is the Idea itself." In fact Schopenhauer differentiates music from the other arts in noting that "it passes over the Ideas." "Music is by no means like the other arts, namely a copy of the Ideas, but a *copy of the will itself, the objectivity of which are the Ideas.*"

Beckett's error is no great matter, and perhaps he was merely unwilling to explain why, if the will is such a bad entity, music is so good. Nevertheless, that explanation must be made if one is to understand the Schopenhauerian conclusion of *Proust*. The explanation begins far away. Early in the monograph Beckett reports some of Marcel's thoughts about death, especially as connected metaphorically with the idea of becoming a new self to whom grief is unknown. Then Beckett moves on to speak of Paradise: "He thinks how absurd is our dream of a Paradise with retention of personality, since our life is a succession of Paradises successively denied, that the only true Paradise is the Paradise that has been lost, and that death will cure many of the desire for immortality" (14). Here Beckett has conflated two quite separate events. Marcel does indeed think of living on after another person has died, on the occasion of being comforted by his grandmother in a strange place, but to this event (*Ombre* II, 97) Beckett joins a quite different one. In the second event, Marcel refuses Saint-Loup's invitation to walk to Doncières, there to visit again the young men with whom Marcel had become friendly at an earlier time. Marcel bases his refusal on his sense that he is no longer the person who enjoyed those young men. This recognition leads him to speculate about an arrival in heaven that brings one face to face with a former self. One would turn away from the encounter, he says, just as one would turn away from Saint-Loup's formerly enjoyable friends. Therefore, he concludes, that untaken walk to Doncières might have prefigured one's arrival in Paradise: "On rêve beaucoup du paradis, ou plutôt de nombreux paradis successifs, mais ce sont tous, bien avant qu'on ne meure, des paradis perdus, et où l'on se sentirait perdu" (*S & G* I, 349).

To this second passage Beckett attaches yet another one. Marcel realizes that his affection for the dead Albertine is weakening, since without her presence the self that loved her is disappearing. He moves from that idea of a fading relationship to consider self-love, another old liaison, as ending with death: "Je n'avais pas cessé de m'aimer parce que mes liens quotidiens avec moi-même n'avaient pas été rompus comme l'avaient été ceux avec Albertine . . . . Notre amour de la vie n'est qu'une vieille liaison . . . . Mais la mort qui la rompt nous guérira du désir de l'immortalité" (*Albertine*, 308).

To this conglomeration of Proustian sources we must add Schopenhauer's remark about a lost paradise. He is describing the "will-less perception" of the artist. In expanding the experience to lesser mortals, Schopenhauer is less positive about its values. "It is also that blessedness of will-less perception which spreads so wonderful a charm over the past and the distant," he

says, "and by a self-deception presents them to us in so flattering a light."
Will-less perception of the past deceives us by eliminating from our memory
the "incurable sorrows" that the will was inflicting upon us then as now.
"Hence . . . the sudden recollection of past and distant scenes flits across
our minds like a lost paradise. The imagination recalls merely what was
objective, not what was individually subjective . . . " (WWR I, book III, §
38). It is this passage especially that Beckett turns into his pessimistic epigram: "the only true Paradise is the Paradise that has been lost."

The consideration of these notions has been imposed upon us by Beckett's
error in asserting that music expresses Ideas, not the will. Schopenhauer
recognizes that in praising music while asserting that it expresses the will,
he has seemed to contradict himself. After much analysis of music he returns to his observation about the lost paradise conjured up when one recalls one's life objectively, stripped of its component of subjective pain. Far
more consistently and extensively, he says, music achieves the same effect,
and without requiring that the listener misremember his own specific past:
"The inexpressible depth of all music, by virtue of which it flows past us as
a paradise quite familiar and yet eternally remote, and is so easy to understand and yet so inexplicable, is due to the fact that it reproduces all the
emotions of our innermost being, but entirely without reality and remote
from its pain" (WWR I, book III, § 52). Beckett also took from this passage
his remark about the "da capo" convention, while improving Schopenhauer's
phrasing above into "an art that is perfectly intelligible and perfectly inexplicable."

Drawing on critics and especially on Proust, Beckett reports that Marcel
"sees in the red phrase of the Septuor, trumpeting its victory . . . like a
Mantegna angel clothed in scarlet, the ideal and immaterial statement of a
unique beauty, a unique world, . . . expressed timidly, as a prayer, . . . imploringly, as an aspiration." The painting is Mantegna's *Assumption*. The
archangel, the prayer, the aspiration, the terms "ideal" and "essence," and
the "mystical experience" of the previous sentence all signal clearly a religious sense in which the unique beauty and world compose a type of Paradise.

Proust's attitude toward this music (Beckett is drawing now upon Marcel's
experience of Vinteuil's Septuor) is thoroughly positive. Beckett's description of the musical statement as expressed "imploringly, as an aspiration,"
takes its last term from Proust's reference to "cette joie inconnue, l'espérance
mystique de l'Ange écarlate du matin" (*Prisonnière* II, 80). So presented,
this music might make Proust's reader believe that salvation was at hand,
and, indeed, Beckett's annotation of his texts suggests that idea. He had

looked closely at Swann's earlier experience of the Vinteuil Sonata. At one point he noted: "Purely musical impression, independent of memory. Compare with the experiences of 'un peu de temps à l'*état pur:* released for P. by fortuitous encounter with certain object, at times when conscious memory is entirely obliterated" (*sic, Swann* I, 288). Another note says simply: "Salvation" (*Swann* I, 291).

Swann hears the Sonata again in the next volume, and it "s'imposait à Swann comme une réalité supérieure aux choses concrètes" (*Swann* II, 32). Beckett's sense of the experience was the same. "Salvation," he noted. When Marcel, listening later to the Septuor, recognizes that Vinteuil and Elstir have created individual universes, Beckett's note (unfortunately only partially legible) speaks of "salvation & non-actual reality" (*Prisonnière* II, 70). We might recall here that Schopenhauer, who speaks often of salvation, characteristically speaks of it as escape; it is "salvation from the world" (e.g., *WWR* I, book I, § 27, and book IV, § 53).

Given Proust's positive treatment of these experiences of music and Beckett's hopeful marginal notes, we might expect Beckett to be developing a positive conclusion to his study of Proust. Surely a paradise is on its way. No such ending occurs, of course. Music's invisible reality ("un de ces réalités invisibles" [*Swann* I, 292]) is not open to human beings. Instead, Beckett sets that invisible reality against human life: "the 'invisible reality' that damns the life of the body on earth as a pensum and reveals the meaning of the word: 'defunctus'."

Part of this passage may be found in Beckett's primary source of philosophical judgments, *The World as Will and Representation* (II, ch. XLV). His immediate source, however, is that essay already noted, "Additional Remarks on the Doctrine of the Suffering of the World." Schopenhauer's German conveys Beckett's use of the passage best: "Das Leben ist ein Pensum zum Abarbeiten: in diesem Sinne ist *defunctus* ein schöner Ausdruck" (*Parerga und Paralipomena* II, ch. XII § 157). It might seem difficult to make Schopenhauer's statement sharper, but Beckett does so. Although he turns his back on those anticipations of salvation, he retains the religious theme: music "damns" the life of the body. A pensum is, as E. F. J. Payne's translation reports, "a task to be worked off," and "defunctus" acknowledges the completion of the task. (Both terms were common in European academic institutions.) Beckett's "damn," however, moves this purgatorial possibility to hell. He has darkened even Schopenhauer's pessimism and has left Proust in the shade. And "pensum" will recur in many later works.

In *Proust*, then, Beckett shows himself deeply dependent upon Schopenhauer not only for terms and passages but for the shaping of a view of life.

He has taken this view of life seriously enough to impose it upon *A la Recherche du temps perdu* not only where it fits easily enough but also where the fitting requires much stress and amputation. (Beckett's unclear presentation and clear dislike of the basic idea of a triumph over time, which constitutes salvation for Marcel, is surely the most obvious instance of his forcing the novel into a pessimistic Schopenhauerian mode.)

One of the basic topics of *Proust* is love. For Schopenhauer, love reduces itself easily to desire, the will's sexual demand made acceptable by the romanticizing intellect. To the extent that any sexual encounter leads physically to postcoital *tristitia,* the drop from a height of expectation to a trough of ennui must cause pain. Similarly, to the extent that a romanticized affair persuades one to expect more from a sexual relationship than temporary sexual satisfaction alone, love intensifies the disappointment and the resultant pain. Since the lover must cope with another human individuality, equally variable and equally subject to these problems, the possibility that love might justify life becomes minimal.

The will seeks to satisfy its insatiable desires. In so doing, it reduces the intellect to its executive officer. In love affairs, even more than in other pursuits, the intellect senses its subservience and its inability to control either itself or the desired other individual. On the topics of the desires of love and the desire for control, Marcel's liaison with Albertine provides Beckett opportunities to speak at length about problems that he will never mention so extensively again. (Belacqua Shuah's and Murphy's affairs are too stylized, and "First Love" enacts different troubles resulting from different desires.) Proust dramatizes the changes in Marcel's self especially by using the metaphor of death, but he does not speak of these changes only negatively. The old ego dies hard, yes, but the new ego is quite indifferent to its ancestor's sufferings. Beckett emphasizes the sufferings, however, and says nothing positive about the new ego except to speak coldly of the necessary numbing provided by habit. Schopenhauer is present in this subject mainly in its connection with the inescapable demands of the will.

Perhaps the most negative Schopenhauerian ideas imposed upon *A la Recherche* appear in Beckett's discussion of life as a tragedy and his removal of salvation and his damning of human life at the end of the monograph. Like most of his grand generalities throughout *Proust,* this bleak sense of existence cannot be found within any single character in the novel—except perhaps briefly, in one of Marcel's depressions during the Albertine affair— and it corresponds not at all to the varied characters and lives of the novel.

What more can be said about Beckett's primary ideas in *Proust?* In the context of the present study, perhaps the most obvious remark is that these primary ideas, most of them derived from Schopenhauer's *The World as Will and Representation,* are not philosophical. One of the most splendid paragraphs in *Proust* is the one immediately following Beckett's grim discussion of life as a tragedy: "Driving to the Guermantes hotel [actually on the train heading for Paris] he feels that everything is lost, that his life is a succession of losses . . ." (49). Beckett then details eloquently the losses of "une existence toute en longueur" (*TR* I, 233). This passage incorporates some twenty specific passages from the novel and concludes with Marcel's understanding of "the dolorous and necessary course of his own life and the infinite futility—for the artist—of all that is not art" (51). This dolorous course is necessary not because of philosophical truths but because of the psychological complexities of the self and its desires. Proust seems to agree. Marcel observes that we learn about ourselves from painful experiences with women: "ces dilemmes douloureux que l'amour nous pose à tout instant nous instruisent, nous découvrent successivement la matière dont nous sommes faits" (*TR* II, 65). Arnaud Dandieu remarks that "un des traits essentiels du romantisme proustien est . . . d'être doloriste" (193). Schopenhauer and Proust have shown Beckett that life is sorrowful and that its sorrows reveal the material of which we are made. Those insights are not philosophical; they are psychological.

*   *   *

The new and essentially Freudian subject of depth psychology reached students of literature early in the century, quickly but vaguely, and because its terminology was unclear to them, they were imprecise in their employment of it. Nonetheless, psychological consideration of *A la Recherche du temps perdu* was obviously appropriate. We cannot look in detail at Beckett's many appropriations from French criticism and from Ernst Curtius (for which, see Edith Fournier's annotated translation), but a quick survey of some critics is necessary.

Curtius, writing in 1924, linked the topic of memory to Proust's distant relative Henri Bergson, especially his *Matière et mémoire* (37). Attempting like many others to adapt to aesthetics Einstein's theory of relativity, he located Proust's relativity in "ces vues psychologiques" (42), but his chapter on "La Volonté" makes no mention of Schopenhauer, Freud, or any other philosophers or psychologists. Two years later J. N. Fauré-Biguet cited the new authorities, asserting that "les trois noms de Bergson, Einstein et Freud ont été prononcés chaque fois qu'a été signalé le rôle joué dans les livres de Proust, par l'intuition, le temps, l'inconscient" ("Réflexions"). Ramon Fernandez, also publishing in 1926, rebuked Proust for "a passive sensibility which manifests no index of maturity, . . . an *ego* larger than life-size which the most lucid analysis fails to render transparent" (57). Two years later, Henri Bonnet published two articles in *Hommage à Marcel Proust*. In one he remarks that "la psychologie proustienne incline au déterminisme intégrale" (45). In the other, "La Psychologie de l'amour selon Marcel Proust," he mentions Schopenhauer briefly—"pour Marcel Proust, comme pour Schopenhauer, l'amour est un leurre"—but he insists that Proust's "subjectivisme n'est pas métaphysique, il est uniquement psychologique" (73).

The critical text that Beckett used most is Arnaud Dandieu's *Marcel Proust: Sa révélation psychologique* (1930), which must have reached the bookstores if not the Ecole Normale Supérieure just as he began his hurried study of the novel. Beckett mined the work extensively. One example must suffice. Discussing life generally before turning to *A la Recherche*, Beckett says of the future that "it seems exempt from the bitterness of fatality: in store for us, not in store in us" (5). The notion that fatality is internal and personal comes from Dandieu's discussion of the liaison between Gilberte and Marcel. It might have been successful, Dandieu says. There is no objective necessity that burdens Proust's love with a pessimistic fatality: "La fatalité est, non dans les choses, mais dans le tempérament schizoïdique du sujet." He adds: "Le pessimisme de Proust ne se borne d'ailleurs pas à l'amour, il est absolument général" (192).

Dandieu claims that after the publication of *Guermantes* and *Sodome et Gomorrhe* most writers considered Proust as "nourri de Bergson et—pourquoi pas?—de Freud," and he praises him for having "poussé à la limite du possible le génie de l'introspection et l'expression du détail psychologique" (9).

Dandieu also asserts that Proust has reversed the conventional notion that an artist must know his material thoroughly before beginning to work. Equating Proust and Marcel, as was common, he says that for the artist the work of art is the "seule moyen de reconnaissance et de traduction de la 'patrie intérieure.' L'art est avant tout une découverte; il est aussi anti-littéraire par essence. Proust échappe à la fois à la littérature et à la morale; il est descendu jusqu'aux racines psychologique de l'art" (24–25). Dandieu's image of psychological roots may echo Proust on the artist as a tree rather than a building (*Ombre* III, 188–89). He surely anticipates Beckett's assertion that the artist's inner self, "the ideal core of the onion," is the goal of proper "poetical excavation" (16–17). Dandieu's use of psychological terms is thoroughly amateurish, but his interesting perceptions survive their phrasing. They were certainly interesting to Beckett.

Only Dandieu's terms appear in *Proust*. Beckett's reasons for using Schopenhauer psychologically without going deeply into a psychological analysis of the text would be interesting to know. (One reason is that he had little knowledge of depth psychology as yet.) Nevertheless, we must move on from the critic and academic manqué to the developing artist. We pause only to note that two terms are surprisingly absent from *Proust*. One is the title of the only work by Proust discussed in that monograph: *A la Recherche du temps perdu*. It is a curious oddity in literary studies that Beckett wrote at length about two of the major works of twentieth-century literature without ever stating the title of either. The second missing term is obvious: "psychology."

2.

Before *Murphy*

Proust shows the young Beckett obliged by *A la Recherche* to analyze and discuss some of the psychological topics that would become central to his own artistic work. His researches, as we have noted, enabled him to study these concerns and become conscious of them extensively. His obligation to discuss Proust's work imposed a useful detachment. Writing about Marcel's problems or the human race's tragic situation, he was able to avoid writing about his own personal views and life. He could deal with plots and characters already contrived. He could use the ideas and terms of experts such as Proust, Schopenhauer, and critics of literature. But all these would not help him much when he began to write fiction.

We are concerned with his use of depth psychology as a source of images, ideas, characterizations, and fictional structures. This is a source he had evaded in discussing Proust and that few readers then or now could easily recognize in fiction. Decades later, when Beckett became the target of worldwide critical analysis, many critics discussed his debts to Dante and Descartes and a host of others, but his uses of Schopenhauer and Freud and Jung were scarcely noted. He had been willing to mention Schopenhauer, at least in *Proust,* but he remained secretive about Freud and Jung throughout his life. James Knowlson's biography has shone bright sunlight on these occult psychological concerns.

In his earliest fictions, however, there was little to be secretive about. We can give these prentice attempts only a passing glance on our way to *Murphy,* and we must settle for four examples: "Assumption," *Dream of Fair to Middling Women, More Pricks Than Kicks,* and "A Case in a Thousand." All four works reveal a writer centrally interested in the psyche but unsure of how to dramatize it and all too willing to settle for heavily metaphorical descriptions.

"Assumption"

This brief story, written even before *Proust*, appeared in the journal *transition* in 1929. Its location promises much. Editor Eugène Jolas retrospectively identifies this story as a "paramyth," a term replacing "short story," he explains, "because we considered that the narrative should be given a mythological prolongation" (*Transition Workshop* 15). By this time T. S. Eliot had praised Joyce's use of the *Odyssey* in *Ulysses* and had acknowledged his own uses of such material in *The Waste Land*. The editors of *transition* had also been reading and in small part publishing C. G. Jung. Jolas relevantly reports Beckett's joining with a few other artists, including his friend MacGreevy, in signing Jolas's manifesto *Poetry Is Vertical* (1932), which "sought freedom from the purely materialistic conceptions then in vogue" (16).

"Assumption" is certainly free of such conceptions. In its brief blur we meet an unnamed and implicitly meaningful protagonist capable of imposing silence upon argumentative speakers by means of an elaborately prepared utterance unquoted but described as a "supreme manifestation of Beauty" (42). Nevertheless, he fears making sounds and tries to remain silent, although he knows that silence increases the pressure of "the torrent that must destroy him. At this moment the Woman came to him . . . " (43). The capitalization and ellipsis signal significance. She keeps visiting and praising him, with dramatic results: "he lost a part of his essential animality," a condition consisting of wordlessness and his "desire to live" (43). Then the dam bursts: "he was unconditioned by the Satanic dimensional Trinity, he was released, achieved, the blue flower, Vega, GOD" (44). This release from Schopenhauer's trinity of time, space, and understanding (*WWR* I, book I, § 4) recurs until "he hungered to be irretrievably engulfed in the light of eternity, one with the birdless cloudless colorless skies, in infinite fulfillment." Reduced to lower case, the woman is "swept aside by a great storm of sound" that "fused into the breath of the forest and the throbbing cry of the sea." She remains calm: "They found her caressing his wild dead hair."

The man may have achieved nirvana by means of music (*WWR* I, book III, § 52; II, ch. 39), but no reader could guess this. Schopenhauer's notions about the mind, the body, the intellect freed from the will, and the negative qualities of women and sex may comprise a paramyth about the artist's reluctant resignation of his principium individuationis, escape from the sexual will, and acceptance of destiny. One might even say that in this story Beckett accepts his own fate. Common sense prevails, however. Beckett had not yet found a way to incorporate depth psychology into his presentations of life.

Dream of Fair to Middling Women

In 1932 Beckett wrote this novel that would not reach print until after his death. It makes use of a verbosely self-conscious narrator uncertain of his abilities and aware that his material escapes his control. Its protagonist, Belacqua, is equally verbose, self-conscious, and uncertain. These overlapping characters are sufficient in themselves to doom the enterprise. To them Beckett adds other characters and incidents from his own life, caricatured and forwarding no coherent plot. The style is choked with allusions and obiter dicta. No chain of associations is left unrattled. Nevertheless, the basing of his novel upon autobiographical materials is of great significance, and the unpublished manuscript became an *aide-mémoire* to which he often returned.

Its most significant theme, here as in the rest of Beckett's work, is the multiple self. The narrative structure cannot support this theme; Belacqua merely goes from woman to woman while shrinking from each into himself and to no end. Beckett, however, inserts into the novel a small paramyth in order to speak about this theme. It concerns a minor character, Nemo, who does not share the others' surface existence in a social world. His descendants will include Mr. Endon and the Unnamable. His name, Latin for "no one," echoes Jules Verne's Captain Nemo. *Dream* makes frequent metaphoric use of water imagery, in which depth and surface are the dual elements.

The other characters "stand for something," the narrator says, but Nemo does not (7). Nemo takes his stand on the O'Connell Bridge in Dublin, over the Liffey. This position acts out his psychic situation. His time complements his space: the narrator speaks of "dusk . . . the magic hour . . . when Nemo is in position" between light and dark (155; see 25). Nemo cannot choose light or dark and cannot move, cannot settle for either side. He thereby acts out the philosophical image of Balaam's ass, dying of hunger between two bales of hay or of hunger and thirst between hay and water. Nemo cannot endure this situation; he jumps. He is pulled out of the Liffey and charged with felo-de-se. (A joke implicit in the legal term is that Nemo has no "se," no self.) The narrator defends him by explaining that he suffers from "a superaboulia" (162, 164)—a condition critics objected to in Proust's Marcel. "Aboulia" is a psychological term for "lack of willpower." Freud uses it; the critics do not.

Nemo acts the part of a part of a psyche, a consciousness powerless to accept the roles it must play. Long before Nemo jumps, the narrator asserts that "suicides jump from the bridge, not from the bank" (24). This situation will recur: the Belacqua of *More Pricks* will die between solitude and married life, Murphy will die between the Magdalen Mental Mercyseat and Celia, and other protagonists will end similarly, neither here nor there. The complementary situation is an endless coming and going, from one bank to the other, as stated most explicitly in Beckett's late poem "Neither."

The seldom mentioned Nemo is a partial projection of Belacqua, to whom Beckett attaches other metaphorical descriptions of this psychic state: "At his simplest he was trine. . . . Centripetal, centrifugal and . . . not" (107); "Apollo, Narcissus and the anonymous third person" (111; see 109). Here Apollo is the bold and outward-looking psychological type, the "extravert" in Jung's terminology. "Narcissus" is the "introvert" and a central type in Freud's psychology. The anonymous third is Nemo. Murphy—Narcissus in his rocking chair—will be lured by Celia into the Apollonian world. He will speak of "the self that he loved" and "the self that he hated." This anonymous "he" echoes Nemo. Jung speaks of harmonizing the extraverted and introverted elements of one's psyche, but the image of Nemo on the bridge offers no possibility of this, nor do the comings and goings. Nor, in fact, does *Dream,* in which settled psyches fix the minor characters in roles that they must repeat unendingly.

More Pricks Than Kicks

In this collection (1934) a few minor themes develop the central theme of the divided self. Most of the stories report again Belacqua's relations with a variety of women. Most of his problems are conventional, though improved by wit. His desire for a woman is set against his desire to be alone, as in *Dream.* Here, however, Beckett adds less expectable dualities, such as "Love and Lethe" and ordinary sexuality versus voyeurism and masturbation. Belacqua's choices are weak and inconclusive. His death is as will-less as Nemo's suicide attempt. Beckett told us that by explaining his characters Proust explains them away. In these stories his acidulous narrator strives for much the same result. Belacqua "was an incoherent person and content to remain so" (38), he says, although he also speaks of "the last phase of his solipsism, before he toed the line and began to relish the world" (36).

In this work Beckett does use the term "psychologically," but only once (127); he also refers briefly to the "psyche," which he equates with "mind" (159, 161). When he develops a psychological matter, however, he turns to metaphors, as when the Nemo motif recurs. In "Yellow," Belacqua decides that "he did not care for these black and white alternatives" and asserts that "between contraries no alternation is possible" (162–63). Shifting to philosophy, Beckett speaks of irreconcilable alternatives, Democritus and Heraclitus. He recalls Proust, Nemo's suicide attempt, and his own citation in

Proust of Baudelaire's "ce gouffre interdit à nos sondes" when Belacqua speaks of "that Delian diver who, after the third or fourth submersion, returns no more to the surface" (164). These are splendid variants of allusion and metaphor. They are also evasions of direct reference to psychology.

The evasiveness is not merely verbal. One example must suffice. In "Love and Lethe" Beckett considers suicide, a central autobiographical concern. The narrator waffles about a motive: "we assume the irresponsibility of Belacqua, his faculty for acting with insufficient motivation" (89). Then the evasion is expanded. Belacqua had no reasons for dying, or at least "he had none . . . that he could offer" (89). The narrator then summarizes the irrelevant reasons: "Greek and Roman reasons, Sturm und Drang reasons, reasons metaphysical, aesthetic, erotic, anterotic and chemical, Empedocles of Agrigentum and John of the Cross reasons, in short all but the true reasons, which did not exist, at least not for the purposes of conversation" (90). Perhaps depth psychology could not be offered for conversational purposes in 1934 in Ireland, but the absence of "psychological" from that list verges on coyness.

Like *Dream* and "Assumption," *More Pricks Than Kicks* contains materials to which Beckett will often return. An example is a physical position that will develop into psychological richness: in "Fingal" Belacqua wishes "to be back in the caul, on my back in the dark forever" (29). In "Yellow" he realizes that "now there was nothing for it but to lie on his back in the dark" (161). Almost half a century later the protagonist of *Company* will be "one on his back in the dark" (7). Such materials, however, are still beyond Beckett's control. In "Yellow" Belacqua acknowledges that the mind he thought to have furnished so well was merely "the last ditch when all was said and done" (161). But there is much more to be said and done before Molloy crawls into his own last ditch.

"A Case in a Thousand"

"Assumption" reflects its declared interest in "applied psychology" and *transition*'s emphasis on the "paramyth," but its vagueness and its arbitrary myth could not have pleased Jung. In *Dream* and *More Pricks* the divided self or psyche recurs often, but the situation is asserted in characterization rather than developed and analyzed, as if the insight, however metaphorical, took us deeply enough.

The most striking anticipation of *Murphy* and the later works is "A Case in a Thousand" (1934). Critics have given it little attention, perhaps agreeing with Raymond Federman and John Fletcher that "the story itself is curiously out of key with the rest of Beckett's fiction; in particular, it has little in common with the *More Pricks Than Kicks* cycle" (15; Bair is more perceptive [184–85]). The story, however, is a forerunner rather than an anomaly.

Its closest source is "Yellow." We are again in a hospital; the "anthrax" on Belacqua's neck is now "tubercular glands" on the neck of a boy who dies during the operation. In "Draff," Beckett had borrowed from Kafka's "A Country Doctor" in order to burn down Belacqua's house; here Dr. Nye's earlier examination of the child includes his lying on the bed next to him, another borrowing from that story. Kafka's child, however, speaks, has a significant wound, plays a major part in the story, and does not die. Beckett's silent child functions indirectly, and Dr. Nye's important relation is to the child's mother, Mrs. Bray. (Bridget Bray was Beckett's childhood nurse for many years [Knowlson, 175].)

Before Nye entered the case, Mrs. Bray had spent so much time at her child's bedside that she had been restricted to two visits a day, one hour in the morning and another in the evening. She spent the day "watching the window and waiting for it to be time to come up," on the bank of a canal. (This setting and situation recur in *Krapp's Last Tape.*) From the clinic window Nye recognizes Mrs. Bray as his childhood nursemaid, and he goes outside to meet her. They speak of her child and "the good old days. 'Yes,' said Mrs. Bray, 'you were always in a great hurry to grow up so's you could marry me,' but did not disclose the trauma at the root of this attachment. On the bridge they parted. . . ." The next detail adds another sexual implication: "A nurse let out a loud giggle. 'Did you see him kiss her?' she said. 'Why wouldn't he kiss her?' said sister, 'and she his old nanny'." (Beckett may glance vaguely here at Proust's Marcel and his mother, in addition to autobiographical material.)

This is a case in a thousand, then, but the case is not the boy's medical case; it is Nye's apparently Oedipal trauma. It is not a simple one. The Oedipal situation is displaced from the Bray boy and his mother (or the Nye boy and his mother) to the Nye boy and his nursemaid. In the past she substituted for Nye's mother; now, especially in lying next to the boy, he seems to substitute for her dead son. Nye's memories of their past relationship have been repressed, but his early feelings recur when he meets the now-married woman, and "the trauma at the root of this attachment" provides a focus for their present involvement and the story's brief plot.

Nye's unexplained trauma is hinted at when he lies down next to the boy and "entered the kind of therapeutic trance that he reserved for such happily rare dilemmas." (The therapy is directed at himself; the boy does not react or benefit.) Mrs. Bray, sitting by her son's bed, did not speak to Nye during his examinations "but was content to watch his face . . . in the hope of recognising him as the creature she had once cared" (*sic*). When he lies down by her son, something is revealed:

> Mrs. Bray, noting the expression, at once aghast and rapt, that over-came his face, was moved in a number of ways: to trouble, at such dissolution of feature; to gratification that at last she saw him as she could remember him; to shame, as the memory grew defined; to embar-rassment, as though she were intruding on a privacy or a face asleep. She forced herself to look at her son instead. Then, very sensibly, she closed her eyes altogether.

His trance enables Nye almost to retrieve his memory of that traumatic event of his childhood. When he awakes, his mind is still on the past: "If only he had a box of peppermint creams to leave with her. Mrs. Bray again closed her eyes as she felt the imposition too pregnant for words of his hand on the crown of her hat . . . , the rapid flutter of his fingers down her cheek, the ineffable chuck to her dewlap."

Beckett's pregnant imposition of psychological concerns upon the medical event continues; the second operation is reported immediately and abruptly: "Surgeon Bor operated, the boy's lung collapsed and he died. Mrs. Bray sud-denly found her tongue and thanked Dr. Nye for all that he had done." Nye then goes on vacation. He returns on learning that Mrs. Bray has resumed her watch outside the hospital after her son's funeral. They meet again on the bridge. Nye says that he has been wanting to ask her something. She replies, "I wonder would that be the same thing I've been wanting to tell you ever since that time you stretched out on his bed."

Nye was introduced as a man whose heart "knocked and misfired for no reason known to the medical profession." (Murphy's heart will be similar but more organized, "one moment in such labour that it seemed on the point of seizing, the next in such ebullition that it seemed on the point of bursting." "No physician could get to the root of it" [3].) Nye is one of "the sad men, but not to the extent of accepting . . . this condition as natural and proper. He looked upon it as a disorder." In his office he thinks: "Myself I cannot save." Then he lies "on the couch, still tossed from the last patient," as he will later lie on the boy's bed.

Obviously the story reports psychosomatic symptoms. Mrs. Bray's rev-elations offer Nye the possibility of therapy:

> Thereupon she related a matter connected with his earliest years, so trivial and intimate that it need not be enlarged on here, but from the elucidation of which Dr. Nye, that sad man, expected great things.

"Thank you very much," he said, "that was what I was wondering."
They watched the water flowing out of the shadow a little longer.
. . . "I brought you a few peppermint creams," he said.

So they parted, Mrs. Bray to go and pack up her things and the dead
boy's things, Dr. Nye to carry out Wasserman's test on an old school-
fellow.

They do not jump, nor do they leave the bridge together. Light shining
into the water flowing out of the shadow enables one to see into its depths.
The story's final sentence returns us from Nye's psychosexual trauma to the
commmplementary world of physical sexual illness and the Wasserman ("water man") test. The reader must connect the story's puzzle pieces to intuit a
possible sexual event that produced the Nye boy's "aghast and rapt" expression and his nursemaid's reactions; to imagine the mother, sitting by her
dying son, concerned with what had been and might have been; to relate the
boy's death, Nye's recovered boyhood event, and Mrs. Bray's return to see
Nye again, on the bridge, and then to take her son's clothes away. That
done, the reader can appreciate such details as the peppermint creams.

Freud's "Analysis of a Phobia in a Five-Year-Old Boy" (1905) concerns
childhood sexuality; Beckett will use it in "From an Abandoned Work."
Consulting Freud's article, quite arbitrarily, and noting a few of the story's
unmentioned details, one might argue that Nye as a child, like Freud's patient, was concerned with the question of whether women have a penis.
Nye's nursemaid may have shown him that they do not. This information,
repressed, led to his present impotence. This analysis would explain Nye's
reported interest in people's buttocks; Freud's child took them to be a substitute for a penis. It would also explain Nye's dissatisfaction with "the
meditative life." In this article, however, Freud notes that the case history
extracted from a patient is quite different from the therapist's later understanding of it: "While the analysis of a case is in progress it is impossible to
obtain any clear impression of the structure and development of the neurosis. That is the business of a synthetic process which must be performed
subsequently" (X, 132).

This is a valuable passage, and not for "A Case" alone. Beckett has presented readers the analytic details of Nye's and perhaps Mrs. Bray's neuroses, leaving to us the synthetic understanding of them. Freud's synthetic
process requires that all the details enter the composition. The hypothesis of
an Oedipal complex, for instance, cannot hold up. There is no mention of
Nye's parents, no emphasis on Mrs. Bray's husband, no serious suggestion
of sexual attraction between Nye and Mrs. Bray. The boy is given no indi-

viduality whatsoever, and Mrs. Bray's concern for him is oddly unemotional and certainly less intense than her concern with Nye.

Even a hasty diagnosis must be dual. The sexual elements, certainly present, indicate dysfunction: impotence and the threat of syphilis. The relation emphasized, however, is that of Nye and Mrs. Bray as son and mother. This long-ended substitute for the conventional pair gave way to normal life; he grew up and she had a son of her own. Now the relation has returned to be recognized for what it was, and its mutual acceptance is signaled by the peppermint creams. It has returned not as a perverse bonding but as a recovered memory, now the possible source of therapeutic recovery for both of them. (The "strawberry mottle of the nose" may fade if Mrs. Bray can settle now for candy instead of drink.) This may be Beckett's only psychological story with a happy ending.

This psychoanalysis is less important than the fact of the story. "A Case in a Thousand" is a surprising work. In writing it Beckett deals directly with a subject previously evaded. Only the term "trauma" explicitly indicates that Nye suffers from a neurosis, but that topic provides a sharp focus for all the materials of the story, including the peppermint creams. And the straightforward narrative does not hide behind a stylistic extravagance of Greek and Roman reasons, Sturm und Drang reasons, etc. Beckett has come far. His next self-imposed task is to write a novel while exercising such control—in short, to write not another *Dream* but *Murphy*.

3.

Murphy

Murphy appears to be well organized. It moves steadily forward along plot lines that are stated and then intertwined. Murphy's isolation is explained as the result of an unsatisfactory attempt upon Miss Counihan's virtue and an equally unsatisfactory attempt at a philosophical explanation of his problem under Neary's guidance. Then Celia upsets his isolation. He attempts to appreciate with her what he had sought with Miss Counihan, balks again at the quid pro quo, and seeks a tertium quid at the Magdalen Mental Mercyseat, which proves no asylum. He decides to return to Celia, but he dies. Meanwhile, the secondary characters engage in their own pursuits, which amusingly if not quite convincingly oblige them all to seek Murphy. Then their plots are also drawn to a close, and the reader is left with Celia. Like Mr. Endon's chess pieces, at the end of her game she is back where she was at the start. *Murphy* needed no structural ideas beyond these, as the plots indicate, but it is also a novel of ideas, beginning with a philosophical uproar. Beckett seems to have rummaged through many books of philosophy for philosophical notions, scanting Schopenhauer but ranging from the pre-Socratics and astrology through Descartes. He also includes a chapter on Murphy's mind.

A glance into the "Whoroscope" notebook in which Beckett began to construct *Murphy* indicates rather startlingly that the finished novel is a smooth film of oil over troubled waters. The notebook's earliest formulation instructs the future novelist to begin with "X who has no motive, inside or out, available," and "H." that gives X "impetus." He adds, "H. any old oracle to begin with." We recognize X. Belacqua's motives for suicide could not be offered, did not exist for purposes of conversation; and Belacqua descended from Nemo, whose superaboulia offered him no motive for moving from the bridge to either bank or for jumping into the Liffey. X will become Murphy; H. will become the horoscope, combining fate and foreknowledge and constituting the external motive, the impetus, that moves X to action.

After a glance, however, at "Racinian lighting, darkness devoured," which suggests that Beckett was imagining a Gnostic treatment such as will be developed in *Krapp's Last Tape*, Beckett turns in the notebook not to Racine or to the Gnostics but to Dante and the climb taken by Dante and Vergil up the mount of Purgatorio: "Purgatorial atmosphere sustained throughout, by stress on Anaximander, individual existence as atonement." Anaximander is said to have created the first map of the stars, and this detail may well connect Anaximander to the horoscope, as does his obscure assertion that death is somehow a retribution or atonement for life. That idea is clearly on Beckett's mind. His notes use the term "defunction," his alteration of Schopenhauer's "defunctus" at the end of *Proust*. Beckett's primary interest, however, remains with Dante and now with the working out of a plot that will show X undergoing purgation through "careers." "But keep whole Dantesque analogy out of sight," Beckett warns himself, a warning that he may have expanded to cover his later uses of depth psychology.

A serious complication occurs in these plans when Beckett notes a new duality arising from the conjoined terms: "Vocation the essence of purgatory, defunction its negation." X is to be purged by working, apparently; Beckett notes the "difficulty of dealing with 'careers,' of which I know nothing." But he assures himself that X's sense of them will be equally vague. The "defunction" will hasten his trip to the summit.

Meanwhile Beckett has made or copied from an Italian scholar a chart that he titles "Purgatorial Distribution." It divides "Peccati d'amore" into three categories (each developed further): "per malo obietto," "per poco vigore," and "per troppo vigore." Beneath the chart he notes: "Cf Purg XVII 90 sqq. & 19–39 & 49–75." This emphasis on love will be retained in *Murphy*.

Clearly Beckett's grandiose Joycean plans become less and less clear, and the notebook's further entries offer us little help in moving from these first ideas to the finished work. Toward the very end of any possible time for working on the novel, there appears one entry not to be overlooked, however. It is set opposite the date "*Germany* 2/10/36," and it simply reports an obvious pun:

Kraft durch FREUDE

*   *   *

The stages between the "Whoroscope" notebook and *Murphy* cannot be traced. One must simply assert that the central theme of Murphy's searches becomes positive—not purgation, but the Desire and Pursuit of the Whole. Through Murphy, Beckett explores the possibility of achieving a wholeness of the self and a union of that self with the world. The theme may sound absurdly pompous for a comic novel (Kraft durch Freude) by an author in his twenties.

Dualism recurs, in Cartesian and Freudian terms. Miss Counihan begins her parroting of a lecture by Murphy with the announcement that "there is a mind and there is a body." That statement is given a Freudian application when Wylie identifies these items as "the little ego and the big id" (218). The division of Murphy into the self that he hates and the self that he loves adds a third item, "he," repeated from *Dream*. Schopenhauer's will or Freud's libido motivates these Cartesian parts. Neary, Wylie, and Miss Counihan spend their time in flight and pursuit, activities that suggest Newtonian motion but primarily demonstrate, as does Schopenhauer, the intellect's responses to the will's unflagging sexual demands.

Miss Counihan's name conceals a term for the female genitals and the mathematical "count." She represents the financial concerns and social proprieties of female desire, with Celia as her complement. Celia is like Miss Counihan in requiring payment for sex, first as a prostitute and then in requiring Murphy to get a job. She has the intimate given name that Miss Counihan lacks; she lacks the socially proper family name and title. Neary's name varies "yearn," while Wylie's name is obviously relevant: Neary clumsily yearns for women, humbling himself to them and then discarding them, while Wylie schemes cleverly. One enacts desire, the other the intellect in the service of desire.

Neary attempts to justify his yearnings through philosophy. He emphasizes the Pythagorean goal that he and Murphy seek: "It was the mediation between these extremes that Neary called the Apmonia. When he got tired of calling it the Apmonia he called it the Isonomy. When he got sick of the sound of Isonomy he called it the Attunement" (3–4). As these pretensions suggest, Neary's philosophical knowledge is superficial. He has encountered the Greek word for "harmony" and has misread its rho as a p, and he mispronounces the Pythagorean term "tetraktys" as "tetrakyt" (5). His own experiences of desire have resulted in no harmony: "Love requited . . . is a short circuit," he notices (5). The metaphor is not Schopenhauer's, but the idea is.

Beckett took much of his own knowledge of the pre-Socratics from John Burnet's *Early Greek Philosophy*. Burnet describes the importance for the Pythagoreans of a rational mathematical basis for existence, and their resulting dismay at the discovery of what Neary calls "the incommensurability of side and diagonal" (47). He is recalling Burnet's "the incommensurability of the diagonal and the side of a square" (105). Burnet also gave Neary and Beckett the Greek term for "harmony" (110), the fate of Hippasos ("drowned at sea" [106]), the problem of the dodecahedron (295), and several other details. Like the topic of harmony, one of these details will recur in later writings: the incommensurable geometrical relation often cannot be expressed except as an irreducible square root. Such a number is irrational, a surd. *Murphy* applies the term to Murphy (77); Murphy himself imagines the depths of his mind as a "matrix of surds" (112). Pythagorean mathematics included astronomical ideas that developed separately and later into astrology. It also included music, a topic that Beckett develops through Murphy and Celia.

It is noteworthy that Neary teaches philosophy as a form of therapy, not as an impersonal academic subject, and that Murphy seeks him out, after abandoning theology and being abandoned by Miss Counihan, for therapeutic reasons. Neary's academy substitutes for a direct treatment of psychotherapy, then.

Schopenhauer asserts that there is a single will that motivates all beings, all representations. Among the will's human representations are intellects, each separate from the others. Filling *Murphy* with characters seeking to fulfill or evade the will's desires, Beckett is faithful to his source, in his fashion. Like Proust and Freud, both influenced by Schopenhauer, Beckett prefers the idea that each individual contains his own will, or at least that the individual takes the will to be his own.

On that topic, however, as on several others, Murphy is characteristically of two minds. As an astrological Pythagorean he seeks in Suk's horoscope evidence for an external force that has shaped his life. In residence at the Magdalen Mental Mercyseat he decides solipsistically that "he was the prior system" and the stars a celestial projection of his self (183). He also tinkers with Descartes, dividing his self into the desiring body, the self that he hates, and the unemployed mind, the self that he loves. The division may be Cartesian, but its unemployment is not; we recall Schopenhauer's Sabbath of willing.

Those who serve the will are tied to the body, even when it is as deformed as Rosie Dew's; Celia is so tied, as are most of the minor characters. Those who evade the will wish characteristically to conceal or repress the body. Mr. Endon wears his gorgeous robe over his, and Murphy, reluctantly on the job path, wraps himself in his absurd suit. His repression, revealed by concealment, occurs most notably when he ties his naked body to his rocking chair. Mr. Kelly, seeking the sky with his kite, is confined physically to his bed and wheelchair.

The genitals are the focus of the will, says Schopenhauer, and the head the focus of the intellect. Celia and Murphy feel this duality most strongly. She is a body, presented statistically, but when Murphy replaces her on the job path she develops speculative yearnings (s'il y a). Her physical comings and goings then occur, like Murphy's, in the rocking chair. Murphy's yearnings for Miss Counihan seek sublimation in philosophy until Neary gives him up for a Cartesian reason: his conarium has shrunk to nothing, thereby cutting the connection between mind and body (as the waiter does more bloodily [6, 138–39]). Then he must pacify his demanding body ritually, in the rocking chair, since he is irredeemably *morphe,* form. That form must be put to sleep (Morpheus) before his mind can be freed from the will's demands. When Celia arrives, this repression ceases.

Because Celia and Murphy are at once complementary and potentially complete beings, body and spirit, they act out a Pythagorean success story: they harmonize. In *Dream* Beckett's narrator labored obscurely to connect the task of characterization with the composition of music. In *Murphy* Beckett compresses the topic into a few metaphors. Celia is Cecilia, the patron saint of music. The couple's sexual relations are formalized: serenade, nocturne, and albada. These musical events add up to a harmonious humming: MMM, music, music, music (236, 252).

Pythagoreans emphasized mathematics in part because of the distinction between matter and form. Numbers give form to matter and thereby set a limit to the unlimited. Neary has composed a tractate called *The Doctrine of the Limit* (50). When he applies music to his philosophical understanding of love, however, he tells Murphy that "all life is figure and ground" (4). Duality has slipped in, as his next image indicates: "the face ... or system of faces, against the big blooming buzzing confusion" (4). Neary's faithlessness obliges him to multiply the single face. He claims a system nevertheless, but sets it against William James's background of confusion. (James's phrase occurs in his essay "Percept and Concept—The Importance of Concepts." James is also important to later works, especially *Molloy*.)

In *Proust* Beckett recalled Schopenhauer's parody of Leibnitz's description of music: "an unconscious exercise in metaphysics in which the mind does not know it is philosophizing." Schopenhauer's own description divides music into harmony and melody, both of which are necessary. Melody needs accompaniment, while "music . . . is also perfect only in complete harmony." Celia and Murphy's MMMusic predicts their harmonious future. Then, however, making clear his analogy between music and the will, Schopenhauer points out "the will's inner contradiction with itself." The analogue of that contradiction in music is that "a perfectly pure harmonious system of tones is impossible not only physically, but even arithmetically. The numbers themselves, by which the tones can be expressed, have insoluble contradictions" (*WWR* I, book III, § 52).

We are reminded yet again of our hero's name. A murphy is an Irish potato, the first of many irrational roots in Beckett's writings. (Note the radishes, turnips, and carrots in *Godot*.) Because an irrational root is mathematically a surd, Murphy is incapable of harmony. ("There seems to be a certain disharmony between the only two canons in which Murphy can feel the least confidence" [76].) Murphy's music with Celia is insufficient for another reason. It demands a complement in the outer world. His evasion of work leads him to a job, but in another private world. The harmony of MMMusic is replaced by the MMM of the Magdalen Mental Mercyseat, where patients separated from that sensual music may worship the mind. (The mercyseat replaces the rocking chair.) Murphy sublimates his libidinal interests, and Celia succeeds to his rocking chair.

Celia too may have undergone such a transposition, structurally at least. The conclusion to Schopenhauer's discussion of music is relevant. The artist studies "the spectacle of the will's objectification," as does the philosopher. The saint, however, goes further. "His power, enhanced by this contemplation, finally becomes tired of the spectacle, and seizes the serious side of things. The St. Cecilia of Raphael can be regarded as a symbol of this transition" (*WWR,* I, book III, § 53). Celia, a Magdalen repenting her service of the will, turns to contemplation. Her reprieve is only a sabbath of willing, however. By the novel's end she has returned to coming and going on the job path. The boy's inability to harmonize his double kites and Mr. Kelly's connection between his body and his self, severed when the kite string breaks, reinforce this final triumph of the will. The serenade, nocturne, and albada are musical forms that imply harmony, but the names identify segments of time, and time's changes continue.

* * *

In continuing this hasty summary of Beckett's use of philosophers, we will need to examine chapter 6, on the subject of Murphy's mind, and also consider Empedocles, who underlies Murphy's death, a death so often misconstrued that it too demands study. First, however, it might be helpful to note where we are now. What is mentioned above and what we know from *Murphy* itself suggest a line simultaneously of plot and of character development.

Before he entered the novel, Murphy had studied theology. Then he sought the hand, or the body, of Miss Counihan. Kept at bay by her material demands, he turned to Neary for a philosophical explanation of his painful life. (Pythagorean philosophy aimed at the establishment of a proper way of life, leading to salvation.) Murphy failed his course of therapy with Neary because he could not love. The diagnosis was Cartesian: "I should say that your conarium has shrunk to nothing" (6). Murphy's mind could not connect to his body. Consequently, he turned to the rocking chair to silence his body, and he sought that "amor intellectualis quo Murphy se ipsum amat" (107)—an intellectual love, replacing Spinoza's God with Murphy as the god of his own idolatry.

Then he met Celia. Impelled by the will (or his star chart) to attempt again a connection with sensual life and his body, he abandoned his rocking chair for an apparent harmony between his increasingly physical self and her increasingly mental self. The result was MMMusic, but music is not the only food of love. Obliged by their bodies to find financial support for their physical existence, he is obliged by his dualism to abandon his mental self. (This reasoning is Murphy's.) Through Ticklepenny he acquires a physical job in a mental world. That connection promises him a new harmony, for which he abandons Celia. Her replacement is Mr. Endon. His name, "within" in Greek, signals the return of philosophy and a search for internal harmony. The emotional and sensual music of Murphy's relation with Celia is replaced by the comic intellectual harmony acted out and denied by his chess game with Mr. Endon. Attempting to look into Mr. Endon's eyes, he can see only himself. Mr. Endon remains within, as his chess pieces remained detached from Murphy's. Murphy cannot achieve a solipsism à deux.

At this point in the narrative, with only a few pages of life left, Murphy abandons his job and strips off his uniform. Quickly he finds himself detached from the external world, abandoned by all the people who once inhabited his mind. What he does next is straightforward and simple, when its structure is examined. Fleeing Mr. Endon, he hurries to his garret at the Magdalen Mental Mercyseat, "intending to have a short rock [he had reclaimed the chair from Celia] and then . . . back to Brewery Road, to Celia, serenade, nocturne, albada" (252). His mental self having failed to connect with Mr. Endon, he will abandon that goal for his harmonious physical existence with Celia. He wishes to have things both ways, however, by enjoying a brief recreation in the dark of his mind before he returns.

Instead he dies.

Romantics, idealists, and materialists here unite to grieve over the sad irony or the inhuman bad luck or the tragic astrological fate of Murphy's death just when he has toed the line and accepted the human condition. Pragmatic readers, on the other hand, note that if Murphy had returned to Celia, he would have returned jobless. There would be no resumption of the

MMMusic until he found another job. In short, the plot would be obliged to enact another variation on the story so far. (We may recall Beckett's early "Whoroscope" notes about "careers.") These readers might conclude that Murphy has failed at two versions of harmony, the MMM of external harmony with Celia and the MMM of internal harmony among the parts of his self, by way of Mr. Endon. Literary economy therefore requires him to die.

This line of reasoning presupposes deeper meanings in the characters and events thus far, a presupposition surely justified by the complexities of planning in the notebook, the philosophical notions scattered through the text, and the characterizations of the major players. But if these meanings do inhere in these materials, then consistency obliges Beckett to make equally meaningful the two major matters still awaiting our consideration: Murphy's death and chapter 6, the description of Murphy's mind.

* * *

Space precludes complete consideration of Murphy's death and the description of Murphy's mind, but we can make some useful observations. (A complete consideration would show that Beckett contrived both matters with reference to the thematic structures we have already noted, generated by philosophy and the mind-body problem and Murphy's search for harmony.) Murphy's death is distressingly complicated. One must assemble many scattered clues: the gas heater in Murphy's garret and its odd chain (similar to that on a toilet tank), the candle that will cause the inadvertently turned-on gas to explode, and the derivation of "gas" from "chaos." These details enable Beckett to conclude Murphy's life with a single sentence: "the gas went on in the w.c., excellent gas, superfine chaos" (253).

On that last night someone inadvertently flushed Murphy, thereby anticipating the instructions in his will. When the chain was pulled, the gas went on. It flowed into the radiator in the garret. Back in his garret after leaving Mr. Endon, Murphy had noticed "the dip and radiator, gleam and grin." He had lighted his way up to the garret with a candle, the dip. Its light reflected from the radiator as a grin, the horizontal row of gas outlets as its teeth. Murphy did not light the radiator, but he did not die of gas poisoning.

"The gleam was gone, the grin was gone." These assertions may suggest that the candle's flame went out, and its reflection along with it. "The starlessness was gone" too, however. It is Murphy's world that is described here. As in the aborted rocking with which the novel opens, so here—rocking, Murphy leaves the world of the senses (gleam, grin, starlessness) to sink inward into chapter 6. In the outer world the flame of the candle continues to burn, and when sufficient gas has accumulated, that gas explodes. Murphy dies from "severe shock following severe burrrns" (262).

Why did Beckett not dispose of the now redundant Murphy abruptly, as he had done with Belacqua and the protagonist of "Assumption" and the boy of "A Case in a Thousand"? Why all these details, this complicated explosion? Quid pro quo?

Murphy's death results from the Rube Goldberg device that Ticklepenny rigged to provide Murphy with fire (the central element for Pythagoreans, a source of light and heat but also a spiritual light). In that climax the major themes of *Murphy* reach a comic resolution. Murphy failed to achieve harmonious relations between himself and Celia and also among the parts of his self. The transitory connections and disconnections among the minor characters reinforce this pessimistic presentation of external harmony while reducing the self to an agent of the will. The novel also suggests, however, the possibility of harmony. Rosie Dew has her dog. Celia and Mr. Kelly have each other. There are metaphoric harmonies. Celia envies the happy tug and barge. Mr. Kelly looks forward to flying his kite, an image of his psychic self. Its tail needs attention, and we learn that Mr. Kelly's "caecum . . . was wagging its tail again" (19). Imagining his kite-flying, he locates himself in the world of the spirit: "already he was in position, straining his eyes for the speck that was he, digging in his heels against the immense pull skyward" (25). Body and spirit pull in opposite directions, but Mr. Kelly is in control and holds them together. More complex is another kite, "a tandem, coupled abreast like the happy tug and barge, flown by the child from a double winch" (152). Mr. Kelly and his kite act out an internal harmony, while the boy controls a harmony between two individuals. Like music, these characters and metaphors intimate a possibility, although all except Rosie Dew will lose in the end.

To consider the possibility of harmony after Murphy's death may seem pointless, but in light of this possibility let us return to the topic of his death. When the gas went on for the last time, it was described as "excellent gas, superfine chaos." These terms were first connected in Murphy's sleepy working-out of "the etymology of gas" on his first night at the MMM: "Could it be the same word as chaos? Hardly. . . . Chaos would do, it might not be right but it was pleasant" (175). Gas, not yet the ignited element of fire and light that Murphy will demand, was named by the Belgian J. B. van Helmont, who derived the term from "chaos." Empedocles, following Pythagoras, contrived a cosmology from the four elements—earth, air, cosmic fire, and water—and the two powers—love and strife. The cosmos consists of elements separated by strife. Love intermingles them, producing chaos. Murphy's meaningful end is not yet clear, but his gassy explosion has been connected with fire, light, chaos, and Miss Carridge's interest in A. E.'s *Candle of Vision.*

The issue of *The Bookman* in which "A Case in a Thousand" appears contains a review of "Recent Irish Poetry" by Andrew Belis (236). Belis, actually Beckett, says of his friend Thomas MacGreevy's poetry: "It is in virtue of this quality of inevitable unveiling that his poems may be called elucidations, the vision without the dip." Those last six words elucidate Murphy's end.

In a passage often annotated with a reference to Empedocles by way of Aristotle and Aquinas, Dante reports difficulty in climbing down into the ditch where the violently angry are punished. Vergil explains that the ruined path had been destroyed since his last visit. He speculates that the destruction occurred when Jesus harrowed hell and

> da tutte parti l'alta valle feda
> tremò sì, ch'i' pensai che l'universo
> sentisse amor, per lo qual è chi creda
> più volte il mondo in caòsso converso. . . . (XII, 40–43)

[the deep foul valley trembled on all sides, so that I thought the universe felt love, whereby, as some believe, the world has many times been converted into chaos.]

With much creaking of a chaos ex machina Beckett has contrived Murphy's meaningful end. His final movements almost simultaneously toward Celia and his rocking chair reveal him, Mr. Endon discarded, as loving both parts of his self, mind and body, for the first time. His system now feels love throughout. The gas, therefore, elucidated by the dip, merges the formerly separate parts of his cosmos into chaos. Murphy's end results from his comic success in achieving harmony, which cannot exist in our divided human cosmos. He has achieved that absence of strife, that absence of opposites, that Schopenhauer defined as nirvana.

This triumphant explication has feet of clay.

* * *

As Murphy achieves chaos, *Murphy* forms a cosmos of detached elements. The novel's organizational principles are implied in its many parts of a single coherent subject, Philosophy. Among its topics are those of Newtonian motion—that whirling acted out especially by Neary, Wylie, and Miss Counihan—and the Cartesian dichotomy of mind and body taught by Murphy to Miss Counihan and reflected in his angry distinction between being and doing when he argues with Celia (37, 40). Pythagoras contributes the themes of harmony, music, and astrology. The dual MMMs express two versions of this harmony. The horoscope and the narrator's astrological details develop a third and imply determinism as well. The chess match, which might have intruded strife into harmony, results in harmony. Murphy's attempts to escape the will echo Schopenhauer. Empedocles, with Dante's aid, provides the climax. No further explanation appears needed; nothing but the odd detail remains to be explained.

The odd detail, however, is Murphy's mind as reported in the sixth chapter. This chapter is a deliberate set piece amusingly intruded into the plot line at an exciting moment. Detached, like the passage in *More Pricks* explaining Belacqua's interest in suicide, from any auctorial responsibility, it reports Murphy's mind as "it felt and pictured itself to be" (107). The description presents itself as philosophical. The mind is a Leibnitzian monad, "a large hollow sphere, hermetically closed," that "excluded nothing that it did not itself contain" (107). Dismissing Bishop Berkeley's "idealist tar," Murphy accepts both the ideal—his mind—and the tar—his body. That body is then dismissed as having an unintelligible connection to the mind (109). No Cartesian conarium is mentioned. The mind's closed system is then divided into three parts—the light, the half light, and the dark. An unexamined self, *he,* "was split, one part of him never left this mental chamber" (110), while another part experiences the body and the external world. (So much for the hermetic seal.)

In the zone of light the materials of the external world are "available for a new arrangement," and "the whole physical fiasco became a howling success" (110). Murphy imagines punishing sinners in a childish version of Dante's Inferno: "Here the kick that the physical Murphy received, the mental Murphy gave. . . . Here the chandlers were available for slow depilation, Miss Carridge for rape by Ticklepenny, and so on" (110). In the second zone unearthly forms are on view, and "here the pleasure was contemplation" (111). In the dark third zone, time and change replace space and stasis; that zone contains "neither elements nor states, nothing but forms becoming and crumbling into the fragments of a new becoming, without love or hate or any intelligible principle of change" (112).

"Love or hate" as a principle of change identifies one element of Murphy's mind as presaging the Empedoclean arrival of chaos in the Magdalen Mental Mercyseat. Hate motivates the nastiness of the first zone; the other two zones offer merely "pleasure." That pleasure is unpersuasive. The second zone offers only contemplation of a Dadaist art gallery. In the third, the claim that "it was pleasant" to sense oneself "a missile without provenance or target" while "in the dark, in the will-lessness, a mote in its absolute freedom" (113), offers some escape from Schopenhauer's will, but no nirvana.

Much can be said about the materials of this mind, but not here. Here only two points must be made: chapter 6 is irrelevant. This point is dual because it can be supported in two ways. Flatly, the chapter does not fit into the novel because it describes an impossible Murphy. In the rocking chair and therefore "alive in his mind" (2), he imagines punishments for Miss Carridge, Ticklepenny, and the chandlers. There is no time in the novel, however, during which Murphy simultaneously knows that those characters exist and uses the rocking chair, apart from his last night on earth. (He is also not depicted elsewhere as so hostile, especially in sexual matters.) In addition, the claim that he has had only mental experience of caresses (108) denies his MMMusic with Celia.

Furthermore, the chapter does not bring together the bits and pieces of philosophy and philosophical descriptions of the mind with which it and the novel are filled. In fact it offers no intelligible description of a mind, philosophically or psychologically. In short, which this dismissal must be, chapter 6 of *Murphy* constitutes Beckett's last attempt to evade what will be the major subject of his artistic concerns not only for the next decades but for the remainder of his making of the novel.

Our original description of *Murphy* is no longer convincing. The structural principles of the novel were identified as fragments from one subject, Philosophy. They remain fragments. *Murphy* offers no fictional world based on a philosophic system or functioning as a critique of a system, as do *Rasselas* and *Candide,* for example. Implying a philosopher's world, it offers only fragments. Describing Murphy's mind, it gives even less. Chapter 6 reports Murphy's self-conceived mind, and that conception does not hold together either within itself or in its relations to the rest of the novel.

* * *

Finnegans Wake includes punningly all the names of rivers that Joyce could collect, but it tells nothing about them and draws no conclusions from them. (Anna Livia Plurabelle is an obvious exception.) Yet it would be absurd to complain that the *Wake* is fluvially shallow. As Beckett asserted, the *Wake* is not *about* something; it enacts something. Its rivers and music and linguistics and characters and places enact its existence, which is other than these.

Similarly, although in a much lesser way, one may assert about *Murphy* that it enacts a subject, and that its philosophical materials are an enriching part of that enactment. *Murphy* enacts Murphy's adventures from philosopharium to crematorium, followed by the dispersal of his literal and social ashes. That description, however, does not offer a basis for Beckett's choice of specific adventures. Mere literal cause and effect will not suffice.

Nor is the novel a bildungsroman. Murphy's childhood and family are not even sketched; the child is not father of the man. And the novel is not political, social, or economic.

This list leaves out an obvious type of novel: the love story. Part of *Dream* tells such a story, and much of *More Pricks* is made up of flight-and-pursuit varieties of the love story. In *Murphy* Murphy and Celia act out another variety. Beckett's extended consideration of Dante in his "Whoroscope" notebook emphasizes love. Murphy's, Neary's, and Wylie's pursuits of Miss Counihan and her pursuit of Murphy develop the novel's comic treatment of the topic. Perhaps *Murphy* is a stylized love story. But despite the claims of MMMusic, passion produces little more than the momentary byplay of Wylie and Miss Counihan. Murphy himself is a cold potato, though we must consider the "amor intellectualis quo Murphy se ipsum amat." Murphy's inability to love was asserted early on by the expert Neary (6), and Murphy's love story received a sour review from a later avatar: "Are we to infer from this that I loved her with that intellectual love which drew from me such drivel, in another place?" (*First Love* 23). This is the right track, however. *Murphy* is a love story. Love drives the plot as well as the characters, though the term has such sentimental overtones that one might do better to invoke Schopenhauer and speak of desire instead.

Certainly Beckett had used Schopenhauer often in *Proust,* and it is possible to find additional references in *Dream* and *More Pricks*. There is no point, however, in claiming that *Murphy* is Schopenhauerian. It is, but to say so advances one's understanding scarcely at all. Schopenhauer cannot easily motivate a plot or develop a character. He tells us what life is, was, and will be. In the will's endless devouring of its representations by its representations, there is no change. The creator of characters and plots requires materials that work themselves out in time, as Beckett recognized in attempting to describe the unfinished *Wake:*

> In what sense . . . is Mr. Joyce's work purgatorial? In the absolute absence of the Absolute. Hell is the static lifelessness of unrelieved viciousness. Paradise the static lifelessness of unrelieved immaculation. Purgatory a flood of movement and vitality released by the conjunction of these two elements. . . . Neither prize nor penalty; simply a series of stimulants to enable the kitten to catch its tail. ("Dante," 22)

Admittedly, "a flood of movement and vitality" scarcely describes *Murphy* (or Dante's *Purgatorio*). Rather, *Murphy* reveals Beckett's working out of all Murphy's possible relations to the world and to himself. This is a new idea.

On what basis could this presentation be organized? The "Whoroscope" notebook indicates that Beckett had the will to organize but could not find the way, and analysis of the novel has revealed some structural weaknesses and contradictions (especially in the chapter on Murphy's mind). Acknowledging imperfection, one can find a structure that props up the whole novel. With love or desire as a basic motivating force, it displays that force as inciting movement and vitality (with complications, including diversion, suppression, and a dead end). Murphy's intellectual self-love and a hint from "A Case in a Thousand" offer substantiation for these assertions.

Murphy reports theology and philosophy as composed of unemotional intellectual assertions. The cold intellect suggests that "intellectual love" is an oxymoron. Murphy's intellectual love of himself generates his desire, even while most engaged with Celia, to preserve his self unchanged. Predicting that a job would change that self, Murphy accuses Celia of not sufficiently loving it. Such details, and the hint from "A Case in a Thousand" that psychological analysis might reveal the cause of an inability to love, suggest a source of the structure with which *Murphy* presents a lover. Here is a description of Murphy:

> In the Oedipus complex the libido was seen to be attached to the image of the parental figures. But earlier there was a period in which there were no such objects. There followed from this fact the concept (of fundamental importance for the libido theory) of a state in which the subject's libido filled his own ego and had that for its object. This state could be called narcissism or *self-love*. A moment's reflection showed that this state never completely ceases.

The author of that description, Sigmund Freud, is surveying the development of psychoanalysis in his *Autobiographical Study* (XX, 56). His observations may seem irrelevant insofar as they mention the Oedipus complex and parents. Murphy's parents do not appear; more accurately, they fail to appear (251). Nor is Murphy a pre-Oedipal infant. Beckett's concern is narcissism in adult life.

Each adult is the protagonist of plots motivated by his libido (Freud's basic term for desire, usually sexual). Like Schopenhauer's will, the libido seeks objects in the outer world, but often in vain. (Beckett discussed this topic in *Proust* before Freud entered the matter.) Sometimes the object desired does not offer a satisfactory return of love. Sometimes, Freud explains, the lover's self becomes that love-object's rival:

> Thus narcissistic libido is constantly being transformed into object-libido [desire for another person], and *vice-versa*. An excellent instance

of the length to which this transformation can go is afforded by the state of being in love, whether in a sexual or sublimated manner, which goes so far as involving a sacrifice of the self. . . . [This repression of self-love initiates the rivalry.] The process of repression was seen to be a process occurring within the libido itself; narcissistic libido was opposed to object-libido, the interest of self-preservation was defending itself against the demands of object-love, and therefore against the demands of sexuality in the narrower sense as well. (XX, 56)

These notions already make Murphy a clearer and more interesting character than Belacqua. Belacqua's multiple alternatives to love report him as merely evasive and indecisive. Murphy becomes intelligible as a narcissistic lover throughout. First he desires Miss Counihan, displaying Freud's object-libido. Because she withholds desire for him until he gets a job, his unrequited desire for her results in too much expenditure of libido without response. He retreats into his self, seeking to find in philosophy an intellectual and therapeutic explanation of his personal problems. Neary diagnoses him as incapable of loving because his conarium has shrunk. In Freudian terms, he cannot alter his narcissistic libido into object-libido; he cannot submit to an object of desire outside his self. He turns increasingly inward, using the rocking chair to sedate his body and free him for "pleasure" in his mind. This indulged narcissism increases his sense of self-importance. Neary is replaced by Pandit Suk and impersonal philosophy by astrology, which claims that the very stars in their courses concerned themselves with shaping and guiding the individual Murphy.

Then Celia appears. Desiring, his body distracts him from his psychic self, and she becomes the object of his libido. Her compliant response encourages him to offer still more. This increase in object-libido stirs his neglected self-love into rivalry (neglected because he does not use the rocking chair while with Celia [30]). Then she ceases to harmonize with him and obliges him to request his star chart, which she hopes will force him to go on the job path. Until that search occurs, she will withhold herself—and she moves out. In reaction he indulges his self-love in the rocking chair until her telephone call from the outer world upsets his heart. ("The part of him that he hated craved for Celia, the part that he loved shrivelled up at the thought of her" [8].) When she finds him thoroughly and literally upset, he quickly claims that only her staying with him can stave off his death. (Actually, it was her announced return with the horoscope, his "life-warrant," that upset his narcissistic heart.)

Already, then, narcissistic duality has clarified the plot of *Murphy*. In this reading the last pages of chapter 5, so sadly at variance with the assertions of chapter 6, convey relevant meanings. The details hold together. Murphy is in the park, experiencing dismay at his mind's being "nebulous and dark, a murk of irritation from which no spark could be excogitated" (105). A reading of chapter 6 would make puzzling his dismay at darkness and "his efforts to rekindle the light that Nelly had quenched"; in these details light is used honorifically, although in chapter 6 the dark of the mind is the best zone. When narcissism is made relevant, the values alter. In chapter 5 Murphy, forced to take Ticklepenny's job, seeks escape without his rocking chair into a world that contains nothing external—not biscuits, not Rosie Dew, not even Celia, "but only Murphy himself, improved out of all knowledge." This passage describes a narcissistic lover seeking his love-object, that is, his self. For the narcissist the mind is the source of light, not the dark outside world, and is the object of that light as well.

Murphy's narcissistic search for himself in chapter 5 contradicts those sequential experiences of chapter 6, where the light of ego gratification fades into the half-light of forms without parallel, observed but undesired, and then the dark of passive and unfocused selflessness. That sequence throws out the baby with the bathwater; Murphy's self disappears, leaving neither subject nor object for that "amor intellectualis quo Murphy se ipsum amat." More clearly than before, chapter 6 now appears easily detachable because irrelevant.

These simple solutions pose complicated questions. Freud's *Autobiographical Study* has intruded into our reading of *Murphy*, but it offers few connections to the novel. Freud does note "the large extent to which psycho-analysis coincides with the philosophy of Schopenhauer" (XX, 59). There is also a tantalizing unannotated fragment in which Freud ascribes to Otto Rank "the replacing of astral explanations by a discovery of human motives" (XX, 69). Did this passage encourage Beckett to plunge into astrology in order to set Suk's horoscope against Murphy's mind and then let Murphy decide that "he was the prior system"? (183). It is amusing to think so, but the early references to H. (the horoscope) in the "Whoroscope" notebook offer no supporting evidence.

Beyond that detail there is nothing relevant in the *Autobiographical Study*. Freud makes much of "the importance of infantile sexuality and of the Oedipus complex" (XX, 53), but Beckett moves from Murphy's vagitus to his theological studies without describing his life in between. Even Murphy's failure to visualize his parents is not presented in a Freudian way. In the *Study* Freud speaks of the superego, but Murphy's mind contains no censor and no morality. For the purposes of this survey only the topic of narcissism is relevant to *Murphy*.

*   *   *

Narcissism is no trivial topic for Freud or Beckett or *Murphy*. The *Autobio-graphical Study* first appeared in 1927 (2nd ed. 1935). "On Narcissism" appeared in 1914. A significant essay on a topic that will recur throughout Freud's writing, it compresses many of his still earlier remarks on the topic. Its terminology develops his ideas about the structure of the mind, antici-pating the triad of id, ego, and superego that he would describe in *The Ego and the Id* (1923). In "On Narcissism" the superego has not yet appeared. Anticipating it is the "ego ideal," an idealized image of the self that the ego (not yet distinguished clearly from the self) strives to imitate, or should.

In his *Study* Freud separated love into object-libido and narcissistic li-bido. In "On Narcissism" the first type is called "object-love of the attach-ment type" or "the anaclitic type." The self-directed second type of love is, generally, the "narcissistic type." Freud tells us that "complete object-love of the attachment type is . . . characteristic of the male. It displays the marked sexual overvaluation which is doubtless derived from the child's original narcissism. . . . This sexual overvaluation is traceable to an impoverishment of the ego as regards libido in favour of the love-object" (XIV, 88).

Both Neary and Wylie conceive of their external sexual targets as irre-placeable, though Wylie is wily enough to protect his ego from any risk of impoverishment. Once their love-object is attained, however, a short circuit occurs and their self-love asserts its priority again, as Neary's discarded wives and mistresses indicate. Wylie and Neary are willing agents of Schopen-hauer's will. But their humility or dominance and their sexual overvalua-tion of their prey find more specific explanations in Freud's pairing of ob-ject-love and self-love. These lesser characters have their object-cathexes relevantly and savagely judged when Miss Counihan learns that there is a Mrs. Murphy (that is, Celia): "Miss Counihan . . . was inclined to regret her reflection in the linoleum. [Beckett puns here, combining both self-love and love of the anaclitic type: *anaclitic* means *leaning, inclined.*] Similarly be-fore Claude's Narcissus in Trafalgar Square [at the National Gallery], high-class whores with faces lately lifted have breathed a malediction on the glass" (228).

Narcissism shapes this passage, most obviously through the image of Nar-cissus. The whores curse him; beautiful and in love with himself, he has no need for a woman. Beautiful here in a work of art, he is untouched by the ravages of time that require face-lifting. (The glass over the painting reflects the whores' faces; what they see is inferior to what he sees in the water.) Inclined to see his face in the water, he need not negotiate with it in the quid pro quo world that the whores inhabit. (There is no hint of Celia in the passage.) This harshly negative passage supports Murphy's leaving Celia for the MMMercyseat, but that preference leads to other problems, also explained in "On Narcissism."

The narcissist loves himself, but his affection is not necessarily mutual, like that of Narcissus. Freud divides a narcissist's love-objects into four types:

(a) what he himself is (i.e., himself),
(b) what he himself was,
(c) what he himself would like to be,
(d) someone who was once part of himself. (XIV, 90)

The second possibility suggests the boy in such works as *Godot* and *Endgame,* but it is almost irrelevant to *Murphy.* (The kite-flying boy is potentially such a love-object, but Murphy does not encounter him.) The fourth possibility appears to be a limiting case of the second type. With the epigraph to chapter 6 in mind, one might seek the first type in *Murphy.* Mr. Endon qualifies. Murphy, however, hates a part of himself, and Beckett's phrasings modify the object of Murphy's self-love to exclude imperfection. At one point, for instance, Murphy seeks "Murphy himself, improved out of all knowledge" (105). At another, he is obliged to renounce "all that lay outside the intellectual love in which alone he could love himself, because there alone he was lovable" (179). More will come of this.

Beckett develops the idea that Murphy's narcissism has as its object "what he himself would like to be." The precursor of Freud's superego is the ego ideal. Murphy's obvious ego ideal is Mr. Endon, who is both separate from Murphy and a part of him: "It seemed to Murphy that he was bound to Mr. Endon . . . by a love of the purest possible kind, exempt from the big world's precocious ejaculations of thought, word and deed. They remained to one another, even when most profoundly one in spirit, as it seemed to Murphy, Mr. Murphy and Mr. Endon" (185).

Since one implication of "Murphy" is "form" and since "endon" suggests "within," the two comprise a whole ("as it seemed to Murphy"). That Mr. Endon is both the ideal internal complement to the external Celia and the object of Murphy's narcissistic love is made clear by Murphy's actions and Beckett's terms. Mr. Endon has "a psychosis so limpid and imperturbable that Murphy felt drawn to it as Narcissus to his fountain" (186). Murphy leans over the comatose Endon in a lover's pose: "Murphy could see . . . in the cornea, horribly reduced, obscured and distorted, his own image. They were all set, Murphy and Mr. Endon, for a butterfly kiss" (249). This is the pose of Narcissus, bent over the stream to see himself. The butterfly is a traditional image of the psyche.

Murphy's narcissism is extensive, but not a source of happiness. It does not underlie a successful love. Mr. Endon does not respond; the butterfly kiss never occurs. Considering this failure and the chess game, we return to "On Narcissism" for narcissistic love of this third type:

> What possesses the excellence which the ego lacks for making it an ideal, is loved [Mr. Endon's apparent satisfaction with his own solipsism, for instance]. This expedient is of special importance for the neurotic, who, on account of his excessive object-cathexes [Miss Counihan, Celia, Mr. Endon], is impoverished in his ego and is incapable of fulfilling his ego ideal. He then seeks a way back to narcissism from his prodigal expenditure of libido upon objects, by choosing a sexual ideal after the narcissistic type which possesses the excellences to which he cannot attain. This is the cure by love. . . . (XIV, 90)

The experience of object-love depletes one's store of self-love. One must be loved in return, then, in order to restore one's supply of libido with the object's love (or to recharge one's battery, given Neary's "short circuit" image).

In Murphy's case, however, no cure by love occurs. Leaving Mr. Endon, Murphy is frightened by the utter loneliness of his situation—prefigured by Mr. Kelly's loss of Celia to Murphy and by the isolation of Rosie Dew, Miss Carridge, the butler, and Celia after she is abandoned. He turns back toward "Celia, serenade, nocturne, albada" (252), but first he returns to the rocking chair to recharge his depleted narcissistic ego with self-love.

Murphy is a love story, then—a story of the failures of love. Beckett's use of Freud's descriptions of the narcissist's love-objects is both careful and witty. The personifying of the ego ideal as a homunculus in a padded cell, itself in a sanatorium, outdoes Freud in topological exemplifying. The description of Murphy's "love of the purest possible kind" in terms that include "ejaculations" and "butterfly kiss" amusingly evokes Freud's insistence upon the sexual nature of all libido and the psychopathology of everyday language. Since Freud identifies narcissism as the infant's first form of love, we might consider Murphy in his rocking chair not only as a comic reduction of the "come and go" motif but also a re-enactment of the parental rocking of one's earliest years.

Beckett is not through with "On Narcissism," however. Consider the vexed question of Murphy's prehistory with Miss Counihan. He did not feel for her the sentimental passion, the "complete object-love of the attachment type," that the yearning Neary felt for Miss Dwyer. Murphy defined his "commerce with this Miss Counihan" as "precordial, . . . rather than cordial. Tired. Cork County. Depraved" (6). His heart was not in it. His feelings were corked up. Neary's analysis is immediate: "for whatever reason you cannot love in my way, . . . for that same reason . . . your heart is as it is. And again for that same reason . . . I can do nothing for you." We can appreciate "commerce," since Miss Counihan withholds her love until Murphy makes enough money. Freud relevantly suggests bookkeeping, with psychic debits and credits: "The aim and the satisfaction in a narcissistic object-choice is to be loved. . . . Libidinal object-cathexis does not raise self-regard. The effect of dependence upon the loved object is to lower that feeling: a person in love is humble. A person who loves has . . . forfeited a part of his narcissism, and it can only be replaced by his being loved" (XIV, 98). Neary, who displays this humility, perceives that Murphy cannot love. Freud continues his description of the narcissist's attempt at object-love by asserting that "the realization of impotence, of one's own inability to love, in consequence of mental or physical disorder, has an exceedingly lowering effect upon self-regard" (XIV, 98). We know that Murphy hates his body and that he will seek in Mr. Endon an ego ideal.

"Your conarium has shrunk to nothing," Neary observes. As Freud discusses this retreat from the physical, he suggests, rather abruptly, the next plot event of *Murphy:*

> When libido is repressed, the erotic cathexis is felt as a severe depletion of the ego, the satisfaction of love is impossible, and the re-enrichment of the ego can be effected only by a withdrawal of libido from its objects. The return of the object-libido to the ego and its transformation into narcissism represents, as it were, a happy love once more [Murphy in the rocking chair]; and, on the other hand [with which Freud offers Celia], it is also true that a real happy love corresponds to the primal condition in which object-libido and ego-libido cannot be distinguished. (XIV, 99–100)

Freud does not use the term "harmony," although the last-mentioned state suggests that quality. But his opposing of a narcissistic "happy love" to a "real happy love" comprised of both types prepares us to recognize that narcissistic love is neurotic when substituted for object-love.

Freud's dramatization of narcissism was obviously useful to Beckett. The narcissist who "is impoverished in his ego," who "seeks a way back to narcissism," and who "chooses a sexual ideal" acts out plots satisfyingly similar to those of *Murphy,* and in doing so tells a kind of love story not conventional in fiction. Rivals in love are commonplace, but that the lover is his loved one's rival for his love is not.

Another oddity in this psychological love affair is that the egotistic Murphy is so passive as he is with others, far more the one sought than the one seeking. Even when he thinks seriously of suicide after failing to make contact with any of the patients in the Mercyseat, he is basically passive. Even with Mr. Endon, he simply responds to what he takes to be an invitation to chess (240 ff.). Yet Beckett, seeking elements of a plot, must connect Murphy with the minor characters. How can he be connected when he is even more self-centered than Belacqua? (His true ancestor is perhaps the protagonist of "Assumption.") Yet by the last days of the plot "Murphy . . . is actually being needed by five people outside himself" (202). The narrator ticks off their various motives, but Freud provides an ur-motive:

> It seems very evident that another person's narcissism has a great attraction for those who have renounced part of their own narcissism and are in search of object-love. The charm of a child lies to a great extent in his narcissism, his self-contentment and inaccessibility, just as does the charm of certain animals which seem not to concern themselves about us, such as cats and the large beasts of prey. Indeed, even great criminals and humorists, as they are represented in literature, compel our interest by the narcissistic consistency with which they manage to keep away from their ego anything that would diminish it. It is as if we envied them for maintaining a blissful state of mind—an unassailable libidinal position which we ourselves have since abandoned. (XIV, 89)

As a motive for seeking Murphy this envy may seem far-fetched. It is true that the need of another is a basic motive for most of the other characters. Murphy himself, however, appears to be driven by need, fleeing one part of his self and seeking another. To understand why this Murphy is desirable, then, requires that he be seen from the characters' viewpoints, not from our intimate one. One simple distinction by the narrator is relevant here. The narrator reports Neary as weeping. Then he generalizes: "All the puppets in this book whinge sooner or later, except Murphy, who is not a puppet" (122). Reviewing a translation of Rilke in 1934, Beckett rebuked Rilke's Malte Laurids Brigge for being "a kind of deficient Edmund Teste, . . . a Teste who had not 'tué la marionette'" (Disjecta, 66).

This sense that people in the normal world are manipulated (by the will, by society, or by their need for object-love, for instance) usefully aids us to see Murphy as separated from the other characters by his ability to avoid that normal world and therefore the role-playing and the whingeing it causes. (Paul Valéry's Monsieur Teste exemplifies the intellect detached from the will; he has cut the connection.) The other characters see Murphy in this way.

Puzzling over the question of "what women see in Murphy," Wylie settles for a phrase: "his surgical quality." "It was not quite the right word," the narrator says (62), but Beckett develops the metaphor. When Murphy returns to Celia with the news that he has found a job, he cannot hold her attention. She is troubled by the suicide of the butler upstairs. (He was her male counterpart. His "soft padding to and fro" echoed her own movement on the job path [69]. When Murphy leaves, she moves into his room.) Murphy dismisses her grief over the butler's suicide: "A decaying valet severs the connexion," he complains, "and you set up a niobaloo" (139). As the allusion to Niobe reminds us of the whingeing puppets, so the butler's severing of the connection recalls Murphy's own surgical quality.

Wylie's explanation (and Freud's) that such narcissistic self-centeredness attracts women may still seem unlikely, but if we recall the high-class whores cursing Narcissus, we may understand him (228). They need others, even to the point of undergoing facial surgery, but their long plying of their trade has brought no return of love, either from others or from their own ego. Celia's account of accosting Murphy at second sight (12–15) indicates that his indifference to her motivated her. (Her first reaction was to consider suicide, as Murphy would do when the patients ignored him.) Increasingly, Freud's sense of narcissism and his discussions of that topic offer a structural basis for the concerns of *Murphy*.

*   *   *

When Beckett uses Schopenhauer and Freud, he tends to echo in his text bits and pieces from the text he is consulting. *Murphy* provides clear examples of this habit. His caricatures of object-loves (two women demanding money for sex) and the type names Wylie and Neary suggest that Beckett was thinking in general terms appropriate to a general discussion such as Freud's of narcissism. In the Dickensian chapter 5, Murphy on the job path encounters these in particular: the chandlers, Ticklepenny, and Rosie Dew. All of them may seem uniquely and trivially Beckett's contrivances, but they are not mere decoration and actually are closely connected to Freud's text.

The term "chandler" is derived from "candle." (Miss Carridge's use of A. E.'s *Candle of Vision*, with a sexual implication, and Murphy's use of the "dip" in his garret set this kind of light against A. E.'s spiritual one.) One of the children is referred to as "the chandlers' eldest waste product" (77). "Waste product" is Beckett's marginal note against a phrase that Beckett partially underlined when reading *A la Recherche*: "si la réalité était cette espece de *déchet de l'expérience*" (*TR* II, 39). The job path, as well as the children, is located in mere reality as waste experience, the sort that one would be obliged later to purge, according to the "Whoroscope" notebook notes. Two paragraphs later there is a reference to "Antepurgatory." That Proust's term is attached to the chandler's children illustrates Murphy's narcissistic indifference to object-love and its fertile results.

Murphy's reaction against the chandlers is only one in a brief series of steps that will lead him to the Mercyseat. Beckett still must get him there. The means might be simple: rejected by the chandlers, Murphy consults another advertisement. Beckett ignores Occam's razor, however. His complicated solution requires three more entities—Ticklepenny, Rosie Dew, and Lord Gall. Why? By this late stage in writing *Murphy*, Beckett has begun to use Freud on narcissism. He must move Murphy from his new object-love, Celia, toward an ego ideal and self-love, a narcissistic cathexis. That intention might produce Mr. Endon immediately, in the Mercyseat's psychological monad, but Beckett is methodical; first Murphy must be turned inward.

In the final paragraph of "On Narcissism" Freud discusses type c, the narcissist's love for "what he himself would like to be." The internal image of this loved one exemplifies Freud's ego ideal. The ego ideal "binds not only a person's narcissistic libido, but also a considerable amount of his homosexual libido, which is in this way turned back into the ego" (XIX, 101). All self-love is technically homosexual, one might suppose, but the last-minute appearance of this idea is startling. (In Freud's brief earlier mentions of narcissism, homosexuality was a major concern.) Murphy's close encounter with Mr. Endon will have sexual overtones and will involve chess. Beckett introduces both chess and homosexuality in this earlier chapter, in association with the ad-hoc minor character Ticklepenny.

Ticklepenny enables the author to move Murphy from Celia to Mr. Endon, but the author leaves himself out: "The merest pawn in the game between Murphy and his stars, [Ticklepenny] makes his little move, engages an issue and is swept from the board" (85). Ticklepenny also makes a literal move, engaging Murphy's knee, but he is physical and imperfect, not an ego ideal. He is homosexual and "an Irish bard" (88). A bard, as distinct from a mere poet, speaks for a group or nation. Freud connects homosexual libido with group psychology: its ego ideal "is also the common ideal of a family, a class or a nation" (XIV, 101). Did Beckett's antic imagination contrive Ticklepenny from this paragraph? Nothing in his astrological and philosophical material would suggest such a character. Coincidence seems unlikely, especially when we turn to the next minor characters. Rosie Dew is also seeking an essence—not a national or ego ideal but a family ideal, Lord Gall's assurance of family identity.

Rosie Dew, like the unseen horoscope-maker Suk, acts a role in the opposition between external (astrological) destiny and internal (theological, philosophical, and finally psychological) destiny. Much has changed since Beckett's early notebook formulations, but his continued intensity of interest is suggested by the brief passage describing Rosie Dew's search for justification of Lord Gall's family identity: "spado of long standing in tail male special he seeks testamentary pentimenti from the *au-delà*, . . . the protector is a man of iron and will not bar . . . " (99). That amazing phrasing condenses intense research into the topic.

But the topic itself? Beckett's father had died in 1933, but he left no difficult will. However, Freud begins "On Narcissism" by apologizing for the necessity of contriving hypotheses about the instincts in order to think about the new subject of psychoanalysis. This necessity leads him to describe sexuality biologically and then metaphorically: "The individual does actually carry on a twofold existence: one to serve his own purposes and the other as a link in a chain. . . . He is the mortal vehicle of a (possibly) immortal substance—like the inheritor of an entailed property, who is only the temporary holder of an estate which survives him" (XIV, 78). That image of the inheritor (unusual in itself, it occurs only once more in Freud's works) continues in his next paragraph: "This primal identity may well have as little to do with our analytic interests as the primal kinship of all the races of mankind has to do with the proof of kinship required in order to establish a legal right of inheritance."

Freud's presentation of this comparison is both awkward and attention-getting. Its topic, entailed property, especially as connected with the problem of kinship and the legal right of inheritance, is even less common in Beckett's works. Its appearance in "On Narcissism" and in *Murphy* cannot be simple coincidence, especially since Lord Gall's sexual problem continues a plot topic, as does Rosie Dew's crippling. She has a body crippled by Duck's disease. The narrator suggests that for "the psychopathological whole-hogs" its etiology consists in her desire to repress her body. It is therefore "simply another embodiment of the neurotic *Non me rebus sed mihi res*" (98). This casual bon mot anticipates Murphy's neurotic decision that his psyche is a prior and deterministic system, the stars a mere reflection of it.

Thus Beckett moves Murphy past two characters, Rosie Dew and Lord Gall of Wormwood, themselves distant from the sexual and fertile world. Rosie Dew has turned to her Ouija board and to a dead Manichean who, both physically and spiritually, has also rejected the physical world (104). She does, however, work for money. Lord Gall is impotent ("spado of long standing" is a limp joke); he believes in the spiritual world but seeks an earthly inheritance. He too has not severed the connection. Murphy's hunger for tea and biscuits indicates his own tie to the world of the chandlers; we hear of "the dip . . . that the biscuits had lit in his mind" (102). With the help of "On Narcissism," however, Murphy is moved from his object-cathexis, Celia, toward his narcissistic ideal, Mr. Endon. These details, then, connect *Murphy* to Freud's ideas about narcissism and specifically to "On Narcissism." They develop psychologically that essay's specific references.

The encounters in chapter 5 act out Murphy's shift from Celia to Mr. Endon. Murphy rejects and is rejected by the chandlers, who are fertile and thereby set against Miss Carridge—her name is relevant—and her *Candle of Vision*. He is propositioned by and rejects the homosexual Ticklepenny. Ticklepenny's infertile homosexuality continues the line from the chandlers to Rosie Dew, crippled and with a dog as her object-love, and to Lord Gall, impotent and with an inheritance as his object-love. Having agreed to enter the Magdalen Mental Mercyseat, Murphy the successful narcissist detaches himself from Rosie Dew and Celia and sinks into himself in Hyde Park.

*   *   *

As a novel of ideas, then, *Murphy* uses conventions of the love story, as well as literary, theological, and philosophical allusions, in order to develop and support a thesis that is never stated simply and directly. That thesis is psychological. *Murphy* acts out these Freudian propositions: the bodiless self is contained in a body that links it to a world of bodies; this self is motivated by a positive desire, love or libido, that is directed both outward and inward; love draws the self to the outer world at its own cost and to the inner self at the cost of the outer world. Developing this proposition, the novel shows that no self can choose one direction only and that most selves choose the outer world while attempting to retain their self-centered control over it. *Murphy* also acts out a truth that Beckett had partially asserted in *Proust*: the love-object cannot be attained because it remains beyond one's possession, whether in the outer world or within the psyche.

Beckett's dramatization of narcissism and more generally of the century's new subject, depth psychology, is no simple matter. (Freud and Jung were recurrently dismayed by writers' attempts to use their ideas.) In 1935 neither the reading audience nor the novice writer and analysand Beckett knew much about these subjects. Nevertheless, Beckett manages some skillful sleights of hand to accomplish his task. His characters move through actual streets and cities (a Joycean characteristic, not to be reused) on identifiable days. Yet they are scarcely visible in that realistic world where the street names and public buildings suggest significance. They never greet casual acquaintances. Murphy's telephone exists only as a brief plot convenience.

We never learn how Celia and Murphy pass their daylight hours, although their dark is noted by serenade, nocturne, and albada. Murphy neither rocks nor reads; Celia has forsworn the job path. Because Beckett is concerned only to animate psychological situations, he distracts us from such questions. If Murphy loves Celia, the cause must not involve such irrelevances as similar interests or friends. She exists only to provide his libido an object-cathexis and to stand for general ideas with her emphasized body's coming and going, need for money, and indifference to any self not acted out. ("'I am what I do,' said Celia" [37].)

Beckett gives his characters a local habitation and a name, but little more. Neary and Murphy and Wylie can speak of philosophy and desire, and Miss Counihan can parrot Murphy. Beyond these topics they have little on their minds but money. Their concerns are almost exclusively with attraction and repulsion, pursuit and flight, desire and dislike. Compared to the crowded scenes and conversations of "Dream" and parts of *More Pricks*, *Murphy* is impressively expurgated, accelerated, improved, and reduced. Yet by the standards of the trilogy, *How It Is*, and the later dramas, *Murphy* may seem a cluttered social comedy. Beckett will go much deeper into the onion.

Even when we turn to the Freudian underpinnings of the plot, we must acknowledge that they appear to have been added late and to be rather skimpy. Beckett offers no relevant description of a psyche. (Chapter 6 will not do.) We cannot find in Murphy an ego, an id, and a superego, much less the minor mental figures that Freud had already contrived. (Some will surface twenty years later.) Instead we have the unanalyzed Murphy observing and judging a self that he loves and a self that he hates. (Even Wylie's definition of mind and body as little ego and big id is scarcely echoed in Beckett's characterizations.) Murphy's identification of the hated self with the body owes more to Schopenhauer than to Freud. Murphy's loved self has no psychological meaning, as we saw in examining chapter 6 and as we might see in examining Mr. Endon (not that an ego ideal could substitute for a self in any case). And the tertium quid, that detached and unquestioned Murphy who gives and withholds approval, is an arbitrary contrivance psychologically.

Still more at home with philosophical ideas than with Freud and depth psychology, Beckett emphasizes not Freud's mechanics but Freudian emotional problems. Obviously the problems of narcissism concerned him most. Beckett has not merely understood Freud's discussions and then contrived a fictional case history. He has built his own understanding upon Freud's basis, as he had done in "A Case in a Thousand." By overlaying the narcissist's possible psychological relationships with recondite theological and philosophical notions and with the practical details of rocking chair and bed, nakedness and the monadic green suit, Murphy's inverted coma and the job path, Beckett has given narcissistic desire comic extensions beyond the psyche. (Perhaps his later respectability has kept readers from noting that the seventh scarf with which Murphy impossibly ties himself to the rocking chair represses his penis.)

Comedy allows Beckett to stylize his simplifications of character and event. Many writers have posed the problem of a solitary self in a world clamoring to engage that self in its activities. Typically the self wishes to be alone to spend time with a mistress, to love nature, to seek wisdom, to pray, or to be an artist. Beckett, on the other hand, completes the inversion of desire by making Murphy turn in toward his self for no purpose beyond that turning, and in an asylum. Beckett thereby takes narcissism to an extreme, just as he takes Murphy's involvement with the external world to an extreme by embodying that world in a prostitute described by her physical measurements.

Like any good novel of ideas, *Murphy* does not simply act out conventional ideas. It implies new ones, and it has a thesis, despite Beckett's explicit dislike of theses. It marks a substantial advance over his previous writings. Belacqua learned to toe the line and settle for the world; he even married. Before doing so, he often avoided the outer world. Each decision, however, was simple and not related to previous decisions. Isolated, he fed his body's desires on highly spiced foods, alcohol, and masturbation. Suicidal, he supported his desire with reasons of all sorts except the psychological. Impelled toward the outer world, he sought sex. No psychic goal was implied. Beckett permits Murphy no such accommodations and fresh starts. Murphy cannot solve his problems by altering their origin; he cannot stop desiring to love himself, he cannot love himself, and he cannot combine self-love and object-love. A lobotomy might reduce him to the level of the simply motivated puppets in the novel, but even those puppets whinge.

This is no simple matter, then. Beckett dramatizes the psychological condition of narcissism with the aid of Freud's analyses, but he goes further than Freud did. Aided by his own pessimism, he shows that the narcissist is victimized by a psychic dilemma that has no solution. Beckett has incorporated the isolated Nemo of *Dream* into a plot that gives substantial definition to the image of the two banks of the Liffey, and he obliges the isolated self to come and go from one bank to the other but to find rest in neither world. That basic image will recur for the rest of Beckett's literary life.

The Freudian material in *Murphy* therefore has a value beyond its shaping and annotating of this passage and that. It differs from the other intellectual materials. The philosophic references carry no more weight than those to astrology, but they are valuable in that they create an ambiance in which readers are entertained by ideas as well as by character and event. This ambiance permits readers to experience the novel's intellectual argument, and in experiencing it, they are suborned. They are encouraged to expect a rational solution to Murphy's difficulties. Deprived of one, they must face his psychological state. But his neurosis, even if explicable rationally, cannot be cured by the intellect. Readers must settle for a painful end and for an acceptance of Beckett's painful thesis. The philosophical and astrological references also illustrate the complexity of human awareness; explanations contrived by the rational intellect are of many sorts, although the problems explained are shown to be psychological. The intellect is of little use, then, although the intellectual comedy of the novel may have sweetened what was probably a bitter pill for Beckett, his understanding of narcissism.

In retrospect we can see that Beckett had been concerned with that psychic condition for years, most obviously in *Proust* and "Assumption." Freud gave the condition a name and an extensive description. Beckett will not forget them. Years will pass before his literary abilities and his increased understanding of psychological matters can produce his mature bitter comedies on such subjects. Nevertheless, his first publishable novel undertakes a tentative exploration of territory not yet claimed for fiction. It provides evidence of a future artist in Schopenhauer's sense of the term, someone for whom the miseries of the psychic world are miseries, and will not let him rest.

4.

"First Love"

Beckett's use of Freud's depth psychology and especially of "On Narcissism" marks a considerable advance over his hesitant and limited uses of psychology in "Assumption," *Dream, More Pricks Than Kicks,* and "A Case in a Thousand." With some help from the minor characters, and with the prostitute Celia as the unhappy but psychologically healthy norm, *Murphy* covers the condition and possibilities of narcissism imaginatively and thoroughly.

Beckett is not dutifully Freudian. He suggests that Murphy's infant narcissism never significantly weakened, for instance, and his later treatments of neuroses take the same position. Freud's expectation of a childhood trauma appears in Beckett's works only in details of early events; these can be understood as suggesting the protagonist's sense of isolation, lack of affection, and occasional harsh treatment, but not as indicating their cause. Such details are diffuse, not fragmentary evidence of a single trauma.

Beckett surveyed the narcissist's dilemma methodically. Dilemmas afford only bad choices, and Murphy's choices constitute a prognosis for all narcissists. Philosophy, theology, and a happy object-love are shown as powerless to cure the neurosis. Whether the condition is imposed by the astrological stars or is innate in the determined psyche, narcissistic libido creates and maintains a neurotic existence. Awareness of the problem is no help, since the connection between the thinking mind and the acting body has been severed.

Murphy employs a narrator, but he and we can see beyond Murphy only to note weaknesses in his reasoning. In the Magdalen Mental Mercyseat, Murphy decides that a psychosis should be his goal, and the narrator comments: "*Quod est extorquendum*" (184); that is, this is a decision "which has been extorted" from his twisted reasoning. "The sad truth was, that while Mr. Endon for Murphy was no less than bliss, Murphy for Mr. Endon was no more than chess" (242). Such remarks by the narrator characteristically identify Murphy's failings without offering any improvements attainable by the neurotic psyche.

Murphy was not easily published, but its rejections apparently included no complaints about its use of depth psychology. One might expect Beckett to build more confidently upon his developed interests in that subject, but he turned to other concerns. His next earnestly psychological text, "Premier Amour," would not be written until the autumn of 1946, after "La Fin" and "L'Expulsé" and before "Le Calmant" (Federman, 63). During that decade he wrote little—mostly poems and book reviews—except for the substantial novel *Watt*. *Watt* and World War II filled much of his time between *Murphy* and "Premier Amour."

Watt and "Premier Amour"

Watt and "Premier Amour" can receive only passing mentions here. Material in *Watt* will be mined now for psychological use later. "Premier Amour" is a thoroughly disappointing return to depth psychology. Both texts will get short shrift.

Watt ends *Watt* in a sanatorium that echoes the Magdalen Mental Mercyseat and foreshadows St. John of God in *Malone Dies*. Poor Johnny Watt (so called on the cover of the fourth of Beckett's *Watt* notebooks) shares Murphy's inability to understand life but is not troubled by a shrunken conarium; he is indifferent to love. The possibility that he is motivated by psychic difficulties is left in embryo. Beckett notes in the first of the *Watt* notebooks: "Quin never properly born." Shortly afterwards he returns to the phrase: "The fact of the matter seems to be that Quin had never been properly born." This idea is worked out briefly but not psychologically in the notebook. It does not appear when Quin, now Watt, reaches the novel. Despite this indifference to a psychological sense, the source of the remark is C. G. Jung. He and his remark will appear seriously in *All That Fall*. When Beckett wrote *Watt*, he may have been unprepared to explore that topic.

Like Murphy studying under Neary, Watt seeks rational and verbal explanations of life, but he seeks no systems, Greek or modern. Brief swallowflights of verbal clarification are all he hopes for, words persuasively connected to things and events. He fails to find them. Molloy will succeed and will not like his success.

The novel's central theme develops Watt's desire to connect specifics or accidents to essential ideas. This theme is stated first by means of the fall from a ladder that implicitly gave Mr. Hackett his hunched back. He fell when he was one year old, a comic age for ladder-climbing. His report of the fall ends with his recalling the fallen ladder, the yard, the fields, walls, and hills, and the summer sky in the distance. These discrete entities comprise a paradigm of existence in time and space, reported by someone hunched over and seeing horizontally (15–16). The paradoxical fortunate fall from paradise is surely implied in these details.

With Mr. Hackett's report the narrative lets the ladder image fall. It rises again in the splendid monologue by Arsene, whose body is bent over like Mr. Hackett's: "my spine and sternum have always been concentric." (Beckett may have in mind Leopardi's scoliosis.) Arsene describes the sudden change in his life that occurred when "something slipped" as if grains of sand were to shift on "a great alp of sand" (42). A result was that his breast, "on which I could almost feel the feathers stirring, . . . relapsed into the void and bony concavity" that it is now. No more prospect of flying. "What was changed," Arsene explains, "was existence off the ladder" (44).

Scholars have connected this ladder with Ludwig Wittgenstein's statement 6.54, at the end of *Tractatus Logico-Philosophicus*: "My propositions serve as elucidations in the following way: anyone who understands me eventually recognizes them as nonsensical, when he has used them—as steps—to climb up beyond them. (He must, so to speak, throw away the ladder after he has climbed up it.)" Beckett's doubts about the reason encourage this connection. One climbs Wittgenstein's ladder and then rises beyond it, however. Climbers no more, Hackett and Arsene are left crippled on the ground.

Beckett's probable source, William James, will return again in *Molloy*. (He described our external world as the "big blooming buzzing confusion" in *Murphy*, 4, 29, 245.) In *Some Problems of Philosophy* James devotes a chapter to "Percept and Concept," in which he speaks of "trains of concepts" in the adult mind. He connects percepts to conceptual terms empirically and pragmatically: "the significance of concepts consists always in their relation to perceptual particulars." He describes that important relation as a ladder. He praises Hegel because he "connects immediate perception with ideal truth by a ladder of intermediary concepts—at least I suppose they are concepts." This image is retained: "Hegel doesn't pull up the ladder after him when he gets to the top, and may therefore be counted as a non-intellectualist, in spite of his desperately intellectualist *tone*."

Hackett fell off the ladder and was left bent over among the immediate percepts that he lists. Arsene reached the top and for a while was contented by the concepts there. Then the sand slid on the alp, down among the percepts, sending him back to the earth, the round of the seasons, and the recurrent percepts. Now any distant truths arrive by post, horizontally, and they are seasonal. For instance, the roses are blooming in Picardy. Arsene imagines the ladder as still in place: "it would be an easy matter [to explain to Watt the significance of Knott's service] and so descend, so mount, rung by rung, until the night was over." He chooses not to do so, though he supposes that those higher truths were not illusory: "in my opinion it was not an illusion, as long as it lasted, that presence of what did not exist . . . , though I'll be buggered if I can understand how it could have been anything else" (45). Skeptical at best, he is now back on the ground floor and about to leave Knott's educational service. Sam and Watt will end up in the sanatorium because they cannot rise above the discrete particulars of existence, which include the negative and changeable Knott himself, and because language itself cannot express generally such particulars. Probably.

Without the ladder image, Freud had offered a similar structure relating abstractions to observable facts in "On Narcissism." Discriminating between "a speculative theory and a theory erected on empirical interpretation," he chose the second, "with nebulous, scarcely imaginable basic concepts. . . . For these ideas are not the foundation of science, upon which everything rests: that foundation is observation alone. They [the concepts] are not the bottom but the top of the whole structure, and they can be replaced and discarded without damaging it" (XIV, 77). Beckett's characters occasionally seek views from on high, but no elucidations result. From the many "demented particulars" of existence (*Murphy*, 13) they, like Watt and *Watt*, can rise to no reliable concepts.

* * *

"Premier Amour" was written in 1946, along with "La Fin," "L'Expulsé," and "Le Calmant," but it was not published with the others. Deirdre Bair says that it was withheld because "it was too autobiographical, for he was still struggling to perfect the techniques of disguise and concealment that infuse his later writings" (358). We can put the matter differently, with the published work before us; Beckett was probably dissatisfied with his attempt to infuse into the story structures and meanings from Freudian psychology.

Such dissatisfaction is unsurprising; "First Love" is a poorly made story. One cause is his Freudian source. *Murphy* developed Freud's general theories about narcissism, which afforded Beckett a complex structure. For "First Love," on the other hand, he turned to Freud's report of a single case, "From the History of an Infantile Neurosis" (1919), and that report is complicated, anecdotal, and not coherent. (Although Freud treated the patient for adult problems, his article reports not those but the patient's troubles in youth. Because of an obsessive fear, the article is misleadingly known as the case of the Wolf-Man.) Bair suggests that Beckett had autobiographical materials in mind, and perhaps the story is cobbled together from two discrete confusions.

In haste, one reduces Beckett's uses of Freud's article to a few central topics: sexuality, the father, evasions of the outer world, constipation and doubt, and childbirth. If these have any common theme, that theme is love.

Freud's patient had a "first love" (XVII, 90), a nursery maid named Grusha. She was not his first sexual partner; he had previously been involved with his sister. He associated Grusha with a peasant girl, Matrona, from whom he later caught gonorrhea. With these females the patient played a passive role. In "First Love" the unnamed protagonist is also passive; he cannot recall whether the prostitute who took him in was Lulu or Anna; and she "was not the first naked woman to have crossed my path" (28).

"First Love" seems to begin irrelevantly, since the protagonist speaks at length about his father's death and his consequent expulsion from the family home. (His mother is not mentioned.) He wished to stay and even offered to swap his inheritance for the privilege of staying at home and doing domestic chores, but he was thrown out. He is connected to his father by many details, especially related to gardening. They develop elliptically Freud's diagnosis of his patient's "obsessional piety" toward his father. That piety, far more than his youthful experiences with Grusha and Matrona, inhibited the patient's mature sexuality. The same result is implied for Beckett's protagonist, and in both cases the connection between cause and effect is expressed in symptoms of neurosis.

The patient's most extensive evasion of sexuality expands to include the outer world. Freud reports his curious visual difficulty:

> The world, he said, was hidden from him by a veil. . . . That veil was torn . . . when, as a result of an enema, he passed a motion through his anus. . . . Nor did he keep to [this metaphor of] the veil. It became still more elusive, as a feeling of twilight, "ténèbres," and of other impalpable things. . . . He remembered having been told that he was born with a caul. . . . Thus the caul was the veil which hid him from the world and hid the world from him. The complaint . . . was in reality a fulfilled wishful phantasy: it exhibited him as back once more in the womb, and was, in fact, a wishful phantasy of flight from the world. (XVII, 99–100)

Beckett gives his protagonist a single window in his bedroom; it is "frosted over" (29). He wishes it curtained as well, and he turns his sofa around to avoid the faint light coming through it. As he reduces the light, his satisfaction increases. He reports a surprising connection: "Already my love was waning, that was all that mattered" (30). (We may recall Proust's connection between Albertine's death and the waning of Marcel's love for her.)

Freud's patient suffers from constipation, and Freud connects the problem with deliberate doubt: "We know how important doubt is to the physician who is analysing an obsessional neurosis. It is the patient's strongest weapon, the favourite expedient of his resistance." Freud promises to cure this constipation; the patient doubts him; and as therapy continues the constipation ends (XVII, 75–76).

Beckett's protagonist is thoroughly doubtful. Mentioning his uncertainty about the song that the prostitute Lulu/Anna sang, he says that he preferred to avoid doubting "at that period," but he immediately adds: "I lived of course in doubt, on doubt, but such trivial doubts as this, purely somatic as some say, were best cleared up" (25). "Purely somatic" suggests his awareness of a psychic cause for his general doubt. He had already associated his constipation with his exile from home and with anxiety: "One day, on my return from stool, I found my room [in the family home] locked and my belongings in a heap before the door. This will give you some idea how constipated I was, at this juncture. It was, I am now convinced, anxiety constipation. But was I genuinely constipated? Somehow I think not" (14). That doubt provides more psychic connections: "Or am I confusing it with the diarrhoea? It's all a muddle in my head, graves and nuptials and the different varieties of motion" (15). The graves and nuptials generalize his father's death, the resulting inheritance problems, and his cohabitation with Lulu/Anna. Freud connects feces with babies and relates his patient's constipation and occasional involuntary bowel movements, some in bed, with his concerns about inherited money (XVII, 72-76, 81). Beckett's protagonist does the same (14–15), and his "one night of love" on the sofa leads him to examine his makeshift chamberpot (30–31).

Freud says that for his patient, feces constituted a neurotic equivalent of babies, of a sort that would not compete with his self-love. Lulu/Anna, who has been emptying the stewpan/chamberpot once a day, claims that she is pregnant by the protagonist (31). She forces him to acknowledge her real pregnancy by opening his window to admit light and then showing him her pregnant body. We recognize from other Beckett stories that the view out that window evokes the protagonist's childhood. It is a relevant background for the announced arrival of another child. The light forces upon the protagonist the fact that Lulu/Anna, for once not in twilight or darkness, is acting out the process that he has been parodying with his constipation and diarrhea. She has not, however, brought his psyche into the external world.

Freud's patient was relieved from his sense of a veil or caul when he was given an enema: "then he saw the world and was re-born. The stool was the child, as which he was born a second time, to a happier life. Here, then, we have the phantasy of re-birth, to which Jung has recently drawn attention and to which he has assigned such a dominating position in the imaginative life of neurotics. . . . The tearing of the veil was analogous to the opening of his eyes and to the opening of the window" (XVII, 100–101). The connection to "First Love" is obvious. The window is not enough, however. "What finished me was the birth" of the baby, says the protagonist. "It woke me up" (35). He flees the apartment.

The theme connecting these multiple topics and details in "First Love" is, as the title suggests, love. The term occurs quite often in the story, but the occurrences fragment its sense rather than developing a single meaning. The "one night of love" is a comic event; the protagonist is a passive participant whose memory of it is clouded by repression (30–31). Before it occurred, he said that in his darkened room his love was already waning. At its most intense, he had celebrated it by such acts as writing Lulu/Anna's name on a cow turd and then sucking his finger. These matters may seem to constitute rather harsh caricatures of sentimental and physical love. The protagonist connects himself with the lover in an earlier work, Murphy, when he breaks off his description of this love to ask: "Are we to infer from this I loved her with that intellectual love which drew from me such drivel, in another place?" (23). (He refers to "Amor intellectualis quo Murphy se ipsum amat," the epigraph to chapter 6 in Murphy.) The entire passage composes a complex run-through of sexual attraction from "love-passion . . . that's the priapic one" through "platonic love"; he rejects both extremes. But this analysis precedes his long report of Lulu/Anna's bringing him to her apartment.

He explains, evasively, why he went to stay with her: "I did not feel easy when I was with her, but at least free to think of something else than her, of the old trusty things, and so little by little, as down steps towards a deep, of nothing" (27–28). This explanation links him again to Murphy. "You can want what does not exist, you can't love it," Murphy tells Celia. "This came well from Murphy," the narrator notes (36). The idea is basically Schopenhauerian, for Beckett: one can want only what one does not have. That wanted item does not exist, says Murphy. The protagonist of "First Love" puts the matter in terms relevant to Watt and to William James's ladder from percepts to concepts, although his steps go downward, to nothingness and the ideal core of the onion. He must flee from Lulu/Anna, however, to begin the trip. He can flee her only when she is present; when she is absent, she fills his mind. No wonder his earlier analysis of love was vague; his thought is based on doubt. He wishes not to know.

Beckett must communicate through his narrating protagonist but without his aid, one might say. In *Murphy* the amor intellectualis referred to Murphy's narcissistic self-love. The first two references to love in "First Love" are relevant. The first occurs as the protagonist imagines his family rushing out of the house, having evicted him: "All those lips that had kissed me, those hearts that had loved me (it is with the heart one loves, is it not, or am I confusing it with something else?)" (16). We must note the passivity. He does not love; he imagines, ironically, being loved; and he is doubtful about the organ of love. The second reference appears in his description of being masturbated on a park bench by Lulu/Anna. He complains of the act: "one is no longer oneself, on such occasions, and it is painful to be no longer oneself." One recognizes Murphy's narcissism there. Then he develops that idea: "What goes by the name of love is banishment, with now and then a postcard from the homeland, is my considered opinion, this evening" (18).

There are several banishments in the story: from his father's house; from his bed and room and hothouse in that establishment; from his childhood; from Lulu/Anna's apartment. These banishments offer definitions of the self that are externally shaped. It is also a matter of being banished not *from* love but *by* love. What, then, is "the homeland"? Murphy never mentions any literal family or other home, yet he describes life as "but a wandering to find home" (4). It must be that the self is the home or homeland from which one is banished by love—not that intellectual love with which God or Murphy loves himself, but that love that, Freud explains, draws the narcissistic ego away from itself toward a love-object in the outer world.

The protagonist's father requires consideration. The protagonist begins his story, "I associate . . . my marriage with the death of my father, in time." Freud suggests that the son cannot experience a mature sex life until he has freed himself from the Oedipal bond. Moran will have much to say about this topic. Here we learn that the protagonist was not loved by his father; "leave him alone, he's not disturbing anyone," the father told the rest of the family (13). He did not, however, will the house to his son before dying, and the family banished him. Thus we find reason for the protagonist's mixed feelings about his father (and his deliberate killing of the hyacinth). But the dead father is given, not quite seriously, "great disembodied wisdom" (16), and the protagonist says, "my father's face, on his death-bolster, had seemed to hint at some" beauty (27).

Freud speaks of his patient's "obsessional piety" toward his father. In discussing his constipation, he adds these ideas: "The wish to be born of his father . . . , the wish to be sexually satisfied by him, the wish to present him with a child—and all of this at the price of his own masculinity, and expressed in the language of anal eroticism—these wishes complete the circle of his fixation upon his father" (XVII, 101). The absence of the mother from the protagonist's narrative and the presence of a similar irrational attitude toward bowel movements (especially his study of the makeshift bedpan the morning after his "one night of love") suggest that Beckett is transposing Freud's observations into his story.

In the story, however, an actual child is born: "It woke me up." Immediately, the protagonist flees the apartment, ignoring its mother as he has ignored his own mother, but briefly identifying with the child: "What that infant must have been going through!" (35). (Freud saw in his patient "an endeavour to debase his love-object" [XVII, 93].) Outside, he looks up to the stars, seeking the two Wains that his father had shown him. Did he wish to dedicate the child to his father? See a sign from him? Identify himself as part of that starry couple? Echo Dante's emergence from hell? No specific sense can be found, and in any case he did not see the stars.

As for the rest of his life, haunted by those cries: "I could have done with other loves perhaps. But there it is, either you love or you don't." Briefly, one must say that his story settles the matter. Unable to love anyone else and haunted by evidence of his failure, he cannot love himself. Murphy intended to return to Celia and MMMusic; the protagonist of "First Love" is further gone, banished completely. He never sang with Lulu/Anna, and now he can hear only her cries.

5.

All That Fall

The ten years after "First Love" considerably altered Beckett's professional existence. *Waiting for Godot* made him internationally famous. Two novels of the trilogy appeared in 1951, the third in 1953. Such difficult works as *Watt* and "From an Abandoned Work" were published (1953, 1956). In 1955 *Nouvelles et Textes pour rien* was published. His translations were making his works available in both French and English. He was also well enough known that the BBC could ask him to write a radio play.

All That Fall and "From an Abandoned Work" are the last-written of the works that this study will consider. They are usefully complementary. In its style and even its implied audience "From an Abandoned Work" is intensely compact and private. *All That Fall*, written late in 1956, is a public piece for an audience unlikely to know Beckett's works and unable to follow any complex presentation of ideas during the broadcast. Written after Beckett had finished, or nearly finished, *Fin de partie*, this play also focuses on a couple. But Maddy and Dan are quite different from Hamm and Clov or Molloy and Moran or Mercier and Camier.

The setting of the play is an explicitly Irish rural area with clear connections to Beckett's hometown of Foxrock, its railway station and its racetrack. There is no serious plot, only a series of incidents during a segment of Maddy's trip to and from the station. For the most part the characters and situations are sentimentally comic; we laugh at the speeches and actions while we pity those hopeless lives suffused with pain.

The play was composed quickly and from only a few sources, at least by Beckett's standards. One source, besides Foxrock, accounts for the setting and general matters of characterization, and a second source provides the two central characters. If we add Schubert's "Death and the Maiden," the biblical passage from which the title is taken (Psalm 145:15), and a phrase spoken by Jung, we have the thematic essentials of the play. This approach to a text through its sources can occasion no surprise. We expect to find Beckett working from sources. They enable him to connect concepts to his percepts—a desire that continues unabated in 1956, even after he has asserted an aesthetics in which meaning is irrelevant and a semi-philosophical skepticism that finds meaning unfindable. The concealment of his sources also continues. It obliges him again, quite properly, to generate significance in his own texts rather than borrowing it from those sources.

We are far from "First Love." Beckett is now splendidly in control of his writing, even in this new genre of the radio play. What he chooses to do, he does. The dramatic form of *All That Fall* eliminates the distancing narrator, as most of his fictional works since *Mercier and Camier* had done by other means. The play's colloquial speakers and quotidian situations encourage immediate involvement and understanding. Its tightly knit composition keeps the audience focused on those central causes of tears and laughter, life and death. Its primary sources provide a coherent thematic presentation of life and death.

Maddy Rooney brings us at once into both topics. She weeps over her dead daughter and other sorrows, and she expresses her desire for life through her interests in dung and sexual activities and by her own vigorous survival. Dan Rooney, her complement, looks forward blindly to retirement and death. He is associated with the boy's death under the wheels of the train. Behind this odd couple the chorus repeats these themes: inquiries after any person bring a response that links living with dying; "Death and the Maiden" is heard both coming and going; the bicycle and Mr. Slocum's car, though still mobile, are decaying. The listening audience needs no more. These abundant details generalize the idiosyncratic journey of Maddy and Dan, while encouraging our sympathetic recognition of the comic pathos of life and death.

Where are the higher concepts that organize these abundant details? Two basic sources provide implicit contexts, Dante and Freud.

The situation, setting, and character types of *All That Fall* take their basic qualities from Dante's *Inferno* and especially from canto III. Dante and Vergil, entering the gates of the City of Dis, visit the crowds of dead on the near side of the Acheron. Many are eager to cross on Charon's ferry to their ultimate punishments; Vergil explains that Divine Justice turns their fear into desire (III, 124 ff.). But many another soul has no such eagerness and no such destination. Such a soul is lukewarm, "l'anime triste di coloro / che visser sanza 'nfamia e sanza lodo" (III, 35–36; the sad soul of him who lived without infamy and without praise). As a result of their wasted lives, "questi non hanno speranza di morte, / e la lor cieca vita e tanto bassa, / che 'nvidïosi son d'ogne altra sorte" (III, 46–48; these have no hope of death, and their blind life is so low that they are envious of any other fate). Dan Rooney, who has longed to kill a child but has not done so, has a comically important predecessor: "colui / che fece per viltade il gran rifiuto" (III 59–60; him who made the great refusal out of cowardice).

Dan is blind, and the poor sight of several other characters suggests their blind lives. They cannot easily recognize each other. That repeated difficulty evokes another echo of Dante, though not from this canto: the repeated and almost formal identification of oneself or of another, when two characters meet. The irritable Mr. Barrell, presiding over transportation at the railway station, imitates the ill-tempered Charon.

The setting of the play is a flat plain from which a passing motor-van raises a thick cloud of dust before rain begins and turns the dust into mud. There is an increasingly strong wind. The rain mimics Maddy's repeated weeping and evokes Dante's "terra lagrimosa" (weeping land). When she reaches the station, we hear several voices, not always distinct and often raised, and twice we hear Mr. Barrell hitting young Jerry in the stomach. Such sounds give specificity to Dante's general description of the crowd:

> Quivi sospiri, pianti e alti guai
>> risonavan per l'aere sanza stelle.
>> . . . .
> Diverse lingue, orribili favelle,
>> parole di dolere, accenti d'ira,
>> voci alte e fioche, e suon di man con elle
> facevano un tumulto, il qual s'aggira
>> sempre in quell' aura sanza tempo tinta,
>> come la rena quando turbo spira. (III, 22–30)

[Here sighs, complaints, and loud cries resound through the starless air. . . . Various tongues, horrible cries, words of sorrow, accents of anger, loud and weak voices, and with those the sound of hands made a tumult that whirls always in that dark and timeless air, like sand when a whirlwind blows.]

To the blown sand and the darkness from Dante's scene Beckett adds the wasps (III, 66; *Krapp's*, 41). Maddy also speaks of "the viler worms" (*Krapp's*, 44), recalling the "fastidiosi vermi" under the feet of Dante's characters.

Both Dan and Maddy are clumsy mentally. Dan tries to count but cannot satisfy himself with his answers. He wishes to retire from business but cannot reason his way to a decision. Maddy has trouble with language, despite her study of it. Like the minor characters, the Rooneys are among "le gente dolorose / c'hanno perduto il ben de l'intelletto" (III, 17–18; those sad people who have lost the good of the intellect). These poor souls are lukewarm about living. Mr. Tyler says that he is "half alive"; Maddy says, "I am not half alive nor anything approaching it" (*Krapp's*, 41). They speak for all the characters. Because existence goes on and on repetitively in Boghill, time means little. Maddy is late for the train, but she arrives in plenty of time. The cloud of dust raised by the van will be raised again by the next one (*Krapp's*, 41). The characters will come and go again. Their lives add up to nothing; they are going nowhere.

Rather than accept responsibility, they are resentful. Beckett gives Mr. Tyler one of his favorite passages from this canto. When Charon questions Vergil's right to be there, Vergil silences him by identifying the powerful source of his orders: colà dove si puote / ciò che si vuole (there where that which is wished can be done). Hearing this, the envious and weak-willed souls

Bestemmiavano Dio e lor parenti,
    l'umana specie e 'l loco e 'l tempo e 'l seme
    di lor semenza e di lor nascimenti. (III, 103–5)

[cursed God and their parents, the human race and the place and the time and the seed of their begetting and of their birth.]

Mr. Tyler is even more specific: "I was merely cursing, under my breath, God and man, under my breath, and the wet Saturday afternoon of my conception" (*Krapp's*, 39). "Under my breath" suggests lukewarmness as well as caution.

Beckett does not limit himself to canto III. Dan admits to Maddy that he has wished to kill a child. Then he suggests that he and Maddy begin walking backwards. "Or you forwards and I backwards. The perfect pair. Like Dante's damned, with their faces arsy-versy. Our tears will water our bottoms" (*Krapp's*, 74–75; the image was used in *Watt*). The damned so twisted had attempted to foresee the future (*Inferno*, XX, 22 ff.), an attempt Dan has made often. He has been looking forward to retirement and to his evening's reading from *Effi Briest*. The immediate connection, however, is with his desire to kill a child, specifically Jerry. He seems now to have given up that hope. Another passage from the canto just cited is unmentioned but relevant. It also engaged the young Belacqua: "Qui vive la pietà quand' è ben morta" (XX, 28; *More Pricks*, 19). That sentence, with its puzzling pun, is addressed angrily by Vergil to Dante, who is weeping for those disfigured by their attempt to foresee the future: "Here lives pity/piety when it is well dead." In *All That Fall* the sense of the pun is suggested in the theological text for the next Sunday's sermon: "The Lord upholdeth all that fall and raiseth up all those that be bowed down" (*Krapp's*, 88). Pity is expressed in that hopeful text. Piety is expressed by its context: these lukewarm characters have condemned themselves and will not be raised up.

* * *

Although working hastily to compose the play, Beckett did not work casually. Deirdre Bair quotes from a letter he wrote to Nancy Cunard about "a nice gruesome idea full of cartwheels and dragging feet and puffing and panting" (474). The feet and the panting survived; the cart was modernized into a bicycle, a van, an automobile, and a train. The surrounding dark became Foxrock/Boghill and the City of Dis. By way of Dante, Beckett gave those speculative images a local habitation and a name. But who will do the puffing? Dante identifies none of the lukewarm dead, since Vergil disdains them. Beckett can find no characters there. Unsurprisingly, he finds models in one of Freud's writings, the second of his basic sources.

Freud's *The Question of Lay Analysis* (1926), a very minor work, is not addressed to his fellow practitioners or to students. Its audience is comprised of potential voters on a bill that would permit doctors of medicine to practice psychoanalysis in Austria, whether or not trained by Freudians. Naturally, Freud wishes to insists upon the necessity of training the doctors in depth psychology and psychoanalysis.

He begins by emphasizing the differences between physical illness and mental illness. Because of his audience, he is not scientific and technical. He offers examples of people whose symptoms would appear unrelated and strange to a medical doctor but not to a psychoanalyst. This distinction is echoed in *All That Fall* when Maddy Rooney describes to Dan her visit to "one of these new mind doctors." "A neurologist," Dan suggests. "No no," she says, "just mental distress" (*Krapp's*, 82–83). (Her brief description of the mind doctor's lecture draws on Beckett's experience of a lecture by Jung [Bair, 209].)

Freud's examples emphasize specific symptoms. One such symptom is a tendency to faint when agitated. (Maddy: "I feel very cold and faint" [*Krapp's*, 79].) In a lengthy passage he develops other mostly female problems: "Their sensual feelings attach them to people whom they despise and from whom they would like to get free [this desire led Maddy to the doctor's lecture]; or those same feelings impose requirements on them whose fulfillment they themselves find repulsive. [Maddy, much troubled by horses, imagines herself the sexually satisfied wife of a horse-butcher.] If they are women, they feel prevented by anxiety or disgust or by unknown obstructions from meeting the demands of sexual life; or, if they have surrendered to love, they find themselves cheated of the enjoyment which nature has provided as a reward for such compliance. All these people recognize that they are ill . . ." (XX, 186).

Maddy often expresses her sensuality, both positively and negatively. She is excited when Mr. Slocum pushes her up into his car, but she objects to mere unproductive affection and laments her lack of a living daughter: "Childlessness. . . . Minnie! Little Minnie! Love, that is all I asked, a little love, daily, twice daily, fifty years of twice daily love [as does Freud above, Maddy uses "love" for "intercourse"] like a Paris horse-butcher's regular, what normal woman wants affection? A peck on the jaw at morning . . ." (*Krapp's,* 37).

Freud notes that a woman with such problems "is overcome by violent headaches or other painful sensations at times when they are most inconvenient. She may even be unable to keep down any meal she eats—which can become dangerous in the long run" (XX, 186). The obese Maddy may seem immune to such a danger, yet she can imagine it: "What's wrong with me, what's wrong with me, never tranquil, seething out of my dirty old pelt, out of my skull, oh to be in atoms, in atoms!" (*Krapp's,* 43). If such fragmentation is not available (the protagonist of "From an Abandoned Work" also imagined it), then not eating might succeed: "Would I were still in bed. . . . Just wasting slowly painlessly away, . . . till in the end you wouldn't see me under the blankets any more than a board" (*Krapp's,* 51).

Beckett's presentation of Maddy as neurotic is perhaps most obvious when she tells about her visit to the new mind doctor. She explains her purpose: "I was hoping he might shed a little light on my lifelong preoccupation with horses' buttocks" (*Krapp's,* 82–83). We need no medical or psychological training to understand that preoccupation; she is speaking, over the then-proper BBC, about a life spent among people whom she identifies as horses' asses. Several of the play's abundant sexual jokes develop varieties of this image. Almost inevitably they imply negative attitudes toward sexuality along with a compulsive interest in it, lukewarmly verbal rather than sensual. Any hot-blooded positive interest is negated by cold doubt or repression.

The moody Dan Rooney also has psychological problems. He recurs repeatedly to mathematical topics, calculating money saved and money lost, counting steps, and computing his salary and costs (*Krapp's,* 69, 70, 77–78). He rebukes Maddy's refusal to count: "Not count! One of the few satisfactions in life?" (*Krapp's,* 71). But while he looks forward to retiring and then "counting the hours—till the next meal" (*Krapp's,* 72), he is not sure how old he is. "Was I a hundred to-day?" he asks. The number is large enough to imply a Dantean posthumous existence, and Maddy's next speech begins appropriately: "All is still. No living soul in sight" (*Krapp's*, 75). Dan behaves evasively about the event that delayed the arrival of the train, the death of a child who fell "under the wheels" (*Krapp's*, 91). That detail ends the play. Earlier, jeered at by the Lynch twins (Art and Con, from *Watt*, 101), Dan asks, "Did you ever wish to kill a child?" He adds that he has often nearly attacked Jerry while being led home.

These specific details are surely curious enough to puzzle any medical doctor. Freud groups them all in one imagined patient:

> A patient . . . may be suffering from fluctuations in his moods which he cannot control, or from a sense of despondency by which his energy feels paralysed because he thinks he is incapable of doing anything properly [such as counting steps], or from a nervous embarrassment among strangers. [When Maddy asks Dan to kiss her, he exclaims: "Kiss you? In public? On the platform? Before the boy? Have you taken leave of your senses?" (*Krapp's*, 67).] He may one day have suffered from a distressing attack . . . of feelings of anxiety, and since then have been unable, without a struggle, to walk along the street alone, or to travel by train; he may perhaps have had to give up both entirely [as Dan would like to do, by retiring]. Or . . . his thoughts may go their own way and refuse to be directed by his will. They pursue problems that are quite indifferent to him. . . . Quite ludicrous tasks are imposed upon him, such as counting up the windows on the fronts of houses. [The steps again.] And when he has performed simple actions such as posting a letter or turning off a gas-jet, he finds himself a moment later doubting whether he has really done so. . . . But his state becomes intolerable if he suddenly finds he is unable to fend off the idea that he has pushed a child under the wheels of a car or has thrown a stranger off the bridge into the water, or if he has to ask himself whether he is not the murderer whom the police are looking for in connection with a crime that was discovered that day. [Dan: "Say something, Maddy. Say you believe me" (*Krapp's*, 82).] (XX, 185)

The moodiness, the uncertainty, the travel by train, the need of accompaniment on the street, the counting, the child "under the wheels," the sense of guilt, and the threat of legal punishment are grouped together here as Beckett groups them in Dan Rooney.

Maddy and Dan are both mentally ill, then, and characterized primarily by means of these Freudian symptoms of neurosis. They share several of them, but Maddy and Dan are not interchangeable. Dan tries earnestly if disjointedly to concentrate on the question of retirement, looking forward with that single aim. Maddy veers from topic to topic, and she contradicts herself repeatedly and unconcernedly. Explaining in *The Question of Lay Analysis* a difference between the ego and the id, Freud says that "the ego is an organization characterized by a very remarkable trend towards unification, towards synthesis. This characteristic is lacking in the id; it is, as we might say, 'all to pieces'; its different urges pursue their own purposes independently and regardless of one another" (XX, 196). Dan suggests the ego, then, while Maddy ("oh to be in atoms, in atoms!") suggests the fragmentary id. Taking into account the relative sizes of Dan and Maddy, we recall Wylie's phrase "the little ego and the big id."

* * *

Our retrieval of structural sources in these Beckett texts has kept us from attempting a final critical reading of any text. Something must be attempted here, however. Beckett's use of Dante in *All That Fall* locates the characters in hell; they are damned souls. Freud complicates the matter. As psychological beings, Maddy and Dan are not sinful; they are neurotic. Probably Beckett's most extended consideration of morality and sin is that single paragraph in *Proust* based almost entirely on Schopenhauer, in which the youthful Beckett approves of Proust as "completely detached from all moral considerations" (49). With Schopenhauer's aid, Beckett distinguishes in that context between "human justice . . . organised by the knaves for the fools," and "tragedy," concerned with "the expiation of original sin, . . . the sin of having been born."

Even in *Proust* that passage was rhetorical rather than relevant. Now, years after the introduction of psychology into Beckett's literary world, the passage seems almost completely irrelevant to his concerns. In *All That Fall* sin is unimportant, perhaps, but judgment has been passed. The weather does not hold up. Maddy was Dunne before she was Rooney. Gaelic will die. Death makes a promise in the lyrics to Schubert's song "Death and the Maiden":

Bin Freund und komme nicht zu strafen.
Sei gutes Muts! Ich bin nicht wild!
Sollst sanft in meinen Armen schlafen!

[I'm a friend and don't come to punish.
Cheer up! I'm not wild!
You'll sleep gently in my arms!]

The poet Matthias Claudius has an odd predecessor for this passage in Chaucer's Prioress's Tale: "My litel child, now wol I fecche thee," says the

Virgin Mary to the dead boy. "Be nat agast, I wol thee nat forsake." Death's promise here, however, is as doubtful as the promise that the Lord will uphold all that fall. No sleep is offered in Limbo, and Beckett's use of Dante suggests that life is itself hell. The characters are working out a pensum imposed upon them for having been born. Psychological illness is, then, the means by which that pensum has been imposed, or the evidence that they are working the pensum out.

The play also suggests, however, Beckett's characteristic dislike for judging, revealed repeatedly in his personal life. No denunciation of the characters occurs here, there being no one responsible for imposing any obligations upon them. (The bastard, he doesn't exist.) Certainly life is presented as bleak, repetitive, painful, and pointless. The audience, however, is not encouraged to draw pedagogical or theological conclusions from *All That Fall*. It proves nothing, and the briefly mentioned mind doctor offers no therapy. The Dantean and Freudian concepts cohere, but not as part of any system of thought.

* * *

Scholars have shown for years that Beckett's texts can be made more nearly intelligible if they are connected at this and that point with works by Schopenhauer, Dante, Descartes, and Shakespeare, for instance. There is a certain propriety in such connections. Beckett is an important writer, and his alliance with important artists and thinkers from the past honors that greatness. Moreover, he was often quite explicit in his references to those writers. But we have just found him playing the jackdaw or the sedulous ape with an article by Freud that even professional Freudians might excuse themselves from reading. The effect is akin to that of discovering that Thomas Mann used Sunday-supplement newspaper articles in writing *Doctor Faustus*. (He did.) Of what benefit to Beckett could it possibly have been to consult *The Question of Lay Analysis*?

Conveniently, Freud offers an answer in that text. He speaks of the novelty and difficulty of depth psychology and of its unintelligibility even for doctors of medicine. He is expressing a professional concern, since misunderstandings might lead to serious misdiagnoses and mistreatments of patients. Therefore he appeals to his audience to consider their own experiences of psychology in such sources as literature and history: "Have you not noticed that every philosopher, every imaginative writer, every historian and every biographer makes up his own psychology for himself, brings forward his own particular hypotheses concerning the interconnections and aims of mental acts—all more or less plausible and all equally untrustworthy?" (XX, 192).

Beckett took seriously the findings of Freudian depth psychology. As far back as *Proust* Beckett also used the ideas of professional philosophers, especially Schopenhauer, and expressed them in relevant terms. He used the ideas and terms of some professional critics as well. He was properly, if not explicitly, deferential to authority. In acknowledging the discoveries of depth psychology and in presenting them rather than misrepresenting or ignoring them, Beckett was not evasive or arbitrary but responsible. (He had been evasive, arbitrary, and irresponsible in chapter 6 of *Murphy.*) He sought clarity and accuracy, not concealment. He was not proselytizing for these ideas or for Freud and Jung as therapists. Maddy's obsession with horses' buttocks is not eased by the mind doctor's lecture, and Beckett presents Jung's description of a single patient as improperly born only to extend that fatalistic idea to all the play's characters.

After *All That Fall* Beckett's works will seldom leave the realm of the mind. Dan Rooney's comic obsessions and compulsions will deepen into the guilt-ridden repetitions of such works as *Eh Joe* and *Play* as Beckett develops the dismay resulting from one's retrospective realization, as T. S. Eliot puts it in *Burnt Norton,* that

> What might have been and what has been
> Point to one end, which is always present.

After "From an Abandoned Work" and *All That Fall,* however, Beckett is crowned and mitred over himself, as Vergil puts the matter to Dante. He is able to present these painful psychological materials without deferring to other authorities. In fact he did so already, in *The Unnamable,* where Maddy's wish to be in atoms was acted out, with grim evidence that even the bodiless and fragmented mind cannot escape pattern, meaning, need, and the search for a nonexistent self. Beckett will build upon the findings of professional depth psychology, but he will not abandon it.

6.

"From an Abandoned Work"

Although written before *All That Fall,* "From an Abandoned Work" constitutes Beckett's farewell to Freud's texts as specific guides to the conception
and construction of works of art. It is not a lingering farewell, certainly, but
it is an intense one. Even *Molloy* does not compress so much psychoanalyti-
cal reference and understanding into its lines as this brief narrative does.

"From an Abandoned Work" was written around 1955. Its few commentators accept Beckett's own description of it as the surviving portion of a
novel, expressing no curiosity about Beckett's willingness to publish it and
to leave it essentially untitled. Nor do they speculate about its possible development into something of novel size. Because space is at a premium for
this investigation of Beckett's works, much must be asserted, without development and support, in considering "From an Abandoned Work." The first
such assertion is that the title is a pun; the work abandoned is the protagonist's
imagined therapy, for which the story functions as a kind of anamnesis.

In a single block of prose the speaker, beginning abruptly, sets out to
describe three days in his life, long before he reached his present old age and
situation. None of the days is described clearly or coherently, and few details are given for the second and third days. The narrative ends chronologically with the narrator's recalling his walks in the mountains in old age.
Except for a briefly mentioned "ragged old roadman" standing in a ditch,
the only other characters are his father and mother.

The story draws exhaustively though not exclusively upon an important
text, Freud's *Inhibitions, Symptoms and Anxiety* (1926). Like Freud, Beckett
develops the relations among these three psychological problems. Freud's
discussion, at once authoritative and speculative, focuses on two types of
neurosis: hysteria and obsession. Usually Freud considered them as separate
problems with distinct symptoms, but here he suggests that childhood hysteria can develop into an obsessive neurosis.

The essay's three subjects are connected causally: anxiety gives rise to inhibitions; inhibitions are acted out as symptoms. Freud's primary subject is anxiety, and in part the discussion responds to Otto Rank's recent *The Trauma of Birth* (1924). Rank asserts that the experience of being born causes our first anxiety, which is the prototype of all later anxieties. Freud had made this observation some years earlier, but Rank claims that the cause of this primal anxiety is separation from the mother. Freud now argues that this traumatic separation is not experienced during childbirth, since the new-born infant cannot distinguish its mother from itself and is completely narcissistic (XX, 130, 133, 136). Beckett's protagonist claims to regret only being born, but his relation to his mother is crucial, and he obsessively acts out the separation.

Anxiety leads to inhibitions, and Freud connects these inhibitions with the child's Oedipal problems. The child's repressed Oedipal desires are displaced by inhibitions into acts that the psychoanalyst recognizes as symptoms. The inhibitions are manifold. Freud finds "five kinds of resistance, emanating from three directions—the ego, the id and the super-ego" (XX, 160). In defining the five kinds of resistance, Freud says that resistance from the id necessitates "working-through" during therapy. The resistance imposed by the superego "seems to originate from the sense of guilt or the need for punishment; and it opposes every move toward success, including, therefore, the patient's own recovery through analysis." This description is obviously relevant to Beckett's title and the story derived from this article. Because the narrator's anamnesis does not lead to therapy, the work is left unfinished.

*   *   *

Freud speaks of two symptom-forming activities of the ego, "undoing what has been done" and "isolating" (XX, 119). The protagonist's recurrent flights, undone by returns, are primarily physical. His isolating, especially of act from affect, is primarily mental; one symptom of his isolating is "interruption of the connection in thought" (XX, 121). The protagonist's separation of violence and rage is an instance of isolation, and this isolation results from and results in repression. Freud is concerned with symptomatic venting of the libidinal energy pent up by such repression. Beckett's protagonist is also concerned; he walks slowly but undoes that slowness by intermittent quick dashes accompanied by cries of "vent the pent, vent the pent" (*No's*, 142).

Even these generalities remind the reader that the story provides ample evidence of diphasic behavior, isolation, repetition, displacement of affect, compulsive actions, and Oedipal trauma. They are more than enough to show Beckett's use of *Inhibitions*.

Freud warns that "so long as we direct our attention to the ego's attempt at flight we shall get no nearer to the subject of symptom-formation" (XX, 94). It is anxiety that sets repression to the forming of symptoms. Beckett mines *Inhibitions, Symptoms and Anxiety* for his development of the protagonist's anxiety about his relations with his mother and father. Here one must say simply that the alerted reader finds ample evidence, confirmed in Freud's work, about the protagonist's obsessive and diphasic relationship with his parents: unexpressed affection and repressed hostility while they were alive, and savagely expressed hostility with repressed affection now that they are dead. (The protagonist speaks of "the old thoughts born with me and grown with me and kept under"; Krapp will speak of "last fancies" and then scold himself, "Keep 'em under!" [*No's,* 143; *Krapp's,* 25].)

* * *

The protagonist's anxiety about his relation to his parents expresses itself symptomatically, because he represses any direct admission of it. Repression is bad even for analysts of literature. Since Beckett develops "From an Abandoned Work" by means of symptoms, let us vent the pent by considering at least one set of those symptoms.

Movement in time and space may be the most extended topic of the story, even though Freud denies that "whenever there is an outbreak of anxiety something like a reproduction of the situation of birth goes on in the mind" (XX, 93–94). The protagonist's comings and goings from his family home certainly act out such a situation, and motion is extended into many other sorts of imagery. Freud connects a second type of symptom with agoraphobia. Beckett turns that type around; home is the space that the protagonist fears to enter, the outer world his unsatisfactory refuge from it. A third category, by his own admission the most affective, is whiteness.

Whiteness implies both a color and an intensity of light. The protagonist has much to say about whiteness, a topic that illustrates his characteristic movement up the ladder from percepts to concepts, "to the general from the particular" (*No's,* 144). He describes his affective response to whiteness in that way: "White I must say has always affected me strongly, all white things, sheets, walls and so on, even flowers, and then just white, the thought of white, without more" (*No's,* 141). Before this movement from "things" to "thought" he had already noted other relevant particulars: "up bright and early," "nice fresh morning, bright too early," "my mother white and so thin," and "a white horse" ("it was a bright white, with the sun on it").

Many of these white and bright images are ambivalent. He had a "great love in my heart" for flowers, and his extended recollection of the white horse appears positive. On the other hand, he has drastically ambivalent feelings about his white mother, and therefore "sheets" reminds us of her fluttering nightdress and the family home, while "walls" connects with "the house-wall grey and my mother white." References to the day and the weather darken as the story continues. Most whiteness, especially positive whiteness, is associated with the first day and with the narrator's youth.

The narrator's parents are the primary sources of whiteness. For instance, the white horse, which seems a dream animal, suggests a kindly image of the father followed by his son. It is, however, put in some dubious contexts when the protagonist tries to finish his description of the first day, despite the isolating that inhibits him from connecting repressed ideas, images, and events:

> But let me get on now from where I left off, the white horse and then the rage, no connexion I suppose.
>
> Well after the horse and rage I don't know, just on, . . . then home.
>
> Now is there nothing to add to this day with the white horse and the white mother in the window . . . , no, nothing, all has gone but mother in the window, the violence, rage and rain. (*No's,* 143, 145)

In all three cases the white horse is associated with rage despite denial ("no connexion I suppose"). In the third, the horse is also associated with the mother, who is connected immediately with violence and rage. Elsewhere both parents are connected with brightness and rage; picturing them "probably in paradise, they were so good," the protagonist imagines that they look down at him in hell and hear him curse them. An image of light results: "That might take some of the shine off their bliss" (*No's,* 144).

Then there is the never described attack by "a family or tribe, I do not know, of stoats, a most extraordinary thing, I think they were stoats" (*No's,* 145). An attack by a family catches one's attention. (Instead of excitement we hear the undercutting doubt: "I do not know"; "I think.") The grotesqueness of the animals' attack is notable, but whiteness is also intricately evaded and involved. "Stoat" is the common term for an ermine in its summer phase, when its coat is mostly brown; ermine is the winter phase of a weasel. ("Weasel" denotes the genus of which the ermine/stoat is a species.) The protagonist's specifying the brown form of a species that is sometimes white suggests that these stoats are a negative image of the positive white animals that he loves, as well as a negative image of his white and good parents. Stoats can be frightening in the intensity of their attacks on their prey. Their high metabolism causes them to spend most of their life in such attacks and in sexual couplings. (The protagonist is linked to another animal with negative associations; after a day of muttering his voice is "not even mine," it is "like a marmoset sitting on my shoulder with its bushy tail" [*No's,* 143]; marmosets have claws instead of nails.)

Freud begins his discussion of anxiety in *Inhibitions* by considering two cases in which a child is troubled by animals. One case is that of the "Wolf-Man," which we discussed briefly in connection with *All That Fall* and *The Question of Lay Analysis,* and extensively in connection with "First Love." In *Inhibitions* it is treated differently, with an emphasis on the white wolves and the child-father relation. The second case considered here is that of "Little Hans," who as a small child experienced an hysterical phobia focused on horses. One of his fears was that he would be bitten by one. At first, however, he repressed the fear of being bitten, expressing "an undefined phobia in which only the anxiety and its object still appeared" (XX, 101).

Beckett's protagonist reports briefly his vision of a white horse followed by a boy, and he evades the details of his attack by a "family or tribe" of stoats. We would like to connect those two animals as complementary symbols of the father and to understand Beckett as displacing the biting from Little Hans's horse to the protagonist's stoats, but we cannot merely assert those ideas. Little Hans's horse is imagined as biting, stoats attack the throat of their prey, and there is a possible faint pun in the protagonist's complaint: "All this talking, very low and hoarse, no wonder I had a sore throat" (*No's,* 143). These are frail connections, however.

Freud connects Little Hans's fear of horses to "the murderous impulses of the Oedipus complex" (XX, 102), with the horse an image of the father. His relation to his father is compounded of ambivalences. His fear of biting leads Freud to say that "the idea of being devoured by the father gives expression, in a form that has undergone regressive degradation, to a passive, tender impulse to be loved by him in a genital-erotic sense" (XX, 105). We seem to be moving away from any possible connection to Beckett's story. The idea of being devoured by stoats, however, leads the protagonist to a rather surprising impulse. He imagines the stoats as killing him: "Anyone else would have been bitten and bled to death, perhaps sucked white, like a rabbit, there is that word white again. I know I could never think, but if I could have, and then had, I would just have lain down and let myself be destroyed, as the rabbit does" (*No's,* 145–46). Perverse genital-erotic passivity, surely. We recognize also that to be bled white would be a deserved punishment and would result in his becoming white, good, like his parents.

The connection, therefore, between the stoats and the parents is strengthened.

One might expect a real or imagined attack by stoats to generate rage in the victim. The protagonist's imagined passivity is given an explanation besides the sexual one when Freud speaks here about the effects of inhibition. He describes an obsessional neurotic who "used to be overcome by a paralysing fatigue which lasted for one or more days whenever something occurred which should obviously have thrown him into a rage" (XX, 90). The protagonist associates the white horse with rage, violence, and his mother, but primarily it is associated with his father and with the white dream animals he loved. He calls it a *Schimmel*. The German term denotes a white horse, but it also means "mold," in the sense of decay. That double meaning makes the color and the horse ambivalent. The pejorative sense is developed by the image of the sometimes-white stoats. We hear of no raging by the parents against the son. Therefore, the attacking stoats may, like Little Hans's horse, represent the narrator's rage at his parents—or his guilt about his feelings toward them—displaced onto the stoats and turned against himself.

Whiteness disturbs the protagonist, but darkness is not attractive. Considering the three days promised, we find what appear to be four:

The first day: "Nice fresh morning, bright too early as often. . . . The sky would soon darken and rain fall and go on falling, all day, till evening. Then blue and sun again a second, then night." (*No's*, 139)

The second day: "Up then in the grey of dawn. . . . Not wet really, but dripping, everything dripping, the day might rise, did it, no, drip drip all day long, no sun, no change of light, dim all day, and still, not a breath, then black, and a little wind, I saw some stars, as I neared home." "Extraordinary still over the land." (*No's*, 146, 148)

The third day: No weather reported; the day is identified only by the frightening encounter with the roadman in the ditch who leans on his spade and leers. (*No's*, 147–48)

The fourth day: The narrative time of the story, "this night here among the rocks with my two books and the strong starlight." (*No's*, 147)

Light dims and the sun is replaced by clouds and then stars. The encounter with the roadman (who anticipates the toothless old man smiling at the end of *That Time*) suggests death, as the books under starlight suggest a posthumous state (*Ohio Impromptu*). In this dark the narrator looks forward to a

time with no light or dark *(No's,* 148), an end to ambivalence. ("It is because there is not only darkness but also light that our situation becomes
inexplicable," Beckett will tell Tom Driver in 1961 [Graver, 220].) But the
protagonist is ambivalent even about that, as indicated by his alternatives
of a dissolution into atoms and a future in hell cursing his parents. Light,
then, imagistically encompasses all the protagonist's concerns, as does motion.

Of course there is more to be said about Beckett's use of light in the
story, and much more to be said about the story and Freud's text. The
stoats could be traced through that text to "Notes upon a Case of Obsessional Neurosis," usually called the case of the "Rat-Man," which is paired
with the article on the "Wolf-Man" in every standard German and English edition. We would even note that a German term for pangs of conscience is *Gewissen-bisse* (bites of conscience). In those articles we would
find other connections with several matters in "From an Abandoned Work";
but time forbids.

* * *

Bites of conscience forbid us to leave this story without a brief discussion of
love. This task might seem simple, since the protagonist says clearly, "Never
loved anyone. Except in my dreams, and there it was animals, dream animals, . . . lovely creatures they were, white mostly" *(No's,* 142). The white
dream animals are linked to a white horse, a Schimmel, "followed by a
boy" and "going somewhere to be harnessed." (A farm boy would lead the
horse, not follow it as a child his father.) "I had never seen such a horse,
. . . and never saw another," says the protagonist, emphasizing its dreamlike
quality. Thus in context his love of white animals is associated with his
memory of his father.

He speaks also of loving flowers (classed with white and bright objects)
and of loving finality: "There is a soft spot in my heart for all that is over,
no, for the being over, I loved the word, words have been my only loves, not
many" *(No's,* 147). His first mention of love gives the term a similar connection: "Great love in my heart too for all things still and rooted" *(No's,*
139). Here "too" links love to hostility, since he has just reported seeking a
snail, slug, or worm to destroy. His dead father is now still and rooted, of
course, as he was on the mountainside.

The protagonist thus connects love with words (especially "over"), time
("the being over"), objects ("things still and rooted"), and white dream
animals. They are all symptomatic of his anxiety about his parents. He can
say "never loved anyone," but he can sustain this anxiety-producing statement only by these widespread displacements of love.

We must take another brief glance at *Inhibitions* to note Freud's discussion of "Little Hans," whose childish anger at his father was displaced into the belief that his father was angry at him. Freud extends that topic by saying that Hans's phobia "had the effect of abolishing his affectionate object-cathexis of his mother as well." He concludes that "the process of repression had attacked almost all the components of his Oedipus complex—both his hostile and his tender impulses toward his father and his tender impulses toward his mother" (XX, 106). Such a repression enables Beckett's protagonist to say that he has never loved anyone. A commonsensical response to his statement—perhaps he really had never loved anyone; why not take him at his word?—fails to account for his spending most of his reported life in leaving home and returning, for his intense hostility to his parents after so many years and despite the absence of any hostile acts on their part, and for his concern with the topic of love.

Beckett's fictions explain much about death and love. Murphy's death is related to love. The protagonist of "First Love" connects his unloving nature with death; as Lulu/Anna's pregnancy advances, he tells us that "I did not yet know, at that time, how tender the earth can be for those who have only her and how many graves in her giving, for the living" (*First*, 35). The protagonist of "From an Abandoned Work" finds in death his final substitute for his mother as an object of love: "I weep for happiness as I go along and for love of this old earth that has carried me so long and whose uncomplainingness will soon be mine" (*No's*, 145). Unable to love their self, these protagonists cannot successfully love anyone else or accept love from anyone else. Depth psychology explained their predicaments to Beckett, who has explained them to us in these love stories.

* * *

These analyses of Beckett's texts show that in each case the psychological meanings are basic. "A Case in a Thousand" is unintelligible without some recognition of its psychological subject. ("Assumption" may be unintelligible even with that recognition.) *Murphy* has an extended philosophical theme and an amateur psychological commentary (centered in chapter 6), but it requires that the concept of narcissism be understood if Murphy's difficulties are to be made coherent and the narrative recognized as a belated but thorough presentation of the narcissist's dilemma.

The individual analyses above have shown, in part by incremental repetition, that Beckett did not simply draw upon that largely undifferentiated mass of psychological knowledge possessed by perceptive people at any time. He required a clear general understanding and detailed descriptions before he shaped his texts, and he found them in Freud's continuing publications.

Most explicitly in interviews with Israel Shenker (1956) and Tom Driver (1961), Beckett distinguished between the mess of life and the necessity for form in art. He never explained, however, what substitutes for "form" or "system" he used in his writing, and even his sense of "system" is not easy to pin down. His interest in that problem suggests the relevance of one of Paul Valéry's observations: "Une littérature dont on aperçoit le système est perdue. On s'intéresse au système, et l'oeuvre n'a plus le prix que d'un exemple de grammaire. Elle ne sert qu'à comprendre le systeme" (*Oeuvres,* II, 801). As he did not write generically conventional novels and stories and plays, so Beckett did not impose upon life any system of psychological order that might arrange the mess into certainty.

Perhaps Beckett's own most compressed single expression of his separation of form or system from the content, essence, or subject of a work of art is to be found in the last long speech of the third of his *Three Dialogues with Georges Duthuit* (1949). The ostensible topic is Bram van Velde, by this point an occasion for speech rather than the subject of it. Beckett says that "there are many ways in which the thing I am trying in vain to say may be tried in vain to be said. I have experimented, . . . under duress, through faintness of heart, through weakness of mind, with two or three hundred" (123). He extends this distinction between "the thing" and its successful saying when he speaks of the "relation between the artist and his occasion." He insists that this "dualist view of the creative process" is inescapable. Examining this duality, he says that "all that should concern us is the acute and increasing anxiety of the relation itself."

This "anxiety" must remind us of *Inhibitions, Symptoms and Anxiety*. (In the previous dialogue Beckett quoted Freud, though not from that text.) This anxiety is based upon "a sense of invalidity, of inadequacy," Beckett says, and he connects it with the irrational. As if referring to *Murphy*'s Neary and to *Watt*, he suggests that conventional rational understandings of and makings of art shy away from the irrational "with a kind of Pythagorean terror, as though the irrationality of pi were an offence against the deity, not to mention his creature" (125). (We are in a position to understand the term "irrationality" as a popular psychological term for such matters as involve the id, libido, and depth psychology.)

Beckett acknowledges that although the acceptance of irrationality ensures artistic failure, the knowledge of that fact might be construed as "a new occasion [for art], a new term of relation." Therefore, a work of art might still be expressive. Beckett cannot accept this conclusion, admitting that "my inability to do so places myself . . . in what I think is still called an unenviable situation, familiar to psychiatrists." He adds a remark about an hypothesized painting: "For what is this coloured plane, that was not there before. I don't know what it is, having never seen anything like it before. It seems to have nothing to do with art, . . . if my memories are correct."

We can recognize topics of our first and our recent study. Evoking a new painting, Beckett says that "it seems to have nothing to do with art." Dandieu remarked about *A la Recherche* that "l'art est avant tout une découverte; il est aussi anti-littéraire par essence. Proust échappe à la fois à la littérature et à la morale; il est descendu jusqu'aux racines psychologique de l'art" (24–25). Beckett has attempted several hundred ways to fail, he says. The "situation familiar to psychiatrists" is that of anxiety and doubt, which Beckett acts out by adding a doubt ("I think") about his own assertion. (Characteristically Beckett takes thinking as indicating doubt, and he offers no psychiatric term for this "situation"; he gives us the red herring of "unenviable.") Doubt stems from anxiety, which in turn results from a problematic relation—here as so often for Beckett threatening and unmanageable.

His reference to psychiatrists, such terms as "anxiety," "inadequacy," and "the irrational," and the quoting of Freud in the second dialogue indicate that here, as in the texts we have examined, Beckett turns to depth psychology in an unenviable situation. That situation is of a piece with those we have considered: it obliges one to enter into a relationship of a type for which memory cannot prepare one, for which reason can provide no guide, and to which no conventions apply. At once suggesting and evading the problem, Beckett implies the existence of a structure of ideas that is not a "system" and that might be used to make art without distorting the work into a systematic and rational report. Similarly, this structure might enable the audience to experience art without wishing to understand it.

This extensive revelation of Beckett's dependence upon Freudian sources outside *Molloy* might have seemed central to those works examined but of little relevance to Beckett's work in general. If so, *Three Dialogues* shows that Beckett's concern with depth psychology did not come and go as he began and finished writing a text. It was not merely a source of recurrent structural convenience.

We are about to turn to *Molloy*. In *Damned to Fame* Knowlson authoritatively says of the trilogy and *Waiting for Godot* that "they are almost certainly the most enduring works that Beckett wrote" (336). The best of the novels is *Molloy*. It is often admired and discussed, but with an odd silence at the center. That it is a coherent work with characters and narratives generated by a sturdy thematic structure is seldom even asserted. Attempts to connect its two halves usually emphasize the specific physical details shared directly or complementarily by Molloy and Moran—percepts, we might say, that do not rise to concepts.

Beckett's public emphases upon form in art and upon irrationality in life separate form, such as an aesthetic structure, from the mess of subject matter. The texts we have examined imply that any structure in *Molloy* is likely to be psychological and will not deny the existence of the mess. Such a structure does exist in *Molloy*, and, what is more, it exists in so complex and detailed a form that our close analyses of simpler texts constitute a valuable exercise. The analysis of *Molloy* will validate aesthetically both Beckett's study of depth psychology and our own. It will take us, not without tears, close to the ideal core of the onion.

7.

Molloy: Molloy

Molloy is Beckett's master work of fiction. Its major characters, Molloy and Moran, are developed and individualized more extensively than any other of Beckett's characters. It is relevant praise to say that they are Joycean: complex, detailed, intelligent, knowledgeable, witty, and possessed of remarkable personal voices. Even on the surface, they are psychologically persuasive.

The structure of *Molloy* is also praiseworthy. In our century many major fictions have presented multiple interpretations of life by way of multiple central characters. *Doctor Faustus, Pale Fire,* and *To the Lighthouse* are obvious examples, and one necessarily thinks of Stephen Dedalus and Leopold and Molly Bloom. One might think also of Proust's altering protagonist Marcel and the writer Marcel, whose organization of the novel comments on its protagonist. Similarly, the artist Dante presents the changing character Dante in the *Commedia.* Beckett's two characters are both writers, and their narratives (we will call those "Molloy" and "Moran") are at once independent presentations of and by each narrator and disturbingly interconnected stories. They offer new varieties of these doublings and triplings noted above. Finally, the meanings of the novel are also praiseworthy. But that topic must wait until some meanings are found.

Beckett turned from essays and philosophical views of life, presented with no academic rigor, toward fiction and the sense that life is primarily psychological. After the simplicity of "A Case in a Thousand" and the multiple and ill-fitting materials of *Murphy,* he often displayed almost academic rigor in his close reliance on Freud's texts, materials, and interpretations. But aside from *Murphy,* Beckett's presentations were essentially static. Each psychological problem was stated and examined; none was worked through. ("From an Abandoned Work" may be an exception, but it was not yet written.)

In *Molloy*, then, Beckett manages a new and dazzling feat. He shapes his creative imaginings of Molloy and Moran with a close and detailed use of psychological texts. He shapes two distinct psyches, creating each psyche with imaginative as well as psychological care. He creates two worlds—themselves dual, at once Irish and French—as projections of each protagonist's psyche. These two characters and worlds are oddly linked, and they have much in common. Life is but a wandering to find home, Murphy said. Molloy and Moran wander through their psychic landscapes in order to return to a home altered by their psychic changes. Each wandering constitutes also a working through—not a successfully therapeutic one, but the analytical development of a psychic problem. The two complementary problems are acted out to reveal each character's developing psychological awareness.

Beckett's sources of professional knowledge are, again, studies in depth psychology. With their aid Beckett sends each character on a journey within himself, seeking the transformations that might cure a serious neurosis. Molloy begins his journey on a hillside detached from the world, and Moran starts from the level ground of ordinary social life. Both go underground, less literally than will the persona of *How It Is,* into the depths of the psyche.

These assertions follow intelligibly this study's earlier considerations of Beckett's dependence upon Schopenhauer and Proust and Freud. The citations of passage after passage and the persistent connection of Beckettian detail with Freudian and Schopenhauerian detail may seem obsessive, even though admittedly incomplete. If the analyses seem obsessive, however, what must one say of the texts analyzed? Beckett did not write with any concern for economical scholarly discussion. Now, before an examination of depth psychology in "Molloy" and "Moran" can be undertaken, he obliges us to turn to an unpredictable text, William James's *Varieties of Religious Experience*. Before we are through, we will be obliged to touch on Descartes and plunge into Jung. Yet our only concern is the central structures of *Molloy*.

* * *

Beckett's specific borrowings from *Varieties of Religious Experience* are few, limited in topic, and amusing. Let us glance hastily at them and at James's text. In this series of lectures, James discusses individuals who have undergone intense religious experiences of a certain sort—conversions, one might say, although these people were usually members of a religious sect already. For each of them, as a result of unconventional experiences in which James finds a pattern, religious matters become suddenly different and personal.

One recurrent feature of such experiences is the receiving of messages: "visions, voices, raptures, and other openings, supposed by each to authenticate his own peculiar faith" (504). One link between Molloy and Moran is this experience of a voice or voices. Beckett adds two oddities. For Moran, the voice is supplemented by another sort of instructor, the messenger Gaber. For Molloy, the voice or voices are supplemented by a bell or gong. "Having waked between eleven o'clock and midday (I heard the angelus, recalling the incarnation, shortly after) I resolved to go and see my mother," he reports, beginning his voyage of transformation (15; "angelos" means "messenger" in Greek). A bell or gong sounds repeatedly through the forest when he is almost at the end of his crawl (89). The bell or gong and the messenger Gaber are curious forms of spiritual communication. They share a common source in *Varieties*.

Before reaching his "Conclusions," James offers a chapter on "Other Characteristics" of the individual religious experience. One such characteristic is inspiration. His discussion leads him to a primary example of someone inspired, Mohammed. James quotes some details from another text: "Mohammed is said to have . . . heard a knell as from a bell, and . . . this had the strongest effect on him; and when the angel went away, he had received the revelation. Sometimes again he held converse with the angel as with a man, so as easily to understand his words." The odd equivalence here of bell and angel reminds us that Molloy deduces the angelus from the bell announcing it. The passage James is quoting lists the several kinds of inspiration that Mohammed experienced: "1, revelations with sound of bell, 2, by inspiration of the holy spirit in M.'s heart, 3, by Gabriel in human form, 4, by God immediately, either when awake . . . or in dream." Other texts cited by James add details and alternative sources of Mohammed's inspiration, among them "Gabriel in propriâ personâ (only twice)" and "Gabriel in the form of still another man" (471).

"Gabriel" obviously suggests "Gaber." The Gabriel-angel-bell association offers a connection between the two halves of *Molloy* and between the novel and *Varieties*. That Gaber appears to Moran "only twice" is amusing but no more. However, the bell and Gabriel as inspirations (for "M."!) suggest that Beckett finds interesting the religious experience that James discusses. In both *Molloy* and *Varieties* the messages conveyed are similar and significant. They represent an experience that James acknowledges as psychological rather than conventionally religious. He studies individuals who, after a crucial experience, seek salvation apart from doctrine. All religions, he says, offer "a certain uniform deliverance" in the form of a two-part experience: "an uneasiness" and "its solution" (498). Moran is a churchgoer at the beginning, a group member already offered a certain uniform deliverance, but he is made anxious by Gaber's visit.

James defines the uneasiness of this unconventional experience as "a sense that there is *something wrong about us as we naturally stand.*" The solution is "a sense that *we are saved from the wrongness* by making proper connection with the higher powers" (498). This uneasiness, which can overcome even a churchgoer, produces a divided self. "The divided self," this uneasy individual, "so far as he suffers from his wrongness and criticises it, is to that extent consciously beyond it, and in at least possible touch with something higher, if anything higher exist. Along with the wrong part there is thus a better part of him, even though it may be but a most helpless germ. With which part he should identify his real being is by no means obvious at this stage . . ." (498). The divided self is obviously a relevant idea in *Molloy* as in many Beckett works. ("How little one is at one with oneself, good God," remarks Moran anxiously [113].) The existence of "higher powers," put tentatively here by James, is made questionable by Beckett's skepticism until we reverse direction and sink into the unconscious of depth psychology.

The plots of "Molloy" and "Moran" require the protagonists to make contact with a significant other. Since Molloy seeks his mother, it is easy to say that he "identifies his real being with the germinal higher part of himself," as James says that he should (498). Seeking Molloy, Moran denies at first that Molloy is related to him, but he admits to finding his images of Molloy within himself. James speaks of the self as including a "wrong part" and a "better part," with the relative values unclear to the uneasy self. Both Beckett characters appear to discover and act against that wrong part; Molloy attacks a charcoal-burner who much resembles him, and Moran kills a man closely resembling his professional self.

Divided selves undergo a struggle that has similar characteristics, James says, in every "autobiographic document" that he has examined, if one allows for "various theologies and various personal temperaments" (499). These phenomena include "the divided self and the struggle; . . . the change of personal centre and the surrender of the lower self; they express the appearance of exteriority of the helping power and yet account for our sense of union with it; and they fully justify our feelings of security and joy" (499). Security and joy are not characteristic of Molloy's two outcomes, though they may certainly be goals. (Moran explicitly expects "happy days" to come.) The other phenomena are certainly relevant. Molloy claims a Jamesian "sense of union" in asserting that he and his mother were old cronies and that after his return to her apartment he has become much like her. Moran certainly experiences a "change of personal centre," as we see especially in contrasting his Sunday in the garden at the start of his narrative with his summer outside the already sold house at the end. (Although he cannot know it, he also increasingly resembles Molloy.) It is possible to say, then, that for each character an apparently external power has become internal and a lower self has given way. (At the end of his "autobiographic document" each Beckett narrator uses the third person in speaking of the protagonist.)

James asks his audience to allow for "various theologies," but his interests and theirs are certainly religious. However, he did not base on theology his study of his subjects' "uniform deliverance": "So far . . . as this analysis goes, the experiences are only psychological phenomena" (499). James connects these phenomena with depth psychology, especially in describing the "unification of a discordant self" through conversion (472). The details reveal, he says, "a department of human nature with unusually close relations to the transmarginal or subliminal region" (473). He might have said simply "psychological," one thinks, but in 1902 that subject was not quite proper. "If the word 'subliminal' is offensive to any of you, as smelling too much of psychical research or other aberrations, call it by any other name you please," James suggests, "to distinguish it from the level of full sunlit consciousness."

This darker and lower level is not a known region. James explains it at some length. He sets against "full sunlit consciousness" a part of the mind that is "obviously the larger part of each of us, for it is the abode of everything that is latent and the reservoir of everything that passes unrecorded or unobserved. . . . It harbors the springs of all our obscurely motivated passions, impulses, likes, dislikes, and prejudices. Our intuitions, hypotheses, fancies, superstitions, persuasions, convictions, and in general all our nonrational operations, come from it. It is the source of all our dreams, and apparently they may return to it. . . . It is also the fountain-head of much that feeds our religion." Seeking the "more" that is achieved when one identifies his "real being" with the "higher part of himself," James recurs to this subliminal level, assuring his audience that "the *subconscious self* is nowadays a well-accredited psychological entity" (501). He then makes an assertion basic to Beckett's uses of psychology in *Molloy* as elsewhere: "It is one of the peculiarities of invasions from the subconscious region to take on objective appearances, and to suggest to the Subject an external control" (503).

To discuss the subconscious, James needs terminology free of associations troubling to an audience shy of depth psychology. He therefore calls consciousness the "A-region" and the subliminal mind the "B-region." Molloy, labeling the townsman and the other man seen from his hillside, relevantly calls them A and B (changed in the English to A and C). B is the older and more unsocial of the two. Both constitute parts of that psychic self he must learn to know and control.

One final detail is worth noting. Moran praises repression when he reports taking away his son's stamp album. "I knew . . . that this ordeal would be of profit to him," he says. Then he quotes from Goethe's *Faust,* altering the values of the phrase: "*Sollst entbehren,* that was the lesson I desired to impress upon him, while he was still young and tender" (110). Since Freud often discusses repression and often quotes Goethe, we might expect him to cite this command to do without. He does not, but James does, and relevantly (51). (And Fritz Wittels does also, in a discussion of Freud Beckett may have read [96], and Beckett knew *Faust* well.)

Before he wrote *Molloy,* Beckett had often turned to the problem of presenting a divided self in literary form. No thorough itemization is necessary. The Belacqua of "Dream" and of *More Pricks* is divided, like Proust's Marcel, between an inner and a social self. Watt suffers from an uneasiness unrelieved by his search for meanings in the external world. Paired or opposed characters help to express this divided self; Belacqua and his narrators, Watt and Sam, and Mercier and Camier (and that third who is always with them) are early formulations of such A and B characters. Murphy, differing as he is connected to Celia, to Mr. Endon, and to his tripartite mind, is an extension of such characters. Murphy aside, the divided self has been presented as rather static. Divided, Nemo can move to neither riverbank. Divided, Belacqua cannot integrate himself with a woman or with society. We watch the resulting difficulties, but the division itself is not addressed.

James offers a way to make the division itself the central subject of a narrative that can reveal its alterations and possible improvement. He offers not merely theory and not merely the endpoints of uneasiness and solution. He specifies the uneasiness as that of a "real being" confronted by a "better part" and withheld from identification with it by a "wrong part." "The change of personal centre and the surrender of the lower self" are significant events in this plot, as are "the exteriority of the helping power and . . . our sense of union with it" (499). In short, he dramatizes the subject.

James also suggests by his choice of materials a valuable kind of text, the "autobiographic document." Such a work omits the normalizing and judging narrative voice and minimizes social and institutional experiences irrelevant to the religious experiences of the twice-born man. (The concepts of "once-born" and "twice-born," devised by F. W. Newman, are discussed by James [79–80] and made a basis of his lectures on the uneasy twice-born individual.) The first-person narratives and the confessional or therapist's-couch styles of *Molloy* may also owe something, then, to Beckett's reading of *Varieties of Religious Experience.*

Mohammed's Gabriel and gongs and A and B and Moran's churchgoing (and Beckett's citation of James in *Murphy*) encourage one to sense deliberate connection between James and Beckett. It is useful to imagine *Molloy* as being—among much else—an application of depth psychology to two varieties of religious experience. Each character seeks something that he cannot specify, something unpersuasively attached to a human being, and he does so because of an uneasiness not easily traced to a specific source. (The source is not the angelus or Gaber, nor is it some traumatic personal event.) Each character seeks deliverance from that anxiety, and each finds a possibility of deliverance within, not without. Such resemblances may obviate implications of mere case-history specificity as we turn to Beckett's inordinately extensive use of the psychologies of Jung and Freud. Those resemblances remind us of Beckett's explicit interest, from as far back as *Proust,* in "salvation."

Jung

We carry these Jamesian ideas toward *Molloy* only to encounter another traffic delay. We have looked at Beckett's uses of Freudian ideas, mostly about narcissism and the Oedipus complex. *Molloy* will send us deeper. Furthermore, *Molloy* supplements Freudian psychology with Jungian psychology, and therefore a brief introduction to the Jungian ideas that we will encounter might be helpful.

Carl Gustav Jung (1875–1961) was a follower of Freud and then a leading Freudian and then, like Alfred Adler, an apostate and the founder of his own school of depth psychology. He uses many of Freud's terms, sometimes altering their sense; he adds many of his own; and he emphasizes different elements from the already vast materials of psychology. For our purposes his work consists only of those materials relevant to the novel and available when Beckett wrote *Molloy.*

Some basic generalizations might help to differentiate Jung and Freud. For Jung the libido is not essentially sexual, as for Freud; it is a psychic energy with many qualities. The id, ego, and superego are of minor interest; Jung prefers to speak of the unconscious and of the conscious mind or ego-consciousness. Treating a neurosis, Freud looks back into childhood for an initiating trauma. Jung emphasizes immediate etiology and a teleological outcome. Freud hopes to mend the broken psyche and then leave that imperfect self to face an uncertain future in an imperfect society. Jung wishes to guide the imperfect self toward its potential perfection, its individuation. Freud finds in dreams evidence of problems repressed by the superego. Jung finds there advice and warnings from the unconscious. Freud uses dreams for analysis; Jung uses them also for therapy.

Freud imagines that the youthful psyche resolves its Oedipal problems by introjecting parental values into itself, thereby forming its superego; it supplements those values with others from the outer world. Jung prefers to find deeper values in a part of the unconscious psyche that is not personal but racial: the collective unconscious. We have inherited that collective unconscious and its contents just as we have inherited our bodies and their characteristic human qualities. As the human race's bodily inheritance has altered over the eons, so has our collective unconscious, accumulating qualities in response to the dangers and possibilities of existence. From these latent qualities each psyche creates a complete self, or should.

Jung develops, peoples, and dramatizes this collective unconscious. The collective unconscious contains the materials not only of positive developments but of psychic difficulties that occur as one moves from infancy through childhood, adolescence, youthful maturity, middle age, and old age. Since Jung is interested in the psyche's developing individuation, his emphasis understandably falls on the latter half of life rather than the beginnings to which Freud so often returned. (Beckett, however, was much moved by hearing Jung remark, about a neurotic girl, that "she had never been born completely," as we noted in discussing *All That Fall*. Molloy's Jungian childhood is also significant.)

Jung's collective unconscious contains not the conflicting libidinal demands of Freud's id but dramatizations of central problems. In a time of psychic stress, especially, the psyche becomes a theater. Its characters are archetypal forms. The collective unconscious is a repertory company; the archetypes cannot take the stage except in costume. They are embodied in specific identities. One can perceive a beautiful woman but not Beauty itself. The beautiful woman plays that role for the psyche involved with her, not for everyone. Any human may play several roles simultaneously in the psychodramas of others, even without knowing it, but most people play no archetypal part in one's life. Innumerable specific costumes are available to these archetypes. Moreover, in Jung's generalizations and examples each archetype tends to vary its contents considerably, so that it becomes difficult to limit the identifying qualities of any one archetype.

Each psyche, Jung says, has a dominant and an inferior side, determined by sex. In the female the inferior side is made up of masculine qualities and represented by the archetypal animus. In the male the anima is the archetype of his inferior side's female qualities. Each person tends, especially during the first part of life, to develop the primary side and neglect or repress this inferior side. In order to achieve individuation and a complete self, one must integrate the qualities of the inferior side with those of the dominant side.

Jung is as persistently dualistic as Schopenhauer and Freud and Beckett. The conscious male side is dogged by a Shadow, representing its unacknowledged and usually rather unpleasant male qualities. The male's anima is also both desirable and dangerous. As Jung remarks in "The Archetypes of the Collective Unconscious" when discussing the archetype of meaning: "Like all archetypes it has a positive and a negative aspect" (*Archetypes*, 37). Archetypes of character include the Shadow, the anima and animus, the Wise Old Man (also known as the archetype of meaning or the Logos), and the Wise Woman.

These archetypes are supplemented by those of another class, especially during major developments of the psyche. Psychic dramas require situations as well as characters. "The process," Jung explains, "involves another class of archetypes which one could call the *archetypes of transformation.*" Archetypes of character "are of a kind that can be directly experienced in personified form." The archetypes of transformation "are not personalities, but are typical situations, places, ways and means, that symbolize the kind of transformation in question" (*Archetypes*, 37–38).

Any difficult transformation of personality may involve many of these archetypal situations, as well as many appearances by archetypes of character. The transformation, like the archetypes, is dualistic: "The symbolic process is an experience *in images and of images*. Its development usually shows an enantiodromian structure . . . , and so presents a rhythm of negative and positive, loss and gain, dark and light. Its beginning is almost inevitably characterized by one's getting stuck in a blind alley or in some impossible situation; and its goal is, broadly speaking, illumination or higher consciousness, by means of which the initial situation is overcome on a higher level." Where does this drama occur, and when? Actual situations in daily life may be experienced archetypally, for good or ill, but Jung's discussions emphasize the psychic experiences provided by dreams and works of art. "As regards the time factor, the process may be compressed into a single dream or into a short moment of experience, or it may extend over months and years . . ." (*Archetypes*, 38–39).

The general relevance of these complex materials to *Molloy* is obvious. Moran's travels cover an approximate year. Molloy's cannot be calculated, but if we had to know, we would have been told. The important matter is the process of transformation undergone by each character. The narratives are not both Jungian. Molloy's psyche is Jungian, and his narrative is composed of archetypal characters and situations. Moran's psyche is Freudian, but Moran's narrative also employs the basic Jungian and Jamesian element of psychic dramatization. (Jung was influenced by James.)

Both Freud and Jung recognize that a patient's sense of his mother, for instance, does not constitute an objective description of the actual woman, though Jung likes to suggest that for Freud it does. One passage in which he suggests this is useful for another reason. It offers, in terms from Jung's psychotherapy rather than Freud's psychoanalysis, a description of Beckett's procedure in creating the central characters of *Molloy*. Unlike Freud, Jung says, "I attribute to the personal mother only a limited aetiological significance. That is to say, all those influences which the literature [of psychiatric studies] describes as being exerted on the children do not come from the mother herself, but rather from the archetype projected upon her, which gives her a mythological background and invests her with authority and numinosity" (*Archetypes*, 83). We will see much that is relevant to this projection. *Molloy* profits from Beckett's mythologizing—that is, making fabulous—Molloy's and Moran's searches.

Like Freud, Jung recognized a personal unconscious containing repressed as well as latent and potentially available information. He acknowledged that this personal unconscious might be involved in mental illness, but it did not greatly interest him: "So far as a neurosis is really only a private affair, having its roots exclusively in personal causes, archetypes play no role at all" (*Archetypes*, 47). Art seeks to expand the personal into the general and, James might add, to connect percepts with concepts. These elements of Jungian psychology offered Beckett many ideas and materials with which to dramatize and generalize his psychological themes and to turn Molloy's and Moran's autobiographical documents into public affairs.

Molloy

Structurally, the most remarked feature of *Molloy* is its duality. The reader experiences a novel that is titled *Molloy*, narrated by Molloy, and concerned with Molloy's search for his mother, and then discovers halfway through this novel that the narrator Molloy has discarded the character Molloy in a ditch, far from home and mother, and has closed his report. Then a priggish minor bureaucrat takes center stage to narrate his search for Molloy—a search interminably postponed, poorly conducted, and abortive. The two narratives constitute only a parody of halves, since no whole can be perceived.

In 1961, well after the composition of *Molloy*, Beckett spoke eloquently of the formal problems facing an artist. Accepting the necessity of form in art, he rejected traditional forms because they can report only clear materials or because those clear forms imply the clarity of their materials. In our time, life—and therefore the material of art—is chaotic. The artist therefore must find ways to admit the chaos into art without imposing form upon it: "The form and the chaos remain separate. The latter is not reduced to the former." Because of this need, the old forms cannot be used: "To find a form that accommodates the mess, that is the task of the artist now" (Graver and Federman, 219). Beckett takes it as axiomatic that life "now" is not the same as life "then." His writings can be understood only if we accept, with him, the primacy of the individual self's psychic experience and the neurotic psyche's generation of a discordant, formless existence.

Beckett did not imply that one single literary form might be found, of course. Each selection of chaotic materials poses its own problems. Long before 1961 he had used psychological problems as structural elements, shaping character and situation with them while finding in such shapes no psychological or aesthetic implication of clarity, order, and solution. Responses to *Molloy* suggest that these qualities have not been found in *Molloy* either. Beckett does offer some conventional structural elements in *Molloy*, including the basic element of symmetry. Putting *Molloy* together out of two quests, two landscapes, and two narrators, Beckett has encouraged readers to find elements that link them. Devising overlapping details of character and appearance, he has added to that symmetry another basic quality of artistic form, complementarity. No harmony results, however. Each narrative takes the reader from beginning to end of a quest posited at the start. Each quest is given the conventional form of a journey, and each journey is varied by encounters with strangers. Conventionally, such encounters during a quest provide the protagonist with clues that lead him, mislead him, and test him on his way.

In addition to these conventional plot materials, the narrators' direct addresses to the reader or listener allow for a wide range of remarks, some retrospectively autobiographical, some relevant to the journey, and some obiter dicta. These state or imply areas of meaning.

So described, *Molloy* is obviously a conventional novel made up of conventional structures. What these structures house, however, is chaotic. Despite the geographical extent of the journeys, they are curiously claustrophic. No mere scenery or clear location is offered. Relations between places are unexplained. No maps are consulted. (Moran's description of Bally darkens its topic.) No vehicles are used (except for bicycles), and only a few farmers' carts are seen. Food and drink are scarcer than minor characters. Weather is intermittent. Personal relationships are questionable, even Moran's quotidian parochial relationships in Turdy. And though the narrators make conventional remarks, they make also some very strange remarks, and they take for granted situations that are odd indeed, such as Moran's job and Molloy's inability to remember where his mother lives. Thus the conventional forms of narrative contain chaos without presenting it as something else.

* * *

But chaos, however formally presented, cannot qualify as art. The two narratives "Molloy" and "Moran" do have a structure. They act out linked and sequential psychological events suggested by James's *Varieties of Religious Experience* and by Jung and Freud. They reach problematic psychological conclusions. The acting out of these situations—a formal notion simple in itself—imposes upon the apparently picaresque novel a tight order.

In this psychological structure the minor characters, events, and settings are projections, embodiments, archetypal forms of the psychic matters that constitute each narrative's developing situation. The narrators are at once actors in their psyche's situations and spectators of them. Each functions as an individual human and also as the Freudian conscious ego or the Jungian ego-consciousness of that human's psyche. As spectators, they impose some shape upon their narratives by their choice of relevant materials and by their rare retrospective recognitions.

So understood, the narrators and narratives give these varieties of symmetry and complementarity meanings profitable to speculation. *Molloy* is a complex mosaic composed almost entirely of small details. The picture created by their arrangement results from Beckett's unstated psychological postulates, of which the following are central and familiar to us.

Human experience is the experience of an individual self isolated from others and needing others. The self's needs are emotional, not rational, often unconscious and often denied. They result from an early loss of some unspecifiable harmony, comfort, and security. (We have already encountered several varieties of this former state, such as the Paradise of "unrelieved immaculation" in "Dante . . . ," the "paradise lost" and "salvation" of *Proust,* the "wandering to find home" of *Murphy,* and the "homeland" of "First Love.") The protagonists' basic need is to restore this lost situation. The restoration requires another person, both literally and figuratively. The Jungian Molloy must come to terms with his mother; the Freudian Moran must win Youdi's approval by finding and dealing with Molloy.

Each protagonist's self consists of Freudian or Jungian parts, but each self is fragmented; Molloy and Moran represent severely neurotic selves. (What "the self" might be—as separate from these parts—Beckett will attempt to learn in *The Unnamable*.) In both cases the most troubling fragment of the psychic self, generating the strongest need, can be described as parental: the mother for Molloy, a paternal authority for Moran. But in both cases the merely personal element is slight; both characters have lived for decades beyond any simple Oedipus complex (unlike the protagonist of "From an Abandoned Work"). In both cases the protagonist—here Jamesian—experiences a sudden change in his situation, a sudden obligation to do something about his unsatisfactory psychic life. The "something" is vague and metaphoric, however, and no single response is decisive; each act moves him into other situations, other obligations, and other revelations. The characters' goal is that of Jungian or Freudian therapy, although they do not know this.

"Molloy"

Molloy is an old man, but he has not yet come to terms with his mother. Like the age of the narrators of "First Love" and "From an Abandoned Work," his age is psychological. That is, it implies that the character is set in his psychic ways, that his failure to develop properly began long ago, and that the chance of therapeutic success is therefore slight. Molloy is involved primarily with women who represent varieties of his psychic need. His biological mother is transformed into a grotesque and barely human creature unable to share rational ideas, and she quickly exits from the drama. She is replaced by another woman on whose estate Molloy spends a large part of his story. When he leaves her, after telling us about yet another woman, he finds no fourth figure. After traveling to the seaside and back through a forest, he ends abruptly in a ditch. Only the opening pages of the narrative inform us that he did somehow reach his mother's room, though not his mother.

Molloy is a typical Jungian patient, in the latter half of life and still far from individuation. He has not yet raised his anima out of his unconscious and made it a part of his self. Impelled to do so (not for the first time), he encounters his anima externally as a series of archetypal images. They are predominantly maternal, since it was in his childhood that his development was derailed. Mag is a caricature of motherhood, and Molloy's hostility to her is explicit. She is not, however, a personal object of dislike. Jung tells us that "the personal mother [has] only a limited aetiological significance" and that it is "the archetype projected upon her" that "invests her with authority and numinosity." The later women provide complements of this form of the maternal anima.

Molloy is a soft character, lacking Moran's sharply drawn early identity. His identity is transitional; he is a self in the making. If we give him a Jungian ego-consciousness and a collective unconscious characterized by repressions, we know him well enough to go on with. But granting Beckett his use of Jung obliges us to know something more about Jung's ideas and especially about the anima.

* * *

Jung offered Beckett several discussions of the anima and the mother archetype. We may meet the mother archetype thriftily by way of his lists. He begins "Psychological Aspects of the Mother Archetype" (1938) by dividing her archetypal forms into good and bad ones. His incomplete list of the good forms includes these images: the actual mother, grandmother, stepmother, mother-in-law; nurse and governess; goddess, Mother of God, Virgin, Sophia; Demeter, Kore, Cybele; "things representing the goal of our longing for redemption, such as Paradise, the Kingdom of God, the Heavenly Jerusalem"; and "Many things arousing devotion or feelings of awe, as for instance the Church, university, city or country, heaven, earth, the woods, the sea or any still waters . . . , the underworld and the moon. . . . The cornucopia, a ploughed field, a garden. . . . the baptismal font . . . The magic circle or mandala. . ." (*Archetypes*, 81).

That large and varied list of available items may lead one into doubt; quantity seems to drown quality and probability. But no one image necessarily constitutes a maternal archetype. The psyche must project archetypal qualities upon it before it can qualify.

Jung's short list of evil forms of the maternal archetype is less evocative: witch, dragon, the grave, the sarcophagus, deep water, death, nightmares, and bogies. Perhaps only the ditches and the sea in "Molloy" are immediately relevant. We must recall, however, that dualism is rampant among archetypes, and therefore all the positive images have potentially negative attributes.

The maternal qualities projected upon these images are also multiple, and again Jung offers a list:

> maternal solicitude and sympathy; the magic authority of the female; the wisdom and spiritual exaltation that transcend reason; any helpful instinct or impulse; all that is benign, all that cherishes and sustains, that fosters growth and fertility. The places of magic transformation and rebirth, together with the underworld and its inhabitants, are pre-

sided over by the mother. On the negative side the mother archetype may connote anything secret, hidden, dark; the abyss, the world of the dead, anything that devours, seduces, and poisons, that is terrifying and inescapable like fate. . . . There are three essential aspects of the mother: her cherishing and nourishing goodness, her orgiastic emotionality, and her Stygian depths. (*Archetypes*, 82)

The reader of "Molloy" quickly recognizes relevant qualities, especially in that final triad. The positive ones may seem unpersuasive, however, since Molloy is extremely critical of women and extremely hostile in reporting instances of solicitude, helpfulness, wisdom, and fostering. Jung notes that "in a man, the mother-complex is never 'pure'; it is always mixed with the anima archetype, and the consequence is that a man's statements about the mother are always emotionally prejudiced in the sense of showing 'animosity'" (*Archetypes*, 82). Unmentioned by Molloy, the positive qualities exist implicitly as positive reasons for Molloy's search, since his present identity obviously lacks them.

Jung believed that he could follow and direct the progress of patients undergoing therapy by hearing and investigating their dreams and observing archetypes at work. This practice provides Beckett with a major structural form. The dramas of both "Molloy" and "Moran" are constructed on the Jungian model of dream sequences. Event is linked to event by psychic cause and effect rather than by rational probability or even chronology, and occasional remarks by Molloy suggest the presence of a judging listener.

To reach psychic maturity, Molloy must raise from his unconscious and understand responsibly his obsessive relation to his mother. This mother is not an individual human being. She is composed of various human beings onto which he projects qualities of his repressed maternal archetype. Thus each necessary encounter with his maternal anima is not a literal meeting in a photographable world; it is psychic throughout.

The angelus sets him going, down to the world of the unconscious and back to his past. Bit by bit and character by character, elements of the maternal archetype emerge from his collective unconscious. To become conscious of them is important, but only as a beginning. He must gain control over his maternal archetype. As it is raised from the unconscious, however, it threatens his ego-consciousness and therefore his masculine rationality and control.

Jung tells us that the development of the psyche "presents a rhythm of negative and positive, loss and gain, dark and light," with "illumination" as its goal (*Archetypes*, 38–39). Molloy begins in an untenable situation, halfway up a mountain and far from his fellow human beings; he recurrently seeks shelter in or is stopped by a ditch; after leaving Lousse he shuffles out of the rain into several blind alleys. Dark and illumination are recurrent themes.

Let us approach the search and that sought-for mother in a relevant, rather than a conventional, frame of mind. "'The search for one's mother': this phrase has almost obligatorily touching overtones," Jung says, "and it implies such phrases as 'the lost child' and 'the maternal bosom'": "This is the mother-love which is one of the most moving and unforgettable memories of our lives, the mysterious root of all growth and change; the love that means homecoming, shelter, and the long silence from which everything begins and in which everything ends. Intimately known and yet strange like Nature, lovingly tender and yet cruel like fate, joyous and untiring giver of life—*mater dolorosa* and mute implacable portal that closes upon the dead" (*Archetypes,* 92).

Even as we recognize relevant details in that sentimental passage (and note its darkening close), we must admit that Molloy is not a lost child but a hairy, dirty, ill-clad, antisocial old man. He describes his mother as "happy to smell me" (17), but that joyous and untiring giver of life "did all she could not to have me, except of course the one thing" (18). Molloy's characterization of this mother and child reunion warns us against sentimentality. Jung also warns us: "It is just this massive weight of meaning that ties us to the mother and chains her to the child, to the physical and mental detriment of both. . . . That is why mankind has always instinctively added the pre-existent divine pair to the personal parents—the 'god'-father and 'god'-mother of the newborn child—so that . . . he should never forget himself so far as to invest his own parents with divinity" (*Archetypes,* 92–93). Beckett emphasizes this second maternal form. Mag is supplemented by a "god"-mother, Sophie Loy or Lousse, and Molloy's stay with her is central in many ways.

Given Jung's interest in individuation and the achievement of one's potential self, one might expect him to urge his masculine patients to make peace with their troubling feminine archetypes, but he does not. Molloy must raise his mother archetype up into the light of consciousness, out of the darkness of the collective unconscious. The Jungian intent, however, is quite different from that of making peace; the successfully developed masculine consciousness, which includes the Logos, is judgmental:

There is no consciousness without discrimination of opposites. This is the paternal principle, the Logos, which eternally struggles to extricate itself from the primal warmth and primal darkness of the womb; in a word, from unconsciousness. Divine curiosity yearns to be born and does not shrink from conflict, suffering, or sin. Unconsciousness is the primal sin, evil itself, for the Logos. Therefore its first creative act of liberation is matricide, and the [masculine] spirit that dared all heights and all depths must . . . suffer the divine punishment, enchainment on the rocks of the Caucasus. (*Archetypes*, 96)

An ominous conclusion—and we recall that Molloy was on a hillside when he started his journey. Molloy, however, develops no admirable Logos. (The Unnamable will distinguish himself from Prometheus, "that miscreant who mocked the gods, invented fire, denatured clay and domesticated the horse, in a word obliged humanity" [303; Jung quotes Nietzsche's phrase "Prometheus the great friend of man" in *Psychological Types*, 137].) Prometheus will appear before Molloy leaves Lousse, and the disparity between Molloy's reason and the Logos is crucial to Molloy's final state.

The complexities of the anima, the search for the mother, matricide, the paternal Logos and the wise Sophia, submission and control—these are airy general terms; instead, we must seek the solid ground of "Molloy" itself.

The Story Begins

The opening section of "Molloy" is thick with puzzles and oddities, and the conventional phrase "deceptively simple" applies. In our haste to get on, let us say simply that the beginning is quite conventional. We meet a narrator, altered by his adventures, who begins to tell us about those adventures. We can, however, draw on some of the psychological information above. The adventures are the sequential dreams of a psychological series, and they involve encounters between Molloy's ego-consciousness and images of his anima, especially of his maternal anima. Acknowledging these bases, at least tentatively, we may compress the extended presentation of A and B or C.

Molloy's active imagination is obliged to present in dramatic form his psychic transformations. He is uncertain, and details in the opening passage emphasize that he is inept at his work. Admitting that he is cobbling his story out of bits and pieces (14), Molloy describes seeing A and B or C and wishing to meet them. They are sketched as complementary types. The essence of their usefulness is contained in Molloy's reason for imagining them and wishing to meet them: "the craving for a fellow" (15). In the original, his term is "un frère," which makes more emphatic the closeness of the relationship sought.

It is a convention of psychology that the success of one's relations with others depends upon the health of one's own psyche. Molloy's inability to know whether to prefer A or B/C indicates that he does not know himself yet (although he inclines toward leaving town with B/C). The composing Molloy, however, knows where the trouble lies, and he gets to the preliminary and basic problem: his inadequate psychological relationship to his mother. He introduces it with a rhetorical flourish: "An instant of silence, as when the conductor taps on his stand, raises his arms, before the unanswerable clamour. Smoke, sticks, flesh, hair, at evening, afar, flung about the craving for a fellow. I know how to summon these rags to cover my shame" (15). Much is compressed into these images. Together they describe both the writer's position at the start of a work and the psyche's condition as Molloy begins his attempt at individuation. The first relates especially to the problem of finding a form that will contain the mess. The second expresses Molloy's obligation to create characters with which to connect such concepts as the craving for a fellow.

The first image is skillfully ambivalent. The conductor's acts take place "before" the clamor in two senses. He stands before an orchestra tuning up, ready to conduct the performers. His success is uncertain, however; "the unanswerable clamour" implies no harmony to follow. The situation is made more difficult when one consults the French, where "unanswerable clamour" is "le fracas des colles" (20). That phrase explains "unanswerable," since "colles" are both falsehoods and academic questions too difficult to answer. That first sense may relate to Molloy's desire to "cover his shame" and to his later acknowledgment that his story reports an "unreal journey" (16). The second image reports the shaping of a drama out of archetypal characters. It also suggests that through such characters the writer evades direct admission of "my shame."

We may seem far from Jung and Molloy's concerns, but Molloy cannot find a fellow or frère, until he settles matters with his maternal archetype, and he gets directly to that need: "But talking of the craving for a fellow let me observe that having waked between eleven o'clock and midday (I heard the angelus, recalling the incarnation, shortly after) I resolved to go and see my mother." He cannot follow A or C until the primal problem is resolved. That his mother is not merely personal is indicated by the angelus, which gives her religious significance. This is also the first of several connections that Molloy makes between himself and Jesus. They will be crucial, in several senses.

Important decisions tend to be over-motivated. Molloy's craving for a fellow is presented as generating several motives to budge him in his crippled state (itself expressive of his unwillingness to move). They provide a comic image of motivation: "I found my bicycle (I didn't know I had one)." Suddenly he is on the road to recovery. Molloy's ego-consciousness has received its opening thematic message from his unconscious, as Moran will receive one from the messenger Gaber. It has made him anxious, like the twice-born Jamesians. It has required him to change.

This presentation of materials is Freudian, too. Freud begins *The Interpretation of Dreams* by agreeing with Schopenhauer that the sleeping intellect shapes impressions "into the forms of time, space and causality" (IV, 36). Later, Freud notes that "what characterizes the waking state is the fact that thought-activity takes place in *concepts* and not in *images*. Now dreams think essentially in images . . ." (IV, 49). Jung has also told us that the encounter with an archetype "is an experience *in images and of images.*" Molloy's two metaphors constitute Beckett's similar statement.

Molloy cannot complete his Jungian self without finding, knowing, and mastering his anima, especially in its maternal forms. The desire for a fellow, then, states the distant goal of the individuation process: a completed Molloy will be able to take his place among other human beings. Now, however, he is on bad terms with his mother. "I needed, before I could resolve to go and see that woman, reasons of an urgent nature," he says, acknowledging that "I did not know what to do, or where to go" (15). Realistically, such an assertion is absurd; psychologically, it is intelligible. Because repression is strong, his masculine and rational ego-consciousness demands "reasons." It does not know where to go or what to do because the mother it must seek is a Jungian anima. The craving for a fellow has provided a stronger motive than Molloy has previously felt, perhaps because it implies a goal beyond the mother and in the masculine world. Its immediate effectiveness suggests the abrupt impetus reported by William James.

For the rest of "Molloy" we will follow his encounters with varied images of the maternal anima. Beckett will set these against images of the masculine animus. These Jungian images will be associated with psychologically relevant places: home, a police station, a cave, a city, or a country scene. The images and events will be generated basically by desire and fear. Since these meanings and the plot of "Molloy" are closely connected with maternal archetypes, let us borrow a structural division from the later novel *How It Is*. "Molloy," then, is divided into three parts: before Sophie, with Sophie, and after Sophie.

Before Sophie

What we experience first—in many more details than this study has space to consider—is Molloy's failure to screw his courage to the sticking point once he reaches Bally. His basic motivation, we have seen, is his desire for a fellow, but in his present psychological state he cannot function as a man among men. He is taken to the police station, where his social inadequacy is established; he cannot produce his papers. Dismissed with masculine indifference, he flees town, evading male and female archetypes at once. Outside town, however, he encounters two more images of the masculine world, the boatman and the shepherd. Their archetypal threats send him back to town. There again his will collapses and so does he. This collapse enables the dominant Sophie Loy or Lousse to emerge from his unconscious. She takes him in.

*   *   *

Mag is the first of Molloy's archetypes of the maternal anima. Their oddly unfamilial relation is unsettling: "we were like a couple of old cronies, sexless, unrelated, with the same memories, the same rancours, the same expectations" (17). Molloy develops the notion of unrelated cronies by unsexing Mag and having her call him by his father's name. Their merely personal relation is also undercut by Molloy's calling his mother Mag because the last letter spits on the syllable "ma." He claims to have understood some of her "clattering gabble" during past visits, but "in any case I didn't come to listen to her" (18). "I got into communication with her by knocking on her skull"—using pain and numbers, not words. The motive for his knocking was money, but the keys to the drawer that contained it were available without the knocks, and "in any case I didn't come for money." Why, then? He will not realize why until his present journey is almost over.

This relation is no more grotesque than is Mag herself. "Veiled with hair, wrinkles, filth, and slobber," her head "darkened the air" (19). She gabbles; she stinks; she cannot recognize him. Molloy's evocation of her is so dreadful that it demands examination. *Molloy* pairs Mag with Moran's servant Martha. (Martha is the hard-working domestic sister of that Mary who heard the angelus; "Mag" may alter "Mary" and "May" as well as the title "ma.") Moran speaks of Martha's "wizened, grey skull," and Molloy describes Mag's head as "that little grey wizened pear" (97, 19; Beckett altered the French to make this connection). The pairing emphasizes their complementary functions. The Freudian Moran is indifferent to Martha, while the Jungian Molloy needs Mag; Moran seeks a male in his future, while Molloy seeks a female in his past. Molloy's presentation of Mag as a grotesquely emblematic creature signals her central role in his Jungian mythic drama, while Martha plays no such role in Moran's Freudian world.

In a section of *A la Recherche* that Beckett marked emphatically in his own copy and singled out for discussion in *Proust,* Marcel hurries to Paris to see his beloved grandmother. He encounters her unexpectedly, however, with his habitual projections and evaluations in abeyance, and sees her as a doddering old woman. Beckett told us that Marcel's "eye functions with the cruel precision of a camera; it photographs the reality . . ." (27). Marcel's ocular photograph is exaggerated in Beckett's report of "this mad old woman, drowsing over her book, overburdened with years, flushed and coarse and vulgar" (28).

In creating Mag, Beckett has outdone his earlier image, but Mag is not a photographable human being. She is an image of what Jung calls the chthonic mother, projected by an ego-consciousness hostile to her. She is not the fertile and sheltering Mother Earth, but a fearful embodiment of physical and mental decay and imminent death. Jung says that "the mother is the first world of the child and the last world of the adult" (*Archetypes,* 94). Saying so is easy; vividly imagining the first image of the mother turned into the last, as Beckett has done, is not.

Mag is frightening and disgusting, but Molloy must somehow come to terms with his relation to her. He must integrate her into his conscious sense of his self. It is not Jung alone who says that he must; Molloy knows it. He will later admit that he has spent his life seeking her (64–65, 87). He implies as much now, although even as he writes his report, he continues to evade the primary Jungian motive, the creation of his Logos, his Wise Old Man, which would enable him to understand his life: "If ever I'm reduced to looking for a meaning to my life, . . . it's in that old mess I'll stick my nose to begin with, the mess of that poor old uniparous whore and myself . . ." (19). The phrasing of this admission is odd. (The term "mess" anticipates Beckett's interview with Tom Driver.) The anima, Jung tells us, is itself a mess, chaotic. Here, however, the mess is not Mag but the relation between her and Molloy. Molloy's assertion suggests that "Molloy" reports that search, despite the evasive "if ever."

Molloy will remain unclear about this relationship and the mess. He will speak of "this matter between my mother and me" and "our relations" (64–65, 87), but Mag gabbles, and "most of the time [she] didn't realize what she was saying" (17–18). Whatever meaning Molloy might be obliged to find, it is not one that Mag can explain to him. Jung wrote of "this massive weight of meaning that ties us to the mother and chains her to the child, to the physical and mental detriment of both" (*Archetypes,* 92). Molloy needs to acquire that weighty Jungian meaning, while freeing himself from the chain.

Acknowledging a need for his mother, Molloy prepares us by describing Mag and his behavior with her. The description is presented as if merely

preliminary. For Jungian purposes, however, it is no such thing; it constitutes the encounter itself. Molloy's description acts out his encounter with
one version of his maternal anima. After long repression he is able to raise
a single image of the maternal archetype into his ego-consciousness. But
his description of Mag constitutes a parody of the archetype and of communication with it. His hostility cancels the possible good of the encounter. What is more, Mag the chthonic mother is only one form of the maternal anima and contains only some of her qualities. Molloy's problems
with the maternal anima are deeper and more complex than those associated primarily with the family. His journey, unpromising already, has a
long way to go.

"Now that we know where we're going, let's go there," Molloy says. "It's
so nice to know where you're going, in the early stages. It almost rids you of
the wish to go there" (19). The heroic Logos arises in response to a confrontation with the anima, and it obviates psychic anxiety by turning part of this
previously unknown power into rational wisdom. But Molloy has encountered Mag only to back away. Meanwhile, the anima remains unknown and
his psyche's need for completion pushes him on.

The Town

Beckett is composing a novel, not performing Jungian psychotherapy on a
real patient. Molloy's anima gives him no second chance with the same
archetypal image. He will never encounter or even name Mag again. Rebuffed, the repressed maternal anima will try again in different forms, Jung
says. But the anima is not alone in demanding attention during a psychic
crisis. Other archetypes enter the drama, including representatives of the
dominant masculine side, the animus. They too are projected from Molloy's
unconscious into his ego-consciousness, incompletely understood and accepted.

Apparently to find Mag, Molloy goes to town. Jung says that "city or
country, heaven, earth, the woods, the sea" are potential forms of the maternal archetype. Mag's chthonic form has suggested one of these—the earth,
whence we came and whither we shall go: objective, indifferent, inexpres-
sive Nature. In the country, the woods, and the sea of "Molloy" we may
find maternal archetypes, but now we go to the city.

Images are only potentially archetypal, and they can evoke more than one
archetype. A city, a center of rational civilization ruled by law, an embodiment of ideas, can be a masculine image. Since Molloy's town is named
Bally (complemented by Moran's Turdy), we may take it as masculine. Bally
frightens him. It is a busy, external, social world, noisy with the "violent

raucous tremulous bellowing" of cattle on their way to the shambles (22). Its primary building is its police station. Molloy cannot rise verbally to its occasions. He cannot name the town; he barely understands the policemen; he is almost unable to speak.

Bicycling down from his mountainside, he enters Bally quickly. Then his motivation weakens and he stops short to rest on his handlebars. He is arrested for having arrested his progress. This offense and the scene at the police station are comic, and Molloy presents them so as to arouse our sympathy for him and our dislike of the law-governed public world.

But one does not accept unquestioningly a patient's evaluation of his actions. Psychologically, Molloy was wrong to rest on his handlebars, and he knows this: "I was straining towards those spurious deeps, their lying promise of gravity and peace, from all my old poisons I struggled towards them, safely bound. Under the blue sky, under the watchful gaze. Forgetful of my mother, set free from the act, merged in this alien hour, saying Respite, respite" (21). This is not a conventional loitering bicyclist. Concerned with depth psychology, we might approve Molloy's attempt to descend. But he acts in bad faith; he knows that these depths are "spurious" and their promise a "lying" one; and he is "safely bound" by "the watchful gaze" of the policeman and the blue sky. (Studying him with Sophie and by the seaside, we will realize that Molloy has contrived a second depth in response to the actual one of Jungian depth psychology. Jung's contains the maternal archetypes and promises gravity and peace; the spurious other is an empty void, a psychic dead end, and frightening—which is why he speaks here of being "safely bound.")

At the police station Molloy is required to produce an identity shaped by identity papers and speech—categories imposed by the masculine reason. These categories require Molloy to accept a public identity and to turn outside himself. (The terms "extravert" and "introvert" are Jung's.) In this extended scene he is roused from his rest by a policeman, offered tea and bread by the social worker as "something to hinder you from swooning" (23), and stopped from playing with his shadow on the wall ("The shadow in the end is no better than the substance" [26]). All these acts keep Molloy up above, in the sunlit world, and prevent him from evasively swooning into a dark shadow of his self. The social worker offers him something positive, a social communion—feminine qualities in a masculine world. Molloy's rejection of the tea and bread offered by a woman cannot be praised; he replaces them and her with a pebble.

Molloy's responses are of a piece. He cannot understand why he is arrested, nor can he reason with the sergeant. He cannot talk to the social

worker. "I used to be intelligent and quick," he says, equating these qualities with "obedient" (25). When he leaves the police station, he has forgotten where he was going, and he cannot think and act simultaneously (26).
His Jungian masculine qualities are almost as undeveloped as those represented by his anima, their development delayed by his rejection of the anima:
"There I am then, before I knew I had left the town, on the canal-bank."
Molloy is in a bad way, neither moving toward his anima and a more complex identity nor functioning well in his role as a masculine ego-consciousness. Thus this flight ends with Molloy static in a comic image of the mother,
another ditch (27; see 19).

In a Jungian dream sequence, whether within one dream or over a period
of many nights, each event is to be understood as generated in part by pre-
ceding dream events. The events so far offer an intelligible sequence. Molloy's
craving for a fellow requires the psychic wholeness that can make possible
an affectionate relationship to others. (One must love oneself before loving
others; Murphy acted out the problem more simply.) Molloy's flaw is in his
psychic relation to his anima, imaged first as his chthonic mother Mag. The
motivation for change has come from his unconscious and is only partially
accepted by his ego-consciousness. Repressing Mag again after evoking her
and heading for town without thinking about her, Molloy becomes evasive
again. The dominant masculine images are coolly rational: "I asked the
man to help me, to have pity on me. He didn't understand," Molloy complains (26). Passive, he seeks a feminine quality, pity. Soon Lousse will offer
it.

Molloy excuses his misbehavior in society by blaming others: he had not
been taught proper principles. Soon he will describe his whole past life as a
time when, "not knowing exactly what I was doing or avoiding, I did it and
avoided it" (55). Now he finds himself on the canal bank "before I knew I
had left the town." Rational knowledge gives power, but only the power to
obey rules formulated by society. The best knowledge requires acceptance
of facts, reasoning, and finally wisdom generated by the Logos. Life must
be understood and controlled, not experienced ignorantly and passively.
Jung says that "the anima and life itself are meaningless in so far as they
offer no interpretation" (*Archetypes*, 32).

Identifying life with the anima, Jung associates meaning with masculine
rationality: "Man woke up in a world he did not understand, and that is
why he tries to interpret it" (31). Since Molloy has not yet awakened to that
world of the anima, his failures are of a lower order. He cannot understand
the laws that he has broken; he does not know the laws of proper behavior.
These are matters not of the anima or the Logos but merely of "the judging

intellect with its categories" (*Archetypes,* 32). Molloy's judging intellect, however, will become a serious topic. (For an anticipation, see his remarks about the pomeranian [11–12].)

On the canal bank Molloy encounters two more images of the animus. These too are conventional, ambivalent, indifferent to him, and implicitly threatening. In the evening he sees a boatman on a barge; in the morning he is awakened by a shepherd with a dog and a flock of sheep. Both men may be described as images of the controlling and judging male intellect; each image excludes Molloy from its acceptable categories.

The boatman has a long white beard, a pipe, and invisible eyes; he spits in the canal. The conventional image of a wise old man is undercut by the last two details. He is silent and nearly motionless, yet his arrival is signaled by "angry cries and dull blows" (26) directed at the donkeys pulling his barge. That barge appeared first in Beckett's "Eneug I": "at Parnell Bridge a dying barge / carrying a cargo of nails and timber." That these are the makings of crosses is now clearer: "It was a cargo of nails and timber, on its way to some carpenter I suppose." Molloy's role as victim is signaled when he notes that "the horizon was burning with sulphur and phosphorus, it was there I was bound." Then he acts out his acceptance of that role: "I got right down, hobbled down to the ditch and lay down, beside my bicycle. I lay at full stretch, with outspread arms. The white hawthorn stooped towards me, unfortunately I don't like the smell of hawthorn." This grotesque Pietà and his rejection of the late-blooming hawthorn lead Molloy to think of death. Psychologically his world is moribund; the anima—life—has been repressed. He must seek his "mother, who thinks she is alive" (27).

He reports no dreams from his night in the ditch. They would appear awkwardly, since his narrative is itself the dream or dream series. One notes again that essentially "Molloy" and "Moran" are reports from the dream-world of the psyche, the night world, here promoted to full narrative existence, as the narrator's psychic world is in "From an Abandoned Work." Didi and Gogo share a similar situation, parting to experience an external world of angry cries and dull blows, and then returning to each other on stage.

Waking from his sleep, Molloy experiences another threatening image of the animus. Our judging intellect with its categories might say that the bearded and indifferent old boatman approximates God the Father. The shepherd is the complementary Son. Before the Father, Molloy lay cruci-form. Now he imagines another subservient role for himself, another will-less submission: he is one of the sheep. (Moran, encountering a similar shepherd, imagines himself the dog.)

Again Molloy notes a bad smell, not the hawthorn but "the shepherd under whose eyes I opened my eyes." He thinks of his own smell, also improper. It leads him to imagine himself not as one of the flock but as a black sheep or a buck-goat. The image of a black sheep or a scapegoat, following the exile from town and the crucifixion, leads now to a generalized sense of doom. Molloy recognizes that no matter which way the sheep are herded at the moment, they are headed finally for a slaughterhouse. He experiences a nightmarish image of multiple killings (29). By these evocations of the deadly, lifeless world of the isolated animus, Molloy is warned to seek his anima.

He reacts characteristically, making a vigorous start and then arresting himself, obliged by his evasive masculine ego-consciousness to reason the matter out: "I did not lose sight of my immediate goal, which was to get to my mother as quickly as possible, and standing in the ditch I summoned to my aid the good reasons I had for going there. . . . My feet, you see, never took me to my mother unless they received a definite order" (29–30). This comic image has serious overtones. The weather is fine, the sun is shining, it is midday (minus the angelus). Instead of acting or even reasoning, he complains about that sunlight, the light of reason and of the ego-consciousness. Instead of removing himself from the ditch, he removes himself to a winter scene and calculates the rate of his farts. This is an act of "the judging intellect with its categories." Molloy is therefore absurd when he justifies these calculations by praising their result: "Extraordinary how mathematics help you to know yourself" (30). Any self revealed by way of its farts cannot satisfy us, and his later extended resort to mathematics will be even more evasive.

He left town not knowing what he did. He returns increasingly ignorant and evasive. He cannot recognize the town, "and even my sense of identity was wrapped in a namelessness often hard to penetrate." The light of reason—light is both a wave and a particle, his educated intellect notes—is growing dim as he approaches the anima: "Yes, even then, when already all was fading, waves and particles, there could be no things but nameless things, no names but thingless names." The Jungian masculine intellect, like Adam, puts names to things and thereby gains control over them. Molloy, however, here abandons that responsibility: "truly it little matters what I say, this, this or that or any other thing" (31).

If masculine reason is a guide and the animated body a masculine machine, then a comic image of human life guided by reason might be a man on a bicycle. Molloy found the bicycle he did not know he possessed when the angelus provided an initial motivation to find his mother. This interpretation of the bicycle may seem as absurd as it is ill-timed. However, the bicycling Molloy's intellect is decaying further as he reaches town. Then it loses control and acts out that loss. The bicycle veers onto the sidewalk, kills a dog, and falls at Lousse's feet. It is a submission. He has discarded his darkening reason, dismissing his halfhearted search for his mother as "my insane demands for more light." (This echo of Goethe's possible dying words, "mehr Licht," necessarily suggests another death of the psyche, as "insane" dismisses the value of rational enlightenment.) Since Molloy had been bicycling in full daylight, his phrase may be obscure. If so, the French sheds light on its psychological meaning: "mes folles prétentions de tirer quelque chose au clair" (47). The "something" is his relation with his mother, of course, which must be drawn from the darkness of the unconscious into the light of consciousness.

In abandoning his reason and his search—that is, in losing control of the bicycle—Molloy destroys a relation between a mother and a male child. He kills Teddy, a dog loved "like my own child," its owner says (30). He must make reparation; he takes the dog's place and becomes a child himself when he is taken over by the novel's major image of the maternal archetype.

With Sophie

Moran will reluctantly accept the name "Molloy," even though he prefers the form "Mollose" (112). Whether the proper form of the name ends in "loy" or "lose," Sophie Loy or Lousse remains nominally a part of Molloy. Jung offers more complex connections. "In every masculine mother-complex," he says, "side by side with the mother archetype, a significant role is played by the image of the man's sexual counterpart, the anima" (*Archetypes*, 85). Jung presents the image of Sophia under both headings. She is an anima figure and a mother: "the feminine and motherly Sophia" (*Archetypes*, 64). Her Greek name indicates wisdom.

As an archetype Sophia is also part of what Jung calls a syzygy, paired primarily with the masculine archetype of wisdom, the wise old man, the Logos. This is not her only pairing, however; Jung carries duality much further: "As mythology shows, one of the peculiarities of the Great Mother is that she frequently appears paired with her male counterpart. Accordingly the man identifies with the son-lover on whom the grace of Sophia has descended, with a puer aeternus or a filius sapientiae" (*Archetypes*, 106). Jung links her also with the Virgin Mother. (Sophie denies any physical desire for Molloy [47].) He also connects her with the crucifixion. Beckett utilizes these variants.

Jung explains that the personal mother is the first carrier of the mother archetype because the child lives with her "in a state of unconscious identity." Then "ego-consciousness . . . leads to differentiation of the ego from the mother, whose personal peculiarities gradually become more distinct," as Mag's certainly did. Then "all the fabulous and mysterious qualities attaching to her image begin to fall away and are transferred to the person closest to her, for instance the grandmother. . . . She is in truth the 'grand' or 'Great Mother'. [One may think of Marcel's shift of focus from his mother to his grandmother in *A la Recherche*.] Not infrequently she assumes the attributes of wisdom as well as those of a witch" (*Archetypes,* 102).

For good Jungian reasons, therefore, Sophie enters Molloy's world. She saves him from the daylight judgment of the "bloodthirsty mob" by overcoming them with her wisdom. True, the event is a comic mélange of clichés and absurdities. Sophia is out of her element in a masculine world (she is not verbally skilled), and her wisdom is reported by Molloy, who is unsympathetic. As a representative of the anima, Sophie Loy or Lousse is part of that natural life, unconscious of itself, that must be overcome by "the paternal principle, the Logos, which eternally struggles to free itself from the primal warmth and darkness of the maternal womb; in a word, from unconsciousness" (*Archetypes,* 96). Sophia's estate suggests a wisely ordered womb, with a tripartite feminine moon but no sun. Her wisdom, never described by Jung, will require Beckett for its expression.

Jung is unclear about the relation between the anima and the Logos. His description of the Logos struggling to free itself from the anima is not easily reconcilable with the Logos he described as first evoked by contact with the anima and as raising the anima's wisdom into consciousness. And if its "first creative act of liberation is matricide," then the achievement of any harmonious wholeness appears questionable. Beckett will not resolve Jung's ambiguities, but he will make artistic use of them.

Molloy's stay with Sophie begins with images not of psychic matricide but of masculine submission. His lack of control results in the death of the dog, which was already deaf, blind, incontinent, crippled with rheumatism, and on its last legs. Molloy says that he contributed his presence to the dog's burial "as if it had been my own burial. And it was" (36). This strange statement demands explanation, and not in vain. Molloy interrupts his report of the burial to interject a long passage about the desirability of cutting off his testicles. (Earlier he was unable to recall the name "Bally.") He concludes that he is attached to them and that he must cherish them as others do their family album. (The translation omits a reference to the Jungian shift of archetypal images from mother to grandmother; the album is "photos de grand'mère" [53].) Molloy's imagined self-castration and burial with the dog are relevant to Sophia.

Teddy is buried under a tree, and Molloy thinks he knows why dogs are always buried so. He may have read Jung's *Symbols of Transformation.*

Discussing mythical heroes, Jung speaks there of animal sacrifices in which the victim is "the animal brother of the hero." Molloy has connected himself with Teddy, and he will do so again as he leaves Lousse's estate. Jung explains, "The sacrifice of the animal means, therefore, the sacrifice of the animal nature, the instinctual libido" (423). While with Lousse, Molloy's libido seeks only food and drink. It is therefore relevant that Jung continues his discussion with the example of Attis, "the son-lover of Agdistis-Cybele, the mother of the gods. Driven mad by his mother's insane love for him, he castrated himself under a pine-tree" (423). Teddy and (somehow) Molloy are buried under a larch.

Why do suggestions of death introduce Molloy to Sophia's world? Proust recurrently uses the metaphor of death to identify the end of a worn-out identity. ("The old ego dies hard," as Beckett puts it.) Now we may add Jung to Proust. Jung told us about the supersession of the mother by the "god"-mother. Sophia, a goddess especially among the Gnostics, joins with Mag to form "the motif of the *dual mother*" (*Archetypes*, 45). A dual mother requires a dual birth, and here Jung uses for that event a term that he took from James's *Varieties of Religious Experience:* "twice-born." Molloy identifies Teddy's burial with his own because he will soon be castrated, put to sleep, and reborn.

The Names

New names have entered the narrative. When we reach "Moran," we will learn much from such odd names as Gaber, Youdi, Yerk, and the Obidil. Here, as is appropriate for Molloy and for Jung, matters are less clear, but something can be learned from Sophie Loy or Lousse.

Sophie is Jung's Sophia. "Loy" suggests the Old French for law, reinforcing the idea of feminine wisdom. "Lousse" ("luce," light) also reinforces that idea, offering a feminine light (her tripartite moon is about to appear) to complement the masculine sunlight of Bally. Molloy's insane demands for more light have produced Lousse's irrational light. That light includes the centuries-old wisdom called "the light of nature." Lousse's estate is a natural world, landscaped and cared for, where she wishes to contemplate Molloy's body. Lousse's names are Jungianly significant, then. She constitutes a feminine trinity: wisdom, law, and light. Jung told us that the accomplishment of individuation is a matter of "illumination" (*Archetypes*, 39).

Molloy's Rebirth chez Sophie

Molloy's first approach to his mother ended with his fleeing Bally. His second approach has resulted in another loss of control. Evoking his mother as

Mag, he failed to find reasons for seeking her or value in finding her; his words and things became increasingly detached; he had increasing difficulty in phrasing his thoughts; and he quite literally lost his way and fell. Now he is led away by Lousse, under her control, into a new dream.

Since the events of "Molloy" occur in a psychic world, their sequence is important, and passages of reflection are also events. The extended dream is pushed forward by causality, expressed with the aid of time and space. This causality supersedes mere clock and calendar time. In previous beginnings Molloy located himself in his mother's room, then on a mountainside, then awakening to the sound of the angelus, and then standing in a ditch with the shepherd gone, attempting to motivate himself to leave it. (These are suggestions; dreams are fluid and the partitions often unclear.) Now he must start again.

He reports Lousse in her parlor, tells us of his indifference to her, listens to her parrot, and then falls asleep. The absurdity of this drawing-room comedy is underlined by the parrot's foulmouthed epithets. (The unconscious is amoral.) Molloy speculates that its previous owner must have been an American sailor. But why a parrot? Discussing "the motif of the *dual mother*," Jung says that "the spirit which appeared in the form of a dove was interpreted as Sophia-Sapientia-Wisdom and the Mother of Christ" (*Archetypes*, 45). The parrot parodies that dove, then, and perhaps Athene's owl as well. The parrot's detachment of words from meanings is also relevant to Jung's insistence on Nature's wordlessness and on the male Logos as the source of words. And perhaps the parrot was once the sailor, as Teddy may have been a puer aeternus, before Circe turned them into animals.

Certainly Sophie Lousse is Circean when she works a sea-change on Molloy. He falls asleep at tea and awakens (with a reference to *A la Recherche*) as a child in a strange room, forgetting who he is and therefore able for a short time to move about on his crippled legs. His clothes have been removed, he has been shaved, he is wearing a nightdress, and he is locked in a room crowded with furniture. He sleeps again (children need much sleep) and wakes to find "a huge moon framed in the window" (39). As the sun shone on his first arrival in Bally, so the moon presides over his first day in this feminine world. Molloy develops his new identity slowly, in part because his actions are slowed by thought sequences. The nightgown, the obstructive furniture, the servant, his short attention spans, his brief tantrums, his demand for a knife and a bicycle—all these details constitute a sad parroting or parody of childhood. He has become the puer aeternus or filius sapientiae who companions Sophia.

Much earlier, not yet motivated to seek his mother, Molloy denied that his world contained a moon: "Let me hear nothing of the moon, in my night there is no moon" (15; the present tense foreshadows his condition at the story's ending). Now a three-part moon—explained by Jung as imaging archetypes of the youthful female, the mother, and the dangerous old hag (or Mag)—fills his window and obscures his view of other matters. Attempting to think about it, he sounds rather loony—"How difficult it is to speak of the moon and not lose one's head, the witless moon" (39). ("Witless" translates weakly the antifeminine "Elle est si con, la lune" [58].) He cannot rationalize the three-part anima whose light shines on this revelation.

A neurosis constitutes a solution to a psychic problem, but a bad solution. Jung gives examples of neurotic solutions to the problem of managing the anima. One is verbal, another imagistic: "It is a convenient rationalistic conceit to say that the dragon [as an image of the anima] is only 'artificial,' thus banishing the mysterious gods with a word." In a schizophrenic's dream he finds imagistic rationalizing "for apotropaic purposes": "He is sitting in a dark room which has only one small window, through which he can see the sky. The sun and moon appear, but they are made of oiled paper." "Sun and moon," Jung explains, "as divine equivalents of the parent archetype, possess a tremendous psychic power that has to be weakened apotropaically, because the patient is already far too much under the power of the unconscious" (368–69).

Molloy's difficulties with the moon cause him to retreat for reassurance to his past education in the masculine world. The sequence of his studies reverses Freud's paradigm for the development of culture and imitates the sequence of Faust's studies as presented by Goethe. Molloy began by studying astronomy but cannot speak now of the moon, since he did not learn its psychic importance. Yet his studies took him from objective and inhuman topics (astronomy, geology) to general humanities (anthropology) and thence to the repair of the mind through psychiatry. (The inclusion of psychiatry may reflect Beckett's doubt of its therapeutic value).

That his studies should end with magic may seem an irrelevance. (But see, as Beckett had done by 1927, Ronsard's "Magie, ou delivrance d'amour.") Freud's discussion of magic and words is more immediately relevant. In *Moses and Monotheism* Freud says this:

> In children, in adults who are neurotic, as well as in primitive peoples, we meet with the mental phenomenon which we describe as a belief in the "omnipotence of thoughts." In our judgement this lies in an overestimation of the influence which our mental . . . acts can exercise in altering the external world. At bottom, all magic, the precursor of our

technology, rests on this premiss. All the magic of words, too, has its place here, and the conviction of the power which is bound up with the knowledge and pronouncing of a name. (XXIII, 113)

Freud's comment is significant in the Jungian context of the verbal Logos. "The magic of words" is a concern throughout "Molloy" and especially at its chronological end. Molloy was a true believer when he explained the magical result of adding *g* to *Ma* to make it *Mag* (17), but he lost control of words on his second return to town:

> I had been living so far from words so long, you understand, that it was enough for me to see my town, since we're talking of my town, to be unable, you understand. It's too difficult to say, for me. (31)

> Saying is inventing. Wrong, very rightly wrong. You invent nothing, you think you are inventing, you think you are escaping, and all you do is stammer out your lesson, the remains of a pensum one day got by heart and long forgotten. (32)

> I always say either too little or too much. . . . (34)

It is no wonder that Molloy's forthcoming description of his mind is both significant and unintelligible. Like the sirens' song and the name of Achilles' anima, however, it is not beyond all conjecture.

In this mental outback he finds no evidence of his education except some "vestiges" of magic. Pursuing a "process of individuation" as expressed in a patient's paintings, Jung explains that "Miss X had to turn back to her 'motherland' in order to find her earth again—*vestigia retro!*" (*Archetypes*, 349). In Molloy's arid and lifeless region, however, magic offers no footprints leading to a mother. ("Delivrance d'amour" may explain why.) "I don't know what it is, what it was," Molloy says (39). Although he finds vestiges there, he says that it is deserted by magic and devoid of mystery. He denies emphatically that it is a dream place. There are no events reported beyond a sensed slow decay, nor is the landscape earthly. The reader imagining "these wastes where true light never was, nor any upright thing, nor any true foundation" (40) may plagiarize from landscapes by Yves Tanguy (especially his *The Condition of Now*). In the absence of "true light," whether from the masculine sun or the feminine moon, one must recall that Milton's hell is lighted untruly: "darkness visible."

In this lifeless, entropic landscape Molloy hears a voice. Unlike his later voices, this one only whispers, and neither to him nor about him. The later voices will instruct Molloy to find his mother, but here nothing acknowledges his existence. "If I do not go there gladly," he says now, "I go perhaps more gladly there than anywhere else, astonished and at peace" (40). It is a place "where you find yourself without any pleasure, but with more perhaps than in those places you can escape from."

Schopenhauer and Freud, more than Jung, have prepared this experience. Freud's pleasure principle, originally the unpleasure principle, describes the psyche's search always for minimal stimulation. In effect one undergoes pleasure in order to put an end to the id's demands for it. That motive was stated earlier by Schopenhauer, who said that the intellect panders to the demands of the will in order to gain momentary respites from them. Schopenhauer's borrowed term for a permanent extension of those respites, nirvana, recurs in Freud's own conception of such a peace as the goal of the death instinct: "The consideration that the pleasure principle demands a reduction, at bottom the extinction perhaps, of the tensions of instinctual needs (that is, *Nirvana*) leads to the still unassessed relations between the pleasure principle and the two primal forces, Eros and the death instinct" (*Outline of Psycho-Analysis,* XXIII, 198).

Thus the tension of Molloy's need for Eros in the form of a relation with the anima may tempt him to the shortcut of psychic death. (He will attempt the physical shortcut later.) Yet another passage might connect these Freudian ideas with Molloy's mind. Freud describes the id without any libido as a landscape. "It is clear," he says about the pleasure principle, "that the function thus described would be concerned with the most universal endeavour of all living substance—namely to return to the quiescence of the inorganic world" (*Beyond the Pleasure Principle,* XVIII, 62). Such quiescence is suggested by Molloy's experience of this part of his mind. He tries to speak positively of it, but cannot maintain that attitude: "And I too am at an end, when I am there, my eyes close, my sufferings cease and I end, I wither as the living can not. . . . But I will listen no longer, for the time being, to that far whisper, for I do not like it, I fear it" (40).

Memories are events in "Molloy." As his memory of Mag constituted an encounter with her, so Molloy's memory of this region of his mind constitutes a visit to it, which he can continue no longer. That indifferent whisper, "silent long since and which I still hear," is all that remains of sentient life in this Freudian id devoid of libido.

Putting the region into Jungian terms, we may see a more immediate relevance in Molloy's description. Jung told us that the anima is life itself. Molloy has conceived of a flight from the anima into a mental region devoid of life, with only its posthumous whisper keeping it from complete inorganic quiescence. Jung approaches such a conception once. From an imagining of the collective unconscious, he briefly omits the archetypes. The result resembles Molloy's retreat: "a world quite different from our own; . . . a world where the pulse of time beats ever so slowly; where the birth and death of individuals count for little . . . " (*Integration of the Personality*, 25).

Molloy has described a psychic event that frightens him. Fleeing that impersonal whisper, he attempts to reason. He educes a "principle," only to admit that the principle often escapes him and that "I speak of principles, where there are none" (46). His "sense of values" is gone. In backing away from the lifeless region of his mind and preferring to grapple again with the question of the tripartite moon, Molloy at least negatively accepts his location in Lousse's world.

Nevertheless, his attempt to put the tripartite moon under rational control quickly loses its businesslike masculine tone. The anima obliges him to revise some early pages of his report. He decides that he had seen this full moon "the night before, or the night before that," as a new moon. He connects it with his explanation of C's actions: "And then I had said, Now I see, he has waited for the new moon before launching forth on unknown ways, leading south. And then a little later, Perhaps I should go to mother tomorrow. For all things hang together, by the operation of the Holy Ghost, as the saying is" (42). He admits that "I failed to mention this detail in its proper place."

Originally, the bell for the angelus, recalling the annunciation to Mary and the incarnation of God, motivated Molloy. Now it is C's waiting for the new moon, Molloy's using the same motive, and the Holy Ghost that unite to move him. (That his revision describes him as seeing the new moon through a window when he ought to have been out on a mountainside he leaves unexplained, and he ignores his collapsing of the time spent so far. Realism is secondary, if even that, in dream sequences.) The moon (with a new reference to the Holy Ghost) has supplemented the angelus. Jung explains why. Discussing the Christian Trinity, he says that "the femininity in the Godhead is kept secret, and to say that the Holy Ghost is Sofia counts as a heresy." Therefore, this idea has remained a secret down through history. Yet "femininity must surely be somewhere; so it is presumably to be found in the dark."

Thus Sophia is at once maternal and spiritual. Jung explains, "For the Holy Ghost was the mediator of the birth in the flesh, and thus made it possible for the luminous Godhead to become visible in the darkness of the world" (*Integration of the Personality*, 156–57). This religious context explains why Molloy justifies his mentioning some things and leaving others unmentioned by saying that "it is often in good faith, excellent faith" (41).

Molloy is thus reborn as a comic version of the puer aeternus, and on Lousse's estate he acts out a progression from childhood through adolescence. He demands the return of his clothes, his hat, his knife (a lie), and his bicycle. His demands are childishly emotional, as is his behavior. His sense of life is similarly childish. Noting his faded desire to find his mother, he makes an excuse: "It is difficult . . . to go to one's mother with things in such a state, more difficult than to the Lousses of this world, or its police-stations" (44). The complaint is interestingly plural, and the excuse is common among neurotics. "Things in such a state," the problems of a mentally ill life, constitute a reason for not seeking therapy (in effect, "I'll enter therapy when I feel better"). The bad experiences of the police world and Lousse—subordinations to an externalized masculine or feminine archetype—seem more bearable than accepting one's mother, creating a harmony among these extremes, and so earning a fellow or frère. We recall Molloy's "if ever I'm reduced to looking for a meaning to my life . . ." (19). If ever, but not now. Now it seems easier to regress to a new childhood.

The Ego in the Garden

Jungian individuation is the creating of an individual identity, a self. Molloy's incomplete new identity, however, grows weaker during his extended sabbatical in Sophie's garden, since he is not actively seeking his maternal anima even while in one of her worlds. Though he moves beyond the childhood phase of tantrums and demands, his behavior becomes only that of a spoiled adolescent—jumping and falling, eating and drinking, following his whims and treating other humans (Lousse and the gardeners) with rude indifference. In Bally he complained that he had not been taught "the guiding principles of good manners." He is still indifferent to them; he does not feel any natural affection for his fellows; and the presocial world of his doting "god"-mother imposes no societal discipline on him.

Beckett differentiates this fantasized childhood from Molloy's own. In Lousse's garden he jumps and falls, but he says that "even as a child I do not remember ever having bounded, neither rage nor pain ever made me bound, even as a child" (54). Now he bounds happily, when "the miserable molys of Lousse . . . draw the pleasure out." The distinction is clear. Molloy's actual childhood was characterized by rage and pain. We never see Molloy's actual mother, as distinguished from archetypal images, but the rage and pain offer a hint from his personal unconscious to explain his distaste for these maternal images and to suggest why his individuation is so difficult.

In addition, Lousse's natural wisdom is expressed by her world, but Molloy is not simply natural. ("I was not purely physical," he will say later, tempted by a different form of nature [86].) The repetitive sensual life of Lousse's garden is not attractive or pleasurable. He eats and drinks. Sometimes he overeats, sometimes he eats little. He "would engulf five or six mugs of beer with one swig, then drink nothing for a week." He jumps and falls. He is given stimulants and depressants. He is "terror-stricken" and "bereft of feeling." He experiences a "torpor shot with brief abominable gleams" (54).

Such mechanically paired exaggerations might be called contrasts or oppositions, but Molloy uses a different term: harmony. "Against such harmony of what avail the miserable molys of Lousse," he says (54). That is, even the molys' artificial prolongation of pleasure cannot alter the essential "harmony" of these pairings in which every positive has a negative and the pairs recur indefinitely.

Harmony has a complex prehistory for readers of "Molloy," as we saw in glancing at *Murphy*. Murphy sought harmony; Molloy has no ear for it, as he will remark when he returns to "the pre-established harmony, which makes so sweet a music, which is so sweet a music, for one who has an ear for music" (62). Jung frequently speaks of harmony, but not as an external condition or as Pythagorean musical mathematics. It is a condition of individuation and therefore a goal of therapy. He offers no formula for it: "How the harmonizing of conscious and unconscious data is to be undertaken cannot be indicated in the form of a recipe. It is an irrational life-process which expresses itself in definite symbols. . . . Knowledge of the symbols is indispensable, for it is in them that the union of conscious and unconscious attitudes is consummated. Out of this union emerge new situations and new conscious attitudes. I have therefore called the union of opposites the 'transcendental function'" (*Archetypes,* 289).

Molloy experiences no harmonious relation to Lousse's world, with its associated opposites. Lousse's world consists of a large house and extended grounds, surrounded by a wall. (Readers will connect this site with Knott's house and grounds and with Beckett's childhood home, and they will anticipate St. John of God's in *Malone Dies*.) The grounds are cared for by gardeners who reduce to a minimum the evidence of seasonal changes (52). Those changes are thereby rendered harmonious. The house and gardens display human nature and nature in harmony and under control.

Lousse seeks to incorporate Molloy into this existence, but not by masculine laws and threats. She squats beside Molloy on the grass and sets out "to mollify me, to mollify Molloy." She is so successful that "I was nothing more than a lump of melting wax, so to speak" (47). Instead of masculine power, she uses a strong feminine weakness: "I could not prevent her having a weakness for me, neither could she." Her irrational persistence links her with nature. Her voice blends in with "the deepening night and the smell of the damp earth and a strongly scented flower." He submits wordlessly to her mollifying: "I stayed where I was, with regret, with mild regret."

No wonder that he then speaks of "the faint soughing and sighing stirring at night in little pleasure gardens, the shy sabbath of leaves and petals" (48). He has accepted this natural sabbath of willing with its accompanying reduction of anxiety, so desired by the pleasure principle. His intellect is at rest. His apathy in Lousse's pleasure garden contrasts significantly with his anxiety in that lifeless back region of his mind.

Beckett reminds us of another context by setting this pleasure garden at night against the police station in daylight. Molloy notes in the garden the air "that eddies there as it does not in other places, where there is less constraint, and as it does not during the day, when there is more vigilance" (48). Lousse demands "the right to contemplate from time to time this extraordinary body" (47); in Bally the police displayed their vigilance. (The French reminds us of the day/night pattern: "le jour . . . permit de surveiller et de sévir" [47].) In both worlds Molloy's ego-consciousness is subordinate, not free and not in control.

Lousse is set against the masculine world, then, but she is also set against Mag the chthonic mother, with her wild appearance, unrestrained behavior, and almost unintelligible gabble. Molloy notes the difference without mentioning Mag, saying that Lousse's cultivated garden is separated from "the earth of deeps and wildernesses" (49). It is an artificial and civilized garden of delights, an earthly paradise. Existence there imperils Molloy's soft individual identity: "there were times when I forgot not only who I was, but that I was, forgot to be" (49).

Retreat to the Philosophic Mind

Molloy's flowing and undramatic narration may distract the reader from a basic discrepancy in Beckett's development of the encounter with the Sophia archetype. Molloy is comically reduced to a shaved, washed, and nightgowned child who grows quickly into the jumping boy and the beer- and food-guzzling adolescent. There we saw Beckett's imagining of the puer aeternus. Simultaneously, however, Molloy retreats from the estate into his mind. That behavior cannot be found in any Jungian description of the puer aeternus, nor is it childlike. Beckett recurrently imposes upon his protagonists a vaguely Cartesian mind-body split, such as Murphy's "self that he hated" and "self that he loved." Here the sensual attractions of Lousse's cultivated natural world have easily seduced the childish physical Molloy, but the weakly rational ego-consciousness refuses to listen to Lousse's irrational talk or to acknowledge the pleasures of life in her pleasure garden. Mentally, this puer aeternus cannot remain puerile eternally.

Jung wishes the dominant male animus to raise its repressed anima from the unconscious and to experience, accept, and control its feminine wisdom. Molloy bullied and abandoned Mag, learning nothing. His experience of Lousse is complementary to that with Mag; she has tamed and subordinated him. His ego-consciousness is threatened with absorption into her impersonal nature. Instead of rising above this subordination and taking charge by developing a Logos, Molloy attempts to protect his mind, which he equates with his self, by hiding from that nature. He imagines "a sealed jar" (his more appropriate original term, which will recur, is "cette boîte fermée") that contains his mind but does not protect it enough from Lousse's nature. He imagines the jar or box as giving way, so that the "roots and tame stems" of the garden enter it (49). Molloy will not evade the anima more obviously than this until he retreats to the sterile seaside.

Within this container he must keep asking questions about his existence so as to avoid "losing the thread of the dream" (49). When he loses the thread of his dreamed mental identity, he is invaded by the external world. "I thought almost without stopping, I did not dare stop. Perhaps that was the cause of my innocence," he says. Without specifying the questions, Molloy generalizes them so that they stretch back to his existence in society and widen to include language, nature, and acts—that is, to cover all external sources of knowledge: "And to the noises of nature too [as well as of human voices], and of the works of men, I reacted I think in my own way and without desire of enlightenment" (50). The phrase "in my own way," as set against "desire of enlightenment," emphasizes his willed isolation and his rejection of the much-needed illumination. He acts out the masculine intellect's attempt to avoid the wordless, irrational, and sensual maternal anima.

This passage contains a remarkable dream-compression of time. Ostensibly it describes Molloy's experiences on the night of Lousse's solicitations in the garden, but it quickly generalizes about experiences that "did not happen to me often, mostly I stayed in my jar" (49). These generalizations report a much longer period. The passage thereby conveys Molloy's slowly increasing consciousness of what is happening in his psyche.

So far those happenings have been negative. Molloy admits as if to a psychotherapist that "I no longer know what I am doing, nor why, those are things I understand less and less, I don't deny it, for why deny it, and to whom, to you, to whom nothing is denied?" (45). He "stayed a good while with Lousse" (50), but with no interrelation between them. In his body he moves between the garden and the house (which he does not explicitly re-enter, although he speculates that "I stayed in several rooms one after the other" [51]). He does so, however, "very slowly, as in a cage out of time, as the saying is, in the jargon of the schools, and out of space too to be sure" (51). That cage echoes the image of the box or jar, and that bit of jargon from medieval theology suggests that he preserves his "innocence" from Lousse's temptations by turning toward philosophy. His evasion is rational; he contrives a philosophical position that will protect him from Lousse's wisdom.

Beckett has set himself a complex problem here. Molloy should accept Sophie—that is, the maternal Sophia—into his conscious self by making her wisdom verbal and a part of his masculine wisdom. This act, which would require the creation of the Logos, would enable the transcendental function to achieve a harmony among the parts of the self. Beckett, however, wishes to do more, or different. He must imagine a philosophic equivalent of Sophia's wordless and irrational wisdom (which is expressed in her estate and its orderly natural world). Molloy will not or cannot accommodate this version of his anima and this vision of life. So Beckett must imagine the philosophy that a frightened masculine rationality might contrive in order to evade the anima. What is more, he must dramatize this evasive formulation as experienced by Molloy, not a trained philosopher but an anxious old man.

Lousse is not verbal. (Molloy reports that she talks to him at length, at least in her parlor and during that one evening in the garden, but he does not quote her, and she quickly recedes into the middle distance.) We must conclude from the details of her estate and his experiences there that she acts out an Epicurean philosophical position. Against that position Molloy in his cage out of time pieces together slowly a complementary philosophy.

The Philosophic Center

Molloy begins to recall scraps of academic learning. Two scraps are especially revelatory. Admitting to defective eyesight, he concludes that "it is certain I saw [the world] in a way inordinately formal, though I was far from being an aesthete, or an artist" (50). He analyzes his feelings and offers a basis for judgment of them: "the truth is, coenaesthetically speaking . . ." (54). A weak rationality is emerging. "Inordinately formal" is an oxymoron. His coenaesthetically achieved truth is merely that "I felt more or less the same as usual." (The impressive term means approximately "judged by ordinary feelings.") His experience in a philosophical cage has not much altered the wordless and will-less man who fell at Lousse's feet.

Jung sketched the resistance Molloy exhibits in describing the process of "active imagination" and the reason's negative evasion of that process. In therapy, "one concentrates one's attention on some impressive but unintelligible dream-image, or on a spontaneous visual impression, and observes the changes taking place in it." The experience of Lousse and her garden constitutes such an image, but it is irrational and in that sense incredible. Jung warns that "all criticism must be suspended . . . , since it springs from the anxiety of an ego-consciousness which brooks no master besides itself in its own house. In other words, it is the inhibition exerted by the conscious mind on the unconscious" (*Archetypes*, 190). We have noted evidence of Molloy's anxious ego-consciousness. His masculine intellect distances itself from sensory and emotional experience to protect itself from alteration. His evasion of Lousse's influence is similarly complex and extended.

Molloy's narrative sounds like an unanswerable clamor, with only the claim of a chronological sequence to hold together its shapelessness. The director, Beckett, must convey meanings despite Molloy, then, and here at the literal center of "Molloy" he implies a central meaning. Its essence requires us to recognize that Molloy's unwillingness to confront his Sophia archetype results in the slow strengthening of his rational, masculine ego-consciousness.

This strengthening is neither simple nor positive. Molloy on the mountain-side neither thought nor felt, so far as one can tell. His imagining of A and C dramatized his need for a fellow or frère—that is, for mutual affection. Immediately the angelus summoned him to his mother. (Under Lousse's influence, the moon replaces the angelus, and the desire for a fellow disappears, never to return.) But movement toward any anima figure increases the anxiety of Molloy's rational ego-consciousness, which begins to reason. Failing in his contacts with the police and the charity worker, Molloy blames not his lack of affection for others but his inadequate rational training, by males. "The fault lies not with me but with my superiors, who corrected me only on points of detail instead of showing me the essence of the system," he says, "and how to trace back to its ultimate source a given comportment" (25). He needs "a reasoned theory."

Anxiety obliged him to seek this evasive explanation: "It is only since I have ceased to live that I think of these things. . . . In the tranquillity of decomposition I remember the long confused emotion which was my life, and . . . I judge it" (25). We must recognize Molloy's incorrect use of the Wordsworthian tag from his school days; the emotion he recollects in anxiety, not tranquillity, is that of fear, not affection, and it results not in poetry but in rational judgment.

That sequence occurred back in Bally. Now, in Lousse's world and reacting against her Epicurean and unemotional life of the senses, Molloy reveals that his judgments have a philosophical basis. Seeking it, we recall those earlier terms; we must connect Molloy's judging of his life at the center of "Molloy" with such rational terms as "principles," "the essence of the system," and "the first rules of a reasoned theory." These are not terms associated with the wisdom of the Logos, but they do suggest the masculine judging intellect. One judges rationally by testing specific matters against a code of laws. Lousse's world provides Molloy no such code: "When I talk of preferring, for example, or regretting, it must not be supposed that I opted for the least evil, and adopted it, for that would be wrong. But not knowing exactly what I was doing or avoiding, I did it and avoided it . . ." (55).

This central passage begins with a clue: at first Molloy did not know exactly what governed his behavior, and that behavior was "preferring" and "regretting," "doing" and "avoiding." When Molloy imagined a failed conversation with the character A, he stressed the positive. He said that A left him free: "Free to do what, to do nothing, to know, but what, the laws of the mind perhaps, of my mind . . ." (13). We see the relevance: either in experiencing the events of "Molloy" or in narrating "Molloy," he might learn the laws of his own mind.

The masculine power capable of accomplishing this is the Logos. This archetype requires more consideration now. Even though it is not about to appear, its methods are relevant. Jung's explanations of the functioning of the Logos cannot easily be reconciled, as we have seen. He describes the union of opposites as a form of harmony and as a part of the transcendent function, but he also says that the Logos commits matricide and that "there is no consciousness without discrimination of opposites" (*Archetypes*, 96). What is more, although he does not speak ill of the Logos, he says that all archetypes are ambivalent. These are difficulties that Beckett has faced.

Molloy is now submissive to Lousse. His acquiescence has reduced him physically to a version of childhood. By being fed, he has acquired appetites, and he has learned to evaluate his condition coenaesthetically. Existing physically in the moment and mentally out of time and space, he no longer yearns for a fellow or frère, or for an understanding of the relation between his mother and himself. Those positive desires have been replaced by "my old ataraxy" (42).

Now he says that "one is what one is, partly at least. Nothing or little to be done" (54). He accepts the incompleteness of his identity, only part of which "is." (He will change his mind in the forest [86].) His hostile rationality, however, now justifies itself against Lousse's implicit Epicurean wisdom by producing a defensive philosophical position. Let us examine that central passage, spoken as of his stay with Lousse: "And when I talk of preferring, for example, or regretting, it must not be supposed that I opted for the least evil, and adopted it, for that would be wrong. But not knowing exactly what I was doing or avoiding, I did it and avoided it all unsuspecting that one day, much later, I would have to go back over all these acts and omissions, dimmed and mellowed by age, and drag them into the eudemonistic slop" (55).

Where is any judgment? It is contained in that metaphorical dragging of his acts "into the eudemonistic slop," and it is developed—it has already been developed—in the hostile report of Molloy's stay with Lousse. (It is useful to remember that Molloy is not locked in; he is always as free to leave Lousse's estate as MacMann will be to leave the House of St. John of God.)

This passage cannot be understood quickly. We begin with Jung. The anima represents unconscious life. In Lousse's garden Molloy has evaded examination of that life, rather than deriving from it any appreciative rule or system or wisdom. Now, in the full passage before us, he speaks of judging it retrospectively, perhaps with impertinence. Now he has a basis for judgment. Beckett found it not in Jung but in Schopenhauer.

Leaning on Kant's distinction between pure reason and practical reason, Schopenhauer says that the highest task of philosophy is to describe existence. A secondary task is the practical one of defining the ethics by which man should live. Molloy's earlier complaint that he had not been taught the essence of the system suggests that he will not now aspire to the highest task, but that he is concerned—weakly—about ethics, the essence of behavior in society.

Schopenhauer's highest virtue requires detachment from the will-to-live and from the individual self (that is, detachment from the demands of the impersonal will and from one's submissive intellect). Schopenhauer turns often to Eastern religious thought in developing this subject. He is anxious to separate his ideas from the Western ethical systems that appear to contain them, and in particular from the Cynics and the Stoics. He distinguishes between Eastern virtuous abnegation and Western ethical codes, and he emphasizes the Stoics' rational ethics. "Rational action and virtuous action are two quite different things," he says. "For the Stoic ethics is . . . not a doctrine of virtues but merely a guide to the rational life, whose end aim is happiness through peace of mind" (WWR I, book I, § 16).

"Happiness through peace of mind" is easily connected to Freud's idea of the pleasure principle and the reduction of anxiety. Schopenhauer's distinction between reason and virtue has no clear counterpart in our psychological texts. However, when Jung identifies the anima with life and sets the animus apart from it, he makes a moral judgment. He speaks of the male psyche as wishing to "rot away in his greatest passion, idleness." (Beckett saves the term "rot" for psychic idleness at the seashore [75].) The basis of Jung's moral judgment against the male psyche is not social propriety. In fact, he says that conventional society fosters this idleness: "A certain kind of reasonableness is its advocate, and a certain kind of morality adds its blessing" (*Integration of the Personality*, 76). This idleness is bad because it replaces the search for the complete self, the transcendental function. Stoic "peace of mind" and Jungian "idleness" are near akin.

Among those pairs of opposites with which Molloy describes his life in the garden, two items are not simply natural and certainly not conducive to peace of mind: "brief abominable gleams" caused by the molys of Lousse, and the state of being "so terror-stricken that I was virtually bereft of feeling, not to say of consciousness" (54). These are not like eating, drinking, sleeping, jumping, and falling. They are states of the mind, not of the body and its appetites. Jung remarks, in connection with the lethargic male psyche, that "Heaven and Hell are the fate of the soul and not of civil man." Molloy in the garden is not terror-stricken by existence in the civil world. (He once was, we learn later.) He shrinks into his jar to escape his psyche's demands that he seek his soul, his anima. In Lousse's world he plays the part of the puer aeternus. The timelessness of that childhood is a danger to the process of individuation: "The longing of the child for the mother is a hindrance on the path to [separation from her], taking the form of a psychologic resistance, which is expressed by . . . the fear of life" (*Psychology of the Unconscious*, 335).

Thus, the maternal anima is ambivalent. Molloy's original longing for his mother was proper, but she was to be a stage on his journey toward the fellow or frère, not an end in herself. Chez Lousse, Molloy's inaction reveals a Jungian fear of life. Jung develops this problem: "The more a person withdraws from . . . reality, and falls into slothful inactivity, the greater becomes his anxiety. . . . The mother-imago . . . possesses its power solely and exclusively from the son's tendency . . . to glance backwards to the pampering sweetness of childhood, to that glorious state of irresponsibility and security with which the protecting mother-care once surrounded him. The retrospective longing acts like a paralyzing poison upon the energy and enterprise" (335).

We recall that Molloy associated no jumping, even in a rage, with his actual childhood. For him the pampering sweetness of childhood occurs only chez Lousse—not in his personal psychology, but in the realm of the archetypes. He blames Lousse for poisoning him with her molys—as if they act "like a paralyzing poison upon the energy and enterprise"—but the masculine ego-consciousness must neither hide from the anima nor submit to it. In *Integration of the Personality* the anima is described as containing a cosmos in its chaos. "It takes man's discriminating understanding, which dissolves everything into antinomies of judgement, to recognize this," Jung says (81). "Antinomies of judgement" is a cold phrase, suggesting the detachment of the rational mind from the materials considered. Molloy settles for that cold detachment, while retaining the emotional attachment to life. In judging Lousse's world and his life in it, he reinvents Stoicism.

It is a childish Stoicism, one might say, and thus it need not deal with sexuality. Molloy's life with his "god"-mother Lousse begins with an imagined castration. Jung explains why: "through the incest barrier the sexual libido is forced away from identification with the parents. . . . Hence the neurotic always renounces a complete erotic experience, in order that he may remain a child" (*Psychology of the Unconscious*, 460). Molloy's response to Lousse has created a child's garden or version of the earthly paradise.

The Stoic philosophy devised by Molloy in reaction to his Sophia archetype is partial, of course. His aversions from pain and strong emotion and sexuality are relevant. Schopenhauer explains why, as he had explained to Beckett: "for the Stoic, ethics is . . . not a doctrine of virtues but merely a guide to the rational life, whose end and aim is happiness through peace of mind." The Stoics' rational happiness was also a material one. They "sophisticated themselves into all the amenities of life" by attending banquets and eating well, while claiming to despise earthly pleasures (*WWR* II, ch. 16). Molloy is similarly two-faced about his meals. Schopenhauer notes a general result of this Stoic pose, and Molloy acts it out when he searches high and low for misplaced food: "the will cannot be trifled with, and cannot enjoy pleasures without becoming fond of them" (*WWR* II, ch. 16). Schopenhauer concludes this discussion as he had concluded his first discussion of the Stoics, by asserting that the aim of Stoic ethics, "like that of *Cynicism* from which it sprang, is . . . a life as painless as possible, and thus as happy as possible. From this it follows that the Stoic morality is only a particular species of *eudaemonism*."

With that last term, which we encountered at the center of "Molloy," we find the most obvious link between Beckett and Schopenhauer, between Molloy and Stoicism. (Another linking term is "coenaesthesia." Knowlson reports Beckett's using it while re-reading Schopenhauer in 1937 [248–49].) The term is central to the implicit values of life on Lousse's estate, and it suggests that the narrating Molloy has a conscious awareness of those implicit values.

The narrating Molloy's understanding of his life is not accurate. He has only reached the stage of dragging his acts and omissions into "the eudemonistic slop," and that remark is characteristically ambivalent. Simultaneously, he judges his life by the standards of eudemonistic ethics and condemns that system of judgment. He recalls his admiration of the image, taken from Geulincx, of the man on a sailing ship who demonstrates his freedom by walking in the opposite direction. Then he alters that image to remove from it even its comically ironic freedom of action: "from the poop, . . . a sadly rejoicing slave, I follow with my eyes the proud and futile wake" (51). Any imagined freedom of—or from—the will is at an end, but the Stoic ethic of pleasure and pain has no need of freedom. To take pleasure and pain as one's bases for action and judgment is simply to become subservient to Schopenhauer's will.

Criticizing eudemonism, Schopenhauer points out that pleasure is not always an available choice: "The Stoic is compelled to insert a recommendation of suicide in his guide to the blissful life." He also concludes that the image of the ideal Stoic "remains a wooden, stiff lay-figure." He quotes ironically, in describing the pursuit of a happiness that may entail suicide, a statement by the Stoic thinker Antisthenes: "We must procure either understanding or a rope (for hanging ourselves)" (*WWR* I, book I, § 16).

Beckett uses all these details in characterizing the later Molloy. After Molloy leaves Lousse for a worse world, he finds peace in an alley and decides to perpetuate it, by beginning to slash his wrist with his dull knife. "But pain soon got the better of me," he remarks with Stoic and eudemonistic appropriateness. Reporting this event, he also describes his present state: "my two legs are as stiff as a life-sentence," echoing Schopenhauer's "wooden, stiff lay-figure." In the forest, Molloy thinks again of suicide and perhaps of Antisthenes. He recalls "wondering sometimes . . . if I shall ever see the hated light . . . and my mother, to settle with her, and if I would not do better . . . to hang myself from a bough" (78). These alternatives echo those of "understanding or a rope."

Beckett fleshed out Jung's presentation of the Sophia archetype by suggesting behind Sophie Lousse and her estate an animated philosophy, Epicureanism. But to be an Epicurean in bad faith is to be a Stoic. Stoicism enables Molloy to have his beer and food and to disdain them too. So, during his stay with Lousse, Molloy becomes a Stoic *avant de la lettre*. Later, writing his report, he is able to pass judgment upon his experiences, though unsystematically. His judgment is at once relevant (a philosophy can be judged only in its own terms) and dismissive: "eudemonistic slop."

Two passages from Schopenhauer describing the Stoics are relevant:

[The Stoics] started from the insight that the motions into which the will is put by the objects that stimulate and stir it, and the laborious and often frustrated efforts to attain them, or the fear of losing them when they are attained, and finally also the loss itself, produce far greater sorrows than the want of all those objects ever can. Therefore . . . they . . . fled from all pleasures. (*WWR* II, ch. 16)

It was seen [by the Stoics] that want and suffering did not result directly and necessarily from not having, but only from desiring to have and yet not having; that this desiring to have is therefore the necessary condition under which alone not having becomes privation and engenders pain. . . . It is merely the hope, the claim, which begets and nourishes the wish. (*WWR* I, book I, § 16)

Molloy will flee from all pleasures and will find Stoic justification for so doing. He offers an anticipatory glimpse of that event just before making his central comment about judging and the "eudemonistic slop." Reporting that with Lousse he sometimes hunted for his misplaced food high and low, he adds: "It was then that I regretted my sucking-stone" (55). He regretted its loss not because there were no stones in Lousse's world or because that lost stone had ever satisfied his present appetite for food and drink, but because it evoked his once and future state of existence in which physical appetite has a properly subordinate place.

We still cannot leave Molloy's brief central comment, with its extraordinary halo of ideas. That comment is an event in a dream series, and context is determinative of many meanings for such events. We must consider the context into which the narrating Molloy inserted his comment and in which the comment is both result and cause.

After lamenting his eudemonistic judgments and the need for them, Molloy returns to Lousse's maternal and material world. His physical health is good, he says of the protagonist Molloy. He is growing old, but there have been "no more new symptoms, . . . nothing I could not have foreseen if I could have" (55). That nearly unintelligible phrasing demands justification. Schopenhauer is still on Beckett's mind. Molloy has just said that in the garden he did not make rational decisions; he acted on the spur of impulse. That is, he responded to emotional stimuli. "Every *emotion*," Schopenhauer points out, "arises simply from the fact that a representation acting on our will comes so extremely near us that it conceals from us everything else. . . . Thus we become incapable for the moment of taking anything of a different kind into consideration" (*WWR* II, ch. 16).

To anyone responding spontaneously to such a limited impulse, Schopenhauer opposes the person who reasons, "the man who takes abstract or rational knowledge as his rule of conduct, and accordingly always reflects on its consequences and on the future. . . ." Molloy has not even attempted such cause-and-effect reasonings in this Circean garden of animal appetites. Again, Schopenhauer opposes to animals those humans who, "by virtue of knowledge in the abstract, comprehend not only the narrow and actual present but also the whole past and future together with the wide realm of possibility" (*WWR* I, book I, § 16).

As narrator, then, Molloy is able to evaluate his earlier self and to make that puzzling remark, "nothing I could not have foreseen if I could have." His earlier self could not foresee and could not include in its decisions any extended knowledge. As a damaged psyche he could not foresee the value of encountering his anima; as an adolescent *puer aeternus* he lived in the sensual moment; as a reclusive philosopher he inhabited a cage out of time and evaded considerations of past and future; as a psyche attempting to combine these personae he became an amateur Stoic, responding to each motive for action. Therefore Molloy's rationality while with Lousse cannot be praised; he is still under the sway of his appetites and his fears.

Molloy and the "Eudemonistic Slop" Concluded

Molloy's phrase "the eudemonistic slop" has focused much that was stated, imagined, or implied earlier in "Molloy." It has given specificity to the semiphilosophical thought with which Molloy raised into consciousness and yet kept at bay the unconscious earthly wisdom of Sophie Lousse. Her sensual garden has been tried and found wanting. Molloy in his cage was not out of time, nor in his sensual physicality was he a part of the timeless circularity of nature. Beckett has given Jung's vision of the slow-moving world of the anima a remarkable imaginative analysis. Nevertheless, while we must criticize Molloy's responses to Lousse, Beckett does not show us what might be correct responses. We cannot rise above the narrative.

We may sum up Beckett's treatment of the sensual life here. He probably most strikingly encountered the idea and term "eudemonism" in his repeated readings of Schopenhauer. He often considered Schopenhauer's extensive criticisms of Cynic and Stoic ethics and of suicide, a serious topic in his youth. (Most of the citations from Schopenhauer above come from only two chapters in *The World as Will and Representation*.) Leopardi's long-admired and relevant phrase "non che la speme" appears at the threshold of Lousse's world as a brief leitmotif; Beckett added it in translation (35).

These topics testify to the seriousness of his treatment of the Jungian "god"-mother. Molloy's experience of Jungian archetypes of the maternal anima centers on his extended submission to an image of the Sophia archetype. For one-third of "Molloy" Beckett develops this archetype through Lousse's speeches and behavior and through two related Jungian images, her house and garden. Molloy's experiences on Lousse's estate act out an existence in a state of idealized nature, an eternal youth to which psychic maturity is irrelevant, and a life made meaningful by its satisfaction of physical appetites and by the psyche's submission to the body. (There is no gourmet cuisine chez Lousse, no music, fine arts, or literature, and no rational thought. One must renounce those complications to live life naturally and eudemonistically.)

The dismissal of such an existence, however, by the narrating Molloy does not constitute a dismissal of the anima. We are in Molloy's mind, not Beckett's, and Molloy's relations to the anima are consistently composed of rejection and subordination. We have not encountered a valid image of Jung's Sophia. Molloy's psychic hostility has caricatured that archetype into Sophie Loy or Lousse and her walled world within Bally, as it had caricatured the physical mother into Mag.

Lousse Acquires a Rival

Molloy's eudemonic judgment upon Lousse's garden of delights is negative. He is equally negative in judging that Stoic ethics are "slop." His sour phrasing suggests that the narrator has outgrown Lousse's paradise. The location of this judging in the dream sequence suggests that the protagonist Molloy is also outgrowing that paradise; it is time for him to move on. He has weakened Sophie's domination of him, but her place is quickly taken by a third archetypal image, a caricature of the new moon.

"In a man," Jung tells us, "the mother-complex is never 'pure,' it is always mixed up with the anima archetype" (*Archetypes,* 94). We have seen already that Sophie belongs to both groups. Together, she and Mag act out the archetype that Jung calls the dual mother. (That the mother is sometimes a form of the anima and sometimes separate from the anima is a matter of Jung's imprecise terminology. Perhaps it is Jung's way of avoiding Freud's Oedipus complex by rephrasing its materials.)

Our Jungian expectations are necessarily mixed. Molloy is too old to be so concerned with his mother and the old woman who has replaced her. His neurotically retarded sexuality must mature in order to direct him toward a successor to his mother. He has not yet come to terms with his mother, however, and he must complete that task to achieve individuation.

We visit Central Casting for possibilities. Jung speaks often of the anima *tout court*. When he gets down to cases, though, the anima multiplies itself into many subtypes. Lousse cultivated Mag's distasteful natural world and made it appetizing. The next archetype combines Mag's earthiness with positive sexuality. Like Sophia, she has a masculine partner, another instance of syzygy. "The companion of the chthonic mother is the exact opposite [of Sophia's puer aeternus]," Jung writes; "an ithyphallic Hermes (the Egyptian Bes) or a lingam" (*Archetypes*, 106). As Jung and the three-part moon outside Molloy's window predicted, Molloy's earthy mother Mag was joined by the wise grandmother Sophie and now by the earthy seductive daughter.

Certainly this belated appearance of sexuality in Molloy's life is comic. Molloy shunned Sophie's wisdom while gorging on her physical pleasures. In so doing he moved from the child in the nightgown to the boy wanting a knife and bicycle and then to the adolescent swigging beer and staying out all night (cautiously out in the garden, not out on the town) and then to the boxed or jarred philosopher questioning but not answering. Given this increasing maturity, the complexities of sexuality cannot be evaded. Two Paradises 'twere in one to live in Paradise alone. Molloy's sensuality in Lousse's garden bears sexual fruit.

Ruth/Edith (for it is she) has her own living quarters, as do Mag and Sophie. She resembles the decaying Mag—she first encounters Molloy on a garbage dump—and Sophie in that she encounters Molloy in the outside world and brings him home (but he only visits). Her relation to the other archetypal women is made explicit: she "might have been my mother, and even I think my grandmother," Molloy says, "if chance had not willed otherwise" (56).

This sexually active chthonic figure requires a partner, and Jung has suggested one. Among his other job descriptions, Hermes is the god of thieves. Molloy will steal some of Lousse's silverware, as earlier he took money from his mother. Otherwise, however, he is limply qualified for the Jungian role of ithyphallic Hermes. Molloy's imagination presents his sexual idyll with Ruth/Edith retrospectively and as farce, keeping Ruth/Edith from seriously threatening his masculine identity. Much of the farce derives from his submission to her, his hostile ignorance of feminine and sexual matters, and his lack of affection. He will not even imagine Ruth/Edith as a seductress, thus denying her sexuality. She is a variant of Lousse, who is "a woman of an extraordinary flatness." He speculates that she may actually have been a man or an androgyne. Similarly he said of Mag that "we were like a couple of old cronies, sexless." He evades the feminine, even though he says of Ruth/Edith, "it was she who made me acquainted with love" (56).

Love has finally appeared as a topic, then, but sadly weakened and distanced. Between describing Lousse and introducing Ruth/Edith, Molloy presents himself elliptically in the role of lover. He raises the question "Could a woman have stopped me as I swept towards mother?" (Answer: "Probably.") This sweeping question alludes to Hamlet, who also has a complex relation with his mother, and to Hamlet's response to the Ghost's hint about an assassin:

> Haste me to know't, that I, with wings as swift
> As meditation or the thoughts of love,
> May sweep to my revenge.

Hamlet's sophomoric examples of swiftness, his recurrently blunted purpose, and Sophia's association with philosophy and therefore meditation are amusingly relevant.

Ruth/Edith supplements Mag and Lousse by evoking from Molloy thoughts of love, but his emphasis on the physical while in Lousse's earthly paradise has reduced life to "the body's long madness" (56). His affair with Ruth/Edith is also a bodily matter, leading him to wonder, "is it true love, in the rectum?" (57). He answers that question implicitly by locating love in a brief time as well as a small space: "Not when you are comfortable, but when your frantic member casts about for a rubbing-place, . . . it is then no doubt that true love comes to pass, and wings away . . ." (58). A pedicure and a massage confirm this analysis; that "instant of bliss" signals true love. We may note Schopenhauer's demanding will and Freud's pleasure principle here. "Frantic" is not a term common in discussions of love—"it was love, for she had told me so" (56)—but it is appropriate to "the body's long madness" and to pleasure as the reduction of painful desire. Love, then, is as transient and as merely physical as hunger and thirst. The preferred sexual position recalls Lousse's Circean world and Molloy's resemblance to Teddy: "it seemed all right to me, for I had seen dogs" (57).

Turning to love, Molloy's imagination has briefly set aside Lousse and her garden, although the experiences of love are physical and the judgments passed on them eudemonistic. Nevertheless, desire has been reported, though comically. Molloy's craving for a fellow or frère, has revived, faintly, and with it his need to return to the social world and to come to terms with his mother.

Now the open wicket-gate is accessible. The suddenly detached ego-consciousness finds no obstacle and invents none. Molloy is able to "take my crutches and go away, springing on them through the air" (59). Winging away like love, he pictures Lousse left behind: "she did not try and hold me back but she went and sat down on her dog's grave, perhaps, which was mine too in a way" (59). Escaping his mortality in her paradise of time and space, Molloy leaves Lousse among her plants, so chosen that they light up in seasonal rhythms.

Free at last, we may think, but such a positive response would be generated by Molloy's presentation, not by our hopes for therapy. When we take into account Jung's ideas, we must correct that response. Molloy raised the Sophia archetype from his unconscious only to submit to her and then reject her, as he had done with Mag and Ruth/Edith. Such psychic behavior gives evidence that Molloy is failing his tests and strengthening his weaknesses. Evasion is not freedom. He is not approaching individuation.

Leaving Lousse and Love

We appear to have emerged from Molloy's most extensive experiences of the anima and of the collective unconscious. Let us recall Jung on those topics:

> The unconscious is the mother of consciousness. . . . Consciousness grows out of an unconscious psyche which is older than it, and which goes on functioning together with it or even in spite of it. . . . There is little hope of our finding in the unconscious an order equivalent to that of the ego. It certainly does not look as if we were likely to discover an unconscious ego-personality. . . . But although a "second ego" cannot be discovered . . . , the manifestations of the unconscious do at least show *traces of personalities.* . . . They seem to represent complexes that have split off from a greater whole, and are the very reverse of a personal centre of the unconscious. . . . The anima and the animus live in a world quite different from the world outside—in a world where the pulse of time beats infinitely slowly, where the birth and death of individuals count for little. (*Archetypes,* 281–87)

Molloy has been involved with three women, all even older than he, none of whom has displayed ordinary individuality or a human personality. Each seems the sketch or caricature of a type. Lousse's slow-moving world differs greatly from the social world outside. Her gardeners tame nature into a quiet harmony. There is an order, but, as Jung says, it is not that of the ego. Unconsciousness functions even in spite of consciousness; they are discrete. Now Molloy has ended a complex encounter with Lousse's world, into which Mag and Ruth/Edith have just been woven. As narrator he will look back from the position of a sour Stoic. But what wisdom does he take with him now?

Jung says that "the first encounter with [the anima] usually leads one to infer anything rather than wisdom." Certainly Mag's unquoted gabble, Sophie's haranguing of the mob and lecturing of Molloy, and Ruth/Edith's undertaking of Molloy with her stick offer little promise of wisdom. Jung, however, also offers some hope:

> It is just the most unexpected, the most terrifyingly chaotic things which reveal a deeper meaning. And the more this meaning is recognized, the more the anima loses her impetuous and compulsive character. Gradually breakwaters are built against the surging of chaos, and the meaningful divides itself from the meaningless. When sense and nonsense are no longer identical, the force of chaos is weakened by their subtraction; sense is then endued with the force of meaning, and nonsense with the force of meaninglessness. In this way a new cosmos arises. (*Archetypes,* 30–31)

Even allowing for Jung's melodramatic presentation and Molloy's characteristic ataraxy, we found little of this chaos chez Lousse, of all places, and no rising of the Logos in response to the ego's terror. On the contrary. Lousse is merely passive at the end, and even at the beginning she needed no impetuous and compulsive character to take over the passive and unthinking Molloy. It is indeed true that a new cosmos arises for Molloy as soon as he leaves her: "Outside in the road the wind was blowing, it was another world" (60). But what has Molloy learned from Lousse, and why does it lead him to the windy world of Bally?

One is in the power of archetypes only so long as one cannot recognize them as such, Jung believes. Knowledge affords control. Repeatedly we have heard his description of the struggle with which the paternal Logos frees itself from the unconsciousness of the maternal womb, and we have even heard that "its first creative act of liberation is matricide." Perhaps Molloy's leaving Lousse is a form of this liberating matricide. We have also, however, doubted the positive value of matricide as an aid to individuation. Examining Jung's discussions more closely, we find some blustering in his praise of the matricidal Logos. When he considers specific processes of transformation and individuation, he takes more complex positions with different implications.

Syzygy becomes significant. We recall Jung's pairing of anima figures with male complements. "Anyone," he says, "who does not know the universal distribution and significance of the *syzygy* motif . . . can hardly claim to say anything about the concept of the anima." One must know about these "divine syzygies, the male-female pairs of deities" (*Archetypes,* 56, 59). With

Jungian sanction we have already linked "god"-mother Sophie with a comic puer aeternus and the sexual Ruth/Edith with a comic ithyphallic Hermes. Perhaps because of his split from Freud, Jung was unwilling to admit Oedipus and Jocasta into these syzygies, but we might do so ourselves and add Mag and Dan/Molloy to this group.

"It is a psychological fact," Jung says, "that as soon as we touch on these identifications we enter the realm of the syzygies, the paired opposites, where the One is never separated from the Other, its antithesis. It is a field of personal experience which leads directly to the experience of individuation, the attainment of the self" (*Archetypes*, 106). Molloy may be close to this goal, but Beckett is not creating a paradigm of this process. Besides, experience of these syzygies is not in itself a necessary and sufficient condition for the achievement of selfhood. A proper response is needed. Describing a failure to complete this process of individuation, Jung shows that the woman involved had indeed encountered her unconscious other half, her animus or hero. She was not, however, "able to meet the next phase of the process, namely the assimilation of the hero to her conscious personality, with the right attitude" (*Symbols of Transformation*, 441). Molloy's ego-consciousness must act properly, assert its control, and assimilate the powers of the unconscious into its identity.

The Crucial Event

Did Molloy assimilate the three forms of his maternal anima? Did he learn the right attitude? We must examine more closely the specific event that leads to his abruptly leaving Lousse. This event reports him as suddenly finding meaning in chaos and achieving a clear and conscious awareness of a meaningful psychic experience. That awareness leads immediately—literally so, from one sentence to the next—to the announcement of his departure. The event is as compactly significant as was his loss of rational control and immediate collapse at Lousse's feet.

Before leaving Lousse, he evokes Ruth/Edith and compares her to Lousse. He is "tempted to think of them as one and the same old hag" (59). His acknowledging the identification and the temptation implies an overcoming of repression, with resultant anxiety. That anxiety increases with his next and ultimate admission: "And God forgive me, to tell you the horrible truth, my mother's image sometimes mingles with theirs, which is literally unendurable, like being crucified, I don't know why and I don't want to. But I left Lousse at last, one warm airless night, without saying goodbye . . . ." Perhaps nowhere else in "Molloy" is there such intensity of feeling. It bursts out suddenly and is just as suddenly repressed. Molloy abruptly moves on, literally and figuratively, from the "warm airless night" of this maternal womb into a cold and rainy world.

Molloy has recognized the confluence of the three anima images. For him they are persons, and his recognition is not disinterested and psychotherapeutic. His awareness arises from his collective unconscious, and it is not the anima figures alone that have been blended. Because of Jung's syzygies, Molloy has been paired with each of them. His recognition of their unity entails an awareness of his complex relations to them. ("If ever I'm reduced to looking for a meaning to my life, . . . it's in that old mess I'll stick my nose to begin with, the mess of that poor old uniparous whore and myself" [19].) A Freudian interpretation of this discovery stresses Molloy's recognition of Oedipal incestuousness, and we cannot reject that idea out of hand. Beckett, however, has been emphasizing Jungian psychology and the collective rather than the personal unconscious. Why can we not speak positively of Molloy's raising his tripartite anima into consciousness, when it is a necessary Jungian event?

The immediate answer focuses not on the raising into consciousness but on Molloy's reaction. The intensity of his horror is imaged as a crucifixion, his deepest fear. ("To tell you the horrible truth"; "pour vous livrer le fond de mon effroi" [89].) Yet again Molloy has identified himself with Jesus. Discussing the dual mother, Jung connects Sophia with "the Mother of Christ" and uses Christ as an example of this "dual descent, . . . from human and divine parents" (*Archetypes*, 45). The linking of Christ and the Mother of Christ suggests a syzygy, and Jung has identified Sophia as a "god"-mother. We seek crucifixion, however, not merely a half-divine origin. Early on, Molloy described the "long confused emotion" of his life as a "passion without form or stations" (25). After he leaves Lousse, he will complain that his progress toward his mother has become "a veritable calvary, with no limit to its stations and no hope of crucifixion" (78). He varies his allusions to suit his situation. Neither of these references is emotionally intense, however, nor does either reference link crucifixion to the anima, unless there is a hint that reaching his mother might be the equivalent of reaching the time of crucifixion.

In the article just cited from *Archetypes*, Jung restates his dual-parent and dual-descent ideas, but differently. Attributing to Freud a literal belief in Oedipal incestuousness, Jung substitutes for one's actual parents "parental imagos." Thereby he moves beyond incest. "Apart from the incest-fantasy," he says, "religious ideas are associated with the parental imagos" (61). This association offers us something with which to work. Molloy's "God forgive me" and "crucifixion" cannot be casual phrasings.

In "The Relations between the Ego and the Unconscious," Jung explores some negative results of raising the anima into the ego-consciousness and gaining control over it. One such result, Jung says, is that the masculine ego-consciousness takes itself to be very powerful: "he becomes a super-man, superior to all powers, a demigod at the very least. 'I and the Father are one'—this mighty avowal in all its awful ambiguity is born of just such a psychological moment" (229). No application of this to Molloy is possible. He does compare himself to Jesus, and Mag's calling him Dan has long since made him one with his father, but he has not acted or spoken as a father or a demigod, and his exertion of power has extended only to his leaving Mag and now Lousse.

This sense of "godlikeness," however, can result in feelings quite different from those that improperly inflate one into a superman. Jung discusses Goethe's Faust in this connection, associating the state of "godlikeness" with knowledge of good and evil, as in the Book of Genesis. Earlier he said that "the analysis and conscious realization of unconscious contents" may give rise to a feeling of superiority. We have just set that idea aside. But "this same juxtaposition of good and evil can have a very different effect on a different kind of temperament." The juxtaposition may bring no sense of power. Quite the contrary: "It may . . . seem as though he were a helpless object caught between hammer and anvil; not in the least a Hercules at the parting of the ways, but rather a rudderless ship buffeted between Scylla and Charybdis. . . . Well might he feel himself like a Prometheus chained to the Caucasus, or as one crucified. This would be a 'godlikeness' in suffer-ing" (140–41). "As one crucified": Beckett's comparisons of Molloy and Jesus do not surprise us Jungians; we know that "Christ, from the point of view of psychology and comparative religion, is a typical manifestation of the self." The image of Christ in a Jungian transformation is generally posi-tive, since "the archetype of the self has, functionally, the significance of a ruler of the inner world, i.e., of the collective unconscious" (*Symbols of Transformation*, 392, 368). However, "as one crucified" demands a quite different understanding.

We have now accumulated many passages explaining significances in Molloy's mingling of the three women in his life. They emphasize his own involvement with these dual archetypes. The religious allusions recall the relevance of James's discussions and encourage us to recognize that Molloy's discovery of the importance of the three women and of his relations to them constitutes the basic crisis of his potential transformation. Now Jung sug-gests the possibility that Molloy has realized the significance of the anima only to react like a chained Prometheus or "one crucified."

After a lifetime of ignorant encounters with his mother and avoidance of her, Molloy has been forced to realize that her values and her relationship to him are not merely personal. She represents a collective power within him, and its values and qualities have appeared in Mag and Lousse and Ruth/Edith. Such a discovery ought to aid Molloy in achieving an understanding of important and previously repressed parts of his own psyche. This understanding should lead to the completion of his own individual psyche. These optimistic assertions are Jungian, however; Beckett has not suggested any such positive effect.

Turning yet again to Jung, we find him adding to his rational categories some rhetorical intensity. Describing the mother archetype's negative qualities, he comes to a version of Sophia: "perhaps the historical example of the dual nature of the mother most familiar to us is the Virgin Mary, who is not only the Lord's mother, but also, according to the medieval allegories, his cross." In this vivid imagistic sense she is also the earth into which one returns and other images of death. Jung adds in summary that "there are three essential aspects of the mother: her cherishing and nourishing goodness, her orgiastic emotionality, and her Stygian depths" (*Archetypes*, 82). In "Molloy" these correspond to Lousse, Ruth/Edith, and Mag.

Despite these Jungian negatives, the coming together of these three aspects in Molloy's consciousness may still seem positive. For Molloy, obsessed all his life by a mother with whom he could not or would not come to terms, this discovery is intensely emotional. This cramped moment—to which Molloy gives cramped and minimal expression—is for Molloy the discovery of "the most unexpected, the most terrifyingly chaotic things." It is the encounter capable of evoking the Logos: "Only when the power of judgement with all its categories is abandoned is it possible to experience the archetype within the anima's senselessness" (*Integration of the Personality*, 82). The judgmental categories that separated Mag from Lousse and both of them from Ruth/Edith have now failed, obliging Molloy to recognize their unity. It is a powerful recognition. It should create the wise Logos, but it does not. The failure of the Logos to rise to the occasion testifies to Lousse's power and to Molloy's fear and weakness of will. The crucifixion—fled by Molloy as not by Jesus—evokes that failure. Again, Beckett compresses the important reaction into a few words. "I don't know why and I don't want to," Molloy says, refusing to awaken or create his Logos.

He escapes, but the effects of this great refusal find expression soon after this flight. He takes with him an image that parodies his immobile bicycle, two fixed and identical parts connected in the middle, motionless and useless: the kniferest. It is merely a kniferest, the trivial object with which Moran fiddles while awaiting dinner (115), but it is extraordinarily suggestive, and not merely of the bicycle. It is his souvenir of Lousse. (He also steals some other silverware, which he sells.) He exalts it to meaningfulness by delighting in its unfindable meaning. It contains a double image of the crucifixion. It is comprised of two similar parts fixed at a distance, each the mathematician's x, a sought-for unknown. It suggests his unknown ego-consciousness in relation to his anima. It is also the counterpart of Moran's dancing bees, an association that further emphasizes Beckett's serious intentions.

Since the kniferest is Molloy's souvenir of Lousse, let us examine her yet again. She is the most powerful of the anima figures in "Molloy." Molloy's active imagination reduces Mag and Ruth/Edith to minor figures appearing in brief events, but Lousse takes over a third of the narrative. For most of her appearance she offers only good things, it seems. Her reign is benign, providing food, shelter, attention, and isolation from other humans. (Shelter is not emphasized, since nature in Lousse's world is not threatening and no humans trouble Molloy.)

Archetypes are ambivalent, however, especially when not under the control of the conscious mind. Lousse forced Molloy into her service, using the policeman and the mob as threats. She imposed upon his dark night her moons. She turned him into her puer aeternus. She aroused his sensual appetites. She may be unable to control her desire for Molloy, but this "god"-mother has access to considerable power. (Any god in any pantheon is similar: powerful but obliged eternally to act out the same attributes of power.) Molloy managed to escape her only after that literally crucial revelation forced him to acknowledge her central and inclusive role, making even his escape a capitulation.

His recognition of the triple identity is so awful that he cannot control it: "I don't know why and I don't want to." All the powers of the Jungian Logos, the archetype of wisdom, derive from conscious and verbal knowing, and Molloy renounces that responsibility. Thus his "godlikeness" as a part of his several syzygies becomes "a 'godlikeness' in suffering," with crucifixion the agent of that suffering. (Rejected, it leads to no salvation.) He leaves Lousse still unenlightened, taking with him only that image of potential meaning, the kniferest. We have just noted implicit meanings in it; Molloy treats it otherwise.

A crucifixion is a horrible event, but a small and polished silver cross, with crossbars of equal length and no representation of a body, often serves as a piece of decorative jewelry. Its central meanings have been suppressed. It disturbs no one. Likewise, the double crosses of the kniferest suggest no pain. (Molloy's acquired knife is associated with pain but not with the kniferest.) These considerations are relevant to Molloy's celebration of the kniferest:

> I could never understand what possible purpose it could serve, nor even contrive the faintest hypothesis on the subject. And from time to time I took it from my pocket and gazed upon it, with an astonished and affectionate gaze, if I had not been incapable of affection. But for a certain time I think it inspired me with a kind of veneration, for there was no doubt in my mind that it was not an object of virtu, but that it had a most specific function always to be hidden from me. I could therefore puzzle over it endlessly without the least risk. For to know nothing is nothing, not to want to know anything likewise, but to be beyond knowing anything, to know you are beyond knowing anything, that is when peace enters in, to the soul of the incurious seeker. (63–64)

Molloy's comment develops Leopardi's "Non che la speme, il desiderio" and his own "I don't know why and I don't want to." He goes on from the kniferest to celebrate the endless calculation of pi as an inexpressible decimal.

This passage is often cited with admiration, if not affection. Jung puts it into its psychic context. Molloy is repressing the horrible recognition of his relation to the anima by projecting his psychic situation onto this kniferest, which he does not mention until his narrative has taken him safely away from Lousse's estate. We have found meanings in it, and we can continue to find them in the bar that keeps X away from X and in the utensil's association with Lousse's paradise of food and drink, for instance. Molloy, on the other hand, is celebrating the inaccessibility of any meaning, and he insists on the inaccessibility because it frees him from "risk" and therefore brings him "peace." He speaks of "peace . . . , to the soul of the incurious seeker." The oxymoron is veiled by the rhetoric, perhaps, but if Molloy is to come to terms with his anima, he must accept curiosity and turn it into a much stronger motive. He associates peace with an absence of discoverable meaning and therefore with wordlessness—but his verbal Logos must put Sophia's wisdom into intelligible terms if he is to mature.

Molloy's praise of the kniferest, then, is praise of meaninglessness, celebrated by "the power of judgement with all its categories," as Jung called it. It is therefore praise of the judging power's irresponsibility. Molloy has avoided the anima's world of wordless feelings (he describes himself here as "incapable of affection"), and his unenlightened masculine reason shelters him from any irrational meanings. He is protected from dangerous knowledge, as when he calculates the undiscoverable value of that surd, pi.

He has evaded understanding of his trinity of anima figures and his relations to it. He has celebrated the act of puzzling over the kniferest and pi. He has thereby acted out Beckett's central criticism of reason: it does not seek meaning; on the contrary, reasoning is an act with which the ego-consciousness evades the discovery of meaning. ("I could therefore puzzle over it endlessly without the least risk.") The sucking-stones problem will dramatize this criticism at length.

After Sophie

Molloy's departure from Lousse's matriarchal estate ends the only extensive encounter between Molloy and any form of his maternal anima. He will encounter no more human forms of that archetype, but his anima has not given up. Jung divides archetypes into two classes. One consists of personifications such as Mag, Ruth/Edith, and Sophia and of images such as the tripartite moon. The second class is composed of "archetypes of transformation": "They are not personalities, but are typical situations, places, ways and means, that symbolize the kind of transformation in question" (*Archetypes*, 38). We have noted already such examples as the town of Bally, Lousse's house and garden, and Molloy's various ditches. More will appear.

By his comments and behavior in such situations and places, Molloy will act out his future encounters with the maternal archetype. One significant result has already occurred: his refusal to learn from the blending of his mother's image with those of Lousse and Ruth/Edith. That refusal negated any creation of his Logos, and it distanced his anima while increasing his identification with his rational ego-consciousness. In this final phase he will emphasize reasoning—drawing conclusions from simple facts, engaging in mathematical calculations, and strengthening the judgmental character of his masculine ego-consciousness.

The terms used above may seem honorific, but the factual particulars bring them down to earth. Molloy's verbal existence is dual, compounded of the voices that he hears and the words that he uses. He says that he leaves Lousse because of "the still small voice saying, Get out of here, Molloy"—a voice he has heard for some time without understanding it (59). The voice is negative—it makes no mention of his need for his mother—and Molloy does not connect it with the fear of crucifixion that is his obvious motive. His own increasing verbal dexterity is displayed in trivial details, as when he finds a shelter from the cold rain falling in Bally. Such a shelter might be an image of the anima, but Molloy is concerned only to control it by naming it, as Adam named the wordless world. "Shelter," "lodging-house," "alley," "recesses," and "alcoves" dissatisfy him; he settles on "chapel" (60–61). That term recalls Jung's linking of Sophia with religious imagery, but Molloy ignores all overtones. He turns to mathematics to identify his "hypotenusal posture" there (61).

His reasoning is also displayed in simple exercises. He explains that "a fine rain falling . . . seems to exclude all idea of wind" (61). He says that "there are things from time to time . . . that impose themselves on the understanding with the force of axioms, for unknown reasons." This fine-sounding academic assertion follows upon his identification of lavatory windows, and "unknown reasons" evades the reasoner's basic justification. When his reasoning leads to an act, the same comic unimportance recurs. Should he take off his hat? "I had two good reasons for taking it off and they were none too many, neither alone would ever have prevailed" (61). The reasons are merely two feelings of discomfort caused by the hat; he is still in the "eudemonistic slop." And he does not discard the hat that may be associated with reasoning: "I threw it from me with a careless lavish gesture and back it came, at the end of its string or lace" (61). Retrieved after his arrival chez Lousse, it had no lace (44), but the dreaming psyche recycles images irrationally, and Molloy is more firmly attached to reason now than he had been.

Now Molloy combines reason with Stoicism. Propped at his absurd hypotenusal angle, Molloy was "in peace for as long as I could endure peace" (61). So, with his hat off, "I began to think, that is to say to listen harder." The result of his thinking is explicit: "For the space of an instant I considered settling down there, making it my lair and sanctuary, for the space of an instant. I took the vegetable knife . . . and set about opening my wrist. But pain soon got the better of me." We follow the train of his thought easily. Time threatens him; peace cannot last. Death will stop time and make peace last. But pain . . . Stoic eudemonism obliges him to live.

Before we move on, we must finish off Beckett's presentation of reason in the regained world of Bally. It reaches a climax in a few abrupt sentences, as did Molloy's collocation of Lousse, Mag, and Ruth/Edith. Molloy apologizes for reporting these details and many others. He promises to go faster and to provide "vast frescoes, dashed off with loathing." Then he justifies the previous "wealth of filthy circumstance" by aphorizing: "Homo mensura can't do without staffage" (63). Here Beckett compresses ideas that he put together in his article on "La Peinture des van Velde" (1945). That article uses the term "boîte cranienne" to describe the mind, recalling Molloy's retreat to a "boîte" or "jar" in Lousse's garden. Molloy's condemnations of the "eudemonistic slop" and the "miserable molys" that extend pleasure are reflected in Beckett's mocking of the "amateur (éclairé)" who "ne pense qu'à son plaisir" (120). "Éclairé" is ironic about enlightenment, of course.

These details reflect and mildly reinforce judgments we have already reached. The topic of reason is more serious. Jung makes that clear in describing what happens when the Logos studies the unexpected and terrifying acts of the anima. The Logos contrives to divide the meaningful from the meaningless: "When sense and nonsense are no longer identical, the force of chaos is weakened by their subtraction; sense is then endued with the force of meaning, and nonsense with the force of meaninglessness" ("Archetypes of the Collective Unconscious," 31). After Mag's gabble, Lousse's unrecorded talks in the garden, and Molloy's recently developed reason, we might expect Beckett to side with Jung and the Logos. In "La Peinture," however, he takes the other side. Setting up an hypothesized painting "immobile dans le vide," he describes it: "la tableau est là, un non-sens" (119). Then he supports this nonsense against the analytical critic and his demands for meaning in art.

Molloy has just defended his presentation of details of reasoning: "homo mensura can't do without staffage." The epigram is admirably condensed. "Homo mensura" abbreviates the phrase "homo omnium mensura" — "man is the measure of all things." The rational act of judging requires staffage, cheap building materials for temporary constructions. ("Smoke, sticks, flesh, hair, at evening, afar, flung about the craving for a fellow. I know how to summon these rags to cover my shame" [15].) The term "staffage" is common in the construction industry; Beckett probably learned it from his father. In his Van Velde article he suggests that Claude Lorrain is the kind of painter whose works are acceptable to humanist critics seeking sense, not nonsense: "Les paysages de Claude ne doivent-ils vraiment rien au staffage?" (122).

Finally, in the article, Beckett turns his attention to those humanist critics. Protagoras is the source of Molloy's "homo mensura." Beckett's article ends, awkwardly, with a series of isolated statements affirming humanistic values. They are to be read ironically. Only one concerns us: "Le philosophe qui dit: Protagoras avait raison" (132). Translated out of irony, the statement asserts that Protagoras is wrong, as are his followers. The idiomatic "avait raison" functions as a double entendre: Protagoras is wrong because he has reason; reason cannot judge art. Beckett understands Protagoras to use "man" generically; the rational bases for the judgments of homo mensura are those of his society. Thus Molloy's epigram identifies him as on the wrong side, distant from the nonsense of the anima.

Molloy's Questionable New Shape

The aborted suicide in the chapel suggests another appearance of the Proustian metaphor of death to signal a substantial change in one's identity. The old ego dies hard, however, and Molloy ends his report of the failed suicide by accusing himself of "backsliding." His French term "récidiver" makes clearer the criminality of his failure; he has committed again Calderòn's sin of being born. Moran, thinking of Sisyphus, will use the same French verb (206) and conclude that making the same journey over and over "would keep hope alive, ... hellish hope" (133). If Molloy is clearer about the crime in French, he is clearer about the rebirth in English. The neutral French contrasts Molloy's present state with that in Bally: "mon existence actuelle dont celle que je conte ne peut donner qu'une faible idée." In translating, Beckett added an image of rebirth and a new start: "my present existence compared to which this is a nursery tale."

This complex verbal analysis may seem far away from Jung, but it is not. In "The Psychology of the Child Archetype" Jung offers interpretations relevant to Beckett's presentations both in "Molloy" and later (especially in *Waiting for Godot* and *Endgame*):

> One of the essential features of the child motif is its futurity. The child is potential future. Hence the occurrence of the child motif in the psychology of the individual signals as a rule an anticipation of future developments, even though at first sight it may seem like a retrospective configuration. Life is a flux, a flowing into the future, and not a stoppage or backwash. ... In the individuation process, it anticipates the figure that comes from the synthesis of conscious and unconscious elements in the personality. (*Archetypes,* 164)

(Beckett echoes that flux and flowing in "Moran" [148–49].)

Molloy's new identity returns him to the criminal world by recreating this masculine ego-consciousness. It is a virgin birth, with no feminine components. The new Molloy emphasizes rationality, as he had done when he calculated the rate of his farts and exclaimed: "Extraordinary how mathematics help you to know yourself" (30). Under Lousse's spell and deciding that sometimes he said too much, sometimes too little, he had reached a similarly far-fetched conclusion: "Divine analysis that conduces thus to knowledge of yourself, and of your fellow-men, if you have any" (34). Later in Lousse's garden he had asked himself questions "just for the sake of looking at them. ... I called that thinking" (49).

Now this analytical mind sets out into the pre-established harmony that it dislikes (62), fleeing Bally instead of seeking the mother. It chooses a direction by "giving in to the evidence, to a very strong probability rather" (64), after Molloy the narrator has celebrated the undiscoverable meaning of the kniferest. This analytical mind tells us that "there is rapture, or there should be, in the motion crutches give," claiming that "these are reasonings, based on analysis" (64). As for the matter of finding his mother, "these were ancient cares and the mind cannot always brood on the same cares, but needs fresh cares from time to time. . . . But can one speak here of fresh and ancient cares? I think not. But it would be hard for me to prove it" (64). These are examples of reasoning that evades meaning. Molloy is not an admirable "homo mensura."

Before he can continue his renewed existence as the rational masculine ego-consciousness, repressed irrational fears force their way into his narrative (65–68). Acknowledging that he had been seeking his mother all his life, he evades that need only to develop the guilty fearfulness of his life in society. "In the country there is another justice, other judges, at first" (65), he says. It is of the town, however, its justice, and his long residence there that he is now compelled to speak.

Molloy the Town Rat

Molloy's analysis of his dangerous social existence implies the passing of a long period of time, even though he appears to be heading for the city gates on the day after his flight from Lousse. Its general character suggests that it comprises one of the promised frescoes dashed off with loathing. It offers a consistent description of social life as experienced by someone unable to seek a fellow or frère, and as analyzed by the reason. This last assertion may seem incredible. A basic difficulty is that Molloy's rational analysis is applied, as often, to quite irrational premises. They include the sense that life is a matter of dangers to be avoided, in town and country, by an individual sensing himself different from and worse than those who threaten him. The subjective and irrational nature of the resultant premises produce a sense of life in society considerably darker than any in Molloy's earlier reports of Bally, even in his paranoid description of the crowd that wished to lynch him for running over the dog Teddy.

Molloy evokes a far broader experience of Bally than any suggested in his first two visits. So far, the narrative has implied that Molloy had fled from his childhood with the chthonic Mag into the wilderness and onto the mountainside. Now he has fled from a complementary childhood with his organized "god"-mother into conventional society. (Lousse's "dear departed" had "fallen in defense of a country that called itself his" [33].) Neither in the social world complementary to Lousse's nor in the chthonic world complementary to Mag's could Molloy find a fellow, A or C.

Underlying Molloy's present report of dangers, a fresco dashed off with loathing, is the life lived by a social and actual Molloy in a social and actual world. Molloy's dark conceptions of this social world are projections of his own psychic condition. He is not a part of that world, where he has no fellows. He relates himself instead to "many a foul beast." During the day he is "bowed down like a good boy, oozing with obsequiousness." This daytime identity is "less rat than toad" (67). He prefers the toad—a toady—because "I for my part have always preferred slavery to death" (68; Moran claims to have developed a public self in order to preserve a private one [110, 114]). He must endure submission to society during the day and pursuit during the night by "the technicians," the psychic horrors of bad dreams (67). *Waiting for Godot* will report this night life.

One general assumption especially governs Beckett's conception of these details: Molloy is not psychically complete. He is the dark half of a light-dark whole; he identifies himself as one "who himself is night, day and night" (67; this is written after Beckett's experience in his dying mother's room in 1945, later altered and dramatized in *Krapp's Last Tape*. See Knowlson, 319). He has opposed light since he described June as a time when "the sun is at its pitilessmost and the arctic radiance comes pissing on our midnights" (17). This identification with night suggests an identification with his Jungian shadow: "The shadow . . . corresponds to a negative ego-personality; it embraces all those characteristics whose existence is found to be painful or negative" (*Integration of the Personality,* 173). The ego-consciousness's identification with these characteristics results in such symptoms as Molloy describes.

In *Psychology of the Unconscious* Jung's analysis of a patient's dream series leads him to generalize about the need to redirect the libido from its early incestuous fixation on the family, and to connect it with the world outside: "All the libido unconsciously bound up in familial bonds . . . must be brought outside into human contact." Like William James in *Varieties,* Jung is speaking here to a religious audience, and he develops this idea by way of Christianity, associating the freeing of incestuous libido with types of work. In antiquity, he says, "the Redeemer and Physician . . . was he who endeavored to educate man to the sublimation of the incestuous libido. The destruction of slavery was the necessary condition of that sublimation." Therefore, Molloy's preference of slavery to death results in a twofold enslavement, to society during the day and to the technicians at night—the Jungian archetypes Mag, Lousse, and Ruth/Edith and their male associates.

If we associate this enslavement with Molloy's fear of crucifixion chez Lousse and of dying in Bally, and with his clinging to his immature relationship to his mother, then we need only one more link. Jung offers it in continuing his analysis of the Christian value of work: "Indolence is the beginning of all vice, because in a condition of slothful dreaming the libido has ample opportunity for sinking into itself, in order to create compulsory obligations by means of regressively re-animated incestuous bonds. The best liberation is through *regular work*" (*Psychology of the Unconscious*, 453–455).

As is often the case for Beckett's protagonists, psychic distress incapacitates Molloy from working, and therefore work cannot provide therapy for him. (Moran's work is evidence of his neurosis.) In praising work, Jung urges sublimation upon the incestuous libido or its psyche. Sublimation requires the raising of emotion into the ego-consciousness. While the psyche is enslaved to the incestuous libido, the person is fixed at "the stage of ungovernableness and surrender to the emotions" (*Psychology of the Unconscious*, 454). This fixation explains why Molloy coolly reasons out his analyses of lavatory lights, the rapture of crutches, and human behavior in the rain, but finds that his "notions" about dying are "all spasm, sweat and trembling, without an atom of common sense or lucidity" (68). The evasive shadow has access neither to Lousse's feminine wisdom nor to the lucidity of daylight reason; unable to govern its fears, it must surrender to them, hostilely. So too Molloy's description of his life in society is not detailed and exact but dashed off with loathing. He is incapable of affection; "all the libido unconsciously bound up in familial bonds" must be freed before it can be directed toward "human contact."

Molloy's brief narrative passage about life in a fearful society may still appear irrelevant to the rest of "Molloy." So may the briefer references in *Waiting for Godot* to a life lived offstage among other people. Their inclusion in the texts, however, emphasizes the psychic nature of the dramas enacted. We are in internal worlds in *Molloy* as in *Godot,* and their inside-out quality requires that conventionally realistic life be displaced.

Molloy's Immature Reason Finds a Role Model

The inadequacy of judgmental reason cut off from the anima's emotional world is most obvious when Molloy's ego-consciousness is threatened with a positive change in identity. So threatened, it has responded by bullying Mag and then fleeing to the mountainside, by evading and fleeing Lousse, by succumbing to Ruth/Edith without learning affection, and now by evading and then fleeing social existence. Molloy flees again from his goals, mother and town and his fellows, until he can go no farther. He reaches the seacoast and establishes himself there to develop his newly hatched self. "The cycle continues, joltingly, of flight and bivouac, in an Egypt without bounds," fleeing Herod and the promised land (66). He has been to the sea before: "Much of my life has ebbed away before this shivering expanse" (68). He recalls setting out on that sea and perhaps never returning. (We recognize the end of "The End.") Far from Bally, extremes meet; the sea suggests a threatening maternal anima.

Jung develops this anima figure with particular relevance when he considers Brünhilde in Wagner's *Siegfried,* a figure encompassing "mother-sister-wife." Examining the imagery of an aria, he notes that this "anima-image brings with it still other aspects of the mother-imago, amongst others those of water and submersion. . . . The water represents the maternal depths and the place of rebirth; in short, the unconscious in its positive and negative aspects" (*Symbols of Transformation,* 388–89).

Molloy will scarcely mention the sea during his stay on the coast. Describing his world as seen from the mountainside, he was inexplicably abrupt about it: "The sea, of which nothing" (11). Repression now creates a psychic setting composed of a sterile rocky and sandy shore next to a scarcely noticed salty sea. There he is free to develop his reason and thereby contrive a relevant identity.

Molloy and Descartes

Following Jung, Beckett characterized the Sophia figure as Sophie Loy or Lousse, but Jung offered no model for the ego-consciousness's rational reaction against the Sophia figure. Beckett turned to Schopenhauer and to the Stoics for his characterization of Molloy's evasiveness. Now Beckett needs to characterize his attempt to make a self out of his masculine rationality. Again Jung offers no simple model. This time Beckett turns to Descartes for help.

Jung insists that the masculine ego-consciousness must gain control of the anima's wisdom, with considerable effort. Sensing the threat of crucifixion in his own crucial discovery, Molloy evaded the psychic information from which he might have gained such wisdom. Many patients abandon therapy at such a painful crux, as Molloy did by leaving Lousse. Earlier, there were other distancings: he did without a fellow or frère or mother on the mountainside, and he hid in a philosopher's cage in Lousse's garden. Another common escape, besides abandoning the work of therapy, is a rational distancing from the psychic problem. We have noted Molloy's developing reason; now his imitation of Descartes will enact that escape into reason.

Beckett told interviewer Gabriel D'Aubarède: "si le sujet de mes romans pouvait s'exprimer en termes philosophiques, je n'aurais pas eu de raison de les écrire." Beckett is no philosopher, and the old man who leaves town on crutches to lurk in a cave at the seashore is not, on the face of it, a rational human being, much less a philosopher. Only comic irony makes it possible for Beckett to model the aged Molloy's rationality upon that of the young Descartes. This modeling results in a comic sketch of the old Molloy as Descartes embarking drily upon his life of reason. (Michael Mooney offers a wider view, q.v.) The man noted for his "cogito ergo sum" described his early preparations for that life of reason in his *Discours de la méthode*. From that text Beckett takes his materials.

Molloy at the seaside does without food and drink and pays minimal attention to his surroundings. He acts out Descartes' description of himself in the *Discours* as "une substance dont l'essence ou la nature n'est que de penser, et qui, pour être, n'a besoin d'aucun lieu, ni ne depend d'aucune chose materielle." His self is his "âme . . . entièrement distincte du corps" (604). Molloy's conclusion from his farts (30), his "divine analysis," and the "things . . . with the force of axioms" that explain lavatory windows (60) have prepared us for his movement toward Descartes. The sucking-stones will provide its climax.

We need not note all the connections between Descartes' maxims and precepts and Molloy's imitations. The terms "analysis" and "axioms" will recur. Descartes' first precept is "de ne recevoir jamais aucune chose pour vraie, que je ne la connusse evidemment être telle" (586). Therefore Molloy immediately identifies lavatory windows. Descartes approves the behavior of voyagers lost in a forest who move straight ahead; if they do not find the hoped-for exit, they will still leave it, which is better than remaining in it (595). This is the method Molloy adopts in leaving Bally: "it seemed to me that if I kept on in a straight line I was bound to leave it, sooner or later. . . . And my pertinacity was such that I did indeed come to the ramparts, . . . having described a good quarter of a circle, through bad navigation" (65). Deciding to leave the forest, later, he will improve on Descartes' method (85). In neither case does he doubt the correctness of his behavior. It is rational.

Descartes concludes his discussion of his precepts by explaining their use. They train the mind to think successfully. In his own case "je sentais, en la pratiquant, que mon esprit s'accoutumait peu à peu à concevoir plus nettement et plus distinctement ses objets" (590). Molloy will repeat these qualities several times, as in praising his success with the sucking-stones. His attempt "to suck the stones in the way I have described, not haphazard, but with method" (Molloy uses "method" often, in this latter end of his report) enables him to see better: "Let me tell you something, my sight was better at the seaside! Yes, ranging far and wide over these vast flats, where nothing lay, nothing stood, my good eye saw more clearly and there were even days when the bad one too had to look away" (74).

In Molloy's material world clarity of conception becomes merely literal vision. His having to turn away from a world where nothing lay or stood (his own possible poses) emphasizes the unattractiveness of this mental landscape in which he is isolated, shunning his own self, devoid of fellow, frère, and mother, and turning away from what he sees. His emotional existence is as dry as this wasteland. ("Flats" omits the shivering sea, and the thriving vegetation of Lousse's nature is nowhere to be found.)

Even before Descartes entered our considerations, we might have sensed his approach in noting Molloy's increasing analyses and his enlarged vocabulary. His excited announcement of clearer vision mentions those matters: "And not only did I see more clearly, but I had less difficulty in saddling with a name the rare things I saw." By the end of his narrative Molloy will have more to say, and painfully, about clear and distinct perceptions and a world thoroughly named. Here he is delighted with his eyesight. He has changed a great deal since he described Mag's appearance and added, "Not that seeing matters, but it's something to go on with" (19).

The solving of the sucking-stone problem is a splendid comic set piece that reduces to absurdity Molloy's response to Descartes' third maxim: "Ma troisième maxime était de tâcher toujours plutôt à me vaincre que la fortune, et à changer mes désirs que l'ordre du monde; et généralement, de m'accoutumer à croire qu'il n'y a rien qui soit entièrement en notre pouvoir, que nos pensées . . ." (595–96). Molloy changes his desires for the maternal anima rather than attempting to change his world, and he emphasizes thinking because only there is he in control. He thinks of a rational substitute for a mother and settles for rational control of that.

His solution to a mathematical problem is the climax of Molloy's imitation of Descartes. It bears on a central flaw in his psychic life: existence without a satisfactory relation to his mother and thus without access to the unrepressed affections needed for a fellow. Paradoxically, he achieves success at the cost of illumination.

The Sucking-Stone Problem

Molloy's first act on reaching the potentially maternal sea is to find a stony substitute womb, his cave. His next is to develop and complicate a rational substitute for the maternal breast: the sucking-stone. He had used a stone much earlier: "a little pebble in your mouth, round and smooth, appeases, soothes, makes you forget your hunger, forget your thirst" (26). He first calls it a sucking-stone when, chez Lousse, he finds that it has been taken away (45). Lousse does not oblige him to repress his appetites; she provides food and drink, thereby developing an appetite for maternal nourishment and sensual life that no stone could satisfy. Now Molloy returns to a cold, hard, rational equivalent for a relationship with a mother. His arranging of sixteen sucking-stones is a comically rational success. He acquires a multiplicity of indistinguishable, timeless, and passive mothers.

His problem is to get them under his rational control. As in Molloy's reasonings about farts and the dangers of social life, so here: the sources of his problem are irrational, emotional, and psychological. His rational ego-consciousness, however, turns the need for a mother into mathematical abstractions and generalities, and it solves the problem in such a way as to evade its actuality. The stones lack even mineral individuality when translated into numbers. Although sucking implies infantile dependence, the arranging of the stones emphasizes a control that Molloy never achieved with Mag, Lousse, or Ruth/Edith.

The arbitrariness of the problem is no accident. A utilitarian difficulty, even if mathematical, might generate too much anxiety, but this one is inferior to those set by the kniferest and pi because a solution is possible. Once solved, this problem can no longer distract the rational ego-consciousness from central concerns. Therefore, Molloy will throw the stones away, or give them away, or lose them. Finding a solution, however, kills time. Its extended presentation also enables Molloy the narrator to suggest the passing of "the months and perhaps the years that followed" his flight from town and mother and society and death (68). Beckett folds more meanings into the sucking-stone problem than those already noted. A major implication can be unfolded from the voice that speaks to Molloy and hints at the answer to his problem. This voice, in part because it is given a religious source, recalls James's *Varieties of Religious Experience*.

Puzzling through his calculations, Molloy finds himself at a standstill: "I was beginning to lose all sense of measure" (70). Homo mensura is sinking under his obligation to measure all things. "Revolving interminable martingales all equally defective, and crushing handfuls of sand"—thereby lulling "my mind and part of my body"—he experiences an "illumination." That term alerts us, here as always, because of Jung's report about the symbolic movement toward individuation from "some impossible situation" to "illumination or higher consciousness, by means of which the initial situation is overcome on a higher level" (*Archetypes*, 38–39). Since mathematics was not included in Molloy's education (39), "martingales" has surprised us. We expect a mathematical discovery when "illumination . . . suddenly began to sing within me, like a verse of Isaiah, or of Jeremiah" (71).

Many authors and characters would intend those names to suggest simply a religious aura around this illumination. A trained reader of Beckett, however, will seek illumination in the literal writings of Isaiah and Jeremiah, and in the King James Version on which Beckett was raised, even though *Molloy* is written in French. One can afford to leave no sucking-stone unturned. Isaiah, Jeremiah, and the Lamentations provide contexts unexpectedly relevant to "Molloy." One of them will not connect until its end; in the Lamentations, Jeremiah reminds God that "Thou drewest near in the day that I called upon thee: thou saidst, Fear not" (3:57). At the end of his narrative Molloy will crawl through the forest calling upon his spiritual hope, "Mother," and will hear "a voice telling me not to fret, that help was coming" (90–91). "Fret" is an amusing parental diminution of "fear."

While speculating about his sucking-stones, however, Molloy says that "the meaning of this illumination . . . I did not penetrate at once, and notably the word trim, which I had never met with, in this sense, long remained obscure" (71). We must therefore seek materials relevant to sucking-stones and "the principle of trim." The suckling of infants is certainly a recurrent image in these biblical texts. Jeremiah laments the absence of the mother's breast: "the tongue of the sucking child cleaveth to the roof of his mouth for thirst" (4:4). Isaiah offers several images of the sucking child and of masculinity comically taking over from the mother, such as "thou shalt suck the milk of the Gentiles, and . . . the breast of kings" (60:16). Some images place adults in a nursing posture: "rejoice with Jerusalem, and . . . suck, and be satisfied with the breasts of her consolations" (66:10–11). Since Mag cannot recognize Molloy, we ponder Isaiah's question: "Can a woman forget her sucking child that she should not have compassion on the son of her womb?" God's answer is not reassuring, given Mag's forgetfulness and Lousse's passive response to Molloy's departure: "Yea, they may forget, yet will I not forget thee" (49:15). Yes, the relevant image of the sucking child recurs, but it establishes a context of only dubious maternal nourishment.

We seek some allusion to "trim." The reader of the French text of *Molloy* must be at a loss, since Beckett's term there is "arrimage" (108), which concerns the loading of a ship and the professional trimming of that load. The Bible in French offers no corresponding term, but the King James Bible offers what we seek, with predictable ambiguity. In Jeremiah, God asks Judah angrily, "Why trimmest thou thy way to seek love?" (2:33). No wonder Molloy was puzzled. In Jacobean English "trim thy way" means "go purposefully," as by the shortest and quickest way. Molloy's understanding of "trim" as "balance" is therefore an error. It enables him to solve his sucking-stone problem, but a solution reached by error must put reason in doubt. And what a solution: reason has succeeded in replacing a mother by an absurd arrangement of sucking-stones, with four pockets to replace breasts.

Molloy's journey was incited by his desire to trim his way toward an object of love, a fellow or frère (quickly amended to his mother). God's objection to such trimming casts darkness rather than illumination upon Molloy's concerns. Why should a voice with such honorific overtones object to his search for love, why does he misunderstand the message, and why does his misunderstanding provide a solution to the sucking-stone problem? Answers are available in Jeremiah. Jeremiah's God objects to Judah's trimming to seek love, not because he opposes the search for love, but because the quickly found object of Judah's love is improper. God describes Judah as "saying to a stock, Thou art my father; and to a stone, Thou hast brought me forth" (2:27). Judah has taken a short cut, replacing God with idols. Molloy seeks or should seek his maternal anima rather than settling for a sucking-stone. (Moran, concerned with a father-figure, will admire the stock, or staff, carried by the old man he meets on the moors.)

Molloy trims his way to love, concerned only with sucking-stones rather than the difficult path to psychic health. He takes "trim" to permit an unbalanced arrangement of the stones. The pun cannot be overlooked; a neurosis is an unbalanced solution to a psychic problem. Molloy's solution indicates neurosis and settles for it.

Jung Upstages Descartes

Molloy concludes his description of life at the seaside with a positive statement about his newly acquired identity: "Perhaps it was I who was changing, why not? And in the morning, in my cave, and even sometimes at night, when the storm raged, I felt reasonably secure from the elements and mankind" (75). Careful not to take him merely literally, we recognize him as a philosopher distanced, as in a cave or cage out of time, from his fear of life in society. This philosopher does not objectively view mankind from China to Peru. He evades man and nature even while saddling with a name the rare things he sees, and he distracts himself from his psychic obligations in his cave as earlier on the mountainside.

Stasis is temporary, however. Even while telling us of his sense of security, Molloy is about to leave. Before we follow him, we should notice how his stay began. He reported casually that "I spent some time at the seaside," as if on holiday. Then he became curiously specific: "Much of my life has ebbed away before this shivering expanse. . . . Before, no, more than before, one with, spread on the sand, or in a cave. In the sand I was in my element, letting it trickle between my fingers, scooping holes that I filled in a moment later or that filled themselves in, flinging it in the air by handfuls, rolling in it" (68). Molloy claims to have been "one with" the sea but immediately retreats to dry land. His play with the sand, like his play in Lousse's garden, signals the childhood of an identity. The sand is as soft and formless as his character; no wonder he takes it as his element.

He left town and mother, however, to be like Descartes. What has Descartes to say about this predilection for sand? He says he withdrew from mankind's errors: "Non que j'imitasse pour cela les sceptiques, qui ne doutent que pour douter, et affectent d'être toujours irrésolus: car, au contraire, tout mon dessein ne tendait qu'à m'assurer, et à rejeter la terre mouvante et le sable, pour trouver le roc" (599). Descartes wishes to "rejeter la terre mouvante et le sable," desiring a firm foundation. Molloy moves the sand aimlessly, not rejecting it but "le jetant en l'air à pleines mains" (104). He is playing, not excavating down to the rock, not seeking the ideal core of the onion.

We have seen Molloy rejecting or repressing or rationalizing aids to a Jungian individuation. His mathematics gave him no therapeutic help: his numbered knocks on Mag's head established no relationship and communicated no ideas, and he derived no useful knowledge of himself from the discovery that he farted at the rate of 16.58 f.p.h. Equally, his solution of the sucking-stone problem had no valuable outcome. His reasoning here is as formless and sterile as the shifting sand of its geographical location.

Molloy achieves a stasis at the seaside. His never-never land of mathematics and philosophy, set in the plane geometry of the coastal region, offers clear days (but stormy nights, like those of his social existence, when the technicians are at work). There are no seasons; time and space scarcely exist. He is in his element. He has achieved a comic version of philosophical detachment. He had reached a similar stasis with Lousse (51)—slow physical movement between house and garden, slow mental movement in a cage out of time. Now as then, however, the cycle of flight and bivouac continues. The loose sand slips, Arsene might say (Watt, 43), and all is changed.

The imitation of Descartes is of no positive use to him; his problems are not philosophical, and reason itself is a problem for him. Molloy therefore leaves the seaside. He does not thereby cease to be Cartesian; indeed, he is indelibly scarred by Descartes. Leaving the forest, he will improve upon Descartes' advice for the lost traveler (85, 90). His movement through future obstacles will include a scattering of philosophical allusions. Descartes, however, emerged from his Dutch *poêle* with the bases of a methodical philosophy; Molloy leaves the seaside with nothing.

Beginning with systematic doubts (Molloy's questions without answers, intended to preserve his identity), Descartes discovered that "je pense, donc je suis," and thereby located "le premier principe de la philosophie que je cherchais" (603). Molloy found in thought no principle and no identity, only a means of evasion. Descartes thought himself a mind, "un esprit," in a cage out of time and space. Molloy hoped for the same, thinking back to his box or jar in Lousse's garden, but he failed, as he acknowledges now: "In your box, in your caves [at the seaside], there too there is a price to pay." Worse, "you cannot go on buying the same thing forever, with your little pittance. And unfortunately there are other needs than that of rotting in peace, it's not the word, I mean of course my mother whose image, blunted for some time past, was beginning now to harrow me again" (75–76).

"Rotting in peace"—but "peace" is not the word. Jung offered a better one when he said that the male psyche, detached from the anima, wishes to "rot away in his greatest passion, idleness" (*Integration of the Personality*, 76). Not peace after Jungian individuation, but Belacquan idleness and evasion of God's word characterize the would-be Cartesian's experience of rot by the seaside. He cannot settle, as Descartes did, for a self consisting of a rational soul indifferent to an emotional body.

Molloy's just-cited formulation is worth another comment. Descartes complains of philosophers who try to think in images even when considering those immaterial entities God and the soul. Molloy, whose existence is determined not by abstract thought but by psychic needs, is driven by his psyche's image-generating active imagination: "box," "caves," "pittance," "rot," "image," "blunted," "harrow." Images, Descartes says, can never assure us of truth (609); Jung, however, claims that "the symbolic process is an experience *in images and of images*" (*Archetypes*, 38). Thus Molloy and Descartes must part, and Molloy must give up rotting in peace for trouble and change.

Back to Bally

Molloy has not responded to the archetypal possibilities of *cave* and *sea*. His return offers him a *forest*, where he encounters a *dark man* and a *mandala* as he moves toward a *town*. He hears *voices*. He ends up in a *ditch*. The pursuer of Jungian imagery and the maternal archetype is given little to excite interest in this final section. The clear, bright expanses of the seaside supported Descartes' belief that "les choses que nous concevons fort clairement et fort distinctement sont toutes vraies" (604–5). No mythic connotations there. Now these clear expanses give way to the darkness of overhanging trees; the ocean is replaced by forest. The young women on the shore are briefly complemented by the old charcoal-burner. And near-stasis by the sea gives way to sluggish progress through the forest. These details are surely systematic and symptomatic. Beckett knows the colloquial phrase "to be in one's last ditch," which is where we and Molloy are heading.

The sketchy psychic landscape has none of the complexity of Mag or of Bally, and certainly it cannot match Lousse's gardened estate. In addition, one is increasingly distracted from the narrative by Molloy's developing tendency to lecture. He has left his Cartesian lair, but not his rational ego-consciousness. Analyses flourish in this third section. Jungian matters also persist, however, and all may yet be well, or at least explicable. Let us divide Molloy's return into sections, in order methodically to evaluate them. The two basic sections, with Cartesian appropriateness, are the material and the mental worlds.

The Material World

The material world is made up of the landscape and Molloy's body. The body is collapsing. Its movements are increasingly mechanical as it levers itself forward on crutches, pulls itself over the ground as a serpent does, and rolls into a ditch. The landscape is primarily forest, although Molloy begins by describing his hometown, as he began his first trip to town by describing his mother. He never reached her; he will never reach Bally.

Heading inland, he speaks knowledgeably about that town. Then his tone alters, and he describes his body, emphasizing the legs, rectum, and urinary apparatus. Next he reports his movement through the forest. He stumbles on an anecdote: his encounter with the charcoal-burner. That obstacle dispatched, he continues to hobble and then crawls. He reaches the plain and falls into a ditch, from which he hears a voice. Waiting for help, he glimpses fragments of his past life as convention demands. Then he abandons his identity and his report.

Factual materials are detailed and the voice chatty, especially with reference to Bally. His account of the swamp, the town, and the Public Works Department comes oddly from a man who cannot remember the name of that town. (Also curious is his mention of anything "said to the contrary" about the location of Bally—specifically, that "all were agreed . . . that their town was on the sea" and that its principal beauty was a tidal creek. None of that has been said. It will be said, yes, but by Moran [134], who also says that the creek [not swamp] was actually an underground lake. Does this confusion mean that "Moran" was conceived first or was placed first?) The swamp is to be drained or transformed into "a vast port and docks, or into a city on piles for the workers," but at present "an incalculable number of human lives were yearly engulfed" in it. Molloy experienced its dangers himself "at a period of my life richer in illusions than the one I am trying to patch together here" (76).

This area is soaked in psychological implications, yet the topic appears and disappears in half a page. Molloy will neither encounter nor avoid any wetlands. Beckett requires us to interpret psychologically the bog, Molloy's cold indifference to the lives lost in it, and its disappearance from his world. Leaving the clear divisions of sea, shore, and sky, Molloy reluctantly heads for town and mother. Leaving the rational ego-consciousness, he seeks "the within, all that inner space one never sees" (10), the Jungian collective unconscious and his maternal anima. Now sea, shore, and sky have become regions of psychical experience.

But "you will not, of course, have pictured sharp frontiers like the artificial ones drawn in political geography. . . . A pictorial representation of something so intangible as psychical processes" must be presented less precisely. "After making the separation we must allow what we have separated to merge together once more." This explanation is not Molloy's or Beckett's or even Jung's. It is Freud's remark about a literal sketch of the psyche that he has just presented in his *New Introductory Lectures*. Molloy recalls it, noting that "regions do not suddenly end, as far as I know, but gradually merge into one another."

Molloy is about to avoid the swamp and hobble into the unconscious. Freud goes on from his sketch and his warning about blurred boundaries to speak of the possibility of knowing the activities of the unconscious. He mentions the means by which "our perception may be able to grasp happenings in the depths of the ego and in the id which were otherwise inaccessible to it." Perhaps thinking of his rival Jung's interest in mandalas (soon to be found in Molloy's forest), Freud speaks of "certain mystical practices" and acknowledges that they may promote such a perception of the unconscious. "It may safely be doubted, however," he adds, "whether this road will lead us to the ultimate truths from which salvation is to be expected. Nevertheless it may be admitted that the therapeutic efforts of psycho-analysis have chosen a similar line of approach" (XXII, 80).

"This road" leads into the topographical metaphor of Freud's drawing. That appropriate image may not have fixed Freud's discussion in Beckett's imagination, but another one surely did. Freud concludes his discussion of the search for the unconscious by mordantly extending his geographical image. It is the intention of psychoanalysis, he says, "to strengthen the ego, to make it more independent of the super-ego, to widen its field of perception and enlarge its organization, so that it can appropriate fresh portions of the id. Where id was, there ego shall be. It is a work of culture—not unlike the draining of the Zuider Zee" (XXII, 80). (The appropriation of fresh portions of the id approximates Jung's requirement that the masculine ego-consciousness raise into itself the maternal anima.) At that time the Zuider Zee was a large marshy inlet from the North Sea on the north coast of the Netherlands (an appropriately named location for the unconscious). Attempts to cut it off from the sea and turn it into a navigable lake had failed, and attempts to drain it were also failing. Freud's apparently straightforward comparison was therefore drily ironic, and Beckett is even less sanguine about the effectiveness of therapy than was Freud.

Thus the swamp between Bally and the sea, in which many lives were lost, takes a psychological sense from Molloy's situation, from his psychological landscape, and from Freud's skeptical image of the doubtful appropriation of the id by consciousness. Molloy, however, is indifferent to the lives lost, he who once longed for a fellow or frère. He will stay dry during his present trip toward town. If it is troubling that after the introduction of this complex image nothing should come of it, then what troubles us explains our troubles. Molloy's dismissal suggests a rational fending off of the unconscious.

Imitating him, we ignore the connection of that "stinking steaming swamp" (76) with the "palude che 'l gran puzzo spira," the stinking swamp that surrounds the City of Dis and that Dante and Vergil cannot cross because they lack anger (*Inferno*, IX, 31). We plunge into the forest, and we hasten toward Molloy's encounter with the charcoal-burner, which curiously lacks anger.

The Mandala and the Charcoal-Burner

The man who once doubted whether anyone's identity could be much changed has undergone several changes. He has set out for his mother and then fled from her and all anima figures. He has mentioned and then evaded the swamp of the unconscious. As we will see, he has abandoned his trust in clear ideas. He will conclude so detached from his identity that he will speak of Molloy in the third person.

The most extended acting-out of his changes after Lousse is his encounter with the charcoal-burner. Since one's identity determines one's relation to others, and since Molloy's psychic self is incomplete, he naturally hesitated over which man to follow, A or C, in search of a fellow or frère. He imagined being rejected by A; C was no more accessible. Therefore, he set out to set things straight between him and his mother, even while making it clear that he had no love for her. Molloy's early craving for a fellow generated two possibilities. Now a possible fellow appears, the charcoal-burner. Molloy says: "I say charcoal-burner, but I really don't know. I see smoke somewhere. That's something that never escapes me, smoke" (84).

The vagueness and smoke recall Molloy's first description of A and C. Wondering if he will ever see them again—"and what do I mean by seeing and seeing again?"—he turned to the twin images of the orchestra conductor and of "smoke, sticks, flesh, hair, at evening, afar, flung about the craving for a fellow" (15). Here the smoke, sticks, and so forth recur to form a charcoal-burner, and Molloy's craving for a fellow is thereby recalled. In this variation, however, it is the dark solitary figure who feels the craving, while the force implied by C's stout stick now activates Molloy's crutches. Molloy's need for affection is reanimated negatively; he projects it outside himself and punishes it.

Because the encounter is part of a dream sequence, we must respect its context. To recognize C in the charcoal-burner and to note these shifts of craving and force constitute only a beginning. The context is Molloy's slow journey through the forest. He has just emphasized a curious feature of that forest. Before describing the charcoal-burner, Molloy reports that "from time to time" he came upon "a kind of crossroads, you know, a star, or circus." The original phrasing is "une sorte de carrefour, une étoile" (127); Beckett emphasizes a significance by adding "circus." The images are Jungian variants of the mandala, which represents the center of a labyrinth, the organized wholeness of a psyche, and the achievement of order out of chaos. (A few sentences later Molloy will add a Dantean mandala image by misremembering Ruth/Edith's name as Rose.)

In "Concerning Mandala Symbolism" (this convenient text was published after *Molloy*), Jung lists "the formal elements of mandala symbolism." He speaks first of the circle (Latin: *circus*). Then he adds some of its developments, with his own italics: "2. The circle is elaborated into a *flower* (rose, lotus) or a *wheel*. 3. A centre expressed by a *sun, star,* or *cross* . . ." (*Archetypes*, 361). "Mandala" means "circle" in Sanskrit, he says. For Jung the term extends to almost any drawing, painting, sculpture, or verbal image in which a complex of materials is presented as harmoniously organized, especially around a center. These materials are taken to represent the maker's active psychic components. Noting the mandala, we notice also the "cross" associated with Molloy's near-crucifixion.

Molloy's reaction to the crossroads in the forest is extensive: "Turning then methodically to face the radiating paths in turn, hoping for I know not what, I described a complete circle, or less than a circle, or more than a circle, so great was the resemblance between them. Here the gloom was not so thick and I made haste to leave it. I don't like gloom to lighten, there's something shady about it" (83). He encountered such crossroads "from time to time. What tenderness in these little words, what savagery." "Hoping," "tenderness," "savagery"! Molloy will soon sum up his encounter with the charcoal-burner as "an incident of no interest in itself, like all that has a moral" (85). The disparity between event and emotion in these juxtaposed scenes obliges us to seek morals in both.

Jung says that the mandala is relevant to a search for one's mother: "Because of the protection it implies, the magic circle or mandala can be a form of mother archetype" (*Archetypes*, 81; see *Symbols*, 370–71, for crossroads, mother, and Hecate). Jung does not take an encounter with a crossroads or other mandala as the equivalent of an important encounter with the maternal anima. This image of the mother may be offered by Molloy's psyche as a place where all roads meet and as a promise of enlightenment. Something hidden in the darkness of the unconscious might be brought to light, but Molloy, making a bad pun, rejects the offer. As far as he can manage, he retreats from the crossroads the way he came. Soon he will report that "all my life, I think I had been going to my mother. . . . And when I was with her, and I often succeeded, I left her without having done anything. And when I was no longer with her I was again on my way to her, hoping to do better the next time" (87). The elements of this later realization are imaged in these events in the forest.

The arrival at the crossroads is not unique; "from time to time" he has had that experience. The tenderness lies perhaps in the repeated opportunity for enlightenment, the savagery in its repeated failure. Even in his cage out of time Molloy could hear clocks chiming "from time to time" (48). Now, in the wilderness, time still warns him that he cannot delay forever. A voice will soon add its own warning: "nimis sero." His past trips to his mother were undertaken while "hoping to do better"; now he turns around in the crossroads "hoping for I know not what."

Molloy says that his intention in finding his mother is that of "establishing our relations on a less precarious footing" (87). In fact, however, his footing is getting worse; he is on crutches now and will soon abandon his "erect motion, that of man" (89). He also has no sense of direction. In one of these crosses, stars, circles, circuses, he turns "methodically," but his achievement of a "complete circle, or less than a circle, or more than a circle" suggests at best the approximation that characterized Descartes' traveler's success in escaping the forest, and at worst an unacknowledged desire to go backward, not forward.

Molloy's bad joke—there's something shady about gloom lightening—may originate with Jung: "The anima also stands for the 'inferior function' [of a male psyche] and for that reason frequently has a shady character; in fact she sometimes stands for evil itself." Jung adds that in Christian theology "the feminine element in the deity is kept very dark, the interpretation of the Holy Ghost as Sophia being considered heretical" (*Psychology and Alchemy*, 150, 152). When gloom lightens, Sophia is no longer kept very dark; she has a frightening shady character.

Molloy flees the crossroads, objecting to its shadiness (set not against illumination but against the preferable darkness) while associating it with hope, tenderness, and savagery. His narrative moves quickly to a projection of himself who mixes light and darkness and to an action in which hope and tenderness are overcome by Molloy's savagery.

The charcoal-burner is a "dirty old brute" whose work turns the dark forest into black charcoal and potential fire, but Molloy does not like gloom to lighten. The man is "sick with solitude probably." (This from Molloy!) He wishes Molloy to "share his hut," as Lousse and Ruth/Edith and Mag had variously wished him to do. Molloy knocks him down and kicks him "with method," adding that he "always had a mania for symmetry." ("Mania for symmetry" combines a rational value with its irrational motive; we recall "inordinately formal" [50].) His rational account of savage acts detaches him from them and from the charcoal-burner. He boasts that he was "showing what stuff you are made of." His original idiom expresses the link between attacker and victim: "il est quelquefois permis de montrer de quel bois on se chauffe" (130).

Moran kills an image of himself and does not recall the event. Molloy's report of attacking this partial self is similarly detached. His tone differs completely from his emotional reaction to the phrase "from time to time." He describes in cold detail an absurd series of acrobatics on crutches. Like his assertion about the rapture of using crutches, this attack dramatizes absurd reasoning motivated by irrational desire; it is a contrivance. The event is "an incident of no interest in itself, like all that has a moral." The French is ambivalent: "comme tout ce qui instruit, ou avertit." Molloy takes no instruction or warning from the encounter, which does indeed show what stuff his ego-consciousness is now made of.

Jung offers a partial explanation for this attack. Analyzing a series of dreams, he reaches one that is set in "a primeval forest" and features "a large ape-man, bear, or cave-man . . . with a club," who threatens the dreamer.

This figure is interpreted as "the god who has become an animal," "the animal divinity of the primordial psyche." The threatening savage is driven away by a third dream-figure associated with Goethe's *Faust* and "Mephisto and his matter-of-fact point of view" (*Psychology and Alchemy*, 89, 91). Molloy's matter-of-factness is rational, and the charcoal-burner offers only emotional hospitality.

To stay in the forest, to become a fellow charcoal-burner, would necessitate Molloy's subordination to the forest, that wild version of the anima, and to an existence of irrational emotionality. Molloy observes that he might have loved him when younger. This speculation suggests that the charcoal-burner might once have served as a fellow or frère and also that solitude had taught the charcoal-burner the value of love. But Molloy quickly turns to mathematics to persuade himself that he would not have loved the man. Then he adds: "I never really had much love to spare, but all the same I had my little quota, when I was small, and it went to the old men, when it could. And I even think I had time to love one or two . . ." (83). Molloy evokes father-figures, not his biological father; we are in the collective unconscious. He does not mention a mother.

Molloy's report of childhood love emphasizes our awareness that love has long since disappeared from his stock of feelings, as his many harsh comments about Mag, Lousse, and Ruth/Edith have especially shown. His strongest feelings (and that phrase is itself too strong) concern himself, and they are not positive. In unemotionally rejecting the charcoal-burner he appears to reject even himself. He still must seek his mother, however: "I could not, stay in the forest I mean, I was not free to. That is to say I could have, physically nothing could have been easier, but I was not purely physical, I lacked something . . ." (86). The simple charcoal-burner may offer an evasion of Molloy's psychic task that his anima will not accept. His ego-consciousness now demands his attention and ours.

The Mental World

Molloy leaves the seaside after praising his eyesight and the views it gave him—of few items and those material and factual, and all "clear and distinct," a phrase recurrent in Descartes' *Discours de la méthode*. Now, however, he moves through a Dantean dark wood of error, bereft of enlightening embodiments of the rejected anima and reduced to unrecognized archetypes of transformation. Unable to see into them, Molloy's rational ego-consciousness turns inward. It discovers a relatively safe area, its memory of the external world, and passes some time by recalling civic-history details about Bally and its swamp, as if his return to town were to be merely touristic. Then the ego-consciousness is obliged to think. Rather than thinking about psychological concerns, it thinks about its thinking. That subject, like the outer world, is obscured by darkness. Rather than plan a rational future, Molloy raises the subject of "presentiments," which he divides methodically into false and true.

Descartes' first precept obliged him "de ne comprendre rien de plus en mes jugements, que ce qui se présenterait . . . clairement et si distinctement à mon esprit" (586). He emphasized these terms in claiming that "les choses que nous concevons fort clairement et fort distinctement sont toutes vraies" (604–5). The equation of clear and distinct with true, which Molloy had accepted at the seaside, now no longer applies. He speaks not of pre*views* but of pre*sentiments,* and when he examines false presentiments, he reports that they are clearer and more distinct than true presentiments: "I think that all that is false may more readily be reduced to notions clear and distinct, distinct from all other notions. But I may be wrong" (82). This attitude is a final one. We have heard it in the narrator's distrust of thought when evoking A and C: "I wouldn't know myself, if I thought of it"; "a pomeranian I think, but I don't think so. I wasn't sure at the time and I'm still not sure, though I've hardly thought about it"; "Yes, it was an orange pomeranian, the less I think of it the more certain I am. And yet" (10–12).

For Jungians this discarding of masculine analytic rationality must be at least potentially admirable. The anima hath its reasons that the reason knoweth not, and Molloy may be moving toward its irrational wisdom. That wisdom should include feelings, sentiments, but Molloy will soon discard sentiments.

Heading into the forest, he recalls and alters the Cartesian advice that enabled him to leave Bally. Descartes recommended that the lost traveler move in a straight line. Molloy has heard that someone so doing will move in a circle. Therefore, "I did my best to go in a circle, hoping in this way to go in a straight line. For I stopped being half-witted and became sly, whenever I took the trouble" (85). Slyness (consider Wylie) is a form of reasoning. Molloy relevantly adds that "my head was a storehouse of useful knowledge." Readers still approving of homo mensura may approve. Beckett's own judgment appears belatedly, in *The Unnamable.* There Mahood repeats the temptation to approve of knowledge: "No denying it, I'm confoundedly well informed." Yet he sets out on his own version of Molloy's circular path, the "inverted spiral" that will lead him, on crutches, back home. (Molloy's attempt to go straight by circling might straighten out an inadvertent circle but might turn it into an inverse spiral.) "No good wriggling," Mahood now says, "I'm a mine of useless knowledge" (317). Molloy's useful knowledge must be classed with those clear and distinct false presentiments. Knowledge, like rationality, is of dubious value for Molloy's therapy.

The weakness of rationality and the possible irrelevance of knowledge to this psychic search do not guarantee the usefulness of irrationality. Molloy finishes off his discussion of clear and distinct notions with a passage unclear and indistinct, but not therefore better. Having divided his presentiments into true and false, he denies their existence, claiming only episentiments. "I knew in advance," he explains, and adds that this advance knowledge disappeared "when the time came . . . and when the time was past I no longer knew either, I regained my ignorance" (82). Molloy or Beckett may be varying a passage in the *Inferno* (X, 97–108), about the fleeting knowledge possessed by the damned. (H. R. Huse suggests that the placement of that passage exposes the "fallibility of human reason" displayed by the heretics of that canto [53]. Moran offers another variation of this topic [133].) Molloy's stumbling explanation reinforces the implicit criticism of Cartesian reason. It also emphasizes the connection of words with the masculine intellect as the journey continues.

A complementary topic takes on increased significance during this journey: religion. Molloy has often referred to religious matters, of course. It was the angelus that made him think of going to his mother; his first arrival in Bally occasioned an obscure assertion about "one day" telling "you" of his "passion without form or stations" (25); he misunderstood an illumination from Isaiah or Jeremiah; recognizing that he could not stay in the forest, he confessed that "I have greatly sinned, at all times, greatly sinned against my prompters" (86); and most obviously fear of crucifixion caused him to leave Lousse.

Now—even before his rejection of clear and distinct ideas—he reports, again directly to the imagined listener, that his progress toward his mother has become, "saving your presence, . . . a veritable calvary, with no limit to its stations and no hope of crucifixion"—a progress that he calls "the immemorial expiation" (78; "expiation" gives a retrospective religious connotation to "pensum" [32]). "No hope of crucifixion" might well surprise us, set against his incapacitating fear of it chez Lousse. Now, when only "episentiments" remain, passion—even intensely painful passion—is unavailable to this intellect detached from the decaying body.

Yet Molloy cannot celebrate this detachment; neither passion nor fear of passion remains. A curious instance of this detachment is compressed into a brief moment as Molloy bumbles through the dark forest. He wonders if he will ever see the light. We know, and he knows, that light illuminates a serious topic. In the past he has often spoken of it harshly, while occasionally celebrating an achieved illumination. Now he evaluates the sought-for light as "hated," then as "at least unloved," and then as meaning nothing to him now (78). In two sentences he detaches himself from any interest in light—that is, any desire to understand the relation between him and his maternal anima. He unplugs any emotional motive, even hatred. Illumination and salvation are dismissed.

The Voices and Molloy's Mind

After his encounter with the charcoal-burner, Molloy explained that he could not stay in the forest because he was not merely physical. He added a concern itself not physical: "I was not free to. . . . I would have had the feeling, if I had stayed in the forest, of going against an imperative" (86). He says much on that subject. On the mountainside he had imagined being rejected by A and left alone and free: "Free to do what, to do nothing, to know, but what, the laws of the mind perhaps, of my mind" (13). Soon he doubted that freedom: "Can it be we are not free?" (36). Now he knows that he is not free to stay in the forest, but he has not accepted this imperative as his own desire. He has not understood freedom as the recognition of psychic necessity.

Earlier he had spoken of the obligation to encounter his mother, but always briefly. Now he is able to stay with the topic, develop it, and discover one of the laws of his mind. No wonder he will conclude this discussion by remarking that "this is taking a queer turn" (87). Any reader hearing its narrator explain "Molloy" might say much the same thing, but to us Jungians the event is particularly intelligible and promising. Nearing the end of a series of Jungian dreams, Molloy begins to become conscious of his psychic condition.

His ego-consciousness—nearly detached from the rest of his psyche—almost ceases to evade its psychic responsibilities. No mathematics now; Molloy investigates the voices. He is reasoning, yes, but about a proper subject. He develops the subject, not with Cartesian method, into several parts. Recognition of the voice's repeated imperative leads to a wider consideration of his experiences of that voice. Their chronological extent leads to an admission of their importance. His present verbal expression of these and other psychic matters leads him to recognize the falseness, the artifice, of his report's dramatized presentation of them. That is, he senses truth outside the words but still within the dream-series of the narrative, truth not intelligible as reported. Nevertheless, his rational ego-consciousness implicitly accedes again to the irrational obligation to express—that is, to raise into verbal consciousness—its repressed materials. So doing, it continues the narrative just acknowledged as a lie.

These discoveries deserve consideration. Molloy is free physically to stay in the forest, away from town and mother. He has food—roots, berries, mushrooms, carobs—and shelter (the forest itself; see the Unnamable's recollections of it [399]). "But I was not purely physical, I lacked something." The acknowledgment that he lacks something is important. Its comic last phrase catches the attention, since one expects another component beyond the physical, not an absence. That Beckett added the phrase in translation also suggests its significance.

Molloy has a psyche, not physical and motivated by what it lacks. Molloy lacks a secure relation with his mother and senses a psychic need for one. The need as experienced by his rational mind is verbal. Therefore "I would have had the feeling, if I had stayed in the forest, of going against an imperative." He has heard such imperatives before. Hearing "something new" in the latest imperative, he identifies it as a warning: "Perhaps it is already too late. It was in Latin, nimis sero. . . . Charming things, hypothetical imperatives" (87). Molloy has none of our Jungian training and terms, but while evading psychology he has dabbled in Stoic and Cartesian philosophies. He can identify these imperative messages philosophically, and he can understand the Latin tag. (Beckett may have retrieved Molloy's Kantian term from his "Whoroscope" notebook of c. 1936. There, following a long passage copied from Kant, he added in quotation marks: "His rare imperatives were hypothetical." This iambic alexandrine is probably his own, noted for later use.)

Considering imperatives, Molloy properly turns his hypothetical (that is, personal, individual, not categorical) imperatives into psychological ones, while associating such imperatives with religion and the theater. First he recognizes that his imperatives have a single subject: "They nearly all bore on the same question, that of my relations with my mother, and on the importance of bringing as soon as possible some light to bear on these and even on the kind of light that should be brought to bear and the most effective means of doing so." His mention of light is no surprise, but he adds a surprising religious judgment: to resist an imperative is "a fault, almost a sin"—in this context a sin against the light.

Continuing to speak of sin, he adds another metaphor, this one from the theater. "I have greatly sinned at all times, greatly sinned against my prompters." The conjunction of these two sources of metaphor suggests that to avoid sin one must *act* as prompted. We recall his regret, during his first visit to town, that no school eduation had taught him the "systematic decorum" underlying behavior, and his claim, in another theater image, that his "repertory of permitted attitudes has never ceased to grow" (25). To the theatrical term "prompters" he adds in the French several others, in speaking of this most recent imperative: "Dans la forme je crus remarquer un detail inédit. Car après le couplet habituel vint se placer l'avertissement solonnel que voici, Il est peut-être déjà trop tard" (133). Here "inédit" suggests a new theatrical work and "couplet" an actor's tirade. Molloy's unconscious is, yet again, prompting him to take on a new role.

The voices expressing hypothetical imperatives may be distinguished from the prompters. The voices are not concerned with social behavior. They voice the demands of the maternal anima, or they express the Jungian psyche's need for its fulfillment, its individuation. They push Molloy toward his mother—only to abandon him on the road, he says. The sense of this abandonment is not that the voices fail Molloy but that his ego-consciousness will not accept responsibility. Therefore it represses either the information or the needed motivational force. Molloy's present recognitions do not indicate that his lifelong evasion has ended, but this new imperative is specially intense. He presents it as from outside him, and he tries briefly to be skeptical. Its intensity, however, is indicated by its raising of his consciousness; he acknowledges that his voices "nearly all bore on the same question, that of my relations with my mother."

We heard of the faint voice in the back regions of his mind that does not speak to him (42) and "the small voice saying, Get out of here, Molloy" (59) that badgered him to leave Lousse. Left to his own resources in the rainy town, he "began to think, that is to say to listen harder" (61). None of these voices spoke of his mother. Now he claims to have heard this positive voice often. There is no contradiction here; the dream recycles its materials to convey new information. The new information is that Molloy now acknowledges his psychic need as long-lasting, important, and expressed by voices different from those of the prompters.

Perhaps the prompters speak for society and tell Molloy to act properly, as the superego might be expected to do. Freud says that the superego's "compulsive character . . . manifests itself in the form of a categorical imperative" (XVIII, 25). Perhaps this is why Molloy recognizes a hypothetical rather than categorical imperative, to stress that it comes not from society but from his individual psyche. The voices are not at odds, however; both imperatives and prompters speak about his need for Jungian individuation; outer and inner worlds concur in urging Molloy to seek town and mother.

Jung takes a great interest in the phenomenon of the voice, in contexts relevant to Beckett's composition of "Molloy" as a narrative that stitches together psychic experiences peopled with archetypal figures and situations, all acting out the attempts of Molloy's ego-consciousness to come to terms with his maternal anima. Jung's sense of such a dream series, especially when generated by a patient undergoing therapy, is of a narrative that shapes itself toward a clear conclusion. The unconscious gives the patient trouble because his ego-consciousness has repressed or evaded its therapeutic messages. With professional aid, repression and evasion are removed or at least weakened, and then the messages can be transmitted intelligibly and acted on by the ego-consciousness.

Molloy is nearing the end of his dream series. He has been notably unwilling to understand his experiences, even turning a biblical injunction to seek the true object of love into a mathematical hint about sucking-stones. He never reflects on his past life, about which we hear only bits and pieces, nor does he think over such narrative events as his stay with Lousse. He says that his encounter with the charcoal-burner has a moral, but he reports none. More understandably, he has remained vague about his intentions with regard to his mother.

Nevertheless, even after the anima figures faded into archetypal images of situation, the voices persisted. Now his ego-consciousness accepts some some meanings. They are not grand ones, and Jung's explanation of the event will appear overstated: "The phenomenon of the 'voice' in dreams always has for the dreamer the final and indisputable character of . . . some truth or condition that is past all doubt. The fact that a sense of the remote past has been established, that contact has been made with the deeper layers of the psyche, is accepted by the unconscious personality of the dreamer and communicates itself to his conscious mind as a feeling of comparative security" (*Psychology and Alchemy*, 87). Explicitly, Molloy's voice offers only an imperative demand for action coupled with a warning, not a final truth or condition, but Molloy is able to interpret this demand so as to discover deeper meanings in it (86–87).

Beckett does not use Jung's idea simply. Molloy acknowledges the importance of bringing some light to bear on his relations with his mother, but for "a feeling of comparative security" Beckett substitutes evasiveness. (Jung's patients were willingly undergoing therapy; Molloy is not.) Admittedly not free because he lacks something, and obliged to obey an order, Molloy imagines a counter-order: "the unspoken entreaty, Don't do it, Molloy" (87). This attempt to wriggle out of his duty is only momentary. He quickly refuses to blame "this so-called imperative"; "fortunately it did no more than stress, the better to mock if you like, an innate velleity." The French expands this acceptance while using yet another theatrical term, "apostrophes": "Heureusement qu'en somme il ne faisait qu'appuyer, pour ridiculiser par la suite si l'on veut, une disposition permanente et qui n'avait pas besoin d'apostrophes pour se savoir velléitaire" (134).

The Jungian dreamer's submissive acceptance of a verbal "contact . . . made with the deeper layers of the psyche [that] communicates itself to his conscious mind as a feeling of comparative security" has not yet occurred. At the very end of "Molloy," the man who once struggled against the social worker's and the young woman's offers of food will hear "Don't fret, Molloy, we're coming." He will accept this offer of charity: "Well, I suppose you have to try everything once, succour included, to get a complete picture of the resources of their planet" (91). Even then he will keep his distance; it is their planet, not his. Once returned, he will describe his missing mother's possessions not as "hers" or "ours" but as his own. Sharing is beyond him. We may still find in the present passage, however, something positive in his acknowledgment of a velleity.

The Narrator's Lying Voice

Having acknowledged the need to get matters straight between him and his mother, Molloy discusses his reliability as narrator. All the narrative occurrences of "I said," of "a voice saying," and of other characters' reported speeches, and even of such rhetorical figures as "I had the impression," were not factually correct and therefore not true, he now says: "I am merely complying with the convention that demands you either lie or hold your peace" (88). Outside the psychological context of "Molloy" this admission might be no more than another literary reference to the age-old problem of locating fiction in relation to truth and falsehood. Molloy, however, develops a different topic, one that he spoke of more assuredly early on ("Not to want to say, not to know what you want to say . . ." [28]) and that the Unnamable will also try to work out (396). This topic is psychological rather than moral.

Molloy avoids the Jungian images of his story; he says that the motive for speech is something going wrong with the silence, thereby causing "a kind of consciousness." Anxiety results. (We recall James's *Varieties*.) It must be allayed: "Somewhere something had changed, so that I too had to change, or the world too had to change, in order for nothing to be changed" (88). For Watt a similar difficulty was essentially verbal; his "need of semantic succour" sent him in search of "a pillow of old words, for a head" (83, 117). But for Molloy the words are lies. Anxiety is now a much more serious matter.

Beckett had put it psychologically, with Schopenhauer's aid, as early as *Proust*: "Life is a succession of habits, since the individual is a succession of individuals; the world being a projection of the individual's consciousness (an objectivation of the individual's will, Schopenhauer would say), the pact must be continually renewed. . . . The creation of the world did not take place once and for all time, but takes place every day" (19). By the writing of "Molloy" these adjustments have become more serious and inconclusive. Molloy's worlds are psychic projections not merely for the day but of long and painful duration, and peace treaties have been replaced by the flight or submission of his ego-consciousness. Jung's notion of a psyche not yet complete, an individuation still in process, makes basic to existence the problems of these earlier "countless subjects."

Molloy adds an additional problem in doubting the truth of words. This doubt is partially a result of the ego-consciousness's verbal reasoning as it describes Molloy's psychic state. With Lousse, Molloy reported that "my sense of identity was wrapped in a namelessness often hard to penetrate" (31). Now naming is no solution, since he denies the accuracy of any naming. Worse will come before that subject is completed, much worse.

Molloy insists that in making his report he has merely invented speeches (and, by necessary extension, scenes and characters). He thereby removes one basis for the credibility of the report. His labeling of these inventions as lies removes even the fiction writer's claim of general truth. We know another kind of truthfulness, however, that of psychology. Molloy's comments are not analytical but evasive. A patient's dreams and his discussions of them reveal psychic truths even when the dreamer denies or misunderstands their meanings. In fact, his denial and misunderstanding are themselves a part of the psyche's true testimony. So when the evasive narrator stops denying and finishes his story, we continue to listen carefully.

Into the forest he plunges again, unprompted. He abandons human motion, "crawling on his belly, like a reptile," his hat jammed down on his head. "From time to time I blew my horn"; "from time to time I said, Mother, to encourage me I suppose" (89–90). Mostly his eyes are closed. When he reaches the plain, his report implies no success. He realizes—or asserts—the impossibility of crossing it and the absurdity of such questions as whether that distant town is his and whether his mother is still alive. They are questions "of undeniable interest on the plane of pure knowledge," he notes, dismissing the rational intellect with a plain pun. He wonders about the birds absent from the forest. As instructed, he does not fret. In one last flicker of negative velleity his identity expires: "I longed to go back to the forest. Oh not a real longing. Molloy could stay, where he happened to be."

Those scattered materials replace any increasing focus on his goal, and the narrator's abandoning the third-person Molloy in his ditch suggests indifference to that identity's psychic health. In his last ditch and unable to move, Molloy submits to the voice while remaining passive and detached.

Success seems far away. But especially in the company of a cripple we cannot leap to conclusions.

The Overtones and Implications of the Ending

Jung emphasized the idea that psychic problems involving the collective unconscious are distinguished by their expression in archetypal images and mythical situations. Beckett has used such images and situations, adding materials from literature, philosophy, and history. These latter sources expand his psychological materials into cultural areas that share the impersonal, collective nature of his psychic material. In Molloy's thoughts and images as in his experiences, the psyche is not merely personal. One such source dominates the end of "Molloy," where Beckett employs almost structurally Dante's *Purgatorio* and especially the Earthly Paradise, that goal of Dante's climbing. Already one may sense metaphoric relevance; will Molloy purge himself of his psychic sins?

The allusions are not straightforward. Dante climbs to the top of a mountain and is purged there of his sins and of any further dependence upon another's aid. Molloy, long since down from his mountainside, crawls horizontally. He remains dependent and will end up where his life began, in his mother's bed. Crowned and mitred by Vergil, Dante is told: "Libero, dritto e sano è tuo arbitrio, / e fallo fora non fare a suo senno" (XXVII, 140–41; free, upright and healthy is your will, and it would be wrong not to do as it wishes). Molloy, on the other hand, responds to the sufferings caused by his unconscious and his ego-consciousness with evasions and errors. He is not a self-sufficient individual. His report must be submitted to others, and it will be criticized from the start by the messenger and his employers (7).

As Dante rises to the peak of Purgatory, his increasingly perceptive intellect is emphasized in images especially of blindness and seeing. Beatrice's eyes are important. She is moved to aid him by love, and she communicates that love. When she appears in the Earthly Paradise, Dante responds immediately: "d'antico amor sentì la gran potenza" (XXX, 39; [my spirit] felt the great power of old love). Beatrice immediately scolds him, however, and he compares her to a mother, himself to a child:

Così la madre al figlio par superba,
   com'ella parve a me; perché d'amaro
   sente il sapor de la pietade acerba. (XXX, 79-81)

[As the mother seems harsh to her child, so she seemed to me; because the taste of stern pity is bitter.]

That stern mother is a good one, but Dante does not present Mother Eve so positively. He speaks of the Paradise lost by Adam and Eve as "quantunque perdeo l'antica madre" (XXX, 52; all that the old mother lost).

The comparisons and contrasts are clear. The bright-eyed Beatrice in the Earthly Paradise provides a strict but desirable goal, far different from that evoked by *l'antica madre* Mag, who is blind and poisons the air (91) and who inhabits no Paradise. Beatrice, turned maternal, rebukes Dante for his slowness (he too trimmed after an easier love), but Molloy displays much worse error in his wanderings, while his saying "Mother" mechanically from time to time as he crawls through the forest suggests no intense desire for or faith in his goal. (It may, however, suggest the continuation of the early parent-child relation, since in French he uses not "mère" but the intimate "maman.")

Dante hears ritual hymns as he climbs the mountain of Purgatory, and he notes the many birds singing in the Earthly Paradise, undeterred by the strong breeze. Molloy speaks of "the bronze-still boughs, which no breath ever stirred" (85), and he hears no birds. He also hears no "forest murmurs" and is curiously disappointed: "to have been looking forward to the celebrated murmurs if to nothing else, and to succeed only in hearing . . . a gong" (89). The murmurs missing here suggest those explained to Dante by a lovely lady: "il suon de la foresta" (XXVIII, 85–108). Molloy cannot explain their absence and has met no woman in the forest. The gong (which will sound later for Moran's dinner and sounded for Mohammed as one voice of his angelic messenger) may be reminding Molloy of the passing of time: nimis sero, from the town across the plain. Molloy's response is merely to blow his own horn.

Dante emphasizes seeing as a means of learning and light as enlightenment; therefore, when night comes to the mountain of Purgatory, all upward movement must cease (XXVII, 74–75). Molloy has little use for light. He moves in the dark and horizontally, with his eyes closed, on his belly like a reptile. Dante's Earthly Paradise helps to identify Molloy's lost paradise, in which the toad or rat of Bally society is now a serpent.

When Beatrice rebukes Dante, he is overcome by her anger and beauty, and he falls unconscious. He wakes to find her towing him across the Lethe. Molloy falls into a dry ditch, after no such meeting or enlightenment. Lethe is suggested only by his forgetting how he was towed thence to his mother's bed. Dante is accompanied by a well-wishing fellow or frère, throughout his journey to the top of the mountain, while Molloy rejects any companion. The contrasts go on and on. Dante's faint negative presence shows us what we see in any case, that the end of Molloy's journey is painfully unattended by any cumulative or sudden wisdom, that its outcome is uncertain, and that no salvation is achieved. The allusions to the *Purgatorio* offer meaningful contrasts to a proper Jungian individuation.

Our comic distancing from Molloy here is also reinforced by echoes of Freud. This Jungian story of a search for the mother ends without a mother and without a climax, but a diligent Freudian interpretation might deny this negation. The shut-eyed Molloy crawls like a blind phallic serpent into a ditch, saying "Mother." There he collapses, all energy spent. These images and acts would make the event the comic sexual climax of an Oedipal yearning. The voice that urges him not to fret since help is on the way suggests a therapist coming to cleanse him of his guilt. Then—sexual union being "the little death"—scenes of his past life flash before his eyes as his existence ends. So interpreted (and what Freudian could resist?), "Molloy" does have an ending, and a happily incestuous one. But we Jungians cannot take this interpretation seriously.

Of course, the Freudian might aim higher, concentrating not on comic intercourse in the ditch but on Molloy's achievement of stasis, his unfretful final recollections that indicate no anxiety. This Freudian might quote Freud on the end of a series of psychological events: "In the theory of psychoanalysis we have no hesitation in assuming that the course taken by mental events is automatically regulated by the pleasure principle. We believe, that is to say, that the course of these events is invariably set in motion by an unpleasurable tension, and that it takes a direction such that its final outcome coincides with a lowering of that tension—that is, with an avoidance of unpleasure or a production of pleasure" (XVIII, 7). The reader finishing the last page of "Molloy" for the first time surely turns the page expectantly; for him there has been no release of tension. For Molloy, too, there is more to come. He must reach his mother's room. In a sense, however, a painful sense, he has indeed reached a condition of stasis, as we shall see. That stasis is not Freudian, however, but meaningfully Jungian.

When thou hast done thou hast not done,
for I have more.

The conclusion of "Molloy" is deliberately inconclusive. Like the conclusion of *Finnegans Wake*, it obliges us to return to the beginning to recall that Molloy did reach his mother's room and that she was either dead when he arrived or died later. His indifferent ignorance on this point, inexplicable back then, now indicates that he had not been "reduced to looking for a meaning to my life" (19)—or that he had not been enlightened about their relation and had not managed the individuation that would have made his life meaningful.

"While the analysis of a case is in progress it is impossible to obtain any clear impression of the structure and development of the neurosis," Freud told us. "That is the business of a synthetic process which must be performed subsequently" (X, 132). The synthesis in this case must be compressed vigorously; "Moran" awaits. Readers of this analysis already have a clear and distinct impression of the structure and development of "Molloy," and so we may move quickly.

As Jungians we find serious reasons for discontent with Molloy's claim to resemble his mother. The intrusion of Sophie Lousse and Ruth/Edith into his search for Mag indicated that his psychic problems were not merely personal. Those characters deepened his difficulties to the level of the collective unconscious and its archetypes. Therefore any merely personal rapprochement with a personal mother would not solve them. Molloy told us that "it's good to have a change of muck, to move from one heap to another a little further on, from time to time, fluttering you might say, like a butterfly, as if you were ephemeral" (41). We Jungians see in that passage a psyche (an entity whose images include the butterfly) engaged in sequential encounters with earthy images of archetypes. We also note that this narrative is written in the mythological present (26). In short, the Jungian psychology beneath the narrative obliges us to bring that narrative to a relevant psychological close.

In fairness to the patient we must emphasize the intensity of his psychic events, beginning with a hasty look back. Having read deeply in Dante and Joyce, Beckett was already no stranger to psychic events in literature when he studied *A la Recherche*. There among much else he found Marcel, Albertine having disappeared, going over and over his memories of her, attempting to understand them and, if one wishes, dragging them into the "eudemonistic slop." Marcel reported many scenes and relations, with a keen eye for their ambiguities and hidden meanings. Even while acknowledging that Albertine was not, probably, any of the identities he had seen in her, and that she was not the person he had hoped her to be, Marcel recognized positively her striking and positive effects. She had evoked in him "de rêves, de désirs, d'habitudes, de tendresses, avec l'interférence requise de souffrances et de plaisirs alternés." These experiences created, and memory preserved in him, "la vie réelle, qui est mentale." Past scenes were thereby transformed, so that "cette terre, comme un pays mythologique conservé, rendait vivantes et cruelles les légendes les plus anciennes, les plus charmantes, les plus effacées . . ." (*Albertine disparue*, 171–72).

Marcel's analysis is very satisfactorily Jungian. The effect upon Marcel's masculine ego-consciousness caused by these encounters with the anima has been to bring sensual, emotional, and mythological life to his world by adding to its material facts her enlivening mythology. "La vie réelle, qui est mentale," is not restricted to the exercises of the analytical reason.

Marcel's exuberantly intense voice emphasizes a singular quality of Molloy's voice. He can be as eloquent and perceptive as Marcel, perhaps, but his voice is stripped of emotional energy, weakened, flattened, so that we have found it intense only negatively and in brief spurts (as in his remarks about being crucified and about the phrase "from time to time"). In *Molloy* even Moran's voice, bursting out at us from the opening pages of his section, startles the reader by its contrast to the voice that has been creating the life abruptly and faintly ended. Where in Molloy's world, then, is the intensity of experience that Marcel has associated with discovery of the mythological psychic world that we know as the anima? Mag, Lousse, and Ruth/Edith gained considerably in meaningfulness when their Jungian significances were brought to the attention of our own ego-consciousnesses. They were not, however, transformed into real people, and the encounters gained no dramatic liveliness.

Speaking of Hölderlin's "Patmos," Jung finds in that poem a retrospective longing for mother and childhood. He connects that longing with a patient's contrivance of a maternal fantasy-character. This character "was really not much more than the personification of a regressive and infantile reverie, having neither the will nor the power to make good [the patient's] aversion from this world by fishing up another from the primal ocean of the unconscious." Lousse offers Molloy the food and drink that Mag had not offered and a version of childhood in which Molloy could jump and fall and escape rage and pain; but Lousse and Mag remain personifications of a regressive reverie. They cannot justify Molloy's flight from the real world of Bally. Hölderlin manages better than Jung's patient. In "Patmos," Jung says, this infantile longing is expressed and then properly supplanted by "the recognition, that one must give up the retrospective longing which only wants to resuscitate the torpid bliss and effortlessness of childhood" (*Symbols of Transformation*, 414). We saw a version of such torpid bliss in the early days of Molloy's stay with Lousse. Its brief replacement by comic sexual activity and pedicures with Ruth/Edith did not constitute a lively step forward.

Molloy reacts, as befits an ego-consciousness, while identifying his motive as external to him. He reacts most strongly when he reacts negatively, but the proper sacrifice of infantile longings requires a strong positive effort: "Such a sacrifice can only be accomplished through whole-hearted dedication to life. All the libido that was tied up in family bonds must be withdrawn from the narrower circle into the larger one. . . . Such a step includes the solution, or at least some consideration, of the sexual problem . . . , for unless this is done the unemployed libido will inevitably remain fixed in the unconscious endogamous relationship to the parents . . ." (*Symbols of Transformation*, 414). Molloy engaged in some consideration of the sexual problem when he turned his psychic attention from Lousse to Ruth/Edith. But his quick association of both women with his mother broke off that consideration. He remained fixed in that unconscious relationship. It should not be completely unconscious after his painful recognition, but that relationship among the three anima figures is never mentioned again, even when crucifixion is mentioned.

The voice urging Molloy to leave Lousse did not urge him toward his maternal anima or any social affections. Molloy's report of his adult life in the outside world—spent in fear, duplicity, and concealment—suggests that he was still fixed unhappily in childhood dependence. He extended no libido to that outer world from which he fled to the seaside.

Marcel's retrospective appreciation of his experiences with Albertine did not lead him to psychological perfection. His morbid affection for his mother shifted its focus to his grandmother and then to Albertine, while spreading to include more and more of his social contacts. Especially because of Albertine, he found himself attached to the world by love. But this is an overstatement, surely; his need for control and his own detachment remain. Molloy's only impulse to positive action is not love for anyone, including himself, but the imperative voice that puts into words his innate velleity and his lack of something. Nor does he lovingly seek a fellow or frère.

His flight from Lousse, his indifference to Ruth/Edith, and his hostile evasion of Mag have kept him from those experiences of the anima that Marcel celebrates intensely and that Jung emphasizes. Jung stresses the values of these experiences especially with reference to Sophia: "Wisdom dwells in the depths, the wisdom of the mother; being one with her means being granted a vision of deeper things, of the primordial images and primitive forces which underlie all life and are its nourishing, sustaining, creative matrix" (*Symbols of Transformation*, 413). Because this maternal matrix is experienced by Molloy's hostile ego-consciousness, Mag and her home and Lousse and her garden provide only a parody of sustenance, nourishment, and creation. Even when Ruth/Edith completes Mag and Lousse, the trinity constitutes no goal worth Molloy's search, no source of the wisdom that Jung ascribes to the anima.

Such an objection seriously affects our evaluation of Beckett's text. Imagine a *Romeo and Juliet* in which Juliet is a gum-chewing dullard, an *Aeneid* in which the hero battles his way from London to found the town of Slough, or a *Faust* in which the hero descends to the Mothers to learn that he should wear his galoshes and eat chicken soup. Do Mag, Lousse, and Ruth/Edith show that Beckett produced an equivalent of such grotesque failures? Is "Molloy" an inadvertent satire of Jungian mythology? No. Considered as individuals with merely personal existence, the characters in "Molloy" lack impressiveness. They and the events of "Molloy" can be understood as more than fragments of a picaresque novel only by accepting Beckett's persistent clues to their psychic nature. When Jung speaks of dreams and archetypal images and events, he does not include in his generalizations about the dream-work and its analysis the rumpled figure of the individual dreamer, report-ing dreams from the office couch. Jung gives the dreams and archetypes a melodramatic grandeur, often with classical associations. Readers of *Molloy*, however, cannot omit the dreamers, since their voices are in our ears through-out and they force on us their decaying bodies.

"Molloy" is not a paradigm of Jungian myths. *It is the dreamwork itself,* unexplicated. Molloy is a central figure in it, a valetudinarian obliged to report his travels for a messenger who works only on Sundays and who pays him by the page—but even this is part of the psychic report. In this report three women act as befits archetypal images—except for their lack of archetypal wisdom. The lesser male images share the fixed and simple char-acterization given to the women. The events, too, have the discrete nature and inconsequentiality that dreams typically possess.

These faults or facts are not Beckett's or Jung's but Molloy's. A work of art so imagined—constructed with intensity, knowledge, and specific de-tail—cannot permit itself any inconsistency in its basic presentation. This is a story expressed entirely in psychological images and events. Molloy is not a novelist writing his autobiography. At the seaside he is entitled to shelter himself in a maternal cave and puzzle over maternal sucking-stones, but he cannot take a day off to mail postcards and visit scenes from *Effi Briest*. He is always part of the multicharactered psyche he reports.

He is old, crippled, far from home, and obliged to keep moving in a world of strangers. His social existence in that world is sketched only fragmentarily. He sold the silver stolen from Lousse (except for the kniferest) to buy food; his many months or years between leaving Lousse and reaching the seaside are sketched only vaguely; and his living off the land while traveling from the seaside to the ditch is only suggested. We are deep in his mind, among characters who themselves have no social existence. He is chiefly the ego-consciousness of the psyche called Molloy. His old age is an old age of the psyche; only metaphorically does it bear on the question of whether his mother could still be alive. The better question is whether this crippled and stiffening ego-consciousness, so close to rigor mortis, can mend itself.

The subordinate imagery shares the characteristics of the personnel, as we noted in finding many conventional Jungian objects. Proust is here too, however. Consider Molloy's crutches. "There is rapture, or there should be, in the motion crutches give" — a hypothetical rapture, the result of "reasonings, based on analysis" (64). This passage associates the crutches—which enabled Molloy to leave Lousse—with analytical reason.

Proust's Marcel discovers that his impulse to write has weakened when he returns to Rivebelle. The desire for fame and the joy of the present moment are no longer motives enough. He needs wisdom, "les sages réflexions du passé, qui nous aident à préserver le futur." He had not considered this need for reason and its wisdom: "Or, si déjà arrivant à Rivebelle, j'avais jeté loin de moi ces béquilles du raisonnement, du contrôle de soi-même qui aident notre infirmité à suivre le droit chemin" (A l'Ombre III, 68–69). Marcel needed these crutches of reasoning, but Molloy's "béquilles du raisonnement" take him without rapture away from Lousse and into Cartesian mathematics and emotional dryness. They are a poor substitute for the wisdom of Sophia. Jung agrees. In his "Archetypes of the Collective Unconscious" he dramatizes the proper masculine confrontation with the anima: "We are entangled and confused in aimless experience, and the power of judgement with all its categories has impotently gone to the devil. Human interpretation fails. . . . It is a moment of collapse. We sink into a final depth, to a spiritual death. . . . It is a surrender of our own powers, not arbitrarily willed, but naturally forced upon us . . . a complete and unmistakable defeat crowned with the panic fear of demoralization." At this time, Jung says, when we have lost the power of judgment, "all supports and crutches are broken" (Integration of the Personality, 82).

Such a fear and such a spiritual death arise from Molloy's sense of crucifixion when he links Mag, Lousse, and Ruth/Edith, but he takes to his crutches and flees. They remain when the bicycle fails. Confronted by the charcoal-burner's offer of irrational companionship, he uses his crutches to subdue him. Even when crawling like a reptile through the forest, he clings to them. Only at the very end of his journey does he realize their inadequacy, when he surveys "the vast moor, where my crutches would fumble in vain." Even then, however, he does not "sink into a final depth"; he goes no lower than the ditch.

Molloy's ego-consciousness explains the unimpressiveness of anima figures in "Molloy." Its crutch is reason. His specific acts of reasoning—his imitation of the young Descartes, his arrangement of sucking-stones, and even his analysis of his narrative—are none of them impressive. To the un-impressive manifestations of the anima we must add this unimpressive ego-consciousness.

Perhaps these explanations sound too defensive. The beleaguered scholar might soon be driven to mere rhetoric: What do you want, Coriolanus and his mother? Let us return to Jung. These imagined complaints about the anima figures and the rational ego-consciousness silently postulate value judgments: Life is impressive; the psyche is impressive; the archetypes that inhabit it are impressive. Therefore, to be valid psychologically, Mag, Lousse, Ruth/Edith, and Molloy as ego-consciousness must also be impressive.

Life is impressive because it is so meaningful. The optimistic Jung agrees, but he puts the matter in an unsettling way: "Actually the anima—and so life itself—is without significance, yet it has a significant nature, for there is a cosmos in all chaos, secret order in all disorder, unfailing law in all contin-gency" (*Integration of the Personality,* 81). It is the work of the Logos to find this significance in the anima. Molloy found in Mag, Lousse, and Ruth/ Edith no such cosmos, order, and law, except for the orderly progress of the subdued seasons in Lousse's garden, unshared with him. He learned noth-ing from that progress, nor from the unspecified pre-established harmony of the outer world. He even discarded Lousse's other names, Sophie and Loy, which offer wisdom and law, and he shunned Lousse's moonlight. He found no cosmos because he, like Murphy, is the prior system—and that system is dysfunctional.

As ego-consciousness he is hindered in his conceptions and interpreta-tions of the anima by his self-protective and fearful rationality. He guards himself against encounters with the anima that might result in his sinking into a final depth and experiencing panic fear: "I don't know why and I don't want to" (59). He evades the anima, flees to society and then to the seaside, and develops his Cartesian rationality.

In addition to the anima, Jung offers another source of wisdom, the voice, in concluding his discussion of individuation. A voice with a basic message expresses a vocation. To that redundant semantic explanation Jung adds a warning: "Only the man who is able *consciously* to affirm the power of the vocation confronting him from within becomes a personality; he who suc-cumbs to it falls a prey to the blind flux of happening and is destroyed" (*Integration,* 296). Jung has more to say, but already we recognize both the necessity for control by the ego-consciousness and the possibility of a nega-tive potential personality.

The psychotherapist dealing with a neurosis must confront this problem of "personality and the inner voice" in order for the patient to understand

the voice: "It is extremely rare . . . that this [understanding] happens spontaneously as in the case of the Old Testament prophets [whom Molloy mis-
understood]; as a rule, the psychic circumstances that have caused the disturbance must with effort be made conscious. Yet the contents that come to
light strictly correspond to the 'inner voice' and have the significance of a
fateful vocation. When this is accepted by consciousness and integrated, it
brings about the development of personality" (302). Hearing a wise voice is
not enough. The acceptance and integration of its message into one's ego-
consciousness are needed for successful individuation. One must experience
the chaos and meaninglessness of the frightening anima. Then, with the aid
of the wisdom derived by one's newborn Logos from contact with this chaos,
one must extract a cosmos. Only then can one accept the task of actively
altering one's conscious self, with the aid of this wisdom, toward the com-
pleteness of individuation.

Molloy has shown no sign of such integration, despite his claim to resemble his mother more and more. We have come a long way, however,
from the problems that initiated our current considerations. We began with
the complaint that Mag, Lousse, and Ruth/Edith are inadequate, unwise,
and unimpressive images of the anima. We moved to the identification of
Molloy as limited to his psyche's ego-consciousness. We recognized this ego-
consciousness as developing, during the narrative, into a rational masculine
intellect—not remarkably intelligent or well educated, but increasingly concerned with knowing, naming, analyzing, and expressing verbally. It is evasive—knowing, verbalizing, and analyzing rather than understanding, sym-
pathizing, and acting upon its discoveries.

This Molloy is both the protagonist and the narrator of "Molloy." In that
fact we find the explanation of our original problems. Mag, Lousse, and
Ruth/Edith are indeed archetypal images. Archetypes have no necessary
forms. They are perceived in images conditioned by the individual consciousness. (The Logos might be imaged with equal validity by a European as a
bearded old man and by an Indian as an elephant.) Archetypes do not necessarily make respectable appearances; the individual consciousness affects
the image. Ruth/Edith is quite different from Jung's favorite images of the
seductress—movie stars and Rider Haggard's "She." As Jung's choices imply something about his own sense of that archetype, so Ruth/Edith does
about Molloy's. Mag the uniparous hag is no voluptuously fecund earth
goddess. Sophie Loy or Lousse is a sexless suburban image of nature's wisdom. In each case we are obliged to see with Molloy's almost monocular
vision. In each case the evasive ego-consciousness has darkened counsel to
justify its neurotic aversion to the maternal anima.

It has not acted freely, however. Perhaps it has done its best, but its best is no better because Molloy cannot love. It is love that ennobles and beautifies its objects, whether they are humans or archetypal images.

In a sense, then, the narrating Molloy is correct to say that he must resemble his mother more and more. Like her he is bedridden, impotent, shut off from the world, and subservient to a visitor whose demands are unintelligible. His maternal anima has been so weakened by the end of his journey that he does not know—and, hostilely, does not care—whether his mother is alive or dead.

Free from any obligatory dependence upon the limitations of Molloy's vision, we can see despite his caricatures that Mag offered him a consistent maternal welcome with physical affection (which Molloy would accept only when translated into money). Lousse was the center of a world ruled by natural laws and improved by diligent care, a world providing unquestioning maternal shelter and nourishment and the materials from which to infer a cosmos. Ruth/Edith offered quiet domestic sexuality. All three of these actively offered affectionate companionship, but Molloy could not see such qualities. He reports his unwilling subservience to a disgusting woman who does not know him, to a nature that keeps him childlike and confined, and to an aggressive and demanding sexuality, where we see an open door, an open gate, and open arms.

We must find these qualities despite Molloy's presentations. He recurrently complains of being obliged to fend for himself. Especially he complains that his voice has often sent him toward his mother, with detailed instructions, only to fall silent in mid-journey and leave him "like a fool who neither knows where he is going nor why he is going there" (86–87). He admits that he often completed this journey anyhow, but managed no active contact: "When I was with her, and I often succeeded, I left her without having done anything." Molloy has little willpower or libido of any sort, even negative, and that little bit weakens during his journey. His report demonstrates his psychological troubles: his trips to Bally are increasingly difficult and detailed; his quick trips out of Bally to the canal bank and the seaside go undescribed. Flight is easy.

During his stay in the social world he skulked and toadied. When the woman at the seaside offered him food, "I looked at her in silence, until she went away." In the forest he asked rhetorically: "Look at Mammy [maman]. What rid me of her, in the end?" (81). His strongest desires are for isolation, detachment, and superiority. He achieves them by retreating from relations with others into his reason. Against these desires his innate velleity for a relation with his mother stands little chance. Perhaps no word in French or

English says "desire" more weakly than "velleity." No wonder his increasingly verbal reason uses it.

Exploring "Molloy" for Jung's Logos, we settled for that weaker entity the masculine reason. Molloy's ego-consciousness uses reason self-protectively, to reduce immediate and discrete anxieties. It seeks prompters and rules of social behavior, for example, rather than a permanent reduction of anxiety. Such evasions are common in ordinary life. Jung remarks ironically that, since "the problems of the inner voice are full of hidden pits and snares," we should be "thankful . . . to all the well-meaning shepherds of the flock, . . . when they erect protective walls" (*Integration of the Personality*, 304). Molloy imagines joining the shepherd's flock and notes the literal walls that protect the citizens of Bally. He notes also the threats implicit in that protection: the Jehovah-like boatman bringing materials for a crucifixion and the shepherd leading his flock protectively to slaughter.

Beneath Jung's irony about shepherds is the assertion that one should follow one's inner voice. Molloy's voice calls him to his mother. In his mother's room he hears no voice. With Lousse he heard one voice deep in his psyche but not talking to him, and another telling him to get out. Only comically does this second voice fit Jung's description of "the paternal principle, the Logos, which eternally struggles to extricate itself from the primal warmth and primal darkness of the maternal womb." Molloy denies having a son, shows no paternal qualities, and does not struggle to extricate himself from his mother's room and bed.

The Kniferest, Pi, and the Feast of Reason

We recall that the narrating Molloy spoke of looking at the kniferest "with an astonished and affectionate gaze, if I had not been incapable of affection" (63–64), and that it attracts him because there is no likelihood that he will ever figure out its use. That activity of the reason, specified also in the working out of pi, enables peace to enter "the soul of the incurious seeker." Molloy, however, offers us no example of such peaceful reasoning, except for the sucking-stone problem. There is a good reason. He must write his report.

He must drag his past life into the "eudemonistic slop" and pass judgment upon it. The life to be judged was predicted at the beginning of his report, when he imagined C back from his journey and seeing again the world he had first seen from a tall monument. He would see it "with other eyes, and not only that but the within, all that inner space one never sees, the brain and heart and other caverns where thought and feeling dance their sabbath, all that too quite differently disposed" (10). Molloy's heart and feelings have nearly atrophied, and he too must look within.

Jung is relevant yet again. Discussing the transformation of the psyche, he defines the term "natural man" as implying "the ability to deviate from the law, or what in theological language is known as the capacity for 'sin.' . . . Instead of instinctive certainty [as in the animal and, we add, the charcoal-burner] there is uncertainty and consequently the need for a discerning, evaluating, selecting, discriminating consciousness." We recognize here the rational abilities needed for civilized life. Jung says that "through the sacrifice of the natural man, an attempt is made to reach this goal, for only then will the dominating ideal of consciousness be in a position to assert itself completely and mould human nature as it wishes" (*Symbols of Transformation*, 434). Molloy's attack on the charcoal-burner may suggest such a sacrifice, enacted by a selecting and discriminating Cartesian consciousness with a neatly geometrical attack. Molloy, however, does not seek any "dominating ideal of consciousness," despite his reasonings.

As one might expect of a psychologist, Jung is not wholly in favor of this molding of human nature by the reason. His ambivalence is expressed here by a concern about the value of the reason when its activities are not engaged with or transformed by the wisdom of the anima. "The loftiness of this ideal [of a rationally molded and law-abiding human nature] is incontestable," he says; "yet it is precisely on this lofty height that one is beset by a doubt whether human nature is capable of being moulded in this way, and whether our dominating ideal is such that it can shape the natural material without damaging it. Only experience will show" (434).

In a grim comment that we will soon read, and by his own psychic situation at the close of his narrative, Molloy offers his experience as a response to Jung's speculation. Before we hear his testimony, however, we might recall the lament of Samuel Taylor Coleridge, who also tried to rid himself of his "natural man." For many years Coleridge suffered because he repressed (rather publicly) his love for a woman not his wife. He sought relief in abstract thought. In "Dejection: An Ode," he reports the effects of this evasion on his psyche:

> For not to think of what I needs must feel,
>   But to be still and patient, all I can;
> And haply by abstruse research to steal
>   From my own nature all the natural man—
>   This was my sole resource, my only plan;
> Till that which suits a part infects the whole,
> And now is almost grown the habit of my soul.

Molloy is not in Coleridge's league as a pursuer of abstruse research, but his analyses of farts, crutches, and sucking-stones, his innate velleity, and the acknowledged falsity of his report certainly constitute attempts to steal from his own nature all the natural man and certainly suggest that the undiscovered whole of his nature has been infected by a rational consciousness.

In this context Molloy's pleasure in the unintelligible kniferest and the calculating of pi is easily understood; such sterile mental exercises avoid occasions of sin and are free from anxiety. They are not personal, they have no practical use, and they cannot disappoint either by reaching or by failing to reach a solution. They also require no exercise of emotion, no love. Nevertheless, a refuge in the intellect cannot protect the ego-consciousness from the voices. They are variable, detached, and sexless. They speak in biblical and philosophical tones. There may be pi in the sky when Molloy dies, but on earth the voices finally require him to come to terms with his mother.

We consult Jung's *Psychology and Religion*. (That topic recalls James's *Varieties of Religious Experience* and its reports of gongs, voices, and angels.) Jung considers here the phenomenon of the internal voice as it relates to religion and individuation. He says that the voice issues from "a psyche more complete than consciousness" (like James, he is speaking to a lay audience, as far as depth psychology is concerned). The voice expresses "a superior analysis or insight or knowledge which consciousness has not been able to produce" (49).

Considering faith and religious insight as a psychologist, Jung takes the individual's religious experience to be a relationship: "Religion is a relationship to the highest or strongest value [in an individual's psyche], be it positive or negative. The relationship is voluntary as well as involuntary, that is, you can accept, consciously, the value by which you are possessed unconsciously. That psychological fact which is the greatest power in your system is the god, since it is always the overwhelming psychic factor which is called god" (49). The relevance is obvious. A voice with knowledge superior to that possessed by Molloy's ego-consciousness has expressed, all his life, an innate velleity requiring him to establish a relationship with his mother. Molloy has reported no relationship to compete with it, but he has not accepted consciously the value by which he is possessed unconsciously.

Jung has been speaking of the greatest power in one's psyche as one's god, to an audience of Christians, and with reference to pagan gods. His next remark bears on Molloy's chronologically final location, a room in which the material objects were once his mother's but from which she is gone: "That psychological fact which is the greatest power in your system is the god, since it is always the overwhelming psychic factor which is called god. As soon as a god ceases to be an overwhelming factor, he becomes a mere name. His essence is dead and his power is gone." Molloy's mother has lost her psychic power. During his last crawl Molloy pushed along blindly, eyes shut: "And from time to time I said, Mother, to encourage me I suppose." That doubting explanation suggests that already his invisible mother had been reduced to a name, not even hated and no longer archetypal. Nimis sero was predictive. The psychic energy of his need has faded and grown weak.

In the lectures that comprise *Psychology and Religion* Jung tells his audience about many patients' dreams. Often the anima appears in them as the "overwhelming psychic factor," and "the 'mystery' of the anima is the religious innuendo" (51). Jung does not claim now that the Logos must kill or control the anima. The anima here is essentially the soul, and it is permitted a dominant role. Jung even makes mathematical room for it. As often, he speaks here of a quaternity as an improvement upon the Christian trinity, proposing the anima as the fourth element: "The progression from Father to Son represents a time element, while the spatial quality would be personified by the Mater Dei. (The mother quality was originally attributed to the Holy Ghost and the latter was then called Sophia-Sapientia by certain early Christians)" (89).

Jung offers ecclesiastical symbols to support his interpretation. They include the "rosa mystica," the "hortus conclusus," and "the cross of equal branches" (89). Molloy leaves Sophie's hortus conclusus and experiences the forest as a negation of the Earthly Paradise. He renames Ruth/Edith Rose while at a mandala in that forest, but then he cancels that name. The cross of equal branches, appearing doubly on the kniferest, pleasantly baffles him. (The more complex image, the cross of equal arms enclosed in a circle, appears "from time to time" as the crossroads or circus, the mandala from which he flees.) These details from *Psychology and Religion* reinforce the spiritual nature of Molloy's need and add significance to his unwillingness to accept his anima.

Perhaps those crossroads should be considered yet again, in the context of *Psychology and Religion*. Jung remarks that in the mandalas drawn by his patients, unlike those from the historical past, "there was never a deity occupying the center" (97). He concludes that "a modern mandala is an involuntary confession of a peculiar mental condition. There is no deity in the mandala, and there is also no submission or reconciliation to a deity" (99). In those empty crossroads and in that empty room awaiting Molloy, we see similar evidence that the maternal anima, the soul of the psyche, is dead. Molloy's rational ego-consciousness has taken its place.

The Dead End

Let us look for a final time at Jung's passage about the experience of illumination that should be the climax, though not the conclusion, of the process of individuation: "Only when all supports and crutches are broken . . . does it become possible to experience an archetype that up till then had lain concealed in the anima's significant senselessness. It is the *archetype of meaning,* as the anima is the archetype of life itself" (*Integration of the Personality,* 82). Molloy never has this experience. His intellect learns only to reason, calculate, evade, and cling to its crutches. To the extent that it seeks meaning in its story, it is grudgingly eudemonistic, using an external system of ethics with which it is not in sympathy—and no wonder, since the intellect is rational and that Stoic system is concerned with pleasure and pain.

Molloy fails. Such a negative judgment cannot please any readers of "Molloy" who have come to feel affection for this grumbling, confused, and often nasty old man, but that affection is not shared by Molloy. We must consider what he says. Of course we have done so all along, as when we noted his doubtful claim to resemble his mother, his harsh presentation of all anima images, his abandoned desire for a fellow or frère, his inability to love, and his preference for escapist mental activity. Implicit in these characteristics may appear to be the idea that Molloy, or the ego-consciousness represented by that name, is satisfied with his identity. He is unable to love but does not hesitate to say so. He is hostile to his mother but quite openly so. He is obliged to make a report but is indifferent to its accuracy and meaning; he even says explicitly that it is a lie. He appears to have accepted his present state. He does not, however, except as it constitutes an excuse not to go on. (He can no longer walk.) His return from the seaside to his mother's room, and perhaps all of "Molloy," is "a nursery tale" compared to his present existence.

Intellectually he has come a long way since the near breakdown of his verbal reason just before he fell at Lousse's feet, when words failed him and the light of reason was going out: "even then, when already all was fading, waves and particles, there could be no things but nameless things, no names but thingless names" (31). At that point the anima's world of things was completely detached from the reason's words and ideas. Percepts could not be attached to concepts. (Schopenhauer's "On the Practical Use of Our Reason and on Stoicism" is relevant [*WWR* II, ch. XVI].)

But Molloy did not stop there. Recognizing his considerable change will enable us to understand the bitter terminal assertions he makes about his present state. Basically, he contrasts to his former separation of words from things their present connection. Such a connection ought to characterize a successful union of animus and anima, since it is the primary achievement of the Logos to raise the anima's unconscious wisdom into words. The connection of words with things ought to signal harmony, control, and imminent individuation. But something has gone badly wrong. His report is as abrupt as his report of the identity shared by Mag, Lousse, and Ruth/Edith. He analyzes his current state, though not with detachment or tranquillity. He divides it into two categories: his making of the report and his experiencing of life.

As Beckett docked the tail end of Molloy's journey and placed it first, and as he located Molloy's eudemonistic Stoicism in the middle of his stay with Lousse, so he displaced this final report, which in a conventional and chronological novel of ideas would constitute the climax. For this climactic revelation we must return to Molloy's introduction to Lousse.

Molloy has just described his inability, before encountering Lousse, to connect words with things. Then as narrator he moves to his present state. In that present state, the relation of words and things is strikingly different, worse, and terminal: "I say that now, but after all what do I know now about then, now when the icy words hail down upon me, the icy meanings, and the world dies too, foully named. All I know is what the words know, and the dead things, and that makes a handsome little sum, with a beginning, a middle and an end as in the well-built phrase and the long sonata of the dead" (31). The narrating Molloy has succeeded in matching words to things. A result is the composition of his report, here predicted to be a finished work of art. The whole is a "handsome little sum"; we can hear the Cartesian calculator. It has a beginning, middle, and end; we have called them "Before Sophie," "With Sophie," and "After Sophie." Its well-built phrases and three parts suggest a sonata. But Molloy lacks harmony and is indifferent to music (62).

The words shaped into phrases are icy; their architectural form is frozen music. The icy words and their fixed meanings have killed the world that they describe. Instead of taking life from contact with the anima, they smother that anima with foul names. (The word killeth, but the spirit giveth life.) Molloy has achieved neither intuitive nor verbal understanding of the feminine life of his psychic world. "All I know is what the words know, and the dead things." The barren plain—"the plane of pure knowledge"—between the edge of the forest and his mother still separates him from psychic health. The icy words hail down with Dantean implications. In the *Inferno* that icy cold emblemizes the absence of any trustworthiness or affection, the worst sin against the light. The traitors against life and God are frozen within themselves at the deepest part of hell.

We must return to that condemnation. But first, let us consider a less judgmental summary of Molloy that can be extracted from the Unnamable's comments as he looks back over his earlier fictional "delegates." He jumbles them together, but we can pick out passages clearly relevant to Molloy. The delegates bring the Unnamable "knowledge of my mother. . . . She was one of their favourite subjects, of conversation": "They also gave me the low-down on God. They told me I depended on him, in the last analysis. . . . But what they were most determined for me to swallow was my fellow-creatures. . . . They gave me courses on love, on intelligence, most precious, most precious. They also taught me to count, and even to reason" (298). That the courses might have favored love above Cartesian intelligence and counting and reasoning the Unnamable does not recognize, or perhaps the lecture form—a rational form—killed the love. His sour tone indicates that the Beckettian lectures on love that began with Neary's comment about Murphy's conarium did not bear fruit, and that mother and one's fellow-creatures were merely topics of conversation. The Unnamable's wholesale rejection of depth psychology and its therapies is summed up by his earlier abrupt remark: "Are there other pits, deeper down? To which one accedes by mine? Stupid obsession with depth" (293).

Coleridge spoke of the infection that resulted from his repression of feeling by reason. William James spoke of the ladder by which the mind rises from percepts to concepts. Arsene, experiencing life off the ladder, found experience intelligible only as individual percepts with the simple coherence of time and space, sequence and repetition. Molloy offers yet another formulation: Without the life of the anima, words are dead.

The metaphors proliferate. Let us return to some of Molloy's terms—words and things and the well-built sonata of the dead. Here *Watt* necessarily comes to mind, and "Watt's need of semantic succour" (83). After Arsene's departure, Watt "desired words to be applied to his situation . . . and in a general way to the conditions of being in which he found himself" (81). In *Watt* Beckett reduces that topic to the connection of individual words and things, of "pot" and a pot especially. The concern is essentially philosophical, with nominalism in the forefront, and Watt's interests are directed toward the world outside himself.

That the connecting of words and things might lead to a sonata suggests more than merely a shifting of terms. As notes cohere to form a piece of music, so words might cohere to form a well-built and therefore intelligible description of life. After all, Molloy's report follows his abrupt question, "what do I mean by seeing and seeing again?" The question is immediately followed by "an instant of silence, as when the conductor taps on his stand, raises his arms, before the unanswerable clamour" (14).

Jung's "chaos" recalls the "clamour," the "fracas des colles." But the icy rain of words and their icy meanings freeze the life of things, now known only to and through the rational intellect. That intellect is now dominant. It falls on the world as an icy rain of words. They impose a fixed shape rather than finding in the life of the anima an order, a cosmos. This dead world is contracted, by the double end of "Molloy," to the ditch and to the bed and room of the absent mother. Nimis sero indeed.

Jung Told Us So

Beckett's early exposures to Jung—the emphasis upon Jungian myth by the editors of *transition,* his treatment by a Jungian psychiatrist in London, and his attendance at one of Jung's lectures at the Tavistock Institute, most obviously—were scarcely visible in his writings. We can only speculate about his reasons for turning so extensively to Jung in "Molloy," but it is informed speculation.

Our references to Jung have focused repetitiously on a few texts and ideas, as distinguished from the many Freudian sources that Beckett used in "Moran" and in "From an Abandoned Work" and *All That Fall.* In large part the difference might be explained by the nature of Jung's writings: they tend to be repetitious and general, they use fewer terms than do Freud's, and they are not so prolific in case histories. But they do emphasize psychic life as a matter of internal connections and completions.

Molloy's fundamental flaw—"I lacked something"—echoes "never born completely" in the Tavistock lecture. That diagnosis of incompleteness in a psyche, with the damage traced to childhood, is also recognizable. Freudian thought sends the patient back to childhood (varied in Murphy's wandering to find home). Jung prefers to begin at the present moment and go forward, as Beckett obliges Molloy to do. Because of his dislike for merely personal psychology, Jung also alters that return to childhood into a basic psychological need detached from mere personal experience—in Molloy's case, a need to come to terms with the overtones and implications of the maternal anima. Failure cannot be repaired from without by merely personal substitutes; in retrospect, Celia and Mr. Endon and Lulu/Anna embody oddly factual external possibilities for psychic therapy when set against Lousse, Mag, and even Ruth/Edith.

Jung also tells stories—not about the circumstances that lead to neurosis, but about archetypal searches for the grail of individuation. Such searches and their dramatis personae obviously enabled Beckett to set his own characters into motion. Employing a first-person narrative and making that narrator the ignorant neurotic rather than the omniscient therapist were Beckett's own achievements; and he began both long before *Molloy.* One cannot doubt that he found much in the testimony of both Freud's and Jung's patients to encourage his imaginings of his own characters' voices and to distinguish what in a patient's talk is psychologically relevant.

In short, Jung facilitated the literary expression of concepts that started their Beckettian existence in the Cartesian separation of body and mind, the Schopenhauerian concern with the will and the separation of need from satisfaction, and the Freudian presentation of psychic traumas. To those topics he added importantly the emphasis upon the mother and upon the double sexuality of the psyche.

* * *

Such recognitions lead to no conclusions about *Molloy*, since we have the Freudian "Moran" still before us. Beckett made himself a Jungian to dramatize a severe psychological problem. Let us conclude by restating the basic structure of that dramatized problem.

Molloy, at once a human and his ego-consciousness, acknowledges his need for a fellow or frère, and the dependence of any satisfaction of that need upon an understanding of his relations with his mother. These topics are not "personalistic"; his psychic problems cannot "be reduced to personal reminiscences or aspirations," as Jung explained; "that is, . . . images of the collective unconscious begin to appear" (*Two Essays on Analytical Psychology*, 81).

The primary characters and images represent the maternal anima. Mag's exaggerated qualities and the intensity of feeling with which she is presented obviate mere "personal reminiscences" and suggest her archetypal nature. Then Lousse diverts Molloy. His stay with her almost silences his interest in his mother without generating any positive relation to this Sophia figure, this "god"-mother. Next Ruth/Edith occupies his narrative. The three female characters (with "mother" now replacing "Mag") are recognized as one. The absence of conventional characterization helps to make this conjoining intelligible.

Jung speaks of that absence of characterization in describing archetypal images, explaining what might be taken as a failure of Beckett's vivifying imagination: "There is nothing in their behaviour that bespeaks an ego-consciousness. . . . On the contrary, they show every sign of being fragmentary personalities. They are masklike, wraithlike, without problems of their own or any self-reflection, with no conflict, no doubt, no suffering; something like the gods, who have no philosophy. . . . Contrary to the functions attached to consciousness, they are always strangers in the conscious world" (*Integration of the Personality*, 24). The ego-consciousness absent from the archetypal images is possessed by, or is, Molloy, but he too is only a part; he lacks something. Therefore he seems a stranger in "the conscious world." These archetypes "have no philosophy." Only suggestively is Molloy a Stoic or Cartesian and Sophie an Epicurean.

Molloy encountered three forms of one archetype, the maternal anima. But to what end, if these women give no advice, offer no psychic aid, and cannot hold his attention? We readers can manage the necessary encounter with the anima only marginally better than Molloy. We recognize something of Jungian "secret order" and "unfailing law" in Lousse's estate. We understand why Mag and Ruth/Edith do not represent similar systems of order and law; they have other meanings to embody. They complete Jung's formulation of the maternal anima's basic qualities. As Beckett exposed Murphy systematically to the characters and situations that Freud had found typical of narcissism, so he exposes Molloy to the separable forms of his archetypal mother.

To Molloy's question about his mother, "What rid me of her, in the end?" (81), the answer provided by this Jungian psychodrama is clear: terminal repression. The closer Molloy gets to his mother, the stronger his resistance grows. When magic transports him from the ditch to his mother's room, his protective resistance has become matricidal.

Molloy's exposure to human forms of the anima ended when he fled from Lousse. Beckett continued his presentation of the psyche in need of individuation with Jungian images of situation. Discussing the integration of the personality, Jung connects "the end of the process" with such inhuman imagery. He reports images that ordinarily function as anima images in his psychology, but now they are differently qualified: "To the end of the process belong all the symbols of the self in its various aspects. While the Christian cross is a symbol of the beginning, the *cross with equal arms* appears later . . . , then geometric symbols, the circle, the square, the fourfold opposed to the threefold in all possible forms, the flower, especially the rose, the wheel, star, egg, sun, likewise the child . . ." (*Integration of the Personality*, 94; Jung's italics).

Aided by that list, we can find a serious comedy in Beckett's construction of the last section, "After Sophie." The crucifixion and Christian cross appeared when Molloy encountered the boatman and again when he realized that Lousse, Ruth/Edith, and his mother were one. The equal-armed kniferest appeared later, in the "After Sophie" section. The crossroads in the forest were linked with both circle and star. Mentioned again in the last section, Ruth/Edith is renamed Rose. One of the images with which Molloy in his last ditch sums up his existence is that of a child with marbles. In his final sentences the sun shines. Beckett was industrious in his attention to Jungian images.

They bring from the anima no life, however. The voice that urged Molloy toward his mother urged in vain: "The inner voice is the voice of a fuller life, of a wider, more comprehensive consciousness. That is why, in mythol-

ogy, the birth of the hero or the symbolic rebirth coincides with sunrise. . . .
For the same reason most heroes are characterized by solar attributes, and
the moment of the birth of their great personalities is called illumination"
(*Integration of the Personality*, 302). At the end of "Molloy" our reluctant
protagonist emerges from the dark forest into the illumined plain. At that
moment he opens his eyes, a conventional image of birth. He hears a voice.
In the feminine ditch he attains illumination: "It was in this ditch that I
became aware of what had happened to me." The time? "It must have been
spring, a morning in spring. I thought I heard birds, skylarks perhaps." The
images all point to a Jungian success, and Beckett's choice of bird emphasizes Molloy's failure, since skylarks are noted for their strong upward flight
from the ground. (Then Molloy remembers from the start of his journey the
corncrakes, which do not fly.)

Molloy has failed to rise above himself, as William James might say. He
has not come to terms with his mother and thereby enabled himself to find
a fellow or frère. Rejecting the emotional side of his psyche, he has not
learned to love. His icy words have frozen his life into a fixed form, the
narrative in which his ego-consciousness remains alone and verbal, frozen
beyond change.

The Unnamable, looking at Malone circling erratically around him and
thinking that he might in fact be Molloy, shows little interest: "There will
not be much on the subject of Malone, from whom there is nothing further
to be hoped" (292). In *Molloy* Beckett signals this hopelessness and rejection most startlingly and abruptly by obliging his readers to turn the page
into another world, in which they and Moran will seek Molloy in vain.
Retrospectively, at least, they must agree that "Molloy could stay, where he
happened to be." Molloy's cycles of flight and bivouac may continue in his
ego-consciousness, but now without a mother and without the infant form
of a completed psyche, with nothing new to say and no listener to create
him.

8.

Molloy: Moran

"Moran" is another psychodrama, but it is no more paradigmatic than "Molloy." Nor does its Freudian basis rebut the Jungian psychology of "Molloy." Rather, the coexistence of both psychological models emphasizes truths common to both. Shared limitations are also emphasized. Freud and Jung see deeply into the human psyche, but their analyses leave in doubt any possible therapeutic altering of that psyche.

The question of why "Moran" follows "Molloy" might be raised briefly here. A suggestion is offered by Freud himself. In his *Moses and Monotheism* he points out that historically "the matriarchal social order was succeeded by the patriarchal one." He explains that succession psychologically: "This turning from the mother to the father points in addition to a victory of intellectuality over sensuality—that is, an advance in civilization, since maternity is proved by the evidence of the senses while paternity is a hypothesis, based on an inference and a premiss. Taking sides in this way with a thought-process in preference to a sense perception has proved to be a momentous step." Freud associates this change with the development of speech, "unquestionably one of the most important changes on the path to hominization."

In "Molloy" this sequence appeared, but the value judgment was reversed. Evasion of sensuality through intellectuality crippled Molloy, and words froze the life out of his life. However, Freud's judgments were often ambivalent, and his attitude toward civilization was especially so. He did not think improvements in intellect and speech are entirely positive: "All such advances in intellectuality have as their consequence that the individual's self-esteem is increased, that he is made proud—so that he feels superior to other people who have remained under the spell of sensuality" (XXIII, 113–115).

We understood Molloy's changes in Jungian terms and we recall Jung's perception of a similar arrogance. Jung's terms, however, express a hierarchy of psychic changes rather different from Freud's. For Jung, awareness of concealed masculine psychic qualities constitutes a necessary step toward individuation, but it is not the final step. The animus must then master the anima: "If the encounter with the shadow is the 'apprentice-piece' in the individual's development, then that with the anima is the 'master-piece'" (*Archetypes and the Collective Unconscious*, 29). This "master-piece" is different from Freud's "turning from the mother to the father." Freud requires "a momentous step" past the mother.

"Moran" has little use for the feminine; that step past the mother has long since been taken. Moran, like Molloy, is intolerant of women, but he is more often indifferent to them. No anima figure solicits his attention in his Freudian group world. He does, however, seek a variable Molloy, who may suggest a father. In a sense, then, Moran acts out Freud's "advance in civilization" away from the natural feminine state. Molloy's involvement with civilization is restricted to brief hours in Bally and to that fresco dashed off with loathing. Moran is a thoroughly civilized man, head of a family, parishioner, and concerned citizen of Turdy, at the start. Molloy was obliged to encounter Bally and Lousse's psychic civilization. Moran will be obliged by his Freudian group psyche to go into the wilderness.

Moran, Sedate and Unsettled

Molloy began almost immediately to alter an identity not completely formed; Moran's identity is so fixed, especially by his connections to the outer world, that it will take half his report just to set him on the road. Jung's sense of the psyche is primarily teleological; he asks us to see the present psyche with reference to its goal. Freud's therapy requires the patient to begin with a thorough anamnesis. Unlike the still unwritten "From an Abandoned Work," "Moran" presents no intense and thorough recall of childhood. Moran offers no memory earlier than his fifteenth year, but that date marks the resolution of his Oedipal phase. Accepting his father's (and Goethe's) words to live by, "sollst entbehren," he became the man his father was, doing without, resigned to the rules and boundaries of conventional social life.

Molloy is at once a character and a Jungian ego-consciousness related to the collective unconscious and especially to its feminine archetypes. Moran is at once a character and a Freudian ego related to an id, a superego, and the external world. (This description will undergo excruciating complications.) We meet Moran as the civilized ego in his ordered garden. He is in charge, with none of Molloy's complexities in Lousse's garden. He is a conscious self at the center of its external social world.

Moses and Monotheism aids Beckett to show Moran as embodying and inhabiting the world created by the mature masculine intellect. Moran has established his paternity intellectually by naming his son and heir Jacques Jr.; the son repeats the act by calling his toy bear Baby Jack. Developing the idea of paternity as an intellectual rather than a physical fact, Freud says that it requires words, names, for its social establishment: "the child should bear his father's name and be his heir." A skeptic might suggest that this relationship is a matter of faith rather than of intellect, as Joyce's *Ulysses* suggests. Freud also connects the two terms "faith" and "intellect," though on a larger scale. In more-developed patriarchies, "intellectuality itself is overpowered by the very puzzling emotional phenomenon of faith. Here we have the celebrated 'credo quia absurdum,' and . . . anyone who has succeeded in this regards it as a supreme achievement" (XXIII, 117).

To this puzzling leap to faith Freud adds another set of topics. "Instinctual renunciation and the ethics founded on it" are not essential to religion, he says, but they are intimately connected to it. What is more, "this course of events [in society] is repeated in the abbreviated development of the human individual. Here, too, it is the authority of the child's parents—essentially, that of his autocratic father, threatening him with his power to punish—which calls on him for a renunciation of instinct and which decides for him what is to be allowed and what forbidden" (XXIII, 119). Moran is a conventional churchgoer, and his faith is also conventional. The ego's "renunciation of instinct" results from the development of the superego. That psychic entity begins with the "autocratic father." Moran celebrates this renunciation—"sollst entbehren"—and wishes his son to have the same experience. That renunciation is also required by Moran's job, which complements his domestic role as an autocratic superego.

These details identify Moran as a conscious ego in an external world. It is primarily social, a crowded Dickensian town quite different from Molloy's nameless and underpopulated Bally. Besides Father Ambrose and the verger, Joly, we hear of the dentist, Doctor Py (as in "pyorrhea"; he treats irrational roots); Mr. and Mrs. Clement, the druggists (the source of Moran's painkillers for inclement times); Mr. Savoury (the "savyour" who will take Jacques Jr. in); the musical Elsner sisters; and Hannah, their maid. It is a world of relationships and known names. In its center is Moran, circled by *his* garden, *his* plants, and *his* birds, defining himself by his possessions—including *his* son and *his* servant Martha—and passing judgment on them and the world beyond.

In this external world Moran plays many roles, including those of father, employer, parishioner, citizen, and neighbor. He also has a job; he works for someone with a non-Dickensian name, Youdi, by way of a messenger named Gaber. They and his job must wait. The Freudian ego deals with the demands of two external worlds. One is this literally external world with its continuing spray of phenomena. The other is the psyche, of which the conscious ego is a small part. Even in the first part of "Moran" we see evidence of the demands made by this second world, beginning with Gaber. In the second part, away from home, Moran leaves the external world for the psychic one.

It is worth recalling that James's *Varieties of Religious Experience* describes the "twice-born" situation: the individual senses "an uneasiness" and seeks "its solution." The uneasiness is "a sense that there is *something wrong about us* as we naturally stand." The solution includes "a sense that *we are saved from the wrongness by making proper connection with the higher powers.*" At this point in one's life, James says, the self is sensed as divided, and "with which part he should identify his real being is by no means obvious" (498). Molloy evaded that sense of wrongness even while seeking its remedy, and despite his voices he identified his real being, wrongly, as his isolated masculine reason. Trimming his way to love, he missed a proper connection with the anima and remained incapable of affection.

Moran's story begins with a similar situation, but he is explicit about his divided identity. "Patiently turned towards the outer world as towards the lesser evil, creature of his house, of his garden, of his few poor possessions," he is turned inwards as well, since he acts as an external and social self in order "to remain a solitary." "I clung to that [solitary self], with as little enthusiasm as to my hens or my faith, but no less lucidly" (114).

James, Freud, Jung, and Beckett have all suggested in their various ways that awareness of a divided psyche signals an imminent change. When habit no longer suffices, when something has gone wrong with the silence, "when for a moment the boredom of living is replaced by the suffering of being" (*Proust*, 19), a transformation of identity looms. James associates this state with "uneasiness," Jung and Freud with "anxiety."

The initial event of "Moran" is clear, then. Moran's Sunday peace in his garden, in his Sabbath of willing, is disturbed by Gaber's transmission of Youdi's order. Moran evades for a while the true cause of his disturbance; then his body obliges him to acknowledge it ("The conscious ego . . . is first and foremost a body-ego," says Freud [XIX, 27].): "I stirred restlessly in my arm-chair, ran my hands over my face, crossed and uncrossed my legs, and so on. The colour and weight of the world were changing already, soon I would have to admit I was anxious" (96).

Gaber's visit has activated in Moran repressed desires relevant to his solitary self, desires Moran is unwilling to act out. Schopenhauer would see an intellect reluctant to let the will have its way. Freud offers a more complicated statement, based on his sense of the ego as functioning between two worlds: "The ego seeks to bring the influence of the external world to bear upon the id and its tendencies, and endeavours to substitute the reality principle for the pleasure principle which reigns unrestrictedly in the id. . . . The ego represents what may be called reason and common sense, in contrast to the id, which contains the passions" (XIX, 25). The application of Freud's observations to Moran's situation is not simple. Youdi's demand is not passionate, for example. Before going further, we should examine Freud's assertion and clarify his terms.

The cited passage comes from *The Ego and the Id* (1923), in which Freud developed earlier ideas and terms into the versions now generally taken to constitute Freudian psychology. In addition to the ego and the id, he presents the superego as the repository of ethical rules imposed by the parents, especially the father. These rules include or imply the proper identity of the conscious self, leading Freud sometimes to call the superego the ego ideal. This psychic function is not a part of consciousness: "Not only what is lowest but what is highest in the ego can be unconscious" (XIX, 27).

The forces or desires within the id constitute the libido. However, the values of the superego are also expressed forcefully: "its compulsive character . . . manifests itself in the form of a categorical imperative" (XIX, 35; we recall Molloy's hypothetical imperative). The ego ideal is not a mere compendium of rules. It is closer to a forceful model of the self governed by what Molloy called the essence of the system. It is also related to the libido and thereby to Freud's version of the collective unconscious, the "archaic heritage." Freud's formulation needs to be read closely: "The ego ideal is therefore the heir of the Oedipus complex, and thus it is also the expression of the most powerful impulses and most important libidinal vicissitudes of the id. Whereas the ego is essentially the representative of the external world, of reality, the super-ego stands in contrast to it as the representative of the internal world, of the id" (XIX, 36).

The superego represents the id while it also represents that which is highest in the id and often opposed to the id's demands. This complexity makes difficult the evaluation of any impulse from the unconscious. That libidinal energies impel both the id and the superego makes the libido equally problematic. These are relevant difficulties.

Moran's Sabbath of willing is interrupted by Gaber's delivery of an imperative from Youdi. ("It was impossible for me to refuse," Moran says [95].) Moran desires peace, and that desire opposes this imperative. The ego is "menaced by three dangers: from the external world, from the libido of the id, and from the severity of the super-ego." Each generates anxiety, "since anxiety is the expression of a retreat from danger" (XIX, 56). No wonder Freud calls the ego "a poor creature." No wonder Moran must struggle to be master in his own house. This external Moran is the "creature of his house, of his garden, of his few poor possessions." He owns them, but equally they own him; they constitute the "contrivance" that is Moran in the external world (114).

In that external role Moran's characteristics are obvious: he is aggressive, ingratiating, rational, and sexually immature. He is aggressive verbally and physically to his two dependents. Freud's discussion of the cruel superego (XIX, 54–55) suggests that Moran, suffering under this arbitrary cruelty in his profession, represses his anger in most of his roles and vents it at home. Repressing it, he is ingratiating to Father Ambrose and to the dangerous farmer encountered on the way home. "In its position midway between the id and reality, [the ego] only too often yields to the temptation to become sycophantic, opportunistic, and lying" (XIX, 56), as Moran's contriving his improper communion shows. That Moran is rational hardly needs mention; he too will echo Descartes' *Discours de la méthode,* as in saying "I had a methodical mind" (98).

His sexuality is limited and Freudian. He imagines his son's intrusion on the primal scene, but his version of that primal scene is comically narcissistic and adolescent: "masturbating, before my cheval glass" (102). Moran's praise of "sollst entbehren" emphasizes the strength of his superego. "The super-ego arises from an identification with the father taken as a model," Freud says. "Every such identification is in the nature of a desexualization." When sublimation of the sex drive occurs because of this identification with the father, "the erotic component no longer has the power to bind the whole of the destructiveness that was combined with it" (XIX, 54), and therefore aggressiveness is intensified. Freud's anal and oral stages occur on the way to mature sexuality. Moran, who speaks sourly of sex and lives in Turdy ("Shit" in the French), is anal. ("You know which mouth to put it in," he says to his son about the thermometer [117].) The son is oral; he has trouble with his teeth, which he persists in poking with his fingers. Freud says that "dreams 'with a dental stimulus'" represent in males "the masturbatory desires of the pubertal period" (V, 385).

Beckett's Freudian presentation of Moran requires some redundancy in its description, especially with regard to Moran's superego. The ego attempts to regulate demands from the unconscious with reference to the reality principle, in part, but also and more generally with reference to the ethical values of the superego. A primary result is repression: "As the child was once under a compulsion to obey its parents, so the ego submits to the categorical imperative of the super-ego" (XIX, 48). Freud points out most extensively in *Civilization and Its Discontents* that obedience and therefore civilization result from such repression.

Moran's awareness of this idea is shown when he defends his taking away of his son's stamp albums: "*Sollst entbehren* . . . was the lesson I desired to impress upon him, while he was still young and tender. Magic words which I had never dreamt, until my fifteenth year, could be coupled together" (110). He imagines his son as connecting that idea with his father when he is himself an adult, and of reluctantly sensing truth in it. That is, Moran sets out deliberately to create his son's repressive superego by instigating a Freudian development: "the ego develops from perceiving instincts to controlling them, from obeying instincts to inhibiting them. In this achievement a large share is taken by the ego ideal" (XIX, 55–56).

This trained ego facing the outer one of its two external worlds is therefore a contrivance. This outer ego, this Moran, is an actor obeying what Molloy called his prompters. Moran demonstrates his awareness of role-playing in several ways. Freud says, "The functional importance of the ego is manifested in the fact that normally control over the approaches to motility devolves upon it. Thus in its relation to the id it is like a man on horseback, who has to hold in check the superior strength of the horse" (XIX, 25). This description may recall Molloy's bicycle and Moran's decision to leave on his autocycle. An autocycle has unconscious horsepower that must be guided; Moran associates his decision to take the autocycle with "the fatal pleasure principle" (99).

In his connection with Youdi, Moran is the agent, the actor, the doer. Molloy in Bally complains that he had not been taught to act properly; he scarely even mentions his father. Moran is proud of his successes as an actor. When he puts his sick son to bed, he almost kisses him and then tiptoes out of the room. "I quite enjoyed playing my parts through the bitter end," he says (122). In a different mood he complains that he would have "other parts to play, during this expedition, than those of keeper and sick-nurse" (129). Even when crippled, starving, and abandoned by his son, he reports being "enchanted with my performance" (163). Nevertheless, this pleased actor-ego is also that "poor creature owing service to three masters" (XIX, 56). Moran must get along in the outer world. He must act as the ego and superego of his household, directing and judging Martha and his son. And he is a minor functionary in a business that he knows little about and that begins to crumble when Gaber brings him his latest assignment.

Moran: The Inside Story

As a Freudian ego Moran has appeared at once sedate and unsettled. Sedate and sedentary in his garden on an August Sunday, l'homme moyen sensuel is at ease with himself and his world. Gaber's message destroys that calm. Soon "I did nothing but go to and fro"; "I could not keep still"; and—emphasizing the absence of profitable forward motion—"I did nothing but go to and fro" again (98, 104, 108). Made anxious by Gaber's message, Moran reports his daily existence even as it comes apart. We must sense its former calm and ordinariness. Inside, matters are at once the same and different. The new anxiety remains. Moran's journey will enact another going and coming. Obviously the chief matter of "Moran" is Moran's search for Molloy. After our reading of "Molloy," it is clear that Moran's search takes place in a psyche provided with abundant stage sets and minor characters. It is time to set out on this inward journey.

There is a lion in the path, however. The ego is not solitary, despite Moran's desire for that state. It deals with a crowded external world. Internally it must manage the often contradictory and impossible demands of the id and the superego. It must attempt to reconcile them with the pleasure principle and the reality principle. Such a harried existence makes of the ego in all three of its relations what Jung, not Freud, would call an extravert, an identity turned toward its outer worlds and shaping itself by its multiple relations there while neglecting its internal problems.

The many inhabitants of Turdy are supplemented by characters with names of a different sort, such as Gaber and Youdi. These characters are parts of Moran's psyche. The name of a late third, the Obidil, has for a long time suggested this interpretation by its scrambling of "libido." The social Moran has projected these psychic parts onto the stage of the outer world. He has dramatized an organization in which he has a job, relationships, superiors, and equals. (For a moment it has a directorate [106]. The Obidil may not be a part of this group.) Such an organization has afforded him a solid basis for identity and self-assurance. Gaber's message in the garden causes anxiety because it forces him to acknowledge his weakening faith in this organization.

Beckett has chosen for Moran a particular type of Freudian psyche almost as common as the narcissist, complementary to that type, and particularly appropriate for Freud's concerns about the psyche in a family, in society, and in civilization. Molloy's hasty fresco of these relationships could not suffice. Beckett's primary Freudian source is *Group Psychology and the Analysis of the Ego* (1921). With the First World War over and its effects already preparing German society for the next war, Freud had good reason to consider group psychology and ample materials. (Beckett's travels through Germany in the 1930s enabled him to test Freud's perceptions.) Freudian psychology emphasizes libidinal forces as they link the narcissistic individual first to his parents and then to others outside the family. Expanding that psychology to the group for this study obliges Freud to find comparable forces and comparable results, but without a family center and with strangers instead of family members, lovers, and friends.

Defining libido as "the energy . . . of those instincts . . . comprised under the word 'love,'" Freud supposes that "love relationships (or, to use a more neutral expression, emotional ties) . . . constitute the essence of the group mind." Eros "holds together everything in the world," and therefore "if an individual gives up his distinctiveness in a group and lets its other members influence him by suggestion, it gives one the impression that he does it because he feels the need of being in harmony with them rather than in opposition to them—so that perhaps after all he does it '*ihnen zu Liebe*' [for their love]" (XVIII, 91–92).

Since the social Moran manipulates and judges everyone he meets, one might expect him to need a compensatory psychic situation in which he might work with and for others rather than against them. In his first remarks about his job Moran emphasizes this idea, using the rare word "we": "We agents often amused ourselves with grumbling among ourselves" (95). He begins his longest description of the organization by saying, "The agent and the messenger. We agents never took anything in writing" (106). Even when suspecting that this organization may not exist, he clings to the idea of community: "we thought of ourselves as members of a vast organization" (107). He attributes to his group a godlike power when he imagines extending his disbelief in it to "the extreme of . . . regarding myself as solely responsible for my wretched existence" (107). That the organization should be given such a responsibility anticipates the Unnamable's description of his delegates: "They also gave me the low-down on God. They told me I depended on him, in the last analysis. They had it on the reliable authority of his agents at Bally I forget what. . . .They called that presenting their report" (298).

The "we" is reserved for the other agents. In his meetings with Gaber, Moran neither offers nor receives affection, but he is anxious about Youdi's feelings for him. Gaber, in reporting Youdi's first order, says: "He wants it to be you, God knows why." Moran forces him to rephrase this assertion. The next version is little better: "He said . . . that no one could do it but you." "Scenting flattery for which I had a weakness," Moran must make do with this statement, which simply identifies him as the ego and therefore the necessary actor. "This was more or less what I wanted to hear," he says (94). By the end of his long search Moran is desperate for affection from this group. But Gaber knocks him down, saying, "you are beginning to give me a serious pain in the arse." Moran says, "He was not brutal, Gaber, I knew him well" (164). In this group, however, love is an illusion; fear is the cohesive force.

Freud makes this point. Discussing group psychology, Freud chooses the church and the army as examples of "artificial groups—that is, a certain external force is employed to prevent them from disintegrating." This threatening force is concealed behind an apparently stronger force, that of love. In both groups, "the same illusion holds good of there being a head . . . who loves all individuals in the group with an equal love. Everything depends upon this illusion; if it were to be dropped, then both Church and army would dissolve, so far as the external force permitted them to. . . . In these two artificial groups each individual is bound by libidinal ties on the one hand to the leader . . . and on the other hand to the other members of the group" (XVIII, 94–95).

Freud has much to say about the effects of group psychology upon the ego. In group members he sees a number of common qualities: "the weakness of intellectual ability, the lack of emotional restraint, the incapacity for moderation and delay, the inclination to exceed every limit in the expression of emotion and to work it off completely in the form of action . . . a regression of mental activity to an earlier stage such as we are not surprised to find among savages or children" (XVIII, 117). Moran reports his intelligence indirectly, describing Jacques Jr. as "big and strong for his age. His intelligence seemed at times little short of average. My son, in fact" (94). Moran's lack of emotional restraint and his physical expressions of impatience and anger are obvious, especially in his savage beating of his son, after which the son's room is "a shambles" (127), and in his killing of his double.

His group qualities increase as he withdraws from his social roles in Turdy and intensifies his psychic role. His identities in the two worlds remain similar, however, and Freud offers us a reason: "We are reminded of how many of these phenomena of dependence are part of the normal constitution of human society, of how little originality and personal courage are to be found in it, of how much every individual is ruled by those attitudes of the group mind which exhibit themselves . . . as racial characteristics, class prejudices, public opinion, etc." (XVIII, 117).

Molloy presents social existence in an undetailed fresco. The socialized

Moran's report is a spray of phenomena (111). Let us take refuge under the umbrella of hasty generalizations. His behavior is characterized by contradictions that emphasize his repetitive duality, his insincere acting of roles, and his substitution of cliché for commitment. He is concerned to raise his son properly, but he is nastily critical of him. He speaks with affection of his birds, but he lies about some of them and leaves home without medicating the sick gray hen. As a good citizen he criticizes his fellow townspeople and plays the peeping Tom. He is fond of making judgmental assertions, which he often contradicts later.

Molloy's acts and circumstances present stages in a Jungian sequence, with Jungian archetypes. Beckett presents Moran's Freudian world differently. He shows little interest in conventional Freudian images, Freudian slips of the tongue, and Freudian notions of sexuality. Even the Oedipus complex is merely sketched. Perhaps one general observation will cover much of the material. Throughout "Moran" details from "Molloy" recur. Molloy's imagined slaughterhouse is real in "Moran" (29, 95). Molloy abandons the principle of trim; Moran's keys tip him to one side (126). Molloy hears a gong in the forest, apparently signaling nimis sero; Moran hears a gong announcing that he is late for dinner (89, 115). Molloy complains of the pitiless summer sun and its arctic radiance; Moran basks in the summer sun (17, 175). More details abound. A common quality is that in "Molloy" these details are thick with symbolic meanings; in "Moran" they clutter a world literally and flatly there—no mountains, no seacoast, no metaphors.

Those assertions made, we may now leave the drab external world and enter Moran by a trapdoor to survey his group existence with Gaber, Youdi, and (perhaps) the Obidil.

Youdi's Organization: The Blueprint

Beckett took his conception of Moran's work from Freud, and in so doing he invested it with considerable complexity. In *The Ego and the Id* Freud describes the ego, the id, and the superego, or ego ideal, and he sketches what he calls their topological relations. He also suggests dramatic relations among them. We have heard several versions of the central drama: "Helpless in both directions, the ego defends itself vainly, alike against the instigations of the murderous id and against the reproaches of the punishing conscience" (XIX, 53).

This inenarrable contraption the psyche, composed of occasionally warring elements, is ordinarily united under the guidance of the ego: "There is a coherent organization of mental processes; and we call this his *ego*. It is to this ego that consciousness is attached; the ego controls the approaches to motility—that is, to the discharge of excitations into the external world; it is the mental agency which supervises all its own constituent processes, and which goes to sleep at night, though even then it exercises the censorship on dreams. From this ego proceed the repressions, too" (XIX, 17). The conscious ego Moran speculates and observes his own speculations. He dismisses dreams as unimportant (114). He defends repressions ("sollst entbehren"). He is in charge of his household. He is in control—outside. Inside, however, he is part of a complex Freudian mechanism with different terms and a mechanical faculty psychology. Beckett took this contraption from both *The Ego and the Id* and *The Interpretation of Dreams*.

The Ego and the Id divides the psyche into the unconscious (*Ucs.*) and the conscious (*Cs.*) systems. The *Ucs.* is itself divided into what is permanently and what is temporarily unconscious. This second category is promoted to a separate existence. What is more, in discussing *Cs.*, Freud introduces the ego from his other formulation. Complications result. Let us look at his description of the psyche at work:

> The state in which the ideas existed before being made conscious is called by us *repression,* and we assert that the force which instituted the repression and maintains it is perceived as *resistance* during our work of analysis.
>
> Thus we obtain our conception of the unconscious from the theory of repression. We see, however, that we have two kinds of unconscious— the one which is latent but capable of becoming conscious, and the one which is repressed and which is not . . . capable of becoming conscious. . . . The latent, which is unconscious only descriptively, not in the dynamic sense, we call *preconscious;* we restrict the term *unconscious* to the dynamically unconscious repressed; so that now we have three terms, conscious (*Cs.*), preconscious (*Pcs.*), and unconscious (*Unc.*). . . . The *Pcs.* is presumably a great deal closer to the *Cs.* than is the *Unc.* . . . (XIX, 14)

The ego does not fit neatly into this system, and its lack of fit leads to a revaluation of consciousness:

> We recognize that the *Unc.* does not coincide with the repressed; . . . all that is repressed is *Unc.*, but not all that is *Ucs.* is repressed. A part of the ego, too—and Heaven knows how important a part—may be *Ucs.*, undoubtedly is *Ucs.* And this *Ucs.* belonging to the ego is not latent like the *Pcs.*; for if it were, it could not be activated without becoming *Cs.* . . . We must admit that the characteristic of being conscious begins to

lose significance for us. . . . Nevertheless we must beware of ignoring this characteristic, for the property of being conscious or not is in the last resort our one beacon-light in the darkness of depth-psychology. (XIX, 18)

The ego, therefore, has a permanently unconscious component: "How little one is at one with oneself, good God," Moran exclaims (113). And the *Pcs*. linking the darkness of depth psychology and the beacon light of consciousness is active. Consciousness is "the *surface* of the mental apparatus; that is, we have ascribed it as a function to a system which is spatially the first one reached from the external world" (XIX, 19). But now an intermediary is needed between that external world and *Cs*. It is perception (*Pcpt.*).

Freud first contrived *Pcpt.* and these other functions while explaining dreams in *The Interpretation of Dreams*. His solutions caused problems; for instance, how could *Cs*. understand the reports made by *Pcpt.*, since perceptions are always specific and momentary? *Pcpt.* must attach them to mnemic residues of past experiences (*Mnem.*; XIX, 20).

Freud is primarily interested in the issues of depth psychology. It is this existence that he takes to be our first and in other ways our primary one (V, 566–67). Therefore he turns now from the sequence *external world* $\Rightarrow$ *Pcpt.* $\Rightarrow$ *Mnem.* $\Rightarrow$ *Cs.* to consider its complement within the psyche: *Ucs.* $\Rightarrow$ *Pcs.* $\Rightarrow$ *Cs.* Emotions, he says, arise in the *Ucs.* and are felt immediately in the *Cs.*, without having to move through the *Pcs.* But ideas are different. The primordial *Ucs.*, like the id, speaks no language and is essentially unaltered by time. Its libidinal impulses, when not simple emotions, require translation into language: "The question, 'How does a thing become conscious?' would . . . be more advantageously stated: 'How does a thing become preconscious?' And the answer would be: 'Through becoming connected with the word-presentations corresponding to it'" (XIX, 20).

Freud admits that the unconscious materials might attach themselves to pictures rather than words, as in dreams. But he puts this mode of transmission lower on the scale of evolution, perhaps to be associated with more nearly elementary *Ucs.* activities: "Thinking in pictures is . . . only a very incomplete form of becoming conscious. In some way, too, it stands nearer to unconscious processes than does thinking in words, and it is unquestionably older than the latter both ontogenetically and phylogenetically" (XIX, 21).

These "unconscious processes" originate deep within the unconscious: "Internal perceptions yield sensations of processes arising in the most di-

verse and certainly also in the deepest strata of the mental apparatus. . . .
Those belonging to the pleasure-unpleasure series may still be regarded as
the best examples of them. They are more primordial, more elementary,
than perceptions arising externally and they come about even when consciousness is clouded" (XIX, 21–22).

We need these arcane materials. A simple example relates to what Freud
just said about thinking in pictures. When Moran attempts to imagine Molloy,
he gets into bed as if to nap, thereby shutting out the external world and
clouding consciousness. He sinks below the phenomenal world into "this
slow and massive world, where all things move with the ponderous sullen-
ness of oxen, patiently through the immemorial ways" (111), and finds in
this Freudian archaic world images of Molloy: "As he appeared to me, so I
felt he must always have appeared. . . ." In Freud's terms, Moran was "thinking in pictures" about materials from "the deepest strata of the mental apparatus." This activity is familiar to us as one-time Jungians, especially when
Moran says that his findings would "invest my man, from the outset, with
the air of a fabulous being."

This fabulous being emerges from within: "perhaps I had invented him, I
mean found him ready in my head." It is not a matter of "even the simple
déjà vu," Moran insists. "It was happening to me then, or I was greatly
mistaken." He places his Molloy among other strangers whom one recognizes because (in his cinematic metaphor) they have "played a part in certain cerebral reels" (111 ff.). No one, he says, could have told him about
Molloy, and therefore this image is not a *Mnem.* residue, a memory-trace.
Molloy must come from within. Gaber and Youdi did not describe him.

Freud is less interested in these "primordial" images than in the more
complex process leading from an unconscious impulse to words. The *Pcs.*
connects unconscious ideas with word-presentations, but this notion causes
another difficulty: "Only something which has once been a *Cs.* perception
can become conscious, and . . . anything arising from within (apart from
feelings) that seeks to become conscious must try to transform itself into
external perceptions: this becomes possible by means of memory-traces"
(XIX, 20). Therefore the system *Mnem.* (in which words are among the
memory traces) is necessary for consciousness of internal experiences as
well as external ones. In addition, "sensations and feelings, too, only become conscious through reaching the system *Pcpt.*" (XIX, 22).

A complete spatial formulation of approaches to *Cs.* is therefore this:

$$Ucs. \Rightarrow Pcpt. \Rightarrow Mnem. \Rightarrow Pcs. \Rightarrow Cs. \Leftarrow Mnem. \Leftarrow Pcpt. \Leftarrow external \ world$$

Freud concludes that "the part played by word-presentations now becomes
perfectly clear. By their interposition internal thought-processes are made

into perceptions. It is like a demonstration of the theorem that all knowledge has its origin in external perception. When a hypercathexis of the process of thinking takes place, thoughts are *actually* perceived—as if they came from without—and are consequently held to be true" (XIX, 23).

If we add to this summation Freud's acknowledgment that internal processes may also result in images, then we can understand Beckett's dramatization of Moran's mind. The emotional component of a libidinal urge reaches consciousness immediately. The ideational component is translated into pictures and into words. The translator is the preconscious, which uses memory to compose the verbal message that perception needs in order to communicate the libidinal idea to the conscious ego. The term "ego" takes us back to Freud's major description of the psyche. Now he attempts to mix that description with the mechanical formulation just examined.

Wishing to contrive a topological description of the id, the ego, and the superego, Freud offers his readers a drawing that resembles a potato, or murphy—an irrational root. A slight bump at the top is labeled *Pcpt.-Cs.* Beneath that lump is written *Pcs.* The whole murphy is labeled ID. A shaded portion in the center is labeled EGO. A small box (a hearing aid?) attached to the upper left is labeled *acoust.* On the right side, slightly lower than the middle, a cut is made into the potato as if to separate a portion of the ego from a portion of the lower id. On the side of the cut opposite the ego is written *Repressed.*

The indeterminacy of parts within this murphy makes difficult our perception of its functioning. Freud's description helps, but not by clarifying divisions: "We shall now look upon an individual as a psychical id, unknown and unconscious, upon whose surface rests the ego, developed from its nucleus the *Pcpt.* system. . . . The ego does not completely envelope the id, but only does so to the extent to which the system *Pcpt.* forms [the ego's] surface. . . . The ego is not sharply separated from the id; its lower portion merges into it."

But the repressed merges into the id as well, and is merely a part of it. The repressed is only cut off sharply from the ego by the resistances of repression; it can communicate with the ego through the id. "The ego is that part of the id which has been modified by the direct influence of the external world. . . . Moreover, the ego seeks to bring the influence of the external world to bear upon the id and its tendencies, and endeavours to substitute the reality principle for the pleasure principle which reigns unrestrictedly in the id" (XIX, 24–25).

No starchy solid, this potato ferments actively. The ego is both part of the id and contrasted to it: "The ego represents what may be called reason and common sense, in contrast to the id, which contains the passions," and "the ego is first and foremost a bodily ego" (XIX, 25–26). Freud repeats this connection of reason with the body when he introduces the superego. "We shall have to say that not only what is lowest but what is highest in the ego can be unconscious," he notes. "It is as if we were thus supplied with a proof of what we have just asserted of the conscious ego: that it is first and foremost a body-ego" (XIX, 27).

The superego does not appear in the drawing, but we must examine its dual role before we can reach our goal, Moran's job. The superego is the ego's "critical agency" (XIX, 51) and therefore the imposer of guilt. In this role the superego punishes the conscious ego for any disapproved permissiveness toward the id's libidinal impulses. It also has a complementary role, however: "The ego ideal is therefore the heir of the Oedipus complex, and thus it is also the expression of the most powerful impulses and most important libidinal vicissitudes of the id [that is, troubles imposed upon the libido]. . . . Whereas the ego is essentially the representative of the external world, of reality, the super-ego stands in contrast to it as the representative of the internal world, of the id. Conflicts between the ego and the ideal will . . . reflect the contrast between the external world and the internal world" (XIX, 36).

The patient reader plodding like those oxen toward Moran's job correctly senses that the quarry is almost in sight. First, let us examine one more emphasis on the duality of these psychic agencies. The superego, because it is both "the representative of . . . the id" and "a reaction-formation against . . . the id" (XIX, 36, 55), is an unreliable faculty when examined by the conscious ego. That is too hopeful a statement, however; neither the superego nor the id as distinguished from the superego can be examined by the ego, since they are in the unconscious ("unbewusste," unknown). The ego can know that unconscious only by means of the messages that the preconscious, with the help of memory, makes verbal and presents to perception. Each verbal message may emerge either from the id or from the superego's reaction against the id. Each message is a command, requiring action by the actor, the ego. Like King Hamlet's ghost, the command may come in a questionable shape, even though Moran fears to question it.

Youdi's Organization Itself

Moran is an agent for an organization set up by a directorate. Behind or below that directorate may be the Obidil (162). Both of these entities are distant from Moran, who takes his orders from his chief, or *patron,* Youdi. Youdi also keeps his distance. His orders are transmitted by a messenger, Gaber, who reads them directly from his memorandum-book ("calepin"; 146, 164, 252).

Freud's sequence of mental acts shows the chain of command:

Obidil⇒directorate⇒Youdi⇒Gaber⇒Moran⇒external world

"Messenger" and "agent" are terms used by Moran. In Freud's sequence the "agent" acts upon the outside world, allowing us to equate "agent" and "ego." Messages from the unconscious pass through the censoring super-ego, which communicates them to the ego by way of a messenger. Moran imagines many messengers and agents, but Youdi and the Obidil are singular.

Gaber's memorandum-book represents the *Mnem.* As the *Pcs.* translates libidinal desires from the *Mnem.* into word-representations, so Gaber reads Youdi's message from it. Let us note a confirmatory comic detail: Gaber's "memory was so bad that his messages had no existence in his head, but only in his notebook. He had only to close his notebook to become, a moment later, perfectly innocent as to its contents" (106). Moran emphasizes this "amnesia"; Freud explains the appropriateness of the term. The *Pcs.* must communicate with the conscious ego by way of *Pcpt.*, but this sequence requires the existence of *Mnem.*, because "the *Pcpt.* system has no memory whatever, it cannot retain any associative traces" (V, 539).

One might object that because Gaber reads the order, it must already be verbalized. Beckett forestalls that objection; the only order we hear directly is read twice, and Gaber varies its wording. "Moran, Jacques, home instanter" becomes "Moran, home, instanter" (163). In the French the change is more noticeable: "rentrera chez lui" is changed to "regagnera son domicile" (253). Whatever Gaber sees in the notebook, he must make it verbal. Seeking flattery, Moran asks if Youdi "said he had confidence in no one but me?" In Gaber's reply we hear the scorn of the verbal preconscious entity for its wordless and unconscious boss: "He doesn't know what he says. . . . Nor what he does" (94–95).

"Youdi" has been identified as varying a French slang term for Jew, "yehudi." Since Freud is our source of deep psychic messages here, we can accept that interpretation, but we can also twist the name, with less torsion than "Obidil" requires, into "you/id." The superego faces both the unconscious and the external self, which is "ego" for itself but "you" to others. In this context of libido, *Pcs.*, *Mnem.*, and ego, Youdi also represents the ego ideal. One more twist gives us "di-you," *dieu.* Since the directorate is mentioned only as approving a messenger's code, we may take it to represent the internalized culture, which provides Gaber's language.

G. C. Barnard noted that "Gaber is . . . an hallucination, a projection of Moran's Super-ego, Youdi, the chief whose commands have to be obeyed" (33). On the threshold of complete recognition he halted, however; he derived from these preliminary identifications only evidence of Moran's "schizo-phrenia." Beckett has other interests.

The superego represents ideals, while the ego exists in the physical world. It is therefore not surprising that the superego's messenger is called Gaber. An angel ("angelos" means "messenger") is an intermediary between God and man. The name "Gabriel" combines the Hebrew words "gabher" and "El," "man" and "God" (a patching like "you" and "id"). Gaber works for a secular psyche, so his tail has been docked. The angel Gabriel delivered to Mary God's message that she was to bear his son, that incarnation of which Molloy was reminded by the angelus. In "Moran" this idea of spirit being made flesh is comically reduced to psychic impulse and physical actions. Gaber was "getting into position to make love to his wife" (94) when called away by Youdi, whose message required wording and delivery before being acted out by Moran. Gabriel's greeting to Mary, "hail, Mary," is in French "salut, Marie." At their first two encounters Gaber says to Moran, "salut Moran." William James reported Mohammed's involvement with Gabriel in a simpler sequence.

Moran's organization is wittily and briefly presented. This explication is neither. Homo mensura needs staffage.

Moran at Work

Moran's organization enables him to be part of a group, to sense that he is doing admirable work, and to be like others while acting alone. His mem-bership enacts his group psychology, and the organization amusingly ech-oes the structure of a Freudian psyche. This subject is central to the develop-ing of "Moran." It provides the dramatic conflicts that in "Molloy" were provided by the ego-consciousness's encounters with archetypal figures.

Moran is an active ego, placed between the rest of his psyche and the external world. The conscious ego processes information from the outside, identifies desirable and undesirable matters, and learns both actively and passively. Meanwhile it conducts similar activities with the psyche. Com-pared with our own busy egos, Moran as a professional ego is a poor thing. He works only intermittently, only in response to Youdi, and only for some-one else's good. What does he do, then? His tasks involve peeping and pry-ing (94), yet he must be comically noticeable (124). He regrets taking his son in search of Molloy because "there is something about a father that discourages derision. Even grotesque he commands a certain respect" (125).

He is sent after men termed variously "client," "patient," and "prey." They include three Beckett characters—Murphy, Watt, and Mercier (137), someone named Yerk, and an unnamed youth seeking a woman. Only two specific professional acts are described. One constitutes the climax of "the Yerk affair": "I succeeded in possessing myself of his tiepin and destroying it" (136). The other act is the ostensible arranging of a rendezvous between the youth and a woman he loves from afar. Wondering what to do with Molloy, Moran says that "there were no usual things, in my instructions. Admittedly there was one particular operation that recurred from time to time" (137). He does not describe that operation, however. The rendezvous and tiepin tell us little, as does his saying that each client is part of a conglomerate rock but thinks himself "a being apart": "I arrive, he comes away" ("il se détache" [171]).

Each assignment involves finding an individual male. He must perform some act in order to accomplish some result. The results, essentially the same, must satisfy Youdi. He must dress so as to be conspicuously comic: "To call forth feelings of pity and indulgence, to be the butt of jeers and hilarity, is indispensable. So many vent-holes in the cask of secrets. On condition you cannot feel, nor denigrate, nor laugh" (124–25). The venting of a cask of secrets recalls Molloy's description of his self as a jar, cage, box, and cave (49, 51, 75). Moran must incite pity, indulgence, jeers, or hilarity in each targeted client. Hearing the vented secrets, Moran must not feel, denigrate, or laugh. This situation and relationship might imply psychoanalysis, but no analyst is obliged to be clownish and therefore pitied, indulged, jeered, or laughed with—that is, the target of feeling, denigration, and laughter.

In *The Interpretation of Dreams* Freud discusses a topic to which he will return five years later, in *Jokes and Their Relation to the Unconscious:* the cause of laughter. He associates laughter with repressed impulses. Before such impulses in the irrational unconscious can emerge in dreams (where the *Pcs.* expresses them in words that "exhibit the same displacements and confusions"), repression must be overcome. When it gives way, the repressed material bursts out into consciousness: "Evidence . . . of the increase in [repressive] activity which becomes necessary when these primary modes of functioning are inhibited is to be found in the fact that we produce a *comic* effect, that is, a surplus of energy which has to be discharged in *laughter, if we allow these modes of thinking to force their way into consciousness*" (V, 605).

Dreams and jokes originate in the irrational and ordinarily repressed materials of the mind. Laughter results, or may, from their forceful eruption into conscious expression. An audience's relaxation of repressions in order to enjoy comedy weakens its inhibitions, lowers its resistance, and eases the acknowledgment of difficult material. Many a true word spoken in jest elicits a response that might otherwise remain unconscious. No wonder, then, that Moran is unhappy at having to bring his son along on his search for Molloy. The role of father demands respect, and respect implies repression, which Moran must overcome to tap his client's cask of secrets. (We recall "From an Abandoned Work": "vent the pent.")

What do we know now about Moran's work? In jumbled terms we may say that a superego transmits through Gaber an order that the ego must obey. Youdi's order obliges Moran to find a man and extract repressed secrets from him, with the result that this man is altered. The terms "client," "patient," and "prey" make ambivalent the value of this alteration and its desirability for the prey. He has imagined himself as part of a conglomerate and has wished to be detached from it. In two cases, Moran has staged a false rendezvous for a lover and has destroyed Yerk's tiepin. These absurd events appear negative and of no use to a superego concerned with conventional group behavior.

In *The Ego and the Id* Freud describes the superego as created by the introjection into the child's psyche of his parents' values, here called "identifications" (XIX, 31). The acceptance of these identifications aids the child to move beyond the Oedipal conflict. Moran serves not his father but a group superego, Youdi. He scarcely mentions his parents. In his fifteenth year he learned the value of "sollst entbehren." Accepting this obligation to do without, to repress, he freed himself from a dependent relation to his father. His own superego was created on schedule.

The earliest identifications come from the parents and form the superego. But the superego's values continue to accumulate. A primary cause is the failure of an external object-cathexis. (We recall this terminology from *Murphy;* one loves another person but in vain.) Then a substitute form of that failed external relationship is "set up again inside the ego—that is, . . . an object-cathexis has been replaced by an identification" (XIX, 28). The result is significant for the psyche: "this kind of substitution has a great share in determining the form taken by the ego and . . . it makes an essential contribution towards building up what is called its 'character'" (XIX, 28).

An example may help here. A man finds a woman desirable because he finds qualities of character in that person desirable. While his desire continues, those qualities are contained in that other person. If the relationship becomes unsatisfactory, he may be changed by it. For a serious change to occur, the lover must be rejected harshly or in some other way seriously disappointed. That may cause an introjection of identifications, an adoption of new qualities:

When it happens that a person has to give up a sexual object, there quite often ensues an alteration of his ego which can only be described as a setting up of the object inside the ego . . .: the exact nature of this substitution is as yet unknown to us. It may be that by this introjection . . . the ego makes it easier for the object to be given up or renders that process possible. [We may recall Celia's adoption of Murphy's rocking-chair and his use of it.] It may be that this identification is the sole condition under which the id can give up its objects. At any rate the process . . . is a very frequent one, and it makes it possible to suppose that the character of the ego is a precipitate of abandoned object-cathexes and that it contains the history of these object-cathexes. (XIX, 29)

Schopenhauer says that the will created intellect in order to become conscious of itself. Jung describes the Logos as taking conscious control of the anima. Freud says that psychic development is a matter of becoming conscious of, and thereby acquiring some control over, one's unconscious (the draining of the Zuider Zee). Freud connects this idea of control with the introjection of identifications: "This transformation of an erotic object-choice into an alteration of the ego is also a method by which the ego can obtain control over the id and deepen its relations with it . . ." (XIX, 30).

With these tools and this wiring diagram let us return to Moran's behavior with the wistful young lover and Yerk. The lover loves a woman whom he has never met, an actress. He may know her only in her dramatic roles, perhaps in films. (We recall Moran's "cerebral reels" [112].) When one loves a woman one has not met, it is inevitable that this object-cathexis is an actress in the lover's psychic drama, reflecting values and desires from within his own psyche. Moran leads this lover to a false rendezvous and leaves him there: "I can see him still, looking after me. I fancy he would have liked me for a friend" (137). Moran is no one's friend; it is a condition of his work that "you cannot feel." The young man desirous of a mistress and a friend, however, obviously seeks object-cathexes for his affection. (His desires recall Molloy's need for his mother and a fellow or frère.) The only possible result of Moran's act is that the young man, disappointed in love, will introject into his own psyche the values of the hoped-for mistress and friend. They will become identifications that will alter his character. The nature of the alteration we cannot yet determine.

This interpretation, though incomplete, must apply to Moran's other cases. We turn to Yerk and his tiepin. *Webster's Seventh New Collegiate Dictionary* asserts without explanation that "jerk" as an insulting term is probably a variant of "yerk." Even without this assertion, the name implies foolishness. (Dying, Belacqua experiences "terrible yellow yerks in his skull" [174]. They appear irrelevant.) Moran's task is to approach closely, in his clownish dress, a man so concerned about his appearance as to take a tiepin seriously. (Amateur Freudians will note that it represses a necktie that might otherwise go astray.)

These basic elements resemble some in the case of the lover. He wished Moran for a friend. Moran must have evoked similar feelings from Yerk, perhaps even specifically because of his clownish costume. "To call forth feelings of pity and indulgence . . . is indispensable"; Moran may even have tempted Yerk into sympathetic hilarity. Moran's destruction of the tiepin must have disappointed Yerk as seriously as his abandonment of the youth must have destroyed that client's hopes. By disappointing his hopes of a mistress, Moran also removed that potential object-cathexis. He literally removed Yerk's comically trivial object-cathexis. A tiepin is nothing, but Moran is confident of his success. We must conclude that the tiepin meant as much to this jerk as the actress did to the unworldly young man. The ties that bind. Introjections of the actress's many-roled values and the tiepin's trivial ones must follow. But Youdi's purpose remains unclear.

Moran includes among his patients Murphy, Watt, and Camier. We must imagine Moran as Beckett's surrogate and therefore as responsible for tempting Murphy to see values in Miss Counihan, in Celia, in Neary's philosophy, in the rocking chair, and in Mr. Endon—to be disappointed each time. Here is a complex version of Moran's effect upon the young man and Yerk. Again, however, we must hesitate about Youdi's intention; surely he did not intend to kill Murphy.

In *Mercier and Camier* it is Mercier who makes the final attempt to establish a relationship, only to be rebuffed by Camier. (His failure leads the Unnamable to describe them as a "pseudo-couple" [297].) Watt makes a cameo appearance in that text, and he identifies his situation with that of Mercier and Camier by saying: "I too have sought, . . . all on my own, only I thought I knew what" (113–14). But he did not know Watt; his search failed too. He found only Knott. So Moran led Murphy, Watt, and Mercier to dead ends.

Youdi's Use of Moran

In a pseudo-psychic organization Moran functions to complete a process by which each client separates from the conglomerate mass of humanity and completes what Jung might call his individuation. Beckett denounced friendship in *Proust* as "a false movement of the spirit—from within to without" (65). Moran's disappointing of Yerk and the young lover seems intended to turn their spirits away from that outside world. We might imagine both men as potential peers of those great solitary figures Murphy, Watt, and Mercier.

The probability of a dual meaning weighs too heavily, however. We know Watt's later identity from his appearance in *Mercier and Camier*. No longer a shy introvert developing his internal self, he is a loud-mouthed extravert thriving in the world of quid pro quo. Murphy was returning to Celia and the job path when he burned out. Camier sought Mercier. We cannot imagine Yerk in the role of a solitary.

Freud also stands in our path. Nothing he has said about the superego allows us to believe that this parentally and socially derived ego ideal of values can desire its psyche to shun society and the object-cathexes to be found there. Nor can his description of the ego as a body-ego and as mediating between other parts of the psyche and the external world encourage us to imagine eliminating that external world. Nor can we understand Youdi's organization if such elimination is its aim; to externalize the parts of a group psyche in order to emphasize the value of psychic solitude would not be intelligible.

Insofar as we can relate Youdi to Moran's comments about his own development, we can find no sign of an ego ideal characterized by willing separateness from the conglomerate mass of mankind. On the contrary, a primary message is "sollst entbehren." That is merely negative, just as Moran's control of his son is mainly negative. To repress any ideas not socially acceptable is no way to devise a solitary identity.

A satisfactory emendation of Moran's function and his place in the organization should not only remove these objections but turn them into positive evidence. That emendation is possible. In the discussion above, "Moran: The Inside Story," Moran was described with the aid of Freud's *Group Psychology and the Analysis of the Ego*. To the extent that Moran's job is understood as separating him from the group world of Turdy, one might think that his primary identity is that of a solitary even though he says it is not. But when we consider Moran's relation to Youdi and Gaber, we see that he imagines himself as part of a group. When we recognize Youdi as a superego presiding over this group and guiding Moran's behavior in the external world, then we find another meaning in Moran's professional actions and their results.

Moran's extended description of his work is now useful. He begins with his getting into bed to consider what course to follow in dealing with his quarry Molloy and that quarry's "ludicrous distress" (110):

Far from the world . . . I pass judgement on it and on those, like me, who are plunged in it beyond recall, and on him who has need of me to be delivered, who cannot deliver himself. . . . From their places masses move, stark as laws. . . . There somewhere man is too, vast conglomerate of all of nature's kingdoms, as lonely and as bound. [Missing in the translation is the original's description of this "bloc" as being conventional or determined, "aussi dénoué d'imprévu qu'un rocher" (171).] And in that block the prey is lodged and thinks himself a being apart. Anyone would serve. But I am paid to seek. His life has been nothing but a waiting for this, to see himself preferred, to fancy himself damned, blessed, to fancy himself everyman ["de se croire médiocre"], above all others ["entre tous"].

At this point Moran shifts to other topics, leaving us in the dark about how he delivers his quarry from that conglomerate and with what results.

Considering him an ego working for a superego with group values, we hear some curious intonations and emphases in this passage. Plunged in the world beyond recall, Moran delivers from it the quarry who cannot deliver himself. (Curiously, the original phrasing refers to Moran: "moi qui ne sais moi délivrer," echoing "others he saves, himself he cannot save," one of the taunts to Jesus on the cross.) This sense of Moran as savior implies that to separate his quarry from the world is a good act. That the quarry's distress is "ludicrous," however, implies no sympathy, and more dualities add confusion. That the quarry fancies himself unlike the common person—preferred, damned, blessed—can be understood as approving of the uncommon. But "to see himself" and "to fancy himself" suggest doubt, and the idea (stronger in the French) that this self-estimate could include being "médiocre" can hardly fail to be dismissive. (Yerk comes to mind.) These quarries need help to separate themselves; they merely fancy another role; they merely think of themselves as separable from others; and their fancied roles are drab.

Surely Moran speaks here as a loyal member of the group, a representative of the block, the conglomerate, judging pejoratively these would-be individuals wishing to be unique and "imprévu." Yet as the dutiful agent of the superego, he aids these clients to leave the group. Something remains wrong. The difficulty is clarified, however, if we see this complex passage in the context of the two previous paragraphs. There Moran reports another example of his work with a victim and connects it explicitly with his praise of "sollst entbehren." For this job he needs no order from Youdi; this quarry is his son, and he is at once the judging superego and the agent ego.

Moran finds his son misbehaving, rearranging his stamp collection in order to bring some favorite stamps on the journey. Aware of this act before questioning him, Moran is able to play the omniscient God or conscience. He forces his son to confess and punishes him by taking both stamp albums. For his audience he draws the moral. He is training his son to obey, preparing him for the lesson "sollst entbehren." (Moran learned this in his fifteenth year; his son is "thirteen or fourteen" [110, 94].) Taking this event as a model, we see that Moran does act for Youdi, the group superego. He instills obedience by negative means, not rewarding good behavior but punishing disobedience. Thereby he teaches the negative virtue of doing without. This approach requires the quarry to act out an improper desire and then learn that it must be repressed.

Moran imposes filial obedience through his paternal authority. In his work for Youdi, however, he deals with people in the social world. His aim there, or Youdi's aim, is essentially the same. He leads his quarry into temptation in order to deliver him from free will. He encourages his client's fancying of himself as separate from the conglomerate and then contrives a bad result, thereby sending the client back to the conglomerate group. This professional imposition of group psychology upon the would-be individual must be described speculatively, with the aid of the scarce evidence.

Yerk is one of those who aspire only to be mediocre. His tiepin identifies him as a member of a group concerned with proper appearances. His slowly evoked willingness to keep company with the comically dressed Moran suggests a different yearning. To destroy the tiepin, however, is to force him into the wrong style. He must have rejected Moran's company in dismay. This is not very clear.

The young lover is a more profitable example. He would like Moran for a friend, and he desires for himself a woman who as an actress is an object of group adoration. Moran contrives to disappoint both of the young man's desires, and we must imagine him returning to his group and group satisfactions. He had improperly wished to do wrong, by group standards. Freud explains why: "Two people coming together for the purpose of sexual satisfaction, in so far as they seek for solitude, are making a demonstration against the herd instinct, the group feeling. . . . The more they are in love, the more completely they suffice for each other" (XVIII, 140). Jacques Jr.'s affection for his stamps distracts him from his group role as the affectionate son.

Mercier ends *Mercier and Camier* abandoned again by Camier, with whom he made efforts to stay. Camier is a private investigator, an ancestor of Moran, who carries a memorandum-book as does Gaber. Camier disappoints Mercier as Moran disappoints the young man. However, nothing suggests that Mercier then becomes a member of a group.

Watt is a more curious example. We encounter him last in *Mercier and Camier,* where he makes a startling cameo appearance. ("I'm unrecognizable," he admits [111].) His first act is to call himself to Camier's attention: "A hand landed with a thump on his shoulder" (110). That coarsely sociable thump on Camier's shoulder recurs in "Moran." The stranger who resembles Moran as agent greets him with "a thump of his hand on my shoulder" (150). The Watt we knew was not forceful. The later Watt tries to ingratiate himself with Mercier and Camier by suggesting that he has experienced their yearnings: "I too have sought, said Watt, all on my own, only I thought I knew what" (113–14). His present identity, however, is different. We may say, with slight assurance, that the present Watt's disappointment with Knott and his therapy in the sanatarium returned him to the group.

The later Watt is more complex, however. He insists upon taking the reluctant Mercier and Camier to a bar. There he shifts from his sociable group identity. Suddenly he shouts "Bugger life!" (114). A while later he smashes a table with Camier's stick, shouting "Fuck life!" Those are not the observations of someone encouraging group membership. Yet Mercier and Camier react to his first cry by coming to his aid, defending his behavior against the bar owner who wishes them to leave. After Watt's second cry they abandon him, but they go off together—for the last time. Any comparison with Moran must be forced. A forced comparison permits us to see that Watt, like Moran, displays a double identity, the solitary and the encourager of group life, and in his extravagance of talk and behavior he anticipates Moran's clownish professional costume and destroying of the tiepin.

Murphy is mentioned anonymously in *Mercier and Camier:* "he died ten years ago. . . . They never found the body" (111). He will reappear in the fizzle "He is barefoot," probably written in 1954. There he wears "vaguely prison garb" ("vaguement pénitentière"). He climbs and falls through a rocky labyrinth suggesting a Mount of Purgatory but with no path to the summit. He does not remember his existence in *Murphy.* Beckett's presentation is ambivalent. Perhaps Murphy is purging himself of that early attempt to leave the conglomerate mass through which he now climbs; perhaps he is a prisoner attempting to escape the group, fleeing the job path again, seeking to escape his issueless predicament. ("Murphy had first-rate legs," we are told.) In any case we know with certainty that his disappointments in *Murphy* sent him back toward Celia and civilization.

The evidence from these Beckettian characters is indecisive. Their introduction into Moran's world should be treated gingerly, perhaps more gingerly than here. However much Beckett may wish to make them examples of a single intent, they cannot have had so simple an origin. Their recurrences here are suggestive, not definitive.

Generalizing from these many details, we conclude that Youdi sends Moran after people identified as unwilling members of a group. Shunning respectable roles and appearances, Moran tempts them to strengthen their velleity, to detach themselves and become individual. Youdi requires Moran to lead these people into individuality in order to disappoint them with that state. They will then repress their erring libidinal impulses and return penitently to the conglomerate mass.

Youdi's organization and its assignments exaggerate and caricature Moran's daily behavior in the external world. With his family and with his neighbors Moran reveals by his acts and judgments his own strong superego and his ego's approval of its values. As father, employer, parishioner, and citizen he emphasizes the importance of proper appearances and behavior. He is an excellent group member.

In his psyche Youdi issues the orders and Gaber is the go-between (94). Moran is the agent, the actor. Activity is therefore a primary concern: "I . . . never set out on a mission without prolonged reflection as to the best way of setting out. It was the first problem to solve, . . . and I never moved until I had solved it. . . . And in my ignorance of the reasons against it I decided to leave on my autocycle. Thus was inscribed, on the threshold of the Molloy affair, the fatal pleasure principle" (98–99). Moran's last remark, the most explicit reference to Freudian thought in the novel, is not easily understood. In the next paragraph he describes his behavior as a matter of "inconceivable levity." (He also reports that the weather soon changed from fair to rainy; perhaps this explains why he did not take the autocycle. Molloy left the immobile bicycle behind when he returned to the now rainy Bally.) In an early remark, back when he called the pleasure principle the unpleasure principle, Freud said that "our thinking always remains exposed to falsification by interference from the unpleasure principle" (V, 603). That desire to make matters easy for himself, given his reluctance to seek Molloy, is also acted out in Moran's inability to remember the details of the assignment. He admits that he almost botched the task of deciding what to bring with him, but then his son came to his room, allowing him to strike the pose of the dominating superego and thereby distract himself from his evasions. As that superego he can even assert, despite the evasions he has just acknowledged, "Vagueness I abhor" (99).

These are useful details. They remind us, as does so much in the early pages, that Moran's character is patched together—a conglomerate, not all of a piece. We noticed his saying that he saves his clients, who cannot save themselves; we noticed also that in the French he cannot save himself. He expresses his desire to be saved from the block, the conglomerate. At the same time his membership in that conglomerate saves him from having to make difficult individual decisions.

Describing "the inenarrable contraption I called my life," he admits that he was a contrivance, "turned towards the outer world as towards the lesser evil," and so turned in order to preserve his existence as "a solitary." "Don't wait to be hunted to hide, that was always my motto," he says (114), and we recall Molloy's vague description of his life in society, hiding from those hunters who purge society of its foul creatures. (Beckett makes clear Moran's hunter/hunted connection with Molloy in translation; Moran's original phrase is "faire le part du feu avant la conflagration" [176].)

In the same tightly packed paragraph Moran identifies his external self by connecting it with "his house, . . . his garden, . . . his few poor possessions," to which he later adds his hens and his faith. Now he is their "creature," a submissive change from his emphatic possession of them in the opening scene. Throughout "Moran" this external identity is linked to the material possessions that help to create it. Before he departs, Moran attempts to ease his worries by going out to his garden. "There is something in this house tying my hands," he thinks. Outside, too, his mind moves among his things: shrubberies, beehives, cigar, the ash-tray and waste-paper basket, the dog Zulu, the smells . . . (122–23). These props of his social identity no longer comfort him: "Finding my spirits as low in the garden as in the house, I turned to go in, saying to myself it was one of two things, either my house had nothing to do with the kind of nothingness in the midst of which I stumbled or else the whole of my little property was to blame."

He decides on the second explanation. Packing, "I had the joyful vision of myself far from home, from the familiar faces, from all my sheet-anchors, sitting on a milestone in the dark, . . . coldly hatching my plans, . . . creating time to come" (125). The sheet-anchors recall Molloy's similarly nautical description of himself, when resting on his bicycle, as sensing a "strain, as of hawsers about to snap," but knowing himself still "safely bound" (21). We may also recall the French description of the conglomerate as "aussi dénue d'imprévu qu'un rocher." Moran imagines himself free to create an unforeseen future, but then he recalls that "my son would be at my side." He too would be safely anchored to his group identity.

His vision of freedom on the road reminds us of his secondary identity, the solitary who hides before being hunted. In that packed paragraph in which he describes his two identities, the solitary is quickly dropped: "this took up very little room in the inenarrable contraption I called my life. . . .

And if I had to tell the story of my life I should not so much as allude to these apparitions, and least of all to . . . Molloy" (114).

His remark is curious. "These apparitions" are apparently the chimeras by which he is "haunted and possessed." It appears that Molloy is one of them. That paragraph begins with his assuming that Molloy's face is "hirsute, craggy and grimacing." The next paragraph suggests doubt: "images of this kind the will cannot revive without doing them violence." Considering this doubt, Moran concludes that "the Molloy I brought to light . . . was certainly not the true denizen of my dark places, for it was not his hour." The discrepancy does not trouble him, since during this event he identifies his self with his public role in Youdi's organization: "for what I was doing I was doing neither for Molloy, who mattered nothing to me, nor for myself, of whom I despaired [we may recall "moi qui ne sais moi délivrer"], but on behalf of a cause which, while having need of us to be accomplished, was in its essence anonymous" (114). Emphasizing the vastness and importance of Youdi's group, Moran can ease his anxiety about this denizen of his dark places by taking refuge in his group identity.

But Moran is a potential defector from that group, at once a company man and a solitary, and he leaves his society behind. His material possessions are most easily left, in part because he must replace his daily dress with a uniform and because his house and grounds appear solid enough to await his return. His social connections are less easily broken. He contrives a visit to Father Ambrose, and he acts out a sentimental farewell to Martha. The very notion that he is a defector seems doubtful, in fact. After all, it is his group leader, Youdi, who obliges him to leave.

But Moran's doubting also detaches him, incompletely, from group ideas. Already in the first half of "Moran" we hear his doubts about religion. He concludes one description of Youdi's organization by admitting that "in my moments of lucidity" he doubted Gaber's existence and might even have "gone to the extreme of conjuring away the chief (one Youdi), could I have denied myself the pleasure of—you know. But I was not made for the great light that devours, a dim lamp was all I had been given . . ." (106–7). That pleasure is another reference to the pleasure principle, here the principle of reducing anxiety to a minimum by keeping himself in the dark about this group's existence. Moran's fear of the light reminds us of Molloy's similar aversion, but it also suggests Moran's ignorance of the unconscious.

If the great light that devours would make away with Gaber and Youdi, would it also make away with the Obidil and with Moran's hidden solitary self? (His versions of Molloy are also associated with darkness.) When we hear of the Obidil, Moran will nearly conjure him away: "Perhaps there is no such person, that would not greatly surprise me" (162). But the libido exists by definition in the darkness of depth psychology, where Moran's Molloy seems also to be located.

These doubts and unsympathetic speculations are intelligible to us Freudians as coming from a group member and also as coming from an ego. Youdi's reluctant employee certainly might wish to conjure away his boss and Gaber, if not the Obidil, and to escape his possessions and Martha and his son. "The poor ego," Freud exclaims: "Its three tyrannical masters are the external world, the super-ego and the id. When we follow the ego's efforts to satisfy them simultaneously—or rather, to obey them simultaneously—we cannot feel any regret at having personified this ego and having set it up as a separate organism. It feels hemmed in on three sides, threatened by three kinds of danger, to which . . . it reacts by generating anxiety" (XXII, 77). Moran will not strengthen his doubts about Youdi and Gaber to the point of conjuring those beings away. Even at the end of "Moran" he is still visited by Gaber and still completing his report for Youdi. He never regards himself as solely responsible for his wretched existence.

Molloy as Client: Why?

It is absurd that the Molloy we have seen should become a client of Youdi. However, "client" in French retains the specific sense of a medical patient. Youdi's clients need psychiatric help. The psychoanalyst must lead his patients back to membership in the groups that constitute society, back to Celia and the job path. Jung offered individuation, but Freudian therapy has no such goal. These comments are scarcely relevant, however, since the Molloy we have seen never appears in "Moran." Moran's imagined Molloy resembles him mainly by separating this client from his earlier clients. Moran's Molloy is far more distant from society than Yerk, the amorous young man, Murphy, Watt, and Mercier. He is also explicitly an entity in Moran's mind.

That source allows us to complete our connecting of terms. Gaber is the Pcs. Youdi is the superego. Moran functions professionally as the bodily ego, the agent. Molloy therefore must join the id and the Obidil in the unconscious. But why should Youdi send Moran after an internal quarry? Why would a superego send its ego in search of the id? That formulation shapes the answer, and the answer shapes the plot of "Moran."

Freud's description of the ego as serving three masters may be altered to describe the superego as itself busy on three fronts. It must ensure the obedience of the ego. It must evaluate threats and possibilities from the external world as they reach it through the ego. It must approve proper and repress improper impulses from the id. These tasks constitute Youdi's job description.

Moran has projected his personal psychic group into society, where it serves as a police force. It is characterized by strong emphases on the distant leader Youdi, on the obedience of that leader's executive officer Moran, and on the disciplining of potential defectors from group society—its clients, patients, quarries, prey. Yerk and the amorous young man constituted threats to group solidity. Youdi sent his obedient agent to bring them back, and as usual (according to Moran) Moran succeeded.

But this obedient agent himself contains an embryonic solitary identity. Perhaps almost any member of a group begins sooner or later to criticize its mechanics. He gets above himself, one says. Planning to take communion although he has broken his fast, Moran admits that "God would know, sooner or later" (97). His taking advantage of an administrative delay amusingly illustrates such restlessness, which will develop complexity in his "questions of a theological nature" (166–67). Moran's early doubts may be superficial, but they surface from a turbulent depth, as Moran's images of Molloy suggest. The images quite take Moran over: "I was nothing but uproar, bulk, rage, suffocation, effort unceasing, frenzied and vain." He defensively adds: "Just the opposite of myself, in fact" (113). Soon, however, he will describe his beating of his sick son with his umbrella.

In describing Molloy, Moran uses images related to his description of mankind as a block and a conglomerate. These images assert his own fixed and proper identity, as opposed to Molloy's. "I was a solid in the midst of other solids," he says (108), "a sensible man, cold as crystal and as free from spurious depth" (113). Nevertheless, the Molloy emerging from him leads him to acknowledge a more complex self: "How little one is at one with oneself" (113). He accurately describes his split psyche as "unfathomable mind, now beacon, now sea" (106). Freud made the same metaphoric sense of the matter: "The property of being conscious or not is in the last resort our one beacon-light in the darkness of depth-psychology" (XIX, 18).

That psychic darkness recalls again Freud's ironic image of the psychotherapist's work: "Where id was, there ego shall be. It is a work of culture—not unlike the draining of the Zuider Zee" (XXII, 80). Just previously Freud had corrected his potato-shaped drawing of the psyche: "the space occupied by the unconscious id ought to have been incomparably greater than that of the ego or the preconscious" (XXII, 79). His emphasis upon the size of the id prepares us to understand that this Zuider Zee is beyond draining. Beckett may have recalled that emphasis in altering "incompréhensible" to "unfathomable": "incompréhensible esprit, tantôt mer, tantôt phare" (164). Moran is becoming aware of the libido.

Youdi has ordered Moran to do for himself what he has done for his previous clients. The order is not straightforward; Moran has not been told that he is his own client. Molloy's ostensibly external existence masks Youdi's intention. Moran tricked his clients by pretending to satisfy their desire for an identity and an existence separate from the conglomerate mass of mankind. Now his search for Molloy—that is, for the unrepressed solitary in himself—will send him out into solitude. Youdi expects this experience to send him back to the group as repentant as Murphy and Yerk and the young lover had been.

Later, Moran will acknowledge Youdi's intention and his own resultant submission by acknowledging that he must continue to fulfill his part, to act out his role, now unwillingly, as once he had done willingly and had obliged others to do. He must "continue to the end the faithful servant I have always been, of a cause that is not mine, and patiently fulfil in all its bitterness my calamitous part [mon rôle (204)], as it was my will, when I had a will, that others should" (132).

With extensive aid from Freud, we have considered materials from "Moran" that ordinarily strike readers as puzzling but uninteresting. These materials have made sense of the basic structure of "Moran," or at least of its first half and the journey that begins the second. Moran is a solid citizen, with the virtues and defects of a conventional group member. He acts out those qualities and demands them from others. (He'll be judge, he'll be jury.) Now, visited by a celestial messenger, as William James might say, he may be born again, but with a painful difference. He is obliged to turn his habitual fantasy of a second and solitary identity, his unacted detachment from any group, into the painful experience of such solitary detachment. (An uprooting, it will seem.) The boredom of living will be replaced by the suffering of being.

Now that we think we know where we are going, let us see if we can get there.

The Journey Out

Molloy's problems were relatively easy for Beckett to dramatize, one suspects. Jung offered him not only the idea of a metaphoric journey toward individuation but also many characters and events with which to act out that journey. The necessary encounter with the anima—developed into encounters with the physical mother, the spiritual mother, and the sensual woman—provided Beckett with a sketched sequence and subordinate masculine characters. It also offered him a goal to be reached or missed.

For "Moran," on the other hand, Freudian psychology offers the behavioral symptoms of neurosis, antagonistic relations among parts of the psyche, and the substitution of the group for the family. The proper resolution of any specific difficulty entails no necessary sequence of psychic events, and no specific goal awaits, no climactic individuation. Beckett must contrive his own sequence of events that will act out the problems of Moran's multiple identities as a solitary and as a group member.

Freud touches on the notion of multiple identities only once and briefly, making it an extreme instance of a more common situation: narcissism as displayed in the abandonment of an object-cathexis and the return of one's externally directed affection upon the ego. When that rejected affection returns, the ego alters to imitate the loved qualities of the object-cathexis: "When the ego assumes the features of the object, it is forcing itself, so to speak, upon the id as a love-object and is trying to make good the id's loss by saying: 'Look, you can love me too—I am so like the object'" (XIX, 30).

Here Freud touches on the topic of multiple identities. He suggests that these "object-identifications" resulting from the ego's imitation of the lost object may get out of hand. They may "become too numerous, unduly powerful and incompatible with one another." Rather than mixing into one whole, they form separate identities. For Beckett's purposes in "Moran," one might speak of these identities as Moran does, calling them roles. A simple instance was reported by the future historian Edward Gibbon, ordered by his parents to leave his mistress: "I grieved as a lover; I obeyed as a son."

The result of multiple identities, Freud says, may be pathological: "It may come to a disruption of the ego in consequence of the different identifications becoming cut off from one another by resistances; perhaps the secret of the cases of what is described as 'multiple personality' is that the different identifications seize hold of consciousness in turn. Even when things do not go so far as this, there remains the question of conflicts between the various identifications into which the ego comes apart, conflicts which cannot after all be described as entirely pathological. . . . This leads us back to the origin of the ego-ideal," Freud says (XIX, 30). A strong ego ideal can keep such fragmentary object-identifications from occurring.

In a group situation this strong ego ideal is enacted by the group leader. He is the cathected object of each follower's affections. If he can so satisfy them that the follower does not seek additional or alternative objects elsewhere, then the follower will not develop these multiple identifications. If he does not so satisfy them, competing identifications may develop in his follower's psyche. Then the leader must use the force that lurks behind his show of affection. Youdi has used Moran to carry out such disciplinary procedures against Yerk and the young lover.

Moran was a devout follower of Youdi. In his relations with his son and

Martha he sought no alternative object of affection; instead, he played the role of the superego as well as the ego. Imitation is the best flattery. He also displayed no strong religious faith. Therefore there was no split loyalty or consequent split identity in Moran's external life, but his psychic life is different. He not only acknowledges a solitary within him but claims that he serves the outer world only for the sake of that solitary.

This unacted desire for solitude, a possible cause of future misbehavior, has spurred Youdi to send Moran out in search of his solitary, the Molloy within him. Moran had supported Yerk's yearning for sartorial impropriety by displaying his own comic costume; then he had obliged Yerk to continue dressing improperly by destroying his tiepin. More importantly, he had supported the young man's desire for a friend and for an assignation with the actress by pretending to be a friend and to arrange this assignation. Now Youdi's work is more complex. Moran must be given the solitude he desires. Negatively, the group world of Turdy and the family group must be removed. Positively, he must experience his solitary self.

Moran is aware of his psychic life and its changes with a subtlety of perception far beyond Molloy's abilities. Moreover, Beckett imagines Moran's experiences not only as a drama but in metaphors. These complexities must be set aside in order to sketch the drama and the dramatis personae. Few actors are needed. Jacques Jr., the white-haired solitary man, the agent who is Moran's double, Moran's Molloy, and the shepherd suffice to set Moran's hopes and fears into action. The drama flows inevitably from their influences, although the outcome is surprising. It can be sketched, as here.

Temptations: Home and Family

Immediately a difficulty arises. Jacques Jr. represents Moran's family connections, but these are double, even if Martha is dismissed. There are also the material elements that make up Moran's home, his property, even his livestock. Youdi treats these two connections differently. The son leaves with Moran, but Moran must leave his property as, apparently, he has never done before.

Perhaps most readers do not value Moran's home highly after he has described the comic external world of Turdy so critically. Moran does not agree with them. Making judgments, especially negative ones, is part of his duty, and he likes his work. Even in his garden, during a Sabbath of willing, he willingly passes judgment. That he persistently finds fault with Turdy does not imply his unhappiness there. He leaves home only to carry out his professional duty. At his wicket gate he performs a conventional act; he looks back. "I turned again a last time towards my little all, before I left it," he says, adding that he left it "in the hope of keeping it" (128). He does not imagine himself as escaping from Turdy. On the contrary, a more sophisticated Moran will lament his future as a solitary: "Does this mean I shall one day be banished from my house, from my garden . . . and be banished from the absurd comforts of my home, which it was my life's work to build, to adorn, to perfect, to keep?" (132).

Moran must bring his son with him. He complains of this obligation because paternity makes him respectable in the eyes of others—neither the socially comic agent nor the socially disapproved solitary. He must play the part of a knowledgeable and competent father, a role model for his son. He played this role poorly in Turdy and does not improve on the journey. His acting out of this minimal family situation should therefore exacerbate his desire to be a solitary.

Then his knee collapses. This is not a simple psychosomatic illness. Moran the group member has complained of coming and going; this collapse offers him an excuse to stop, right there in the wilderness, and become a solitary. He is tempted by this opportunity and develops it into an adolescent metaphysical fantasy and anticipation of the Unnamable: to be incapable of motion, mute, deaf, blind, with no memory! "And just enough brain intact to allow you to exult! And to dread death like a regeneration!" (140). But he is afforded no cage out of time, no box or jar to enclose his mind. The ego is primarily a bodily ego, Freud insists. Moran inhabits a flatly realistic Freudian world where he is merely crippled, in a tent, with his son and with a job to do. He returns quickly to his role as agent, bullying his son and sending him to buy a bicycle.

When his son leaves, he is alone. He cannot act out his identity as an agent, a doer of deeds, and he is detached from the son and possessions that constitute his family identity. But he does not enthusiastically develop his latent identity as a solitary. On the contrary, and despite his anger at the son he has humiliated before sending away, he acts a comically sentimental role as the loving father. He imagines his son playing with the bicycle: "It would be my joy to help my son . . . to fit his bicycle with the best lamps . . . and the best bell and the best brakes that money could buy" (145). Reciting these lines with no need of a prompter, he is affected by them. He discovers, "I missed my son!" The next day he acts out his continuing solitude primarily by retreating to his family role, recreating his conventional domestic situation. The makeshift shelter becomes "my little house," and he moves in "vain comings and goings," as he had done before leaving home (148).

After another bad night alone (we will return to those bad nights) he is gripped by guilty fear of society's wrath. Persuading himself that "Youdi will take care of me," he returns to the script of the doting father: "And they can do nothing to my son, rather they will commiserate with him on having had such a father, and offers of help and expressions of esteem will pour in upon him from every side" (154).

Moran is a ham actor, to be sure, but these passages in which he acts the role of the parent might still indicate a valid identity. Freud just warned us, however, that multiple identities may result in "a disruption of the ego in consequence of the different identifications becoming cut off from one another by resistances." The "question of conflicts between the various identifications into which the ego comes apart" is certainly being raised. The paternal Moran concerned for his son's well-being had just asked himself whether he should tell his son that he had killed the pseudo-Moran. Far from answering the question as a doting parent, he had decided not to tell him because his son would denounce him to the police (154).

We must return to this topic of Moran's identity as head of a family, and before doing so we must go on to other temptations. First, however, we must note that Beckett—with characteristic indirectness—has planted at the start of Moran's solitude a most powerful motive against solitude.

When his son leaves, Moran attempts to admire nature ("I surrendered myself to the beauties of the scene" [145]), but this group member cannot appreciate scenery. Beyond the bird songs he hears a vacuum: "for an instant I fancied I heard the silence mentioned, if I am not mistaken, above." Immediately he reverts to his agent role: "I brooded on the undertaking on which I was embarked." In order to appreciate this sequence, we must recall that previous mention of silence, which occurred long since and in no dramatic context. He desires the experience of silence for his son, and it complements his insistence upon "sollst entbehren": "Not one person in a hundred knows how to be silent and listen, no, nor even to conceive what such a thing means. Yet only then can you detect, beyond the fatuous clamour, the silence of which the universe is made" (121).

Such silence expresses an absence of communication and connection, the essence of a solitary existence. It should frighten his son into group membership. The fatuous clamor of group life and the voice of Gaber are preferable to voiceless solitude in a silent universe. ("Fatuous clamour" translates "absurde fracas" [188]; both terms echo Molloy's metaphor of the orchestra and its conductor [15]. "For the righteous the tumult of the world never stops," Molloy noted [29].) No wonder Moran misses his son.

Temptation: Solitude and the Solitary

Excusing himself for not thinking through his experiencing of psychic changes while alone, Moran says that "it was not my nature, I mean it was not my custom, to conduct my calculations simultaneously, but separately and turn about" (149). "Custom" evokes for us the necessary identification or role demanded by a social occasion; we respond habitually by becoming a student, a friend, a family member, a citizen. Moran's explicit replacement of "nature" by "custom" indicates his lack of any "natural" identity containing all his customary roles. Alone now, he encounters two men who oblige him to contrive new identities.

The silence of which the universe is made led Moran first to retreat into his agent role and then to examine his face in a stream. The narcissism of his masturbation before the cheval glass does not recur; drops of water keep shattering the familiar image (145). Beckett will develop this metaphor and similar others with splendid poetic variety. We must turn, however, to the drama's stimulant of a new identity, the old man with a stick.

Like Moran but on a small scale, the old man is a contrivance, patched together arbitrarily. His coat is too heavy for the season; his stick is a hindrance, not a prop, although it is not heavy; his face is "dirty and hairy" but "pale and noble" (146). He seems fifty-five years old but has "a huge shock of dirty snow-white hair." Asking for bread, he "accompanied this humiliating request with a fiery look." (The appearance of the next visitor, the pseudo-Moran, will suggest "great harmony and concord" [150].)

Since we Freudians know that the libido is not coherent but a chaos of often conflicting desires, the old man's inharmonious appearance is suggestive. Yet he is an antithesis of Moran's Molloy, fierce in look but quiet, unthreatening, and essentially emotionless. Moran's response to him is equally unpredictable. He evokes the biblical loaves and fishes in sharing his food with him. He envies his appearance: "His face was pale and noble, I could have done with it." When the old man leaves, Moran does not try to keep him there, but he watches him go: "I wished I could have stood there looking after him, and time at a standstill. I wished I could have been in the middle of a desert, under the midday sun, to look after him till he was only a dot, on the edge of the horizon" (147).

That passage was already extraordinary in its developed emotion; Beckett intensified it by adding "and time at a standstill" in translation. Yearning for a fellow before he leaves his mountainside, Molloy says: "From things about to disappear I turn away in time. To watch them out of sight, no, I can't do it" (12). Moran's action is not merely complementary, however. We must remember his last mention of the young lover: "I can see him still, looking after me. I fancy he would have liked me for a friend" (137). Moran's watching the old man is not, then, the opposite of Molloy's turning away; both men enact the experience of loneliness.

After other painful experiences of the solitary life Moran will deliberately hope that Molloy "would come to me, . . . and grow to be a friend, and like a father to me, and help me do what I had to do" (162). But already we recognize what the fear of silence has done to him. Rather than go off alone into the wilderness like the old man, Moran cuts a branch in imitation of the old man's stick. (Both hold it by the wrong end.) However, he uses it only to poke his fire while waiting for his son's return.

Temptation: Solitude and the Agent

"We agents," Moran said at a more hopeful time (106). The implied camaraderie faded, however, since it became clear that he had never met any other agent. Now he has repressed his experience of the old man and has imagined himself a living torch, when his image appears, speaking heartily and clapping him on the shoulder. This man is dressed oddly, like Moran at work; he is seeking the old man with the stick, as might an agent concerned with someone who has left the group; and he treats Moran as a fellow. But Moran's identity is changing, although he cannot say how, and he sees and recognizes this past identity from outside. Moran's negative acts are consistently far more energetic than his positive acts; his abrupt killing of this double (the work of the unconscious; he cannot recall it) is thorough. It must have been accomplished with the stick, since his umbrella is unscathed.

A quick interpretation: Moran has reacted against his previously dominant identity, that of Youdi's agent; in fact he has destroyed it, even to the extent of recovering the use of his crippled leg. He has acted to protect the solitary old man, using a stick that links the two of them. He has thereby opted for the identity of a solitary.

This interpretation must be quick, since it is quickly proven wrong. Moran busily assembles the materials of his agent costume, comically settling for the keys he can find as if keys are no more than props. He hides the body (to which the wandering dog will be indifferent) and packs up his and his son's equipment. However, he does not go off as a solitary; he awaits his son. He has resumed his agent's role.

This role has even strengthened. We have noted already that he hopes Youdi will protect him from society's condemnation and that he realizes his son would, if he learned of the crime, side with society rather than with his father. The impulse that strengthens his agent role is fear: he fears society, he fears his son's hostility, and he fears to be alone. The irrational claim that Youdi would defend him, even though he killed another agent, is linked to his vague claim that he will be "far away" when the crime is revealed, yet still under Youdi's protection. As for the old man, Moran notes that he would be suspected and probably could not exonerate himself, but he shows no sympathy (154). Now the son he has missed makes his long-awaited return. No sooner does Moran see him than "a wave of irritation broke over me" (155). Dressed as an agent, he behaves as a parent. No new identity has replaced an old one.

Matters have changed, however. In Turdy Moran forced himself upon others—on Father Ambrose, as a parishioner; on his son and Martha, as head of the household; and on his various clients. These relationships are social ones, and not surprisingly Moran tended to consider his identity in each with regard to his face, his clothing, and his voice—the bases of his presentation of his role. After experiencing the alterations in his reflection and the apparent rising up of a faceless mask, and after a brief desire to have the old man's face, Moran's concerns altered. He spoke negatively of the pseudo-Moran's face and clothing. He will not mention his own theatrical equipment until the trip home. He will neither evade nor force himself upon the shepherd.

During the brief last events of his trip outward Moran will report traveling with his son. He will encounter the shepherd and his flock. He will argue with his son, who will leave him. Left alone, he will encounter Gaber. Concerned with his minimal identities as a family man, a householder, an agent, and a solitary, we must draw our materials from these events rather than restaging them.

Temptation: Home and Family Again

Traveling with his son might be expected to develop Moran's identity as a family man. It does not. His gratitude for help is minimal, and it is expressed to the reader, not the son: "I would never have got there [to Ballyba] alone. It was thanks to my son" (157). The sequence of ideas is instructive: "He took good care of me, I must say. He was clumsy, stupid, slow, dirty, untruthful, deceitful, prodigal, unfilial, but he did not abandon me. I thought much about myself" (158). They encounter the shepherd, his dog, and his flock, and Moran is caught up imaginatively by that group. Then, studying the lights of Bally as pointed out by the shepherd, he says: "I knew I was all alone gazing at that distant glow. . . . And I did not like the feeling of being alone, with my son perhaps, no, alone, spellbound" (159). No paternal role remains.

The linked role of householder is enacted with conventional optimism when Moran, warmed by the presence of the shepherd and flock, gazes at the lights of Bally: "I gave thanks for evening that brings out the lights, the stars in the sky and on earth the brave little lights of men." He even adds a Panglossian bit of optimism: "By day the shepherd would have raised his pipe in vain" to indicate the location of the town. If not for dark, one could not see light. After his son has left, however, and Moran faces his solitude, those recently gratifying lights become the "foul little lights of terrified men," and in a comic clash of identities and values he adds: "I might be there now, but for my misfortune!" (162).

Rejecting his householder role, which includes his roles as citizen, parishioner, and neighbor, and abandoned by his unloved son, Moran has dismissed one of his basic identities, and he has done so with negative emotional intensity. Negatively, at least, he appears to seek the role of the solitary.

Temptation: The Role of Agent

Once Moran had bullied his son into pedaling the bicycle correctly, he was free to think of himself. This situation included freedom from his role as an active agent: "I did practically nothing any more," he said, and "I thought no more about" what to do with Molloy when he was found (158). Although Moran did not depart on his autocycle, he now had a clumsy imitation, with his son as the motor, and the fatal pleasure principle was at work.

Dutiful concern for his assignment was replaced by stressless complacence. The fear that led him to assert that Youdi would protect him disappears quickly; the murder will never be mentioned again. Now a splendid image of the group life appears to encourage him to go on to Bally, to deal with Molloy, and to return to Turdy; he encounters the shepherd and his flock. The shepherd "was sitting on the ground stroking his dog. A flock of black shorn sheep strayed about them, unafraid" (158).

We note the context. Moran has recently imagined Youdi as protecting him from the results of his murder; this shepherd tempers the wind to his flock of shorn black sheep. Moran had sought from Gaber some evidence of Youdi's high estimate of him, with little success; this shepherd strokes his agent, the dog. Moran has doubted the size and reality of the Youdi organization; here are many sheep together, under protective guidance. Moran often finds imperfect the members of his society; here the shepherd, dog, and sheep constitute a harmonious and better world: "what a pastoral land, my God," Moran remarks, emphasizing the religious quality of the scene. The weather is "divine" (originally "delicieux" [246]). "The silence was absolute. . . . I looked about me incapable of speech. I did not know how I would ever be able to break this silence" (158–59). The sheep's fearlessness becomes comic when they surround Moran and he concludes that they think him "the butcher come to make his choice."

He imagines himself the shepherd's canine agent. He wishes to say to the shepherd, "Take me with you, I will serve you faithfully, just for a place to lie and a little food." He does not break the silence, however, and in silence the group departs. He imagines the dog following the shepherd toward his cottage: "but the dog stops at the threshold, not knowing whether he may go in or whether he must stay out, all night" (160). That partial rejection of the agent ends the scene. (Beckett added the emphatic "all night" in translation.)

During his journey out Moran sided with the solitary old man but then quickly offered him as a potential scapegoat to law-enforcers seeking the killer of the pseudo-Moran. He solicited Youdi's support in the exile he foresaw. (There are curious echoes of Frankenstein's monster in these acts and elsewhere.) He grudgingly accepted his son's inadequacies and his own dependence on the son's aid. These are all acknowledgments of the security offered by group membership. Now they have produced a wish-fulfilling image of protective care, a glorification of group existence under a benevolent ruler, and a reflection of this starry pastoral group in the brave lights of the distant town.

But the scene is as false as Moran's optimistic report of the lights of Bally. "His dog loved him, his sheep did not fear him." Moran's verbs emphasize the reality of his own group existence, in which the agent fears the master and the group does not love him. (Freud noted that fear is the ruling principle underlying apparent benevolence in groups.) Moran senses this fear when he realizes that he has not been invited to join the group, that his son is not with him in spirit, and that the lights of Bally will soon go out: "I did not like the feeling of being alone. . . . And I was wondering how to depart without self-loathing or sadness." Refused membership in this group, obliged to realize that the group and his son are indifferent to him, Moran cannot turn to any identity as a solitary or any alternate set of values that might sustain him as the old man was sustained.

We recall his treatment of the young man who sought love and friendship. Like the young man, Moran is left alone. The self-loathing is new. Solitude forces upon Moran a sense of self that he loathes and might escape when acting as a group member. We recall Freud's report of an individual's motivation for joining a group: "he does it because he feels the need of being in harmony with them rather than in opposition to them—so that perhaps after all he does it '*ihnen zu Liebe*' [for their love]" (XVIII, 91–92). Moran had been willing even to act as an agent dog in return for group membership, but his application for the job has been rejected.

Temptation: Solitude and Death

Moran sensed himself alone in experiencing the shepherd and his flock. Earlier, he reported about his son that "he did not abandon me. I thought much about myself." Attributing to his son his own lack of affection for him, Moran is rather surprised by his son's dutiful behavior. Now, doubtful again, he acts to banish doubt. Moran is almost always active negatively, even when the negative action is directed against himself. "When a thing resists me, even if it is for my own good, it does not resist me long," he will soon say (165). Here he abandons his son before the son can abandon him, by starting an argument with him.

When his knee stiffened in the shelter, Moran faced "the problem of what I should do." His answer recalled Molloy's condemnation of his own narrative (88): "I shall not expound my reasoning," Moran said. "Its conclusion made possible the composition of the following passage" (140). Now he says, "That night I had a violent scene with my son" (160). Developing the scene, he notes: "In order to make all this sound more likely I shall add what follows." The scene was like many before, and the sympathetic reader has long expected the son to depart.

Moran is now reduced to the solitary identity he had once cherished, had recently evaded, and has just now spoken of negatively. "I was therefore alone" (161). He has lost his paternal identity. The son was his last connection with the group world. He has no way of contacting Gaber and Youdi, and he has failed to find Molloy. Now he is bereft of his equivalents of Yerk's tiepin, the young man's actress and friend, Murphy's Celia and Mr. Endon, and Mercier's Camier. Like those former clients, he has been shown both the unhappiness of a solitary life and the impossibility of a personal relation. He has just dramatized his willingness to return to the fold. Youdi has successfully used the almost forgotten search for Molloy to frighten Moran into subservience. His agent's task is completed, though he cannot know this.

It is no wonder that Gaber now appears and puts an end to Moran's search. (He is literally at a standstill.) Moran has been taught a good lesson. But Gaber arrives a paragraph too late. That paragraph is well worth our attention. In it, Moran eats his last provisions and dallies with "the hopes that spring eternal, childish hopes." He hopes that his son will pity him and return, or that Molloy will come to him "and grow to be a friend, and like a father to me, and help me do what I had to do, so that Youdi would not be angry with me and would not punish me!" These hopes—especially the hope that Molloy would become simultaneously father, friend, and aide—reveal both Moran's fear of solitude and his need for social identities in the external world. He has become more vulnerable and more extensively dependent upon others.

Then, surprisingly, he reacts against this dependency and accepts his solitude. He sweeps away all these hopes. He faces the reality that his son will not return, that Molloy will not befriend him, and that Youdi will not spare him. He sees the lights of Bally as the "foul little lights of terrified men" and he realizes that "I might be there now, but for my misfortune!" This last assertion comprises a puzzling sequence of ideas. The group members in Bally are terrified, yet Moran's absence from that group results from misfortune. Youdi's terrifying power is not denied, even though Moran laughs at it: "And at the thought of the punishments Youdi might inflict upon me I was seized by such a mighty fit of laughter that I shook. . . . Strange laughter truly, and no doubt misnamed" (162). The sudden release of a repression can result in laughter, Freud has told us. Gaber and Youdi are still silent, however.

Much more is to be found in this passage. It is concerned with emotions. Moran yearns for his son's return and for Molloy's aid, as he had depended in an earlier passage on Youdi's support for him and his son after the murder. He hopes for their affection. He hopes for emotional relationships even at the expense of his submission to the superego's rational judgment. These emotions must have escaped repression, since as an agent he cannot feel . . . or laugh (125). We should note that he hopes for affection *from* others; he expresses no affection *for* his son, Molloy, and the terrified men.

There is still more in this passage. Moran reports the absence of that character "of whom I have refrained from speaking." Imagining Molloy, Moran said that he had "no information as to his face" (114). Now—repression having been overcome—he can name and speak of the Obidil: "all I can say with regard to him is this, that I never saw him, either face to face or darkly [this reference to 1 Corinthians 13:12 was added in translation], perhaps there is no such person, that would not greatly surprise me."

We know that Moran has projected his superego outside himself as Youdi and its *Pcs.* as Gaber, and that he imagines himself as working for their organization. We know that the libido, or more properly the id, is also a part, an enormous part, of the psyche, although it was never mentioned as a part of Youdi's organization. Now we must link Molloy's face, which he has not imagined, and the old man's face, which he desires, with his longing to see the Obidil face to face. The Obidil is associated with Moran's solitary identity, not his group identity, and this longing for a face-to-face meeting, not a group relationship, must remind us of the young man seeking a lover and a friend.

His conclusion, "perhaps there is no such person, that would not greatly surprise me," echoes the unspoken conclusion reached by the young man when the actress does not appear for the rendezvous. We are aided by the biblical reference. Paul says that the encounter face to face will have an illuminating result: "then I shall know even as also I am known." In seeking Molloy, Moran was somehow seeking the Obidil, the unknown part of his self. In giving up the possibility of finding the Obidil, Moran is sweeping away the hope of any knowledge of his full self.

We must yet again recall Freud's explanation that psychoanalysis seeks "to strengthen the ego, to make it more independent of the super-ego, to widen its field of perception and enlarge its organization, so that it can appropriate fresh portions of the id. Where id was, there ego shall be. It is a work of culture—not unlike the draining of the Zuider Zee" (XXII, 80).

Moran has made his ego neurotically dependent upon his group superego. That superego, Youdi, is hostile to emotions—libidinal impulses—that lure members away from the group, such as the young man's longing for the actress and friend. Libidinal desires do not comprise a single entity; the libido cannot be personified as Freud and Moran personify the ego and the superego. Moran's weak desire to be a solitary has no clear object-cathexis such as the actress. He can summon up, when Youdi permits him, only clichés of the wild man. His insistence upon projecting his psyche into the outer world enables Youdi to encourage his trip into the wilderness, where his search must fail.

All this acting out has a serious psychological sense, then. Alone at the extremity of his trip—those distant lights are in Bally, not Turdy—Moran experiences his demanding group superego as a source of fear and punishments. In reaction, a need for positive emotion rises from repression into consciousness, but it is passive. Moran needs affection from others, but he feels no positive affection for his son or Molloy or the Obidil. Emotions are not all of a piece, and Moran has access to some that are essentially negative. He sweeps away his hopes; that is, he despairs. His laughter at the thought of Youdi's punishment of him is then projected upon a group of which he is not a member: "I crawled out in the evening to have a good laugh at the lights of Bally."

"As for myself, that unfailing pastime, it was far now from my thoughts," he says. As often, he immediately contradicts himself, but in doing so, he tacitly acknowledges his despair of finding that central identity "my self" by imagining its end and the oddly passive arrival of a new one. He offers three images. In the first, that self ("moi") "did not seem so far from me, when I seemed to be drawing towards it as the sands towards the wave, when it crests and whitens" (162). The image is paradoxical. Its oddity recurs in the next images: the sands, like the "turd" and the "ash," are passive.

Each of Moran's imagined identities undergoes a change after being acted upon by an external force—the wave, the water that will flush the turd, and the fly hovering over the ash in the ashtray. All three images, then, develop Moran's physical situation now: "I remained for several days . . . in the place where my son had abandoned me, . . . powerless to act, or perhaps strong enough to act no more. For . . . I knew that all was about to end, or to begin again, . . . I had only to wait."

The sands continue the earlier image of "a crumbling, a frenzied collapsing of all that had always protected me from all I was always condemned to be. . . . This sensation at first all darkness and bulk, with a noise like the grinding of stones, then suddenly as soft as water flowing" (148). The turd reminds us that Moran is an inhabitant of Turdy; its flushing anticipates the end of Moran's identity as a citizen of that town. The ashes immediately suggest the end of a life. (He had earlier imagined himself catching fire in his sleep and awakening a living torch [147].)

The fly stirring the ashes implies the rising of a phoenix, but the limitations of that new life were emphasized by another earlier image: "I seemed to see myself ageing as swiftly as a day-fly" (148). The brevity of life is emphasized after Gaber's departure. Moran then says: "But to return to the flies, I like to think of those [cluster flies] that hatch out at the beginning of winter, within doors, and die soon after" (166). Moran does not use the accurate term "cluster flies," but his plural and their domestic location suffice to remind us of his own group identities. The flies, the sand, the turd, and the ash offer no suggestion of continued existence. Moran, his food gone and his strength ebbing, looks forward only to losing consciousness.

In short, Moran is dying. The ego is primarily a physical ego. He does not expect or fear immortality, but he recognizes that as a dying man he plays an important theatrical role: "I felt extraordinarily content, content with myself, almost elated, enchanted with my performance" (163). The French stresses this repertory-company identity: "Je me sentais extraordinairement content, content de moi, exalté presque, enchanté de mon personnage" (252). Moran thinks himself about to shuffle off his mortal roles, but Gaber appears "to put a stop to these frolics." We may understand them variously: Moran is literally dying; he is representing himself as sufficiently chastised, so that Youdi will take him back; he is preferring death to his existence as a solitary. Certainly he is still part of Youdi's organization, as Gaber demonstrates by showing up and as Moran acknowledges by obeying Youdi's order.

There is yet another way to put the matter, still Freudianly. Moran is passive. Whether all is about to end or to begin again, the impetus must come from outside. He cannot move. Libidinal energy must come to the ego either directly from the id or by way of the superego. Because Moran has abandoned hope of the id/libido, he requires to be motivated by way of the superego. So Gaber arrives.

Gaber has changed. He is more sluggish and hostile. He seems as slow-witted as Moran's son. He is distant (the translation slightly emphasizes this). There are faint echoes of Moran's encounter with the pseudo-Moran. ("Do you hear me talking to you?" said that character; "I can't hear a word you say," says Gaber. "The voice [of the pseudo-Moran] seemed to come to me from afar"; "I did not recognize that far-off voice" [151, 163].) Beckett plays here with Freud's description of the *Pcs.* We noted that Gaber's verbal function was revealed by his varied wording of Youdi's order and by his sense of superiority to the unconscious Youdi. Here is another game. The *Pcs.* has no memory; therefore, Gaber carries the memorandum-book. As Moran tries to keep Gaber talking, Gaber displays his lack of memory by repeating the last word of Moran's speeches (more clearly in the French), as if he can retain no more.

Moran's connection to his group leader is fainter now. In his garden, Moran extorted from Gaber some faint approach to a compliment from Youdi. Now Gaber will not suggest even that Youdi is angry. Youdi is distant and self-satisfied. As for Gaber's own feelings, he says that Moran is giving him a pain in the ass, and he knocks him down. Needing his group identity now, Moran tries to gloss over this act.

Youdi's final message in this scene was addressed to Gaber, not Moran. It is that life is a thing of beauty and a joy forever. The rejected Moran doubts the application of this notion to human life, thereby distancing himself from his patron's basic postulate. In the French a complementary topic arises. The phrase from Keats's *Endymion* (an idea denied in his "Ode on a Grecian Urn") replaces the assertion that "la vie est . . . une chose inouïe" (255). The immediate sense is "unheard of," but the term reminds us of that silence, heard only by the solitary, of which the universe is made. We Freudians are also reminded of the internal life of the wordless unconscious.

Youdi's assertion ends the meeting. Moran reacts by tearing up the earth on which he lies ("I was literally uprooting"). His rebellion is momentary, however; he stops that "nasty" act and sets off for home, no longer dying. The temptations have ended, and he still serves Youdi.

But now his servitude is complicated. He has imagined other kinds of group existence, sketched ever so faintly—the kindly association of shepherd and flock; the fantasized relationship of doting parent and dutiful child; the relationship with a fantasized Molloy who is at once friend, father, and aide; and even "the brave little lights" among "the towers and steeples" of

Bally. He explicitly abandoned hope of them. On the way home he will generate ironic questions about religion, extending his dismissal of that group. He has also withdrawn all positive emotion from his relationship to Youdi, and he no longer imagines himself and Gaber as among many agents and messengers.

Youdi has begun to suggest a threatening Yahweh, but if one must have no other gods before him, then there must be other gods. A voice arriving from no geographical distance will solicit Moran during his trip home. Like Youdi's, it will not speak a human language, but Moran will work to become his own Gaber. The journey home is not without incident.

Home, Instanter

Moran's bustling activities are contained within the general form of "to and fro," and now his shuttling motion reverses its major direction for the last time. He has been punished by Youdi's withdrawal of personal attention and Gaber's indifferent hostility. He is cut off from his church, his servant, and his son. He will not reestablish these contacts when he reaches Turdy. Gaber and Youdi will be his only significant contacts with a world outside his almost blank ego-identity.

The return is condensed: "It was in August, in September at the latest, that I was ordered home. It was spring when I got there. . . . I had therefore been all winter on the way. Anyone else would have lain down in the snow, firmly resolved never to rise again" (165). A cold coming he had of it, and no wonder. The journey out had stripped him of his connections to the external world. It had also destroyed his brief hopes for a protective and approving Youdi and its metaphoric equivalent, the kindly shepherd and his happy flock, replacing them with the sense that the human herd under the brief lights of Bally is terrified, and with the impersonal order to return. He must also write a report, which suggests that he is not trusted. ("I was never required to prove I had succeeded, my word was enough. Youdi must have had some way of verifying. Sometimes I was asked for a report" [136].)

Motives from the id and the superego require the *Pcs.* to put them into words before they can reach the ego. As a bodily ego in a lifeless external world and as a psychological entity cut off from libidinal energy, Moran was almost lifeless until Gaber's arrival and Youdi's command remotivated him. He was also literally starving, not a slight matter for the bodily ego. Now he sets out for Turdy at once and continues persistently. "When a thing resists me, even if it is for my own good, it does not resist me long," he boasts (165).

He had spoken similarly when his leg had become crippled, remarking on the difficulty of being unable to rise—"because of the will I suppose, which the least opposition seems to lash into a fury" (139). Struggling to mount his bicycle for the first time, he increased the intensity of his assertions: "The more things resist me the more rabid I get. With time, and nothing but my teeth and nails, I would rage up from the bowels of the earth to its crust, knowing full well I had nothing to gain. And when I had no more teeth, no more nails, I would dig through the rock with my bones" (156). This is not merely amusing rodomontade. Extricating himself from the center of the rocky earth recalls his image of the mass of mankind as a block, a conglomerate. Yet his inept search for Molloy was crippled and vague.

An earlier praise of his willpower may explain this apparent contradiction. Here the emphasis is placed not on his manic libidinal energy of action but on the external source of it, that new voice exhorting him to "patiently fulfil in all its bitterness my calamitous part, as it was my will, when I had a will, that others should" (132).

When did Moran have that individual source of energy, "my will"? Perhaps only when he had learned to renounce direction of it—"sollst entbehren"—and submit to Youdi's control. After that submission, his vigorously exercised will displayed only his obedience to Youdi, in whose will was Moran's peace. Now Youdi's pretense of approval and therefore affection has been dropped, and his power to punish and terrify has been recognized. Now, "in obedience to Youdi's command" (166) and in bitterness— which intensifies his energy—Moran can force his way home. (We hear in Moran's description of his purpose—he obliged his clients to fulfil in all its bitterness their calamitous part in Youdi's organization—the tone of an agent punished for the same offense and forced to play the same calamitous part.) Thus Moran's praise of his willpower covers over his submission to Youdi.

His emphasis on physical force is brief. Instead of "the fiends in human shape and the phantoms of the dead," we hear about "certain questions of a theological nature" (166). His crippled leg and near-starvation appear, as does the inadequacy of his umbrella in the wintry weather. They too are relegated to second place. Weakened in his group membership and group beliefs, Moran nevertheless obeys unthinkingly, leaving his rational and analytical mind little to do. His appetites and his emotions have shrunk considerably now that his son has left him, Molloy is no longer a possible goal, and Youdi and Gaber have chilled. He is free to think freely, after instructing himself to eat and drink. "It was in this frivolous and charming world that I took refuge, when my cup ran over," though not with goodness and mercy (167). Thought is scarcely needed by Youdi or the Schopenhauerian will for this return, but the thinking cannot stop. He speaks of this thinking as the "cogitations of a man like me, exiled in his manhood" (169).

Free to think, Moran thinks first of theology. Youdi described life as a thing of beauty. More ambiguously, he called it "inouïe." Both phrases turn us to Freud's discussion of the promises of religion, in the *New Introductory Lectures* we have consulted so often. There Freud imagines religion as justifying its claims as contrasted to those of science: "What I have to offer you is something incomparably more beautiful, more consoling, and more uplifting." It offers something unheard of, then, inouïe, an incomparable thing of beauty. But Freud imagines a dubious reception for this good news: "The ordinary man only knows one kind of truth. . . . He cannot imagine what a higher or a highest truth may be. Truth seems to him no more capable of comparative degrees than death; and he cannot join in the leap from the beautiful to the true" (XX, 172). Nor could Moran, when he heard Youdi's opinion that life is a thing of beauty.

We can only glance at Moran's questions. Two of them recall Freud's objection to "highest truth": "How much longer are we to hang about waiting for the antichrist?" and "Might not the beatific vision become a source of boredom, in the long run?" Both the antichrist and the beatific vision exist in a timeless state. The Freudian superego and its alternative form, the ego ideal, also contain timeless truths and judgments. But Moran's questions emphasize time. (Time is a part of questions 4, 7, 10, 11, 13, 14, and 15, at least.) Time fixes humans in the material world of the bodily ego. Time alters desire, as Schopenhauer, Proust, and Beckett agree. Time has altered Moran's early allegiance to Youdi, weakened in part by his recognition that Youdi changes his mind often and has unrealistic ideas, such as that life is a thing of beauty and a joy forever.

These questions move from religion to include consideration of Moran's family. The church, like all group organizations, is an alternative form of the family, Freud says. The family adumbrates the group's basic structure. But Moran has outgrown that family, and he sees no value in the ultimate profit of church membership, an eternity spent viewing the beatific vision among members of one's family.

Freud's history of reason, in *Moses and Monotheism*, noted that in more-developed patriarchies "intellectuality itself is overpowered by the very puzzling emotional phenomenon of faith. Here we have the celebrated 'credo quia absurdum,' and . . . anyone who has succeeded in this regards it as a supreme achievement" (XXIII, 117). Now Moran has ceased to take Youdi on faith or to trust faith at all, as his arid questions show. Still needing the security of a dominant patriarchy—Moran does not contest Youdi's power—

he is detached from the church group by the critical rationality of the conscious ego. No salvation there. His skepticism sweeps away these hopes of church and family.

His multiple identities persist, though weakly. He judges solitude as a group member, group existence as a solitary. The comforts of neither position are available, but the need for membership continues. Therefore his conscious ego, detached from the libido and the superego, attempts to contrive its own psychic world, even while he continues his obedient journey home. He thinks about the bees.

He begins with some basic facts—bees live together, "dance," and work separately—but he alters these and omits others to contrive an organized and successful group existence. He sets aside the sardonic doubt just displayed by his analytical reason. That was frivolous and charming, but nothing more. About the bees Moran is serious. His imagined organization of the hive alters two troubling features of Youdi's group. Most obviously, given his dislike of women (137) and Youdi and God, there is no queen bee or other superego. Perhaps the whole swarm of bees replaces that figure; only the workers are described. They need no guidance or correction, having been spared those troublesome human qualities associated with the libido: "I would never do my bees the wrong I had done my God, to whom I had been taught to ascribe my angers, fears, desires, and even my body" (169). Purged of them, the bees' workday enacts in time its unchanging timeless absolutes. (Lousse's organized nature is outdone.)

Moran's second major alteration of fact offers a place for the solitary. Here the individual has no explicit obligation to the group. Bees dance on returning to the hive, signaling the location of food, as Moran has discovered; but their dance on leaving attracts him more. It says, "Don't worry about me," he decides. Away from the hive and working, "the bees did not dance. Here their watchword seemed to be, Every man for himself" (168). Both messages stress solitary work and ignore group service. Moran concealed from others his solitary self. This society permits such a self. It even indulges the solitary and cares for him; his anxious fellows worry about the welfare of the departing bee. Moran reluctantly grants that the returning bee might express pleasure, the dance, but he sets that notion aside. His worker bees are asexual and untroubled by any alternative demand upon their allegiance. They do not desire to break off from the conglomerate swarm.

Moran concludes with a cheerful judgment that he will not retract even when he reaches home and finds his bees dead: "And I said, with rapture, Here is something I can study all my life, and never understand" (169). This pleasure demands to be set hastily against Molloy's response to the kniferest:

"I could therefore puzzle over it endlessly without the least risk. For to know nothing is nothing, not to want to know anything likewise, but to be beyond knowing anything, to know you are beyond knowing anything, that is when peace enters in, to the soul of the incurious seeker" (64). We found this attitude and the kniferest itself ominous or worse.

Moran's harmoniously organized hive, an optimistic image, suggests Beckett's description of music at the end of *Proust:* Marcel "spatialises what is extraspatial" and sees in the Septuor "the ideal and immaterial statement of the essence of a unique beauty, a unique world, . . . the 'invisible reality' that damns the life of the body on earth as a pensum and reveals the meaning of the word: 'defunctus'." There's the rub, however. Youdi said that life is a thing of beauty and a joy forever (164). His agent, his conscious ego, responded with the reality principle: "Do you think he meant human life?" Moran's bees act out concepts not relevant to humans. The hive's unattainable salvation from society and from the psyche damns human life even more strongly than does its earlier form, the earthly paradise of the shepherd, his dog, and his flock.

The hive indicates Moran's attachment to group existence. Only in a group organization, with space and permission for his solitary alternative self, can he imagine his highest values. The angers, fears, desires, and bodily existence with which the harried ego must deal are not repressed; they are swept away, with rapture. But these concepts do not rise from human percepts and possibilities. Turdy and submission to Youdi remain unaltered.

* * *

Words and ideas are not magic; they cannot alter the world, as Freud pointed out in *Totem and Taboo*. The ego is primarily a bodily ego, life is a matter of acts, and action is motivated from the id, which cannot be educated. Moran turns from his theological questions and his vision of the bees to his bodily activities. First, however, he mentions verbal motivation: "I have spoken of a voice giving me orders, or rather advice. It was on the way home I heard it for the first time. I paid no attention to it." He dismisses the words, which now give not orders but merely advice. Of his physical appearance, he says: "Physically speaking . . . I was now becoming rapidly unrecognizable" (170). Yet "to tell the truth I not only knew who I was, but I had a sharper and clearer sense of my identity than ever before," a sense apparently achieved by means of an "intuition."

Something can be made of these details, and more easily if one consults the original French. There one finds that "unrecognizable," "did not know," "knew who I was," and "acquaintances"—terms not obviously akin in English—are all forms of "connaître" (263). Freud's term "das Unbewusste,"

we have noted, implies something unexpressed in our term "the unconscious"; that part of the psyche is "the unknown" (see XIV, 165 n.). Although Moran's body is changing, he claims to sense his identity more clearly,
with an emphasis on *knowing*. Has he raised some irrational abilities into
consciousness? He distinguishes this intuitive knowing from his knowledge
of other matters. The unconscious, the unknown, has no coherent identity,
Freud stresses, not even the multiple identities of Jung's archetypes. Despite
all its chaos, however, it does not hesitate: "there are in this system no negation, no doubts, no degrees of certainty: all this is only introduced by the
work of the censorship [later the superego] between the *Ucs.* and the *Pcs.*
. . . In the *Ucs.* there are only contents, cathected with greater or lesser
strength" (XIV, 186).

What is happening to Moran, then? The body is separated from the ego,
and the ego is separating from the intellect, and the new voice offers detachment from responsibility for action. Moran acts out the role of agent; he
wears a tie although he has no collar, and he shelters under his umbrella
although it is in tatters. He thinks little during the journey home. He spoke
of his theological questions as "my rare thoughts" (166), and he says that
"my best thoughts came to me" while standing still in the rain under his
useless umbrella (172). Detachment, then, is a central event of Moran's journey, and it is worthwhile to rise above the narrative and take a summary
view of this topic.

Moran's journey out reached its intended goal when he was detached
from even a physical ability to reach Molloy. Youdi's command to return
also ended a series of detachments from other relationships that had provided him with identities. Considering these materials, the Freudian under-
structure of the story, Beckett's earlier treatments of identity from *Proust*
onward, and Moran's own comments about his changes, we concluded that
Moran's old ego was dying. Let us look back at that old ego.

Before beginning his narrative of the journey, Moran had intuited the
possibility that he might lose all his physical possessions. He was dismayed:
"I am too old to lose all this, and begin again, I am too old!" (132). When
his knee stiffened, he imagined an all but total paralysis of mind and body,
and he added a wish: "to dread death like a regeneration" (140). Still later,
after encountering the old man, he imagined his face as crumbling, "with a
noise like the grinding of stones, then suddenly as soft as water flowing,"
and then rising up in the form of a nearly blank mask (148–49). He responded to these remarkable visions by speaking not of a new but of his old
identity: "my growing resignation to being dispossessed of self."

That response sends us back to James's *Varieties of Religious Experience*.

There James speaks of "the salvation through self-despair, the dying to be truly born, of Lutheran theology, the passage into *nothing* of which Jacob Behmen writes." James then adds a relevant image: "To get to it, a critical point must usually be passed, a corner turned within one. Something must give way, a native hardness must break down and liquefy" (108). Moran's images of a liquifying identity led to the abandonment of hopes and despair of self; the return home literally turns a corner. "The dying to be truly born"—the death of an old ego—requires the appearance of a new one, as Proust and life itself had long since informed Beckett. Moran's sense of an ego must be emphasized. His primary ego-identity has been that of a group member. A group member wears a uniform, and Moran clings to the tattered remains of his costume as an agent. A group member wears a mask, a persona, and Moran is quite aware of himself as acting roles.

The new Moran, almost home, has no soft white hands. His hair and beard are untrimmed. His costume suggests that of a clown: tattered shoes, no stockings, tattered shirt with an unattached tie, tattered trousers and jacket, and little more than the metal structure of an umbrella. His straw hat has not survived the journey. This costume cannot last much longer, and this identity appears equally temporary. The absence of a hat may suggest the absence of an identity or at least of a rational self. (*Godot* is not yet written, however.) Perhaps the blank mask and the missing hat suggest a detachment of identity from appearance. Perhaps the "self" has begun some sort of existence apart from any group, with a voice now internal. Perhaps the remnants of proper dress emphasize the comic costume of the agent at work.

This analysis is unclear. Its subject is unclear to Moran. Before he started his journey, Moran imagined the pleasure of detachment from group identity: "I had the joyful vision of myself far from home, from the familiar faces, from all my sheet-anchors, sitting on a milestone in the dark, . . . coldly hatching my plans, for the next day, for the day after, creating time to come" (125). The pose and "sheet-anchors" suggest Blake's unsympathetic engraving of Newton on the sea bottom of the material world, clearly in rational control of his elements. Moran's pleasure in his vision is cut short when he realizes that the need to bring his son would make this identity impossible. He immediately adds to his equipment "a full tube of morphine tablets, my favourite sedative," and he finishes the morphine after Gaber leaves him (126, 165).

The morphine is a sedative against the pain of change. We may recall the calmative in Beckett's story of that name and also his discussion in *Proust* of habit and existence. Habit "paralyses our attention, drugs those handmaids of perception," while during "the perilous zones in the life of the individual . . . for a moment the boredom of living is replaced by the suffering of being." Any important psychic change "is inseparable from suffering and anxiety—the suffering of the dying and the jealous anxiety of the ousted. The old ego dies hard. . . . It disappears—with wailing and gnashing of teeth" (8 ff.). Bereft of calmatives, Moran overcame the snow that lured him more than it resisted him: "I vanquished it, grinding my teeth with joy, it is quite possible to grind one's incisors. I forged my way through it, towards what I would have called my ruin if I could have conceived what I had left to be ruined" (165). Moran is struggling at once to delay and to achieve his ruin.

Such details emphasize the grinding down of Moran's old ego. We see the collapse of that identity, even after its detachment from many group connections, rather than the construction of a new identity. This negativity answers Moran's question, "Why had I obeyed the order to go home?" Unhappily, insecurely, with suffering, anxiety, and gnashing of teeth, he still serves his group identity and his external superego. It is the bodily ego that struggles to survive, while the detached reason becomes frivolously theological or speculative about the bees. It has nothing to plan, since this is a return, not a new venture requiring rational thought.

"The Methods of My Full Maturity"

Already back home but in part "he who finds" as well as "he who tells what he has found," Moran predicted that he would not "relate all the vicissitudes of the journey from my country to Molloy's." However, he would include a few examples "in order to give some idea of the methods of my full maturity" (132–33). The words and tone suggested confidence and success, back then. Moran's optimistic tone might imply that his encounter with Molloy will especially demonstrate these methods. But no such encounter occurs. The old man and the shepherd depart unaffected, the son flees, the farmer met early is evaded, and the pseudo-Moran is killed. (Moran tries to persuade us that his son left only after he had trained the boy properly, but this claim is dubious, unless we are to understand that he similarly fled his own father.) These events cannot fit the model provided by Yerk and the young man.

Now Moran refuses to record "other molestations than this [cold, rain, snow], other offenses": "Let us be content with paradigms" (172). Only one follows: his encounter with the farmer who looms up in the dark and puts a hand on his shoulder, as the pseudo-Moran had done. This event, then, must encapsulate the methods of Moran's maturity. He lards his anecdote with self-praise: "I did not lose my presence of mind"; "Another would have lost countenance. Not I"; "Ah, Moran, wily as a serpent, there was never the like of old Moran." (Perhaps there was the like, however. Molloy boasted that when he took the trouble, "je cessais d'être ballot et devenais malin"; and he demonstrated his "malin" cleverness in "la motion reptile" [131, 138]. Moran uses the same adjective and image: "ce vieux Moran, malin comme un serpent" [269].) One self-praising comment alludes to the promised methods of his maturity: "This incident gives a feeble idea of my ability, even at this late period" (173). Since he merely evades the farmer's anger, "feeble idea" seems painfully accurate; either Moran or Beckett has failed to produce what was promised. Let us examine the scant materials in a larger context.

On a dark and rainy night Moran is accosted by a private citizen on whose land he has trespassed. Questioned by the farmer, Moran lies glibly. "I have a fairly distinguished voice, when I choose" (173). Developing a new role, he contrives a pilgrimage to the Turdy madonna, asks for tea, and offers money. When the farmer goes for the tea, Moran leaves. The methods of his maturity here reported for Youdi must refer to his methodical work as an agent, not his social or antisocial skills. What is presented in this event beyond Moran's ability to manipulate a group member?

That classification of the farmer offers entry into the event. He is a stereotypical caricature: land-proud, hostile to the stranger, suspicious, and religious. He carries a spade that Moran imagines as available to bury him with, if needed; it recalls the spade with which Lousse buries Molloy's substitute, Teddy. Moran avoids burial here, however. With an absurd tale of a pilgrimage to a madonna he persuades the farmer to behave absurdly, bringing him tea in the rain. We must add to these facts the undescribed conclusion: the farmer delivers the tea and finds no Moran.

Now we may see the methods of Moran's maturity. He treats the farmer as a client. The farmer is no obvious candidate; he is a conventional stereotype, a solid part of conglomerate humanity. But he is not solid enough. Although his religion is superficial (he knows of no shrines), he falls for this story of a pious pilgrimage, and he goes against all his stereotypical qualities in order to aid this solitary. After being duped, then, he must be angry at Moran and himself, vowing never again to be tempted by any unconventional person, though wily as a serpent, and affirming his conventional values. Moran has split him from and then bound him more firmly to his conglomerate group.

Moran's maturity as an agent is not remarkable. Moran is no remarkable agent. The sense is clear, however; his boasting shows a desire to persuade Youdi of his value to the organization. He is still himself. After he crossly sent his son to buy a bicycle, he missed him. When he was abandoned by the noble old man, he reacted by appreciating his shelter-home and his son's return. When he killed the pseudo-Moran, he reacted by assuring himself that Youdi would protect him from punishment. When his son left him again, he imagined Molloy—no longer a wild man—as appearing and caring for him. Indifferent to such connections and indeed to life, he responded to Gaber's reappearance by obeying. In short, Moran has acted out his coming and going from one psychic position to its complement, and in each case he has returned to his group.

Moran's evasion of the farmer also allowed him to return home, obediently. That idea is reinforced by his abrupt next remark: "Now I may make an end" (174). He has completed his report, so far as it testifies to his dutiful professional behavior. Youdi appears to have won the day. Nevertheless, we may anticipate Moran's turning yet again; whatever his nature may be, his custom demands that he come and go.

Banishment

Before he described his journey, Moran paused to report his stylistic intentions and motivations, providing a complex passage to which we have turned repeatedly. The narrative voice, he told us, would usually be that of the Moran who experiences the events rather than that of Moran the reporter: "I am far more he who finds than he who tells what he has found, now as then, most of the time" (133). It is in that double voice that he anticipated the end of his journey, putting as a question the answer that he knows when he writes: "Does this mean I shall one day be banished from my house, from my garden, lose my trees, my lawns, my birds . . . , lose and be banished from the absurd comforts of my home where all is snug and neat and all those things at hand without which I could not bear being a man?" (132). The uncertain voice produces dual judgments; "the long anguish of vagrancy" makes "freedom" a goal little to be desired, but the "comforts of home" are "absurd" even though they help him to "bear being a man." The group member and the solitary both speak, although not with equal force.

Now Moran the traveler has almost caught up with Moran the narrator. The traveler has returned, and the narrator compresses all the complexities of that return into a paragraph. Some of the dualities above are repeated. "I could not bear being a man" finds its first echo in the report that Moran is now doing without electricity: "That is the kind of man I have become." Then, after reporting his detachments from his son, Youdi, Gaber, and Father Ambrose, "I am clearing out. . . . All there was to sell I have sold. . . . I have been a man long enough, I shall not put up with it any more, I shall not try any more" (174–76).

Molloy opted out of manhood when he went from vertical to horizontal.

(He "abandoned erect motion, that of man" [89].) Moran defines manhood as group identity in a material world. In disposing of his possessions (with no concern for his son) Moran discards the public persona of which so much has been said. Nevertheless, he still lives in that house, as does his son; he still sits in that garden; he still speaks of "my birds"; and, though he claims to be clearing out, he basks in "the longest, loveliest days of all the year." No Gaber or angel with a flaming sword banishes him from this domestic paradise. From the garden he returns to the house to begin his report: "I went back into the house and wrote, It is midnight. The rain is beating on the windows. It was not midnight. It was not raining."

Let us return to the opening scene and its origin. On a pleasant summer day, Moran enters his house to begin his work by describing rain at midnight. The weather report is complemented by a fearful warning: "I hear the eagle-owl. What a terrible battle-cry! Once I listened to it unmoved." Soon the bedridden Malone will recall a night of different weather, when "the clouds scud, tattered by the wind, across a limpid ground. If I had the patience to wait I would see the moon" (198; the moon arrives on 201). He describes the scene as "such a night as Kasper David Friedrich loved."

When love is mentioned in a Beckett text, it requires consideration. The gnostic painter Friedrich died slowly of a degenerative illness that left him increasingly unable to paint. In his last years he created many variations on a scene in which he imagined death, as well as that other existence that had long been his central concern. The essential features of this varied scene are a window in a ruined stone church, through which one sees the full moon. The viewer is barred from the moon by a dead branch or some other obstruction. In several of these variations Friedrich places on the windowsill, facing away from the moon toward the viewer, an eagle-owl. In Friedrich's gnostic vision, the owl—able to see at night—possesses wisdom about the death of the body and the other world of spiritual light. (At death the luminous essence of the gnostic adept rises from the dark world of matter to the moon, which every month pours its accumulated light back into the sun.)

The application of such matters to "Moran," essentially on the basis of the moonless night scene and the eagle-owl, must be tentative. Tentatively, then, this scene that brackets "Moran" adds complexity to the imminent death of Moran's old ego, a death not yet achieved at the end of the report despite the verbal shift there when he refers to himself in the third person.

The sunlight in which Moran basks is earthly, and his optimistic tone takes its cue from the splendid weather. He looks forward to freedom from Youdi and anticipates no need for Molloy or the Obidil. Indeed, he emphasizes the contrast between his present circumstances and his gloomy first paragraph. What are we to do with this unpredictably cheerful outcome, this volte-face about banishment? We turn to Freud yet again, of course, to the *New Introductory Lectures* and his ironic comparison of the aim of therapy to the draining of the Zuider Zee. Now it is necessary to look at the specific goals of that therapy. The intention of psychoanalysis is "to strengthen the ego, to make it independent of the super-ego, to widen its field of perception and enlarge its organization, so that it can appropriate fresh portions of the id" (XXII, 80).

A dependent in the service of his group superego, Moran has acted to bring people back to the superego's fold, or flock, or society. That task always necessitated forcing them to obey. He revealed as much in reporting his new voice, which, as we have heard, "exhorts me to continue to the end the faithful servant I have always been, of a cause that is not mine, and patiently fulfil in all its bitterness my calamitous part, as it was my will, when I had a will, that others should. And this with hatred in my heart, and scorn, of my master and his designs" (132). As he obliged Yerk and the young man and Watt and Murphy to return to the group and to obey the superego, so Moran has now obliged himself to return. He repressed his hatred and scorn or redirected them against the obstacles to his return, as he had forced his clients to repress or redirect their more positive libidinal desires. So doing, he or his ego did not appropriate more of his id; he subordinated more of it to the group superego and its negative "sollst entbehren."

At the end of "Moran" he is basking in the summer sun and only beginning his report. It will not be completed in such a pleasant season. His optimistic expectation of setting out for more of these happy days is accompanied by no fierce display of energy—in part, surely, because the journey will be aimless; this time there will be no return. Despite his previous adventures he imagines no obstacles—or only one, as a preliminary: he must first write his report. That is no small task, as the writer Beckett is in a position to know. But Moran summons up libidinal energy easily by associating the obligation with resentment: "He asked for a report, he'll get his report" (120). After that, Youdi will have no power over him.

No Youdi, no son, no Molloy, no Obidil. But he does not anticipate isolation in solitude. He is preparing to follow a substitute voice. That voice displays little authority and demands no activity, except by reinforcing Youdi's demand for the report. It is foreign indeed. Moran says that it "did not use the words that Moran had been taught when he was little." We may understand the new words taught to this suddenly third-person Moran by beginning with "the words that Moran had been taught when he was little." Moran was taught by his father. That teaching was compressed into a phrase perhaps literally as well as metaphorically unintelligible to the adolescent:

"sollst entbehren." "At first I did not know what it wanted," Moran says about the new voice, as perhaps once about his father's. Perhaps, then, Moran as a conscious ego is beginning a second childhood, developing again an obedient relation to a superego. "Does this mean I am freer now than I was?" Moran wonders. We must wonder too, since he intends to abandon his son, house, priest, and town to set off again on his new crutches—but only when his new voice gives the order.

Moran consistently identifies "manhood" as defined by the relations and possessions of group membership. Therefore he imagines his potential solitary identity as a captive inside that group identity: "a man like me, exiled in my manhood" (169). Not exiled from the group but within it; not exiled from his manhood but in it, as if in Siberia: "homme malgré lui" (267). We must recall that image that rose up toward him through the water: "little by little a face, with holes for the eyes and mouth and other wounds, and nothing to show if it was a man's face or a woman's face, a young face or an old face, or if its calm too was not an effect of the water trembling between it and the light" (149).

We must recall this image; Moran does not. When he attempts to think of what remains in wait for him, he says: "I have not enough imagination to imagine it. And yet I have more than before" (131). There is a gap between anticipation and willpower. Continuing that earlier report on his present state, Moran said: "I am still obeying orders, if you like, but no longer out of fear." Then he altered that assertion: "No, I am still afraid, but simply from force of habit" (131). Beckett spoke earnestly about habit in *Proust* and since. Because Moran acknowledges that he is a contrivance, we must take seriously his report of an identity contrived in response to group pressure. Moran "exiled in his manhood" refers us back to *Proust,* where identity changes at moments when "the boredom of living is replaced by the suffering of being" and where the self unable to achieve existence is "the true ego exiled in habit" (8–9). Now Moran conceives of his Freudian ego as exiled in the group habit imposed by the superego.

The test of whether Moran is "freer now" will be his next journey. His crippled leg implies a significant weakness. His inability to imagine a goal implies the need for a directing voice. The negativity of his motive—"I have been a man long enough"—suggests a flight, already begun, from his group identity defined by debts, possessions, family, fellow citizens, and obedience. We might encourage him to set out, but if we acknowledge that he is Freudian, we will restrain ourselves until we consult the master again.

Freud's description of the goal of therapy is two-fold. We have considered one part: the widened field of perception and the ego's appropriation of fresh portions of the id. The second part is relevant to Moran's anticipated journey guided by a new voice: therapy should also make the ego "more independent of the super-ego." If more of the id is available to the ego, and if the ego is more nearly independent of the judging superego, then the improved conscious ego will operate with more feeling and less categorical thought, with more spontaneous emotion and less calculated deliberation, more positively than negatively. Surely Moran has not yet reached this goal. Youdi sent Moran after Molloy to tame his desire to leave the group and develop a solitary identity. Punished and repressing his unfaithfulness, Moran must return to his previous obedient state and acknowledge his subordination explicitly, verbally, in his report. Moran has returned and is writing that report.

We might imagine Youdi's pleased reading of the report, if Youdi could read. Having imagined his solitary self as the roaring and rampaging Molloy, Moran reports setting out costumed as a caricature of a citizen, complete with son. He encounters an attractive solitary figure, but the old man with the stick embodies no rebellious intensity. The absence of Moran's son having weakened his desire for solitude, he imagines only a harmless old man with a solitary's indifference even to aid and admiration. Solitaries do not come in pairs. (Moran will later realize that Molloy would not be a friend or father to him.)

Next (as Youdi reads the report) Moran contrives a hostile caricature of his agent self. Then he kills off that caricature, ending his dutiful pursuit of the old man. (Moran's own pursuit of Molloy has been less than dutiful.) The killing immediately rouses Moran's group conscience, which threatens him with punishment. He takes refuge in his relationship to Youdi, powerful to defend him. Then Moran alters his negative sense of Bally (and Turdy) as embodying unpleasant group existence by imagining the shepherd, his flock, and his dog. This desirable group seems to offer him membership and a role he is willing to play, but it leaves without him. His son also leaves. The church, examined rationally, is beyond understanding. Only one group identity is left Moran, and when Youdi summons him back, he quickly obeys.

Youdi must be pleased. This description of Moran's report makes it that of a dutiful servant, a report of the ego's repression of improper desires in the id, even though Moran is still unaware of his dual role as agent and client.

However, Moran's report provides another sense of that two-fold journey. Youdi's assignment, as experienced by Moran, obliged him to function *without* the autocycle (which he associated with the pleasure principle [99]), *without* the aiding son, *without* clear and explicit instructions, *without* access to Gaber, *without* two functioning legs, *without* the companionship of the old man or the shepherd, *without* reaching Molloy or the Obidil, and even without food. The mild dissatisfaction and doubt that he felt during that opening sunny Sabbath have been intensified, and the painfulness of his journey has strengthened his desire to leave Youdi, to leave the group, to cease being a man. Youdi cannot approve of this report.

Moran puts a good face on the matter. He promises himself happy days during his next journey, even though he reached his sunny summer world through weather like that through which Dante struggles to reach hell: "Grandine grossa, acqua tinta e neve / per l'aere tenebroso si reversa" (VI, 10–11; huge hail, foul water, and snow pour from the dark air). Dante's goal is that "città dolente, / u' non potemo intrare omai sanz' ira" (IX, 32–33; that unhappy city that one can never enter without anger). The weather, Moran's motivating anger, and his earlier description of Bally in the darkness make up a negative Dantean warning. Yet his unlighted and empty house and the dead bees and birds cause Moran no pain or anger, and he foresees no return of bad weather even though he can imagine the storm and the eagle-owl.

Like Molloy, Moran shows little understanding of his report. He does not base his plans on what he has learned. Indeed, he does not plan. He anticipates the characters in *All That Fall* who come and go aimlessly and eternally, having lost the good of the intellect. Moran's uneducated ego will not take control; wondering if he is freer now, he awaits commands from his new voice. Freud's goals of therapy are far away.

This new voice "is rather an ambiguous voice and not always easy to follow, in its reasonings and decrees," Moran said earlier. "When it ceases, leaving me in doubt and darkness, I shall wait for it to come back, and do nothing" (132). Admirable subordination, surely, but poor evidence of an ego freed from the domination of the superego. (Bodily the returned Moran basks in sunlight; psychically he waits in doubt and darkness.) Such freedom as Moran has gained is negative, limited to partial freedom from his former group roles. Without an independent ego capable of summoning up motives for action, what can he do but drift on the Zuider Zee of random impulses? We recall Molloy's complaints that his voice repeatedly sent him toward his mother, but without telling him what to do once he arrived. He too evaded responsibility, waited, and did nothing.

Both characters suffer from disabled motivation and an intellectual crippling. Both characters grow more rational as their reports continue, yet both have lost the psychological good of the intellect. We noted the detachment of Molloy's emotions from his cold reason. Moran's report ends with little harshness; that tone appears only with regard to his son and Youdi. He dismisses the other characters with mere indifference. Regarding Father Ambrose, he says, "I think he really liked me, in his own way. . . . I left him" (although Father Ambrose was the visitor); regarding Zulu and the Elsner sisters, "The news was bad, but might have been worse. There was a bright side. They were lovely days."

Much might be said about these abrupt remarks. The "lovely days," an unexpected tone from Moran since the opening scene, must catch our attention. We must be startled by the meeting with Father Ambrose. Moran's indifference to his affection cannot surprise us, but there is another oddity: "He began to talk. He was right. Who is not right? I left him." Throughout his report, Moran has been judgmental. He made his own judgments in the garden and the family. He carried out Youdi's judgments and reported his successes proudly. Now, suddenly, he accepts all judgments as right and dismisses them all as irrelevant. Such a dismissal must come from a psyche without a superego.

Freud concludes the *New Introductory Lectures* by dismissing the claims of religion and philosophy to the production of valid *Weltanschauungen*. In reporting philosophers' attacks upon science, he focuses upon "intellectual nihilists" and their use of "the relativity theory of modern physics." The nihilists use this scientific theory to refute scientific claims by insisting that all science is subjective: "Since the criterion of truth—correspondence with the external world—is absent, it is entirely a matter of indifference what opinions we adopt. All of them are equally true and equally false. And no one has a right to accuse anyone else of error" (XXII, 175–76). Moran has extended this "anarchist theory" to psychology and religion, in effect; Youdi is no longer to be trusted, and Father Ambrose is irrelevantly right.

"They were lovely days." Moran's earlier fears about "banishment" are replaced by optimism about the next journey. Judgment is not the only mental weakness here, however. The weakness of feeling in this final paragraph reminds us that Moran, like Molloy, cannot feel affection. He is emotive, yes—or he was—but his positive emotions were deliberately and conventionally acted out, as in his care for his son, his kissing of Martha's hand, and even his masturbation. His far stronger negative emotions resulted in the savage beating of his son and the killing of his pseudo-self, as well as his forcing his way back to Turdy through the hellish winter. Now both kinds of emotion have faded. The superficial and temporary "lovely days" are enough.

Youdi is a substitute father, what Jung might have called a "god"-father, an external, group-leader form of Moran's own father as internalized superego. Freud reports some negative effects of attaining a superego: "The super-ego arises, as we know, from an identification with the father taken as a model. Every such identification is in the nature of a desexualization or even of a sublimation." Moran's sexuality is minimal and accompanied by hostility to women. "After sublimation the erotic component no longer has the power to bind the whole of the destructiveness that was combined with it." That is, the child's Oedipal feelings, a fused complex of love and hate, do not enter equally into the psyche. Because his sublimated love cannot be expressed directly, it is weakened and separated from negative forceful action. The force that was combined with it "is released in the form of an inclination to aggression and destruction. This defusion would be the source of the general character of harshness and cruelty exhibited by the [ego] ideal—its dictatorial 'Thou shalt'" (XIX, 54–55).

In his behavior with clients Moran has acted out some of this loveless destruction (more painfully for the clients' egos than for the tiepin). Beckett has extended the superego's positive "thou shalt" to its complementary negative, "sollst entbehren, thou shalt do without." Within the ego of the subordinate son and the subordinate group member, aggression and destruction counter impulses toward individuality and freedom. These forces have been detached from positive erotic feelings, except for the slightest traces. Moran's conventionally sentimental acts follow the script for group behavior. His sexuality is turned inward. His low opinion of himself and his failure to develop the solitary side of his nature suggest that he has never managed even a positive narcissism. (Both references to masturbation emphasize its joylessness [102, 145].) Such positive narcissistic feelings as he had were linked to his "manhood" as the owner of property, son, and servant and to his role as Youdi's agent. No love there, in short. But Freud is not a determinist, and Moran's past does not excuse him from the obligation to improve.

The End of Moran

Moran's failure to love, even in the simple forms needed for comfortable group life in Turdy, is expressed less strongly at the end of his journey than is Molloy's at the chronological end of his. Basking in the sun, Moran is immersed in his static personal existence, where there are no opponents. He has cut himself off from the external human world. That image of the indifferent father and citizen and the complacent landowner is evanescent. Moran is still heeding the command to do without. The electricity has been cut off; his property has been sold; his town citizenship, his religion, and his acquaintances have been rejected. The material world of the opening scenes is now staffage, flimsy props behind an actor about to retire from the stage. Those roles too will be left behind.

No Freud is needed to tell of a man who, having traveled beyond his accustomed town, returns to it so altered that he changes his life, selling his real estate business and opening a travel agency. In "Moran" as in "Molloy," however, Beckett uses the outer world to tell the inner story of a developing neurosis. "Neuroses are asocial structures," Freud says; "they endeavour to achieve by private means what is effected in society by collective effort" (XIII, 73). He develops this assertion into a judgment of group existence complementary to that of *Group Psychology and the Analysis of the Ego.* The positive collective construction of one's psychic identity is achieved by the many social groups of which any individual is a member. Each group demands from him some renunciations, each encourages some positive qualities, and each confers upon him a group identity and membership. Their collective effect is to civilize him. (Freud developed the ambivalent results of this collective training in *Civilization and Its Discontents.*)

The positive civilizing effect depends on the individual's anticipatory acceptance of his social identity. However, Moran distanced himself from these social groups, emphasizing in each his detached judgmental role rather than affectionate membership. In creating Youdi's organization, Moran reacted against his culture's dominant groups—the church, the state, the family—while bringing into Youdi's organization some of the very qualities he dislikes. Yet his motive was the avoidance of displeasure: "The asocial nature of neuroses has its genetic origin in their most fundamental purpose, which is to take flight from an unsatisfying reality into a more pleasurable world of phantasy. The real world, which is avoided in this way by neurotics, is under the sway of human society and of the institutions collectively created by it. To turn away from reality is at the same time to withdraw from the community of man" (XIII, 74). These observations are taken from *Totem and Taboo* (1913), the text with which our consideration of "Moran" started. In his later *Group Psychology* Freud repeats part of this passage: "a neurotic is obliged to replace by his own symptom formations the great group formations from which he is excluded. He creates his own world of imagination for himself, his own religion, his own system of delusions, and thus recapitulates for himself the institutions of humanity in a distorted way" (XVIII, 142).

Moran's re-creation is less complete, at least so far. He has recognized those great group formations, while criticizing them as if outside them. But he has also projected his own dominant psyche upon the social world. This externalized psyche provides him little comfort, however; his neurotic formulations are undercut by anxiety when his story begins. He suspects that he has no colleagues (111–12). The pleasure of having as ancestors "those old craftsmen" is denied him (115). He makes little money. His fellow towns-people often treat him with suspicion or mockery. He is on increasingly worse terms with Youdi and Gaber. Only his exertion of power over others offers him assurance about his motives and abilities. But his victims—his son, Yerk, the amorous young man, Murphy, Watt, Mercier/Camier, the angry farmer—do not figure extensively in his sense of himself. Where, then, is his "more pleasurable world of phantasy"?

We must consider his father the source of Moran's psychic problems. The cause was his submission to his father's negative "sollst entbehren." (Moran makes it clear that submission was painful [110].) A result was his neurotic attempt to compensate for that submission by projecting into the social world a model of the group psyche. Membership in that group distances him from his father by providing a substitute superego; it awards him an agent's aggressive and destructive power over others; and for some time it permits him to cherish his secret solitary identity. (Detached from aggression, the erotic component weakened quickly. Moran's son has friends but Moran none.)

Freud explains that "the aetiology common to the onset of a psycho-neurosis and of a psychosis always remains the same. It consists in a frustration, a non-fulfilment, of one of those childhood wishes which are . . . so deeply rooted in our phylogenetically determined organization." The frustration of this childhood wish is caused by something outside the self, and it is usually the father who embodies this counterforce: "this frustration is in the last resort always an external one; but in the individual case it may proceed from the internal agency (in the super-ego) which has taken over the representation of the demands of reality" (XIX, 151).

The frustrated wish is libidinal, of course. Whether the result of this frustration is neurosis or psychosis "depends on whether . . . the ego remains true to its dependence on the external world and attempts to silence the id, or whether it lets itself be overcome by the id and thus torn away from reality" (151). It is tempting to stop our consultation of Freud right here. The diagnosis seems obvious; Moran, acting as a conscious ego, managed to be functional thanks to his neurotic projection of his superego onto the external world and his repression in the id of his childhood desire to be an emotion-driven solitary. Listening to Youdi in Gaber's voice, he was able to silence his id's messages. (In his imaginings of Molloy that wild figure neither speaks nor communicates emotion directly.) Now, however, he ends his report by cutting all ties with the external world. He must therefore have been torn away from reality by the id—that is, by his childhood's frustrated libidinal desire for solitude. The id's uncivilized messages are implied by Moran's concluding interest in the songs of the wild birds.

Moran's decision is not that simple, as Freud told Beckett: "A complication is introduced into this apparently simple situation . . . by the existence of the super-ego, which . . . unites in itself influences coming from the id as well as from the external world, and is to some extent an ideal model of what the whole endeavour of the ego is aiming at—a reconciliation between its various dependent relationships. The attitude of the super-ego should be taken into account . . . in every form of psychical illness." Here Freud reminds himself that the ego has three sources of obligation. Moran's superego, Youdi, encapsulates the external civilized world's repressive demands, its "sollst entbehren." As that superego's agent, Moran has imposed upon others that dictum. His customary method was to lead his victim into temptation in order to deliver him from evil by disabusing him of his desire for a life separate from the group. The healthy superego is influenced by both the external world and the id, Freud just noted, and the healthy ego may seek reconciliation. But Youdi and Moran demand subordination, not harmony.

Freud is not finished, however. To the passage above he adds this possibility: "We may provisionally assume that there must also be illnesses which are based on a conflict between the ego and the super-ego. . . . We would set aside the name of 'narcissistic psychoneuroses' for disorders of that kind" (XIX, 152). Narcissism necessarily catches our attention in so relevant a context. We have considered "Moran" as reporting such an internal conflict. William James pointed out that voices, a sense of uneasiness, and an awareness that matters are not right and that one's self is divided are features common to the experience of being twice-born. We noted these features in the opening pages of Moran's report. Then we recognized that Moran's adolescent acceptance of "sollst entbehren" instigated his membership in Youdi's group.

Years after that enlistment, Gaber's first message in this report and Moran's reactions ("soon I would have to admit I was anxious"; "I felt a great confusion coming over me" [96, 98]) signal the weakening of Moran's longheld beliefs. This change leads to his experience of temptation, the acting out of his impulses at once to control and to rebel. His ego's growing insistence on its own importance and independence and on Youdi's inadequate respect or affection, combined with its continuing dependence upon Youdi, indicates that "narcissistic psychoneurosis" is a happily appropriate term for Moran's problems as a member of Youdi's organization. Beckett's emphasis on this conflict helps to explain the near irrelevance of its ostensible motive, the desire to be a solitary.

Throughout our analysis Moran's psychic situation has been that of a group member, and *Group Psychology and the Analysis of the Ego* has provided invaluable help in our analysis as in Beckett's conception of Moran. Moran's neurotic troubles have been linked to his membership in Youdi's organization. However, Freud does not treat the group psyche as a neurosis. He does not assert that all members of religious and military groups are neurotic. He describes them in deprecatory terms, but he had no very lofty expectations about the psyche, and he generally settled for the ability to function in society as evidence of psychic health. The group psyche's weaknesses do not distinguish it from ordinary psyches: "many of these phenomena of dependence are part of the normal constitution of human society" (XVIII, 117). It is Beckett, then, who intensifies Moran's group psyche into a neurosis, while remaining Freudian in his construction of that neurosis.

Freud asserts that "a certain external force is employed to prevent [artificial groups] from disintegrating." This force is concealed behind a stronger apparent force, which is love. In religious and military groups "the same illusion holds good of there being a head . . . who loves all individuals in the group with an equal love. Everything depends upon this illusion" (XVIII, 94).

We have noted Moran's desire for evidence of Youdi's regard for him, and also his early unwillingness to reason at length about the organization. "We [agents] thought of ourselves as members of a vast organization," he said. "But to me at least, who knew how to listen to the falsetto of reason, it was obvious that we were perhaps alone in doing what we did." (The clash between "obvious" and "perhaps" is characteristic, and that falsetto voice reminds us of Freud's observation that reason often gives way to faith.) "In my moments of lucidity I thought it possible"; but he admits quickly sinking "back into my darkness" rather than "regarding myself as solely responsible for my wretched existence" (107). Reading the account above of Moran's journey out and of the temptations that he resisted, an earnest Freudian might well feel that the account distorted matters. When Molloy sought his mother, he encountered several opportunities to come to terms with his maternal anima, and his story was so treated. Moran is presented as an unhappy group member because he needs to complete his psyche. The journey in search of his solitary identity, so described, implicitly encourages an even worse neurosis.

In fact, Moran ought to replace his false and narcissistic group identity with the multiple memberships offered him during his journey: the father-son relation, the personal friendship (with the pseudo-agent or Molloy), and the group relationship imaged by the shepherd, dog, and flock and implicitly echoing his church membership. Then he need not regard himself as solely responsible for his wretched existence; then he could experience the affection of other human members of these groups. Temptations luring him away from Youdi's group are better perceived as temptations toward normal human relationships.

All this is true enough, in theory, but readers of "Moran" have already experienced "Molloy," and they are aware of the extent to which a neurotic sensibility distorts what it perceives. They cannot expect Moran to perceive normal social existence without distortion. They have also experienced Molloy's self-centered indifference to potentially therapeutic experience. Moran's response is much more negative, hostile, and active. His beating of his son and his arguments with him have no equal in "Molloy"; his savage killing of the pseudo-Moran makes even more comic Molloy's symmetrical kicking, on crutches, of the charcoal-burner. Moran is beyond feeling affection for others even at the start of his existence.

Solitude is his only goal, then, though it will be bitterly different from his irrational expectation of happy days. At the end, Moran has abandoned his membership in Youdi's organization, or he is still subservient to that super-ego but unloved by it and yearning for a substitute leader, a substitute voice, that appears not to have sufficient force to speak impressively. We recall Freud again: "there must also be illnesses which are based on a conflict between the ego and the super-ego. . . . We would set aside the name of 'narcissistic psychoneuroses' for disorders of that kind" (XIX, 151–52). Moran has nothing left to set out in search of, except a self to love narcissistically. Murphy's wandering to find home has shown that this is a dead end, but Moran has turned his back on all the potential object-cathexes available to him as father, neighbor, parishioner, believer, and citizen.

Of the three varieties of flying things that engaged Moran's imagination earlier—birds, bees, and flies—only one remains at the end of "Moran": the wild birds. They are not individual; like the bees and the cluster flies they exist in flocks. They offer Moran no membership, although he tries to learn their language better. He will not fly with them. He will set out alone, crippled, solitary, and earthbound. We hear the terrible battle-cry of that predatory eagle-owl.

* * *

In this secular version of William James's *Varieties of Religious Experience*, with allusions to Dante's *Inferno* and *Purgatorio* and with many other metaphoric enhancements, to say nothing of the elaboration and complication of Moran's individual character and actions, Beckett hinders our perception of "Moran" as a Freudian case history. Similarly, he built complexities of statement and allusion over the Jungian materials of "Molloy." Nevertheless, the structures remain—Jungian in one case, Freudian in the other, psychological in both. A skeletal conception of *Molloy* might resemble the kniferest that appears in each half. Each narrative is a stimulating and puzzling X, and connections join them as sturdily as that bar, although the connections also become puzzling when one tries to interpret them.

Let us look at *Molloy* and its major characters again, removing our depth-psychology blinders and translating the novel's most obvious metaphors. Molloy was alone and satisfied, Moran in society and satisfied, before *Molloy* began. Between them they represented the conditions of most adult humans. To begin, each thinks about his own type—Molloy about two solitaries, A and B/C, Moran about his fellow citizens. Starting from abstractions, Molloy individualizes two men; starting from named individuals, Moran generalizes about society. Both protagonists are abruptly impelled toward change. Molloy wishes to follow C and add company to his solitude—a fellow or frère; Moran wishes to leave Turdy, preferring a solitude detached first from conventional society, then from his son, and then from Youdi and even from the Molloy he set out after.

That summary omits multitudes, obviously, but it reminds us, after many pages of close reading, that Beckett is concerned with conventional generalities about the human condition. He assumes that, because of our mental individuality, we are each alone and unique, even though composed of the generalities that our shared minds create. Discarding God as a cause and religion as an explanation, he locates our individuality (with its complementary tendencies toward solitude and the group) in existences so primarily mental that any social, economic, and physical activities become merely tangential.

Into that existence he introduces unhappiness, discontent, anxiety. One experiences these states as negative because each implies a previous positive state, for which culture offers myriads of metaphors: the land of lost content, those happy highways where I went and cannot come again, the Earthly Paradise, home, mother, the womb, heaven. These terms and images describe a positive existence projected from the happy, contented, unanxious mind. Their present absence generates attempts to compensate and to explain why one is unhappy, why life is painful.

For Beckett, depth psychology completed the explanations that Dante and Schopenhauer especially had begun. We have seen Beckett's complicating and varying of these explanations and his reliance on their mechanics. We have reasoned our way through many of his presentations of psychological troubles. What we could scarcely notice—since this is scholarship and only a necessary preliminary to criticism and celebration—is Beckett's continuous concern with the primary cause of these metaphoric exiles from heaven, God, home, the Earthly Paradise, and so on.

That cause is lack of love. It sends its victims into themselves and out to the world in search of the love that they need and do not deserve. They seek nectar with a sieve, their rational mind. Worse, they do not deserve love because they are unloving. They do not love others; they cannot love themselves. Nevertheless, we cannot easily denounce them and side with their victims or stride briskly away. Especially in his first-person fictions and his dramas, Beckett obliges us to become them and to understand them through sympathy—that is, through experience of their situation. They become our fellows, our frères—unless we cannot love them.

Conclusion

Exposed to so many detailed reports about Beckett's structural uses of depth psychology, the ideal reader may resemble Descartes' traveler or Molloy lost in the forest—unable to see that forest for the trees and wanting merely to get out. Or the ideal reader is now in the position of the title character of Jorge Luis Borges's "Funes the Memorious." Funes perceives everything in exquisite detail. Worse, he remembers everything that he perceives. Borges points out a negative result; thinking is difficult for Funes: "To think is to forget differences, generalize, make abstractions. In the teeming world of Funes, there were only details, almost immediate in their presence" (66). This concluding chapter obliges us to fumble for abstractions and generalities.

*　*　*

Beckett's multitudinous uses of Freud sketch his sense of Freud. This Freud is a remarkably central version, free from the distortions of his early discoverers and from the overthrowings and alterations of recent times. The skeletal structure of Beckett's Freud is provided by basic tenets of depth psychology: much of our psychic identity is *unbewusste,* beyond knowing and beyond control. Especially beyond control are those libidinal impulses basic to our existence. Beckett's reading of Schopenhauer undoubtedly made easy his acceptance of these elements; Schopenhauer's descriptions of an amoral and almost omnipotent will and subservient intellect had prepared him, as they had prepared Freud himself.

Even before Freud's publications completed his formulation of the psyche as compounded of the id, the ego, and the superego/ego ideal, Freud had recurrently described and dramatized the psyche as multiple and as prone to disharmonies. Moreover, these disharmonies were not simply a matter of relationships between parts of the psyche and the outer world—that one might feel one way and think another way, for instance, or feel and think one way but behave another way. Early on, Freud developed the sense of a psyche at odds with itself and concerned primarily with itself. Fresh from a close analysis of *Molloy,* the reader needs no further reminder of Beckett's applications of these ideas.

This psychic introversion led Freud to the concept of narcissism, which he recognized as a central matter and continued to take seriously throughout his career. Laymen understand the narcissist as loving himself and therefore selfishly ignoring other people, but Freud does not simply repeat that mythical sense. In his analyses the narcissistic psyche is generally at odds with itself, not happy, and its incapacity for domestic happiness spoils its emotional relations with other people.

Beckett picked up that subject early in his own career, as we saw extensively in *Murphy.* Narcissism remains central to his writings far beyond his immediate structural uses of Freud. While his presentations of the multiple psyche develop such complex forms as the voices of *Company* (in which "I" is not the first but the "last person"), the unhappy narcissist increasingly looks outward at emotional relationships unachieved, mishandled, and lost. These variants are lineal descendants of *Murphy* and of Freud's "On Narcissism."

The narcissist is made insecure by being unworthy of love, as are many other Freudian neurotics. Their concern begins early in life: "Children are protected against the dangers that threaten them from the external world by the solicitude of their parents; they pay for this security by a fear of *loss of love* which would deliver them over helpless to the dangers of the external world" (XXIII, 200). This fear is central to one's sense of security in a world in which a basic question is "whether one human creature loves another or kills him" (XXII, 164). In the context of those alternatives Freud again describes the child's dependence on his parents: "The child is brought up to a knowledge of his social duties by a system of loving rewards and punishments, he is taught that his security in life depends on his parents (and afterwards other people) loving him and on their being able to believe that he loves them" (XXII, 164).

These latter remarks are taken from the *New Introductory Lectures,* to which Beckett often refers. He cannot have missed the painfulness of that last phrase; both as a child and as an adult, one must make others believe that one loves them. That persuasion is the essential matter, then; actual feeling is beside the point. Molloy's toadying in society and Moran's recurrent and conscious role-playing are still fresh in our minds.

No sense of security can last—that is, no assurance that one is loved by all potentially dangerous others. When one cannot love oneself, the insecurity is pervasive, as Murphy on the job-path demonstrates. Therefore the ego's intellectual passivity before the id and the superego is complemented by the emotional passivity of the neurotic psyche in need of love.

Again, Beckett follows Freud closely. With the exception of a very brief and caricatural passage in "First Love," characters who actively love another are not easy to find in Beckett's writings. Before Freud, he was much taken by Dante's account of Paolo and Francesca, but his concern for them echoes Belacqua's difficulty with Vergil's scorn for Dante's pity: "Qui vive la pietà quand' è ben morta" (*Inferno* XX, 28; Here lives pity when it were well dead). Dante weeps at the contorted predictors of the future, not at damned lovers, and Beckett seems in both cases more concerned with theological punishment than with love. He was also an admirer of Ronsard's ode to Anteros, "Magie, ou delivrance d'amour" (Harvey, 308–9). Freud's concerns with libido and "desire" rather than "love" may have been preferable. Beckett on love, however, is a topic too large to undertake here.

Recurrently we heard Beckett's first-person narrators suggest that they were speaking to an analyst. The late Freudian story "From an Abandoned Work" seems almost completely a patient's recounting of his psychological life. But there and elsewhere we saw no signs of helpful intervention; no profitable therapy occurs. One might expect any satisfactory presentation of Freudian psychology to include therapeutic success. Here too, however, Beckett is faithful to his source. Again we turn to the *New Introductory Lectures* for much of our material. "You are perhaps aware that I have never been a therapeutic enthusiast," Freud tells his imaginary audience; "there is no danger of my misusing this lecture by indulging in eulogies" (XXII, 151–52). He develops this skeptical beginning at some length. Neuroses are not "unnecessary," he says. "They are severe, constitutionally fixed illnesses, which rarely restrict themselves to only a few attacks but persist as a rule over long periods or throughout life." He notes "the constitutional factor" ("we can do nothing about it"), and finds two other factors worth much discussion: "the amount of psychical rigidity present and the form of the illness" (XXII, 153–54).

The "psychical rigidity" or "stiffening" opposes "the plasticity of mental life" so that "not everything can be brought to life again." We recognize Beckett's use of these metaphors; Molloy and Moran stiffen increasingly as their stories continue. "All too often," Freud says, "one seems to see that it is only the treatment's lack of the necessary motive force that prevents one from bringing the change about" (XXII, 154). Again *Molloy* is ready to hand.

Moran and Molloy and Murphy and the lesser protagonists are individual cases, however, and one might suspect Beckett of contriving them with pejorative intent. Therefore, we turn to Freud's third factor, "the form of the illness": "The second limitation upon analytic successes [that is, besides stiffening] is given by the form of the illness. You know already that the field of application of analytic therapy lies in the transference neuroses— phobias, hysteria, obsessional neurosis—and, further, abnormalities of character which have been developed in place of these illnesses. Everything differing from these, narcissistic and psychotic conditions, is unsuitable to a greater or less extent" (XXII, 155). Freud's grouping of narcissism with "psychotic conditions" suggests strongly his conclusion (as of 1933, when Beckett was seeking therapy) that neurotics unable to love themselves and therefore unable to love others have little chance of therapeutic success. In Beckett's presentation of such characters Neary's formulation is recurrently explanatory: they have cut the connection; the conarium is lacking. Nemo remains a nobody because he cannot leave the bridge for either bank. Molloy's rigid kniferest demands mention.

Some of Beckett's neurotics, however, are also narrators, and they display sharp and well-informed intellects. Why, then, are they so obtuse about their illnesses? Freud's "Recommendations to Physicians Practising Psycho-Analysis" (1912) is relevant throughout, although only a few matters can be mentioned here. Freud dismisses the value of the patient's intellect. In the early days, he says, "we took an intellectualist view of the situation. We set a high value on the patient's knowledge of what he had forgotten." But the neurosis remained even after the patient recalled the past. Therefore, therapy had to address "the resistances which had in the past brought about the state of not knowing. . . . Conscious knowledge, even if it was not subsequently driven out again, was powerless against those resistances" (XII, 139–42).

We recall Moran's complex explanation of his dual role as character and narrator and Molloy's analyses of the falsity of his narrative. When a narrator displays such self-awareness, he reassures us of his validity. However, Freud's narrators, his patients, gave Freud and Beckett another sense of the matter. For one thing, the narrating patients are neurotics. For another, they sometimes do not *remember* their repressed past. Instead of remembering, they are compelled to *repeat* it. They act out their pathology: "In drawing attention to the compulsion to repeat we have acquired . . . a more comprehensive view. We have only made it clear to ourselves that the patient's state of being ill cannot cease with the beginning of his analysis, and that we must treat his illness, not as an event of the past, but as a present-day force" (XII, 151).

Such narrators as Molloy and Moran and the unnamed protagonists of

"First Love" and "From an Abandoned Work" tell their stories variously but well—well enough, at least, so that we can psychoanalyze them in detail. Yet they are worse off at the end than at the beginning. Previously repressed knowledge has not helped them, while their narrative acting out, their repeating, may have done them harm. Freud warns that repeating "implies conjuring up a piece of real life; and for that reason it cannot always be harmless and unobjectionable. This consideration opens up the whole problem of what is so often unavoidable—'deterioration during treatment'" (XII, 152). Beckett makes artistic use of such deterioration, as of the multitudinous other matters that he found in Freud and in depth psychology.

*　　*　　*

Beckett's literary works explore no complexities of religious belief or doctrine, nor do they attack or support political and economic systems. They draw no philosophical conclusions from their characters and stories. Yet most readers agree that Beckett involves them in concerns at least as humanly important as those, despite dramatizing his insights with no great figures and events and drawing from them no eternal verities. The important issues sensed by his audience remain implicit in Beckett's inconclusive presentations, causing persistent difficulties for anyone wishing to raise those issues into consciousness and fix them in icy words.

*　　*　　*

Readers of Beckett who have also undergone the close rereadings demanded by this study are well equipped to agree with the assertions above. They are also aware that the absence of explicit moral, theological, philosophical, and political topics in Beckett's writing signals no failure of responsibility on his part, no evasion of the most serious tasks of art. But how are those unstated topics suggested? How is the great outer world at once avoided and involved? And how is that great complementary internal world to be described, that psychic world that has no material existence, no human shapes, no disinterested onlookers, no objective context? Beckett was no authority on these problems.

Israel Shenker has disclaimed the actuality of his apparent interview with Beckett, from which many critics have taken key passages. Nevertheless, the validity of the ideas in those passages and the Beckettian quality of their phrasing have not been questioned. Therefore we turn again to that text, in search of solutions to the problem of presenting the psyche and its sensed and experienced life.

"The kind of work I do is one in which I'm not master of my material,"

Shenker reports Beckett as saying. "I'm working with impotence, ignorance."
He sets himself apart from "the other type of artist—the Apollonian" (Graver
and Federman, 148). This passage draws on Schopenhauer's praise of the
Apollo Belvedere: "Now as a rule, knowledge remains subordinate to the
service of the will. . . . With the animals, this subjection of knowledge to the
will can never be eliminated. With human beings, such elimination appears
only as an exception. . . . This human superiority is exhibited in the highest
degree by the Apollo Belvedere. The head of the god of the Muses, with eyes
looking far afield, stands so freely on the shoulders that it seems to be wholly
delivered from the body and no longer subject to its cares" (*WWR* I, book
III, § 33).

Not an Apollonian writer, Beckett claims no superiority to his materials,
no knowledge by which he might be detached from and raised above the
bodily cares of his characters. He does not deny the existence of such artists
and of such knowledge. He simply disclaims access to that detached
Apollonian viewpoint. He is working with "impotence, ignorance" insofar
as these are characteristic of his characters. Those qualities, in our psychic
life, describe "the mess" of that life. Moreover, since he is not master of his
material, he also asserts his own impotence and ignorance as an artist.

One might set this humility among the reasons for Beckett's lifelong reliance on the ideas and expressions of other authors. We know that Beckett
was deeply affected by writings in which his own doubts and pessimistic
intuitions were eloquently expressed, as often by Schopenhauer. We know
also that he was affected by writings that eloquently express positive, optimistic, idealistic ideas. He often sympathized with these, surely, but he could
not believe in them. His attitude toward those Apollonian artists—most
obviously Racine and Joyce—gives evidence. (Dante displays that detached
and superior knowledge too, but Beckett's use of him scarcely reflects the
fact.)

Unable to discuss as an Apollonian *A la Recherche du temps perdu,* Beckett
approved Proust's connection of music and salvation, but he could not evoke
this connection for readers of his *Proust* without insisting that music's implicit demonstration of paradise "damns the life of the body on earth." To
be "wholly delivered from the body and . . . its cares" is impossible, he
sensed even then. He had no idyllic childhood as a model for Schopenhauer's
earthly paradise lost. ("Childhood is the time of innocence and happiness,
the paradise of life, the lost Eden, on which we look back longingly through
the whole remaining course of our life," said Schopenhauer in "On Genius"
[*WWR* II, ch. 31].)

Raised by an earnestly Christian mother and taught about the Bible in several schools, Beckett could not escape the concepts of paradise and sin, even before reading Dante. He could doubt the reality of paradise, its truth, as Joyce doubted the truths of Catholicism, but he could not forget religion's incredible ideals. Nor could he dismiss the pervasiveness of sin.

The resultant dualities of evil and good, damnation and salvation, lingered throughout Beckett's career. As he told Tom Driver: "If there were only darkness, all would be clear. . . . But where we have both dark and light we have also the inexplicable" (Graver and Federman, 220). "The family was Protestant, but for me it was only irksome and I let it go," Beckett said. Driver then asked about his plays; do they "deal with the same facets of experience religion must also deal with?" "Yes," Beckett answered, "for they deal with distress." He linked that distress to the physical and emotional unhappiness shown in advertisements for charitable organizations. Such visible, public distress does not figure in his writings, however, nor do "innocent victims," as journalism describes them.

Beckett's youthful pessimistic search for a satisfactory philosophical description of this dual world of darkness and light led him especially to Dante (heaven and hell, with a painful middle term), Descartes (mind and body, with an irrelevant divinity), and Schopenhauer (will and intellect, with an inaccessible Sabbath). He absorbed especially their examples, their characters and scenes, and their psychological components. The advent into Western life and then his own life of depth psychology enabled him to translate philosophical insights into psychological concepts, while his knowledge of philosophy enabled him to expand and dramatize the psychologist's sketchy descriptions of the ego in its role of the self posing as disinterested thinker. ("Can it be we are not free? It might be worth looking into," Molloy wonders [36].)

*   *   *

Our slow journey through many texts has shown that Beckett's discovery of depth psychology was itself slow and probably reluctant. He was not suddenly twice-born. Psychological notions appear in his earliest writings only in immediate connection with mental illness. The vaguely self-destructive artist of "Assumption" and the troubled doctor of "A Case in a Thousand" must be set against the evasions of psychology in *Dream of Fair to Middling Women* and *More Pricks Than Kicks,* with its "Greek and Roman reasons, Sturm und Drang reasons, reasons metaphysical, aesthetic, erotic, anterotic and chemical, Empedocles of Agrigentum and John of the Cross reasons, in short all but the true reasons, which did not exist, at least not for the purposes of conversation" (90).

Beckett attempted many contrivances with which to present an abstractly conceived psychological character, as when he began his speculations about the future *Murphy* by turning a part of the *Inferno* into a narrative structure. Another Irish stew like *Dream* might well have resulted. Even the belated arrival of local habitations and names, Dublin and London and Celia and Murphy, produced a psychologically troubled character who consults the philosopher Neary, the astrologer Suk, his own rocking chair, and the psychotic Mr. Endon, but not a psychiatrist. In the tormenting theatrical light of his later works, the young Beckett can be seen still kicking against the pricks of insight.

* * *

For Beckett the most interesting varieties of psyche are at once dangerous and fragile. They are greatly in need of other psyches, and what they need most is emotional acceptance, unjudging affection. This need cannot be rationalized, tamed, and made a negotiable commodity in the world from which Murphy hears cries of quid pro quo. They are likely to damage others as well as themselves in their improper pursuit of affection or their retreat from such pursuit and from offered affection.

The Beckettian character developed from this psychic need takes many forms. He may retreat from a society in which his demands cannot be met, as Murphy does. He may seek explanations for his unhappiness as Murphy and Watt do, as Doctor Nye does, or as the protagonist of "From an Abandoned Work" does, isolated with his books among the rocks. But he must, if only as passively as Doctor Nye and the protagonist of "First Love," act out the conflicting demands for satisfaction that emanate from his unconscious.

These protagonists are unhappy, but somewhere in their past they found happiness, or at least they conceived of it. It is a source of pain in their mature existence, a paradise lost to them forever. In that happiness they experienced or imagined a gratifying response to their need for love, or at least they think so later. They also learned—often retrospectively—the ethics of paradise, the rules by which good and evil are created and identified, and so they learned of their own moral inadequacies. (Such inadequacies occurred whether the lost happiness was internal and narcissistic or external, as with Krapp's woman in the punt.)

Such a blanket description covers too much too thickly. Some of the characters deny experiencing love at all, for instance. It also implies that the alteration of life for the worse is accompanied by progressive awareness; therefore, that unhappiness is a learning experience, replacing ignorance with knowledge. We have seen that this is not the case. Awareness may not come at all, thanks to repression, as in *Happy Days* and *Not I*. Or it occurs incompletely and too late. The intellect is not able to effect change in any case. Often the experience of unhappiness occurs too late because awareness is not accompanied by the psychic power needed for change. Much of the significance of old age in Beckett's protagonists derives from its physical representation of this psychic impotence.

The character of Frankenstein's monster seems often to lurk in the shadows of Beckett's more developed protagonists, and this matter of conceivable change provides one relevant reason. One passage must suffice. The monster, by now a murderer with a developed ability to hate, demands of his creator "clemency and affection": "Everywhere I see bliss, from which I alone am irrevocably excluded. I was benevolent and good; misery made me a fiend. Make me happy, and I shall again be virtuous" (II, i). A typical Beckett protagonist is driven by a psyche that makes the same amoral demand, and makes that demand with the same dubious honesty. Inability and unwillingness to change are closely linked psychologically, and they recur in Beckett's writings.

After many pages of painstaking analysis, none of these generalities can remain both persuasive and sufficient for long. Murphy found security in Celia's love, but he would not accept responsibility for her (by getting a job and getting her off the job path), nor could he adequately love himself. Molloy offered no return of love to his mother or Sophie Lousse or Ruth/Edith. Moran wanted freedom from responsibility in his role as Youdi's agent, aggressive power over his clients and his son, and solitary freedom from relationships—and he wanted these incompatible psychic states at once, and to them he added the desire that Youdi respect him and his son love him. Even such modifications of earlier generalities do not do justice, however, to Beckett's presentations of characters and psychic events.

Those presentations constitute our basic reason for reading and rereading Beckett's works. One reads Descartes, Schopenhauer, Freud, Jung, and James for didactic purposes; any aesthetic pleasure is gratifying but not essential. Milton reinforced the didactic purposes of *Paradise Lost* by writing *Christian Doctrine* and thereby provided evidence of the moral slackness of his audience, which goes on preferring the poem to its meaning.

When a didactic meaning sticks in the reader's craw instead of passing unnoticed or reinforcing a belief already held, aesthetics may go out the window. The fact that most readers of Beckett show little concern about the unpleasantness of many of his protagonists suggests that they are untroubled by any stimulus to moral judgment. (The Nobel Prize committee may have been troubled, however.) Perhaps Beckett sided with those readers. Despite the present study, he displayed both in the works and in his private comments on life an extensive unwillingness to judge negatively anyone other than himself. ("Two thieves are crucified with Christ, one saved and the other damned," he reminds Tom Driver. "How can we make sense of this division?" [Graver and Federman, 220].) The aesthetic fact of his materials matters, then, far more than moral judgment passed on them. Such a relative emphasis is easy enough when the artist paints colorful bouquets, but Beckett's materials are usually quite grim. Beckett's presentations of his characters must concern anyone who wishes to understand the elements central to his works. As we have seen, those elements are not moral but psychological.

*　*　*

"Not to know what you want to say, not to be able to say what you think you want to say, and never to stop saying, or hardly ever, that is the thing to keep in mind, even in the heat of composition" (*Three Novels*, 28).

This passage constitutes excellent early advice for anyone who, like Beckett, wishes to evoke the psyche in art. One cannot begin with an outline form. In Beckett's sense of the psyche its dominant part is pervasive, dangerous, contradictory, and negative. It is also unknowable. Human consciousness exists in a room darker than Molloy's bedroom chez Lousse. It persistently barks its shins on unseen obstacles—furniture or guideposts or dragons.

At most one may intuit the essence of the psyche, uncertainly, from its accidents. The pun can scarcely be evaded, given the dangers and negativity of this dominant part; the events of one's psychic life are primarily matters of damage, accidental harms, incomplete repairs. However one describes the situation, the result is at least generally clear: the conscious self is aware of damage, error, and danger in the outer human world, but it is essentially unaware of the damage it has done itself and the consequent external dangers that its blurred perceptions incur. The protagonist of "First Love" tells a story in which his behavior is persistently unpleasant, and his accounts of his family life and Anna/Lulu emphasize his inadequate understanding. Similarly, Murphy can leave Celia for the Magdalen Mental Mercyseat with a retrospective concern only for the rocking chair that he left behind. Similarly, the protagonist of "From an Abandoned Work" can with indifference conclude that he has not loved, except for a few words and things.

That story, like so many of Beckett's, is told by a protagonist unaware of being its actual subject. In most of the later texts we hear only the protagonists' foreign voices, with no mediating narrator. These apparently unshaped monologues encourage commentators to apply approvingly Beckett's assertion that Joyce's "Work in Progress" is not *about* something; it is that something itself. We have seen a passage in which Freud clarifies relevantly that idea: "While the analysis of a case is in progress it is impossible to obtain any clear impression of the structure and development of the neurosis. That is the business of a synthetic process which must be performed subsequently" (X, 132). In the monologues especially, Beckett's presentation is mimetic rather than synthetic or didactic. The protagonists are aware of an audience to which they must make their report, as later theatrical characters must respond to the demands of a light, but they can say no more than they know, and they cannot know accurately what they should say or want to say or how to say it, even while they must continue their report.

Their report may impel them to more serious disclosures and recognitions as they go on, as Molloy demonstrates, or it may encourage self-deception, as Moran's optimistic ending suggests, or it may leave them where they were, as in "First Love," *All That Fall,* and *Waiting for Godot.* In any case, no therapy occurs. Partial recognitions of error lead only to partial changes; even the strongest libidinal urges—which lead Molloy and Moran to undertake painful journeys—weaken until they can motivate only retrospective reports.

Simple mimesis, however, would amount to no more than an actor's echoing of a neurotic's anamnesis. Freud does not publish couch-side notes, and in narrating a case he selects and emphasizes dark materials in the light of a later diagnosis. Like Freud, Beckett must have his synthetic analysis in mind as he presents his protagonists' imperceptive and muddled reports. Therefore if, as the apprentice artist, we wish a text to develop, we must move on from Molloy's acceptance of an obligation to compose even while ignorant of what one wants to say. We must move on to Moran's echoing of Dante: "It is one of the features of this penance that I may not pass over what is over and straightway come to the heart of the matter. But that must again be unknown to me which is no longer so and that again fondly believed which then I fondly believed, at my setting out. And if I occasionally break this rule, it is only over details of little importance. And in the main I observe it. And with such zeal that I am far more he who finds than he who tells what he has found . . ." (133).

Structure is necessary, but it must not impose clarity and order on the mess of actual experience. Even Dante does not predict his arrival at the beatific vision while in the Inferno. For Beckett, however, the example of Dante could be of only limited value when the structure of a work was at issue. Like Milton, Dante had available to him more than a thousand years' worth of exegetics. Complex structures of thought underlie his far-from-raw materials with a large vocabulary of clarifying terms. The *Commedia* reports a unique Dantean vision of existence, but its contemporary audiences of pious believers could not doubt the essential accuracy and validity of its postulates, which they had accepted for years, nor could Milton's audience doubt the postulates on which *Paradise Lost* is constructed.

Such certainties belong to the past. Speaking to Tom Driver, then Professor of Literature and Theology at the Union Theological Seminary, Beckett contrasts the "mess" of the present to the clarity of classical art. Using the example of Racine's *Phèdre* and its underlying belief, he says that "within this notion clarity is possible, but for us who are neither Greek nor Jansenist there is not such clarity." In our time, then, art cannot be based on the solid structure of belief; its "form will be of such a type that it admits the chaos and does not try to say that the chaos is really something else. . . . To find a form that accommodates the mess, that is the task of the artist now" (Graver and Federman, 220, 219).

Beckett does not simply oppose the past to the present; clarity of belief may still occur to an individual, despite the mess. (The Jesuit in *Dream* comes to mind.) And when he speaks to Driver of that clarity in classical art, he contrasts it to the fourteenth-century cathedral of Chartres: "There is the unexplainable, and there art raises questions that it does not attempt to answer" (220). Beckett also does not imply that the events of human life once had a clarity that they now lack; it is one's perception of the events that imposes order or disorder upon them.

Beckett spoke to Driver in 1961, well after the writing of *Molloy*. We have seen from his transposition of William James's material into psychological terms that he had no more religious faith when writing *Molloy* than he expressed during this interview. That novel has overtones of religious experience, but no more than overtones. They cannot function as structure.

Art remains formal, however, as Driver pointed out and as Beckett agreed. Depth psychology afforded him the materials that theology and philosophy could not provide, as well as a persuasive internal location for life's most serious problems. His most immediate early professional contacts with the subject—the editorial interests of *transition* and the interests of the psychiatrist he consulted in the early 1930s—emphasized Jung's ideas. Jung's writings are characterized by an authoritative assurance; even as a young researcher he sought the voice of the Wise Old Man. Beckett usually shied away from such assurance, however, and he soon preferred Freud. ("In the quarrel between Freud and Jung," he said, "I sided with Freud.")

* * *

Freud is generally thought of these days as a Wise Old Man himself, or as the Dead Father whose imposed ideas must be condemned. Beckett formed a quite different impression of him. It is not merely that Freud was dealing with improper subjects, such as sexuality and family relations, and was moreover a Jew and therefore an outsider, although those matters are relevant. It is not even that Freud was undercutting the proprieties that propped conventional society.

To read Freud's works closely and in chronological order is to experience the making of a work in progress, but not in the Joycean sense of assured and knowledgeable development. Freud recurrently returns to earlier formulations to dismiss them or revise them. He recurrently and explicitly asserts the tentative nature of his discoveries, even while giving them as persuasive a presentation as he can manage. A professionally trained medical scientist, he is quite aware of the impropriety of his uses of the arts and of the metaphorical nature of his terms. He tells stories about his patients, and the stories offer a wide variety of problems and experiences, variably interpretable and reducible to no ten commandments or categorical imperatives.

In short, his writings offered Beckett an uncommon mixture of professional knowledge and pioneering caution. Where Descartes quickly assured himself that the self exists because its thinking exists, Freud moved away from physical diagnoses and medical treatments by means of unsystematic doubting, and for much of his career he continued to cope with the results of that doubting. Such an irregular approach to the profundities of the mind could not easily win converts, and for much of Beckett's early life Freudian psychology was not considerably more respectable than Yeats's Order of the Golden Dawn. In part for that reason, those who knew Beckett at that stage of his life and heard him speak at length about Schopenhauer and suicide have not reported that he discussed depth psychology. Nor would he in the much later interviews with Shenker, Driver, and D'Aubarède.

We cannot doubt that Freud's discoveries, however tentative, found some confirmation in Beckett's own psychic experiences. He responded to the sense of a fragmented psyche with hostile and inaccessible parts, the sense of an internal judge, the sense of voices within the mind, the sense of a passive and subordinate relation to a force neither rational nor personal— one might easily go on.

Equally, there is a sense that one exists much more in retrospect than in prospect. True, Didi and Gogo are waiting for Godot, and that waiting seems to emphasize the future. But they have no conception of Godot, no idea of the results of Godot's coming, and no plans of their own. True, they also have little past. They speak to pass the time, but they are stripped down; there are few characters in Beckett's fiction so devoid of memories, allusions, ideas, and guilt, and therefore so free of their pasts. The past haunts most of Beckett's characters. Even for that reason alone, Freud's retrospective search for psychic traumas is far more useful to Beckett than Jung's urgings toward teleological goals.

Freud's term for his professional work, psychoanalysis, is appropriate for his writings. He says little in them about the work of therapy. His primary interest is in the detective work of interpreting the patient's largely unconscious revelation of his neurosis. Studying inhibitions, symptoms, and anxiety, for instance, he seeks relations among them. Considering a few cases, he seeks to generalize. For Beckett, consistently distrustful of authorities and final truths, Freud's emphases on the individual illness and on the speculative nature of his own analyses offered both enlightenment and freedom. He could place a tentative trust in the narratives and in Freud's accurate selection of relevant evidence from which to draw conclusions, but he was not obliged to accept any certainties beyond that point. In particular, therapy itself and the positive results of therapy were separable from the analyses.

Let us approach specificity for a moment. The ideal core of the onion that Beckett postulated as the subject of art is given a specific location by Freud: the psyche. The core must be reached by unpeeling many layers. Consider Molloy.

A neurosis is not a psychic illness; it is the psyche's inadequate attempt to cure that illness. Molloy has neurotically evaded society by exiling himself to a mountainside, thereby achieving peace, superiority, and distance. This solution is inadequate, however. Analysis reveals that the original psychic difficulty resulted not from association with others but from its opposite, the need for a fellow or frère. Further analysis reveals that this need has remained unfulfilled because of an earlier unfulfilled need for a relation with his mother. Examination of the mother as she is reported by the patient suggests her inadequacy while revealing his deep hostility to her and dependence on her. Examination of the patient's relations with another mother figure and with a love-object indicates that the failure of love in those relations is due primarily to the patient, not the mother, and that his descriptions of these women are distorted by his own psychic inadequacies, which he is slow to acknowledge. And then perhaps we reach the icy core. Molloy's inability to love himself, combined with his insistence on his primacy and his increasing resort to reason, blocked his emotional connection with his mother, with other women, and with any potential fellow or frère.

This coarse and vulgar analysis is not quite Freudian, not quite Jungian, and not quite Beckett's, but it is a coarse approximation. If one takes the time to match it against "Molloy," one notices more than its inadequacy; one notices also that this sequence of unpeelings does not match the sequence of the relevant details in the story. This is quite intentional. The story presents a case in progress, and as Freud noted it is impossible to obtain any clear impression of the structure of a neurosis during that presentation. A subsequent synthetic process, such as we underwent for many pages, is necessary. We could achieve that synthetic understanding, however, only because Beckett had included in the structure of the story the necessary psychological form. It was not enough for him to produce a mimetic report from a neurotic; he was obliged to know the diagnosis even as he began, in order to give a relevant structure, a significant form, to the mess.

* * *

But all this psychological analysis! one might complain. If he had meant us to read "Molloy" or any other of his works as a psychological case history, Beckett would have made explicit and clear his intentions and his psychiatric assumptions. Since he offered no such explicit information, and since in fact he scarcely mentioned psychology, much less Freud and Jung, in any public writings, we must conclude that he had no desire to turn his audience into psychoanalysts or therapists, nor to pose as one himself.

To assert—after hundreds of pages about Beckett's detailed and specific uses of the writings of Schopenhauer, Proust, Freud, and Jung—that Beckett did not intend his audiences to recognize those uses or to perceive his texts as psychological seems downright foolish. The vulnerable asserter looks around for a shield and finds John Pilling. After many pages of analysis of Beckett's literary sources, Pilling concludes with the suggestion that Beckett increasingly found all that knowledge useless (*Beckett*, 158).

Doctor Nye found no relief for his symptoms in his medical studies; Murphy consulted philosophy and astrology and texts at the Magdalen Mental Mercyseat in vain; the "mind doctor" provided Maddy Rooney with no therapeutic materials; the protagonist of "Abandoned Work" reported no profit from his books among the rocks; and Watt learned nothing from Knott, unless that beneath the complexities of knowledge nothing exists. More seriously, perhaps, Molloy's college career was of no use to him, and Moran was moved by painful experience to extensive doubts about theology and Youdi. Still more seriously, Molloy found even his immediate personal knowledge frozen hellishly in words, evidence only of fixity and lifelessness.

Most seriously and especially in *Molloy*, Beckett consistently presents the rational intellect as detaching one's individuality from concern for others, repressing one's feelings, keeping others at a distance by judging them, and emphasizing one's superiority—that is, the superiority of one's reason. Worse still, for the person centrally concerned, the intellect accomplishes the same repressive fragmentation within the psyche, whether as a superior judge or as an evasive reasoner.

Beckett's characters tend to know. Like Winnie's in *Happy Days,* their thoughts are rich in—or littered with—literary allusions. Words and finely phrased ideas mean much to them. Words are all they have, it often seems. Beckett's audiences, themselves highly verbal, tend to place at least as much trust in these words as do the characters. Beckett's warnings about the characters' reliability are easily forgotten. Moran's admission of the importance of viewpoint—he will speak sometimes as one who knows, sometimes as one who does not—is set aside. Molloy's assertion that one must be silent or lie is equally forgettable, for Beckett's audiences. They trust that in some sense, however unclear, Beckett himself does not lie. They may also assume that the ability to express ideas well implies control over them. (Reminded that at the end of *Rasselas* the young hero, summing up the gloomy knowledge he has gained, is rather pleased by his eloquence, Beckett was asked whether his characters felt a similar pleasure. His answer was abrupt and inclusive: No.)

Beckett denies that he is an Apollonian artist. He rejects the position of the writer who knows all about his characters and about life. His characters reveal impotence and ignorance, and they speak in situations that emphasize their inability to think successfully. Their ignorance, however, does not imply the certain existence of potency and knowledge elsewhere, either in Beckett or in their and our world. That duality exists only in these characters' conceptions or vague suspicions of what might be.

Perhaps the complement to ignorance and impotence in Beckett's texts is no more than the silence of which the universe is made. But that silence seldom can be heard in Beckett's writings. If the character manages to stop thinking, a voice in his head speaks up. Sometimes he thinks in an attempt to drown out that voice. From somewhere, in any case, the words go on. Despite ignorance, assertions continue. ("I was never silent," says Molloy, "whatever I said I was never silent" [34].) The mind can never be satisfied, never, despite the desire of many characters to have done with it, to stop, to reach the silence. Ideas, speculations, denials, conceptions continue to be generated. The self may never express itself in words, as the Unnamable fears, but the words go on.

The words imply communication, too, that contact with another person that Molloy and Moran shun so vigorously. Early in *Watt* the narrator annotates "said Mr Hackett": "Much valuable space has been saved . . . by avoidance of the plethoric reflexive pronoun after *say*" (8). Everyone speaks only to himself; no communication is possible. In a worse mood, Beckett had damned friendship. "The attempt to communicate where no communication is possible," he wrote, "is merely a simian vulgarity, or horribly comic, like the madness that holds a conversation with the furniture" (*Proust*, 46).

With his turn to psychology, Beckett had made the silence of the universe a psychic silence, the indifference of the psyche to the appeals of the conscious ego, as well as the indifferent silence of other people and the inability to reach them and even to wish to reach them. The self no longer turns away from other people of lesser value: it cannot turn toward them; it cannot find a fellow or frère. It is left with its cold intellect and its useless knowledge. No Apollonian, Beckett can see no way out of this labyrinth. He cannot minister to these minds diseased. At most, he can make us uneasy too.

*　*　*

Beckett did not write novels of ideas, despite all their ideas—even the basic structural ideas that we have excavated. Since this study has persistently emphasized those ideas and their origins in other writers, that approach must continue now, even while denying their centrality.

In order to identify Beckett's central literary concerns, let us go back to one of his early images: the ideal core of the onion. That image exists in a necessary context: "the heart of the cauliflower or the ideal core of the onion would represent a more appropriate tribute to the labours of poetical excavation than the crown of bay" (*Proust*, 16–17). Beckett presents here images appropriate to the artist's successful achievement. He does so in discussing Proust's ideas, but as elsewhere in the monograph he alters matters toward his own sense of the subject. A major concern here is his approval of Proust's indifference to "la littérature qui se contente de 'décrire les choses,' de donner un misérable relevé de leurs lignes et de leur surface. . . ." To this superficial art of lines and surface Beckett and Proust prefer "la marche en sens contraire, le retour aux profondeurs, où ce qui a existé réellement gît inconnu de nous" (*TR* II, 39, 48). This return to the depths is given comic expression in Beckett's images of the cauliflower and the onion.

Those vegetable images also grew out of Proustian soil. Continuing past this return to the depths, Proust develops the idea that those discoveries provide materials for the work of art. For Proust, his own life especially lay beneath that surface. Therefore, he develops his life into the image of a seed: "Je compris que tous ces matériaux de l'oeuvre littéraire, c'était ma vie passée. . . . Comme la graine, je pourrais mourir quand la plante se serait développée. . . . Cette vie, les souvenirs de ses tristesses, de ses joies, formaient une réserve pareille à cet albumen qui est logé dans l'ovule des plantes et dans lequel celui-ci puise sa nourriture pour se transformer en graine . . . (*TR* II, 52–53).

Beckett is sympathetic to Proust's values, but he is interested also in giving them amusing metaphorical expression. Therefore, he plants those seeds and raises a cauliflower and an onion. They are comic vegetables and therefore useful for his purposes. Many readers recall the onion, but scarcely anyone mentions the cauliflower. The center of the cauliflower is called its "heart." With that term Beckett reinforces the connection to the onion. The "core" of the onion echoes "heart" through the Latin "cor" and the French "coeur." The proper artist, then, is rewarded by the cauliflower and the onion for getting to the heart of the matter—not to the head, the conscious and rational intellect, but to the emotions.

In presenting *A la Recherche,* Beckett speaks of the primary emotions of love, jealousy, and regret, emphasizing their pain. Some thirty years later he will tell Tom Driver that his plays "deal with distress." Beckett's central concerns, in short, are pain and distress; they affect the heart and they are caused especially by diseases of the heart, failures to love and be loved. The onion, conventionally associated with tears, especially prefigures Murphy and the later surds; it is a prophetic irrational root.

Beckett's works do not leave us meditating on philosophy, theology, and psychology. "The power of the text to claw," he saw later, was his concern. The core of the onion may evoke tears, but it certainly does not suggest hidden knowledge.

We are not shown love at work over any extended period in Beckett's writings. It is characteristically a topic about which a character makes rather abrupt remarks. We recall the epigraph to chapter 6 of *Murphy,* "Amor intellectualis quo Murphy se ipsum amat," and a later character's sour comment about "that intellectual love which drew from me such drivel." Hamlet's academic phrase "meditation and the thoughts of love" might be applicable; we are given the thoughts, not the emotion, and the thoughts tend toward the sardonic. One version of love, however, is made ironic only in expressing a desire impossible of fulfillment. That version is metaphoric, and the metaphor is of home. We have noticed it before. Not surprisingly, that metaphor can be found in Freud's speculations. He develops it while discussing "Das Unheimliche" in 1919:

> It often happens that neurotic men declare that they feel there is something uncanny about the female genital organs. This *unheimlich* place, however, is the entrance to the former *Heim* of all human beings, to the

place where each one of us lived once upon a time and in the beginning. There is a joking saying that "Love is home-sickness"; and whenever a man dreams of a place or a country and says to himself, while he is still dreaming: "this place is familiar to me, I've been here before," we may interpret the place as being his mother's genitals or her body. In this case too, then, the *unheimlich* is what was once *heimisch*, familiar; the prefix "*un*" is the token of repression. (XVII, 245)

Jung's associations with the maternal anima are relevant too, of course, but this desire for home recurs in Beckett's works beyond any simple echoing.

Murphy describes life as "but a wandering to find home" (4). His successor in "First Love" comments that "what goes by the name of love is banishment, with now and then a postcard from the homeland" (18). The recurrent exiles from home and returns to home in Beckett's later fiction do not serve to remove metaphor from this idea. Home is sometimes a place where one feels uneasy and unloved, as the narrators of "First Love" and "From an Abandoned Work" and Molloy and Moran especially demonstrate. It seems sometimes the self, as Murphy and the narrator of "First Love" suggest. Even that self is inhospitable, however. It lacks its ideal core, its heart. Even the narcissist can find no suitable love. Freud and Jung offer Beckett the means with which to say a great deal about such matters, but they offer no solutions to the problems, no calmatives or purgatives, no salves or salvation.

*   *   *

We cannot leave yet the larger subject of Beckett's materials and their treatment. It has been suggested all too glancingly that Proust came back to Beckett's creative mind while he wrote the trilogy. Let us turn once more to those closing pages of *A la Recherche* where Proust lays out his aesthetic notions in eloquent analysis. Spawning metaphors, he considers the question of what one finds when one dives into the depths of the mind. One finds glimpses—photographic negatives—of the past. They are not enough for the artist: "On éprouve, mais ce qu'on a éprouvé est pareil à certains clichés qui ne montrent que du noir tant qu'on ne les a pas mis près d'une lampe, et qu'eux aussi il faut regarder à l'envers: on ne sait pas ce que c'est tant qu'on ne l'a pas approché de l'intelligence. Alors seulement quand elle l'a éclairé, quand elle l'a intellectualisé, on distingue, et avec quelle peine, la figure de ce qu'on a senti" (*TR* II, 49). The intelligence is necessary. One must shed on the negative the light of reason before one can distinguish clearly what it is that one has sensed, Proust shows us. That rational light, however, is an untrustworthy fox fire in Beckett's works, and he was to reject the terms in which Proust stated his position. The clearer an idea is, the less likely it is to be reliable.

This study demonstrates that Beckett did increasingly expand his intelligence over the years, with the considerable aid of Freud, Schopenhauer, and Jung, in order to intellectualize what he had sensed. It also acknowledges, however, that Beckett never admitted any profit from such study and understanding. Indeed, when Gabriel D'Aubarède asked him, about the novels of the trilogy, "Et quelle raison avez-vous eue de les écrire?" Beckett answered: "Je n'en sais rien. Je ne suis pas un intellectuel. Je ne suis que sensibilité. J'ai conçu *Moloy* [sic] et la suite le jour où j'ai pris conscience de ma bêtise. Alors, je me suis mis à écrire les choses que je sens." We have just heard Proust speak of the intelligence and intellectualizing. Beckett may have had Proust's formulation in mind. As he would tell Driver that he was working with ignorance and impotence, so here he rejects the position of the "intellectuel" whose "intelligence" would "intellectualiser" the materials that his acknowledgment of "bêtise" allowed him to "sentir." (We may recall here, from our reading of "Molloy," Beckett's similar rejection of philosophy and reason in "Peintres de l'empêchement.") Replying to D'Aubarède, then, Beckett implies the mimetic nature of his writing by rejecting any philosophical or other intellectual motives.

John Keats had experienced some of Beckett's problems and discoveries and had given them useful expression. He too had sensed the inadequacy of the reason, for instance, noting that "axioms in philosophy are not axioms until they are proved upon our pulses." He gives primacy to the feelings, then—but he lived barely long enough to discover their unreliability and to recognize, unlike Youdi, that beauty is not always truth. Beckett went further and found worse, and he could not retreat to any rational philosophy based on concepts not reached from percepts.

Beckett would recognize his *bêtise* and write the things that he sensed; Keats had found it necessary for the artist not to be omniscient, like Coleridge, but to possess "*Negative Capability,* that is when man is capable of being in uncertainties, Mysteries, doubts, without any irritable reaching after fact & reason" (letters of 3 May 1818 and 21 Dec 1817). ". . . Uncertainties, Mysteries, doubts" describes "the mess" that the artist must put into form. We are back to that similar pair of terms, ignorance and impotence.

* * *

Eyestrain aside, the worst result of reading this extensive analysis of Beckett's use of psychology may be its effect on one's reading of Beckett's works.

Analysis is reductive. It encourages the analyst to settle for detachment and superiority. Such a position must necessarily destroy the dramatic immediacy of Beckett's presentations, which literally or figuratively emphasize the protagonist's subjective existence in time and mental space. The audience must experience this existence with the character, not turning away to meditate, not rising above the character to pass judgment on him, but immersed in his flow of verbal awareness. Not to do this—to shelter oneself from this immersion by climbing into the chair of the official scorer—is to commit the basic fault of the Beckett protagonist—the concealment of complete psychic existence behind the blinds offered by the reason.

* * *

After so long a study of such basic materials in Beckett's thought and writing, the negative warning above must seem unnecessary. Where are the nuggets of wisdom mined from his lifetime of fine writing?

This study began by asserting that the most valuable approaches to an artist's work seek the artist's own ideas. It must conclude in a similar fashion, and anecdotally. Once during a gloomy conversation I attempted to lighten the tone by telling Beckett that a great many people found positive values in his writings. He was not mollified. "They find in them something that I do not," he said.

Bibliography

Anzieu, Didier. *Beckett et le psychanalyste*. Paris: Mentha, 1992.

Bair, Deirdre. *Samuel Beckett*. New York: Harcourt, Brace, Jovanovich, 1978.

Barnard, G. C. *Samuel Beckett: A New Approach*. New York: Dodd, Mead, 1970.

Beckett, Samuel. *All That Fall,* in *Krapp's Last Tape and Other Dramatic Pieces.* New York: Grove Press, 1960.

———. "A Case in a Thousand." *Bookman* 86 (Aug 1934): 241–42.

———. "Assumption." In *Transition Workshop*. Ed. Eugéne Jolas. New York: Vanguard Press, 1949.

———. "Dante . . . Bruno . . . Vico . . . Joyce." In *Our Exagmination Round His Factification for Incamination of Work in Progress*. Paris: Shakespeare, 1929; subtitled *James Joyce/Finnegans Wake*. New York: New Directions, 1972.

———. *Disjecta*. Ed. Ruby Cohn. New York: Grove Press, 1984.

———. *Dream of Fair to Middling Women*. Ed. Eoin O'Brien and Edith Fournier. New York: Arcade, 1993.

———. *En attendant Godot*. Ed. Colin Duckworth. London: George G. Harrap, 1966.

———. *Film*. New York: Grove Press, 1969.

———. *First Love and Other Shorts*. New York: Grove Press, 1974.

———. "From an Abandoned Work." In *No's Knife*. London: Calder and Boyars, 1976.

———. *Krapp's Last Tape and Other Dramatic Pieces*. New York: Grove Press, 1960.

———. *Mercier and Camier*. New York: Grove Press, 1975.

———. *Molloy*. Paris: Ed. de Minuit, 1951.

———. *Molloy*. In *Three Novels*. New York: Grove Press, 1965.

———. *More Pricks Than Kicks*. New York: Grove Press, 1970.

———. *Murphy*. New York: Grove Press, 1957.

———. *No's Knife*. London: Calder and Boyars, 1976.

———. *Proust*. New York: Grove Press, 1957.

———. *Proust*. Trad. de l'anglais et présenté par Edith Fournier. Paris: Ed. de Minuit, 1990.

———. *Stories and Texts for Nothing*. New York: Grove Press, 1967.

————. *Three Dialogues with Georges Duthuit.* In *Proust and Three Dialogues with Georges Duthuit.* New York: Grove Press, n.d.

————. *Three Novels.* New York: Grove Press, 1965.

————. *Watt.* New York: Grove Press, 1959.

Belis, Andrew (pseudonym of Beckett). "Recent Irish Poetry." *Bookman* 86 (Aug 1934): 242.

Bonnet, Henri. "Le Sens de la Recherche proustienne" and "La Psychologie de l'amour selon Marcel Proust." *Hommage à Marcel Proust: Cahier spécial du "Rouge et Noir"* (April 1928): 37–48, 49–75.

Borges, Jorge Luis. "Funes the Memorious." Trans. J. E. Irby. In *Labyrinths.* New York: New Directions, 1964.

Burnet, John. *Early Greek Philosophy.* 4th ed. London: A. and C. Black, 1930.

Coe, Richard N. *Samuel Beckett.* New York: Grove Press, 1964.

Curtius, Ernst R. *Marcel Proust.* Trad. de l'allemand par Armand Pierhal. Paris: Ed. de la Revue Normale, 1928.

Dandieu, Arnaud. *Marcel Proust: Sa révélation psychologique.* Paris: Firmin-Didot, 1930.

Dante Alighieri. *The Divine Comedy.* Trans. and commentary Charles S. Singleton. 6 vols. Bollingen Series, no. 80. Princeton: Princeton University Press, 1973.

————. *The Divine Comedy.* Trans. and commentary H. R. Huse. San Francisco: Rinehart, 1954.

D'Aubarède, Gabriel. "En attendant . . . Beckett." *Nouvelles Littéraires* (6 fevrier 1961): 1, 7.

Descartes, René. *Discours de la méthode.* Ed. Etienne Gilson. Paris: Librairie philosophique J. Virin, 1962.

Driver, Tom. "Beckett at the Madeleine." 1961. Reprinted in *Samuel Beckett: The Critical Heritage.* Ed. Lawrence Graver and Raymond Federman. London: Routledge and Kegan Paul, 1979.

Duckworth, Colin. See Beckett, *En attendant Godot.*

Fauré-Biguet, J. N. "Réflexions." In *Marcel Proust.* Paris: Editions de la Revue le Capitale, 1926.

Federman, Raymond, and John Fletcher. *Samuel Beckett: His Works and His Critics.* Berkeley: University of California Press, 1970.

Fernandez, Ramon. *Messages.* Trans. Montgomery Belgion. New York: Harcourt, Brace, 1927.

Freud, Sigmund. *Complete Psychological Works of Sigmund Freud.* Ed. and trans. James Strachey et al. 24 vols. London: Hogarth Press, 1955–1974.

Gardiner, Patrick. *Schopenhauer.* Baltimore: Penguin, 1963.

Graver, Lawrence, and Raymond Federman, eds. *Samuel Beckett: The Critical Heritage.* London: Routledge and Kegan Paul, 1979.

Guthrie, W. K. C. *The Sophists.* Cambridge: Cambridge University Press, 1971.

Harvey, Lawrence E. *Samuel Beckett: Poet and Critic.* Princeton: Princeton University Press, 1970.

James, William. *Some Problems of Philosophy.* 1911. Cambridge, Mass.: Harvard University Press, 1979.

———. *Varieties of Religious Experience.* 1901–1902. New York: Modern Library, c. 1929.

Jolas, Eugène, ed. *Transition Workshop.* New York: Vanguard Press, 1949.

Jung, Carl G. *Analytical Psychology: Its Theory and Practice. The Tavistock Lectures.* New York: Vintage Books, 1968.

———. *The Archetypes and the Collective Unconscious.* Trans. R. F. C. Hull. 2nd ed. Bollingen Series, no. 20. Princeton: Princeton University Press, 1969.

———. *The Integration of the Personality.* Trans. S. M. Dell. New York: Farrar and Rinehart, 1939.

———. *Memories, Dreams, Reflections.* New York: Vintage Books, 1965.

———. *Psychological Types.* Trans. R. F. C. Hull. Bollingen Series, no. 20. Princeton: Princeton University Press, 1971.

———. *Psychology and Alchemy.* Trans. R. F. C. Hull. 2nd ed. Bollingen Series, no. 20. Princeton: Princeton University Press, 1968.

———. *Psychology and Religion.* New Haven: Yale University Press, 1938.

———. *Symbols of Transformation.* Trans. R. F. C. Hull. 2nd ed. Bollingen Series, no. 20. Princeton: Princeton University Press, 1967.

———. *Two Essays on Analytical Psychology.* Trans. R. F. C. Hull. 2nd ed. Bollingen Series, no. 20. Princeton: Princeton University Press, 1966.

Keats, John. *The Letters of John Keats.* Ed. Hyder Edward Rollins. 2 vols. Cambridge: Harvard University Press, 1958.

Knowlson, James. *Damned to Fame: The Life of Samuel Beckett.* New York: Simon and Schuster, 1996.

Magee, Bryan. *The Philosophy of Schopenhauer.* Oxford: Clarendon Press, 1983.

Pilling, John. "Beckett's *Proust.*" *Journal of Beckett Studies* 1 (1976): 24.

———. *Samuel Beckett.* London: Routledge and Kegan Paul, 1976.

Proust, Marcel. *A la Recherche du temps perdu.* 1919–1927. 15 vols. Paris: NRF, 1932.

Schopenhauer, Arthur. *Parerga and Paralipomena.* Ed. J. Frauenstadt. 2 vols. Leipzig: F. A. Brockhaus, 1878. Rpt. Trans. E. F. J. Payne. Oxford: Clarendon Press, 1974.

———. *The World as Will and Representation.* Trans. E. F. J. Payne. 2 vols. New York: Dover, 1966.

Shattuck, Roger. *Proust's Binoculars.* Princeton: Princeton University Press, 1986.

Shelley, Mary. *Frankenstein.* Ed. Leonard Wolf. New York: Clarkson N. Potter, 1977.

Shenker, Israel. "Moody Man of Letters." 1956. Reprinted in Graver, *Samuel Beckett: The Critical Heritage.* For Shenker's disclaimer, see Bair, 651.

Valéry, Paul. *Oeuvres.* E. Jean Hytier. 2 vols. Paris: Bibliothèque de la Pléiade, 1962.

Wittels, Fritz. *Sigmund Freud: His Personality, His Teaching, and His School.* Trans. Eden and Cedar Paul. London: George Allen and Unwin, 1924.

Wittgenstein, Ludwig. *Tractatus Logico-Philosophicus.* Trans. and ed. D. F. Pears and B. F. McGuiness. London: Routledge and Kegan Paul, 1961.

Credits

Excerpts from the following material are reprinted in this volume by permission of the publisher.

Samuel Beckett, *All That Fall,* in *Krapp's Last Tape and Other Dramatic Pieces,* copyright 1958, 1959, 1960 by Grove Press, Inc. *First Love and Other Shorts,* 1974 edition. *Molloy,* in *Three Novels,* copyright 1955, 1956, 1958 by Grove Press, Inc. *More Pricks Than Kicks,* 1970 edition. *Murphy,* 1957 edition. *Proust,* 1957 edition. *Watt,* 1959 edition. Reprinted by permission of Grove/Atlantic, Inc.

Sigmund Freud, "Analysis of a Phobia in a Five-Year-Old Boy," "From the History of an Infantile Neurosis," "The Interpretation of Dreams," "On Narcissism," "Recommendations to Physicians Practising Psycho-Analysis," "The Unconscious," from *The Standard Edition of the Complete Psychological Works of Sigmund Freud.* Reprinted by permission of HarperCollins Publishers, Inc.

Sigmund Freud, *An Autobiographical Study,* translated by James Strachey. Translation copyright 1952 by W. W. Norton and Company, Inc., renewed (c) 1980 by Alix Strachey. Copyright 1935 by Sigmund Freud, renewed (c) 1963 by James Strachey. Reprinted by permission of W. W. Norton and Company, Inc.

Sigmund Freud, *Beyond the Pleasure Principle,* translated by James Strachey. Translation copyright 1961 by James Strachey. Reprinted by permission of Liveright Publishing Corporation.

Sigmund Freud, *The Ego and the Id,* translated by James Strachey. Translation copyright 1960 by James Strachey, renewed 1988 by Alix Strachey. Reprinted by permission of W. W. Norton and Company, Inc.

Index